CCNA Routing and Switching 200-125 Certification Guide

The ultimate solution for passing the CCNA certification and boosting your networking career

Lazaro (Laz) Diaz

BIRMINGHAM - MUMBAI

CCNA Routing and Switching 200-125 Certification Guide

Commissioning Editor: Vijin Boricha
Acquisition Editor: Shrilekha Inani
Content Development Editor: Abhijit Sreedharan
Technical Editor: Prachi Sawant
Copy Editor: Safis Editing
Project Coordinator: Jagdish Prabhu
Proofreader: Safis Editing
Indexer: Priyanka Dhadke
Graphics: Tom Scaria
Production Coordinator: Shraddha Falebhai

First published: October 2018

Production reference: 1301018

Published by Packt Publishing Ltd.
Livery Place
35 Livery Street
Birmingham
B3 2PB, UK.

ISBN 978-1-78712-788-3

www.packtpub.com

`mapt.io`

Mapt is an online digital library that gives you full access to over 5,000 books and videos, as well as industry leading tools to help you plan your personal development and advance your career. For more information, please visit our website.

Why subscribe?

- Spend less time learning and more time coding with practical eBooks and Videos from over 4,000 industry professionals

- Improve your learning with Skill Plans built especially for you

- Get a free eBook or video every month

- Mapt is fully searchable

- Copy and paste, print, and bookmark content

Packt.com

Did you know that Packt offers eBook versions of every book published, with PDF and ePub files available? You can upgrade to the eBook version at `www.packt.com` and as a print book customer, you are entitled to a discount on the eBook copy. Get in touch with us at `customercare@packtpub.com` for more details.

At `www.packt.com`, you can also read a collection of free technical articles, sign up for a range of free newsletters, and receive exclusive discounts and offers on Packt books and eBooks.

Contributors

About the author

Lazaro (Laz) Diaz, as he prefers to be called, is a Cisco Instructor who has been in both the field and the teaching industry for almost two decades. He currently lives in the State of Florida, USA and migrated from Cuba at the age of six (6) years old. He is a Network Engineer and holds several certifications in CCNA R/S, CCNA Security, CCNA Voice, CCNP, Security+, Network+, A+, MCP, MCTS and the MOS.

However, he is best known for his self-paced courses, teaching over 100K students around the globe. His first book is called *The Only IP Book You Will Ever Need!* However, he knows that this CCNA study guide will be a testament to his commitment in giving students an opportunity to achieve the CCNA R/S certification.

About the reviewer

Gurmukh Singh is a seasoned technology professional with more than 15 years of experience in Infrastructure design, Implementation, and is working in Big Data domain for the past 6 years. He loves coding and solving scalability problems. He has worked with companies like HP, JPMorgan, Yahoo, Amazon and is always looking forward to learn new technologies and meet people.

He is an author of two book on Hadoop and a reviewer on many books covering Security, Application Architectures and Cisco devices.

Packt is searching for authors like you

If you're interested in becoming an author for Packt, please visit `authors.packtpub.com` and apply today. We have worked with thousands of developers and tech professionals, just like you, to help them share their insight with the global tech community. You can make a general application, apply for a specific hot topic that we are recruiting an author for, or submit your own idea.

Table of Contents

.

Preface

Cisco Certified Network Associate (CCNA) Routing and Switching is one of the most important qualifications for keeping your networking skills up to date.

The CCNA Routing and Switching 200-125 Certification Guide covers topics included in the latest CCNA exam, along with review and practice questions. This guide introduces you to the structure of IPv4 and IPv6 addresses and examines in detail the creation of IP networks and sub-networks and how to assign addresses in the network. You will then move on to understanding how to configure, verify, and troubleshoot Layer 2 and Layer 3 protocols. In addition to this, you will discover the functionality, configuration, and troubleshooting of both DHCPv4. Combined with router and router simulation practice, this certification guide will help you cover everything you need to know in order to pass the CCNA Routing and Switching 200-125 exam.

Towards the end of this book, you will explore security best practices as well as get familiar with the protocols that a network administrator can use to monitor the network.

Who this book is for

This book is for you if you are a network administrator, network technician, or anyone who wants to prepare for CCNA Routing and Switching certification. Basic understanding of networking will help you get the best out of this guide, although sufficient information is provided to those new in this field.

What this book covers

Chapter 1, *Internetworking Models*, in this chapter, the reader will be introduced to the basics of networking an introduction the layered approach. Such as, the OSI model and its advantages also, we will be discussing the different layers that exist and make the distinction between the upper layers and lower layers that make up the OSI model.

Chapter 2, *Ethernet Networking and Data Encapsulations*, in this chapter, the reader will be introduced to the networking type called Ethernet, they will be learning how packets flow in a network and when they can flow based on the access method used in Ethernet Network called CSMA/CD. Readers will learn the differences between collision domains and broadcast domains and of course the cabling of this type of network.

Chapter 3, *Introducing the TCP/IP*, in this chapter, the reader will be introduced to a brief history of the TCP/IP model and the DoD model, and you will gain an understanding of what protocols work on each layer and how to map the TCP/IP model to the OSI model and see the comparisons. Also, we will go over the basics of IPv4, it terminology and the hierarchical approach it uses, also to round off the chapter we will learn the different types of addresses that exits within an IPv4 world.

Chapter 4, *Subnetting in IPv4*, this chapter, will show readers how to subnet a Class C, Class B and Class A addresses. Learning how to subnet is an essential part in networking. This is the process of how one can logically segment a network. The readers would learn how to increase the number of broadcast domains while decreasing the amount of broadcast or noise in the Network.

Chapter 5, *Variable Length Subnet Mask and Route Summarization*, readers will learn how not to waste IP address in their networks. Meaning, they would only use the IPs needed to service their network. This will be presented in a form of a diagram or formula that will simplify the process of calculating VLSM. In networks, the goal of an Engineer is to minimize the routing tables on a router. The reason for this, is so that the router is not overwhelmed with the exuberant number of network addresses. Therefore, readers will be learning how to minimize the routing table using Route Summarization. Which simply means, taking multiple, smaller networks and combining them into one big network, by adjusting the prefix length.

Chapter 6, *The IOS User Interface*, in this chapter, the reader will be learning the Cisco Internetworking Operating system. They will learn how to connect to a Cisco Router or Switch, navigate the Command Line Interface or CLI and learn the different router modes and switch modes. We will also go into configuring basic administrative commands on both the router and the switch and of course how to view your configurations, save or delete them.

Chapter 7, *Managing the Cisco Internetwork*, in this chapter, the reader will be learning the components that make up a Cisco router or switch. Readers will also must understand the bootup sequence of the router to be able to troubleshoot a problem, in case one occurs doing this process. We will also dive into configuring DHCP, SYSLOG, NTP, CDP and LLDP the new version of CDP. You will be configuring Telnet, SSH, host tables, and verify that all this works using the CLI. Round off the chapter with basic troubleshooting techniques, to test for connectivity to the destination.

Chapter 8, *Managing Cisco Devices*, in this chapter, the reader will be learning how to manipulate the Cisco Register, to do so you will become familiar with how the register works during the boot process. You will learn to manipulate the register to be able to troubleshoot routers or switches. You will also be learning how to back up your Flash, Startup-config files and how to restore them using an FTP or TFTP server. We will finish up the chapter with Right to use Licenses and backing up and installing the license.

Chapter 9, *The IP Routing Process*, in this chapter, the reader will be learning the process of how a packet traverses the network from source to destination. Reader will be gain the understanding of default and static routing, not only how to configure it but when and on what router should these routes should exist. We finish the chapter with a discussion on Dynamic routing with emphasis on the RIP routing protocol. We will make examples using RIPv1, RIPv2 and RIPng.

Chapter 10, *The IPv6 Protocol*, in this chapter, the reader will be learning be learning the benefits of using IPv6 in your network, we will be breaking down the different components of an IPv6 address, to gain a better understanding of the IPv6 address. We will look at different ways of writing an IPv6 address and the rules or guidelines they must properly write an IPv6 address. We will also look at the main three IPv6 routing protocols, such as, RIPng, EIGRPv6 and OSPFv3. This and much more will give us an understanding how IPv6 works on an internetwork.

Chapter 11, *Introduction to IPv6 Routing*, in this chapter, reader will know the benefits of using dynamic routing. Also, reader will learn how to configure EIGRP for IPv6, including the topology.

Chapter 12, *Switching Services and Configurations*, in this chapter, the readers will be learning how a switch learns mac addresses and what does it do with those Mac addresses once its learned them. We will also be learning how to secure our layer 2 ports using the command switchport security and basic switch administration commands such as passwords, hostnames, gateway addresses and so on.

Chapter 13, *VLANs and Inter-VLAN Routing*, in this chapter, the reader will be learning what is a VLAN and the importance of creating VLAN's in your network not only for security purposes but decreasing the amount of broadcast in your network, while optimizing the bandwidth of each logical segment. They will understand that using VLAN's in a network creates a better administration method as well making your network more scalable. Readers will also acquire the knowledge of how to make different VLAN's talk to each other through the use of trunk ports and the 802.1q protocol.

Chapter 14, *Introduction to EIGRP Routing Protocol*, in this chapter, our focus will be on how EIGRP works, its features, and configuring EIGRP for single autonomous systems and multiple autonomous systems.

Chapter 15, *Advanced OSPF Configurations,* in this chapter, reader will be learning the basics of OSPF, its features and configuration, and much more. We will be creating multiple labs, since OSPF has different aspects that we need to learn for the certification and the real world. Not only will we be looking at single area OSPF, but also multi-area OSPF.

Chapter 16, *Border Gateway Protocol,* in this chapter, you will looking at BGP, specifically the External Border Gateway Protocol (eBGP). Also, you will learn about the differences between iBGP and eBGP and we will see how to configure and verify BGP.

Chapter 17, *Access-Control List,* in this chapter, the readers will be learning about securing their networks using Firewalls and Internal Routers using Access-List. We will learn about the different types of ACL's such as Standard, Extended and Named. We will be configuring all three of them, but to so you must also understand not only the rules that govern firewalls but how to convert a subnet mask into a wildcard mask. We will learn how to control TELNET and SSH traffic using ACL's but apply them to a line not an interface.

Chapter 18, *Network Address Translation,* in this chapter, the reader will be learning about the NAT protocol, why are we using it and how to configure NAT in our network. Once NAT is configured we must make sure that it is working properly, so by issuing the `show IP NAT translation` command we can verify that indeed it's working. We will be discussing the different types of NAT that exist, such as; Static, Dynamic and NAT Overload also known as PAT.

Chapter 19, *Wide Area Networks,* in this chapter, the reader will be learning about Wide Area Networks and will gain an understanding of the terms used in WAN, the different connection types and cabling that is required. This will help the reader make a more informed decision when ordering a WAN connection. Readers will be learning about the HDLC protocol and its drawbacks when compared to PPP, which reader will be configuring and learning the process and the components that make up PPP. We will also briefly touch upon VPN's and their importance when using remote users. We will discuss GRE tunnels, and gain the understanding of their use and how to configure GRE on our network.

Chapter 20, *Advance Networking Topics,* in this chapter we will create a large topology to include what you would need in your LAN and WAN. Also, we will cover layer 2 and layer 3 configurations. In this chapter we will configure everything that we have covered so far in this book.

Chapter 21, *Mock Test Questions,* will consist of mock questions for you to test your knowledge. It tries to cover all the topics from the scope of the exam and challenges your understanding of the topics.

To get the most out of this book

In order to achieve your goal of passing the CCNA Routing and Switching (200-125) certification, which is the reason I decided to write this book, and also the reason you are reading this book, you will need to have certain things, as described in the list following, to get the most from this book and to ensure your success you will need the following:

- First and foremost, you must have a passion for networking.
- You do need to have some basic understanding of networks.
- You must have the dedication and make time to study for the CCNA R/S certification
- You need the drive to get the CCNA R/S certification against all obstacles
- You must have either a simulator/emulator (that is, the Cisco Packet Tracer which is now free by Cisco on their website at `https://www.cisco.com/` or you may want to use the following link: `https://www.netacad.com/courses/packet-tracer/introduction-packet-tracer`. The CPT is one of the simulators used in this book along with GNS3 . Each topology and/or diagram will advise you which simulator has been used. However, you can also use the emulator, VIRL, another Cisco product or Live/Real equipment). The choice is yours!
- You need to commit to do all the practice labs in this book.
- You must answer and review all questions and quizzes in each chapter to include those at the end of the book.

These are the requirements you must have to successfully understand and get prepared to pass the current CCNA R/S certification exam.

I know that this book will give those that read it and follow the instructions herein, the knowledge and information for successfully pass and acquire their CCNA R/S certification exam.

Practice tests

The practice test questions for the book is also hosted on GitHub at `https://github.com/PacktPublishing/CCNA-Routing-and-Switching-200-125-Certification-Guide`. We would be updating questions on regular intervals, it will be updated on the existing GitHub repository.

Download the color images

We also provide a PDF file that has color images of the screenshots/diagrams used in this book. You can download it here: `https://www.packtpub.com/sites/default/files/downloads/9781787127883_ColorImages.pdf`.

Conventions used

There are a number of text conventions used throughout this book.

`CodeInText`: Indicates code words in text, database table names, folder names, filenames, file extensions, pathnames, dummy URLs, user input, and Twitter handles. Here is an example: "Port 20 is listening for incoming FTP traffic and port 21 does the transferring of data."

When we wish to draw your attention to a particular part of a code block, the relevant lines or items are set in bold:

```
CORE1(config)#VTP DOMAIN CISCO
Changing VTP domain name from NULL to CISCO
CORE1(config)#VLAN 16
```

Any command-line input or output is written as follows:

```
R1(config)#ipv6 router eigrp 500
R1(config-rtr)#?
```

Bold: Indicates a new term, an important word, or words that you see onscreen. For example, words in menus or dialog boxes appear in the text like this. Here is an example: "Notice the bit rate is set to **9600**."

Warnings or important notes appear like this.

Tips and tricks appear like this.

Get in touch

Feedback from our readers is always welcome.

General feedback: If you have questions about any aspect of this book, mention the book title in the subject of your message and email us at customercare@packtpub.com.

Errata: Although we have taken every care to ensure the accuracy of our content, mistakes do happen. If you have found a mistake in this book, we would be grateful if you would report this to us. Please visit www.packt.com/submit-errata, selecting your book, clicking on the Errata Submission Form link, and entering the details.

Piracy: If you come across any illegal copies of our works in any form on the Internet, we would be grateful if you would provide us with the location address or website name. Please contact us at copyright@packt.com with a link to the material.

If you are interested in becoming an author: If there is a topic that you have expertise in and you are interested in either writing or contributing to a book, please visit authors.packtpub.com.

Reviews

Please leave a review. Once you have read and used this book, why not leave a review on the site that you purchased it from? Potential readers can then see and use your unbiased opinion to make purchase decisions, we at Packt can understand what you think about our products, and our authors can see your feedback on their book. Thank you!

For more information about Packt, please visit packt.com.

Internetworking Models 1

Before we begin our trek into the world of networking, let's take a quick look back on how it began. In 1962, J.C.R. Licklider and W. Clark coined the *Galactic Network concept*, which encompasses social interaction.

It wasn't until 1969 that the first version of ARPANET (internet) went online. It connected four devices from four different universities: the University of Utah, Stanford Research Institute, UCLA, and the UCSB.

So, in our world of information technology, we have been trying since the 60s to communicate with each other using different types of networks.

The Defense Department was one of the first institutions to develop a system by which we could communicate across the world in case a major catastrophe occurred. Yes, we had the phone system, post office, even through air and sea we could send information across the globe, but we were not satisfied with the scalability, interoperability, and efficiency of how these particular networks operated, and you basically had to have a PhD to even get close to one those monstrosities called computers.

Not until the mid-1980s did computer networks start to appear more in small to large businesses. This was due to the powers that be; they created the TCP/IP network suite and allowed the rest of world to transmit information throughout their business, making them more efficient at getting information into the hands of the people that need it, in a way that was quick and required little effort.

Let me explain that last line – *required little effort*: you could simply share a file, folder, or drive on your network and people could navigate to it and access that information without leaving the comfort of their desk.

So, networks came to the rescue; using a cabling system, internetworking devices, and protocols, we could do the same work at lightning speed.

The following topics will be covered in the following chapter:

- Internetworking devices
- Network topologies
- The OSI model

Internetworking devices

With all that said, let's begin by talking about internetworking devices and the role they play on the network.

Routers

This is the most intelligent device that exists on the network. It handles all the traffic in your network and sends it to the proper destination. Routers have an **Internetworking Operating System (IOS)** that allows the router to have a set of features that will allow you to configure it for the specifications needed on your network to get that data across:

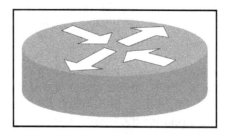

Routers have the following components you need to be aware of, not only for your certification, but for real-world applications: ROM, RAM, NVRAM, and Flash—each of these components serves a unique purpose.

For now, you need to know that routers create multiple collision domains and multiple broadcast domains, and they work on layer three, or the network layer, of the OSI model. Don't fret; we will be getting to that shortly.

Switches

Switches come in different flavors, meaning they could have different functionalities depending on the IOS that they had and the needs of your network. For certification purposes, layer-two switches will be the focus of our studies, but we will briefly cover some layer-three switching features:

The main purpose of a switch on a network is functionality. The switch is where all your devices will be connected for them to communicate with each other, but the switch offers a lot of features we can use to our advantage, in making our network more efficient. The following bullet points concern some of those features:

- VLANs
- Switchport security
- Spanning Tree Protocol
- EtherChannel

And there is much more, depending on the IOS you have. The switch also has the same components as the router, but it maintains a VLAN database file that you need to be aware of. Once again, all of these features and their details will be revealed later in the book.

Bridges

Bridges are like switches, but they are much more limited, with fewer ports, are software-based instead of hardware-based, and offer fewer features:

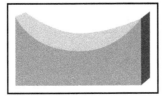

Bridges operates at layer two and their main function on the network is to segment the network. They also create multiple collision domains and broadcast domains.

Hubs

Hubs are not used on a network in today's IT world. Hubs are unintelligent devices. They are a layer one device; their main function is to act like a multiport repeater. It will create one collision domain and one broadcast domain, which is a very bad thing, especially in an Ethernet network. But this will be explained in detail later.

Just remember not to use hubs in your network, because they will slow it down.

Network cabling

I know what you are saying, *Cabling is not an internetworking device*, but know that when building, repairing, or enhancing a network, the type of network cabling used is very important. The following diagram shows the typical **CAT5e** cabling used to connect end devices to internetworking devices to allow them to communicate. We will discuss cabling more in depth later, but for now just keep it in the back of your mind:

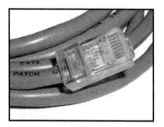

Network topologies

Alright, now that you have been introduced to the internetworking devices, let's talk about topologies. First, let's define what a topology is. There are two types of topologies: you have the *physical topology*, which is how the network is physically connected. The other is the *logical topology*, which is how the path of the data flows. It depends on several factors, such as routing protocols, internetworking devices used, and the bandwidth configured on the interfaces of those internetworking devices.

But let's begin with the basics.

The Bus topology

Bus topologies use a primary cable, to which all end devices are connected. The data travels along this cable, hence the name **Bus**. The problem is that, at the time this type of topology existed, we were using coaxial cabling that at speeds of 10 Mbps, which is considered slow using today's standards. It was considered a **shared medium**, because the bandwidth was divided up based on how many computers you had connected. The following diagram shows the basic structure of Bus topology:

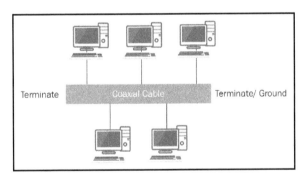

In this topology, Ethernet technology was used, which uses an access method called **Carrier Sense Multiple Access Collision Detection** (**CSMA/CD**). CSMA/CD is the method in Ethernet that end devices use, to be able to transmit their data. As I explained previously, if a device hears any noise on the wire, it will not transmit, it will wait until all noise is gone and then it will send its data. It could be that one node or device does not hear the other device, and both end devices are attempting to send at the same time. That will cause a collision; at that point, a jamming signal is sent, packets are dropped, and a countdown begins to see who transmits; the one whose countdown ends gets to send first.

So, imagine not the five nodes that you see in the figure, but hundreds of nodes trying to communicate. It's insane, since this type of topology creates only one collision domain and one broadcast domain that is running on half-duplex. It was not scalable and hard to troubleshoot, hence, not feasible at all.

Besides all that, if you do not terminate both ends of the cable, you will create something called *reflection*, which the signal that is on the wire reflect onto the cable continuously, creates noise so no one can transmit. The same thing would happen if your cable were cut somewhere in between; that is why troubleshooting this network was a nightmare. But, let's put the icing on the cake: if you don't ground one side of the cable, if a power surge hits your cable, it could fry all your nodes attached to the cable.

The Bus topology was not going to become the wave of the future.

The Star topology

In this topology, all devices are connected to a central device, in this case a layer-two switch. This is still using the Ethernet access method of CSMA/CD. But, since the media that is transferring the data is a switch, each port on a switch is a private collision domain, so you can have full-duplex, which will allow you to send and receive data. If one of the cables from an end device breaks, only that device will not be able to communicate on the network:

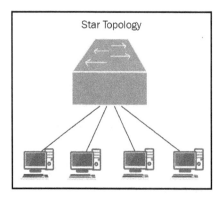

Even though you have increased the number of collision domains and they are private collision domains, which allows for greater bandwidth, one problem still exists: you have, by default, one broadcast domain. This means that when someone transmits on the network, everyone connected to that device, or to be more specific, VLAN 1, which is the native VLAN that all end devices connect to, will also hear that noise and still slow down your network.

The good news is that with a layer two or layer three switch, you can create multiple VLANs. You can logically segment your network so that when someone transmits within their own VLAN, no one else hears that noise.

To explain the obvious about this *Star topology*, you might be thinking, *Hey, that doesn't look like a star*, and you would be right. Just because they called it a Star, does not mean you are going to design your physical network in such a manner. It simply means you are connecting your devices to a central point where all devices can communicate:

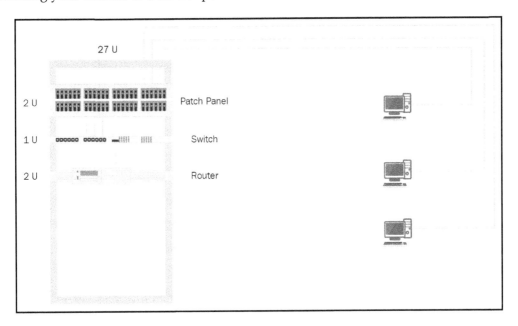

The preceding illustration shows the reality of a common network design. You will run your cable from the office, cubicle, or classroom to the communications closet and terminate your cable at the patch panel. This in turn gets connected to the switch using *patch cables*, which then gets connected to the router.

With all that said and illustrated, I hope that clears up the *Star topology* definition.

The Ring topology

As illustrated in the following diagram, a token ring network is represented as a circle or ring, but there is more to token ring networks. A token ring network uses a central device called a **Multi-Station Access Unit** or **Media Access Unit** (**MAU**) and its purpose is to connect all end devices to it:

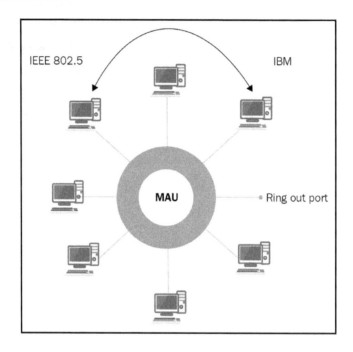

The MAU is not circular; it is rectangular and one could say it looks like a switch. There is a huge difference between them; an MAU has two ports called Ring in and Ring out to connect to other MAUs and concentrator ports for the end devices.

This MAU connects all these devices in a logical circular pattern, but the physical topology is that of a star.

The type of access method is called token passing and is deterministic in nature, unlike Ethernet which is contention-based. By this, I mean a token ring has an empty, free-flowing token that goes around the network waiting for someone to seize the token and send data. Only the person with that token can transmit, and once the token is seized, no other token is generated. Therefore, no one else can transmit until that token has been released by the destination end device back into the network.

With the token ring, there are no collisions and it was reliable, but the speed of it was just too slow. Again, the popularity for designing, implementing, and using a token ring network simply did not catch on for use on LANs.

On WANs, we did have the **Fiber Distributed Data Interface** (**FDDI**) which used token ring technology and ran it up to gigabit speed. But, as you go through this book, the token ring will not be mentioned at all; it is considered an older technology and, for LANs, it is not used. Also, for your certification you will not need to know this information. Just think of it as information to have in your back pocket for interviews and dinner parties.

The OSI model

For anything to work properly and for us to understand how things work, we need to have some sort of standards or blueprints that will allow us to clear the concepts of how particular objects interoperate with each other.

So, for us to be able to network with different types of devices and understand what it takes to get information from a source to a destination, the **International Standards Organization** (**ISO**) came up with a conceptual blueprint called the OSI model. This model is in a seven-layer approach that helps us understand this concept and allows vendors to create devices that can interoperate with each other.

This conceptual layered blueprint gives each layer a responsibility; each layer has a job to do, specific to that layer. You can think of it as a company; every business has departments and each department is responsible for a specific role that the company requires to operate smoothly. If any department within the company fails to do their job, the company will fail to carry out its primary objective.

The cool thing is you can change employees within the department and, if they are trained or at least knowledgeable in their respective field, it will not affect the outcome of what that company is trying to do.

The same goes for networks, each layer of the OSI model has a job to do and if vendors make changes to one layer, it won't affect the other layer from doing its job.

Let's go ahead and look at this seven-layer OSI model:

Layer number	Layer name	Brief description
7	Application	Works closest to the user, data
6	Presentation	Deals with the format of the data
5	Session	Keeps different applications' data separate
4	Transport	Provides reliable or unreliable delivery of information, segmentation
3	Network	Provides logical addressing, which routers use to route traffic, packets
2	Data Link	Deals with frames, error correction, and uses the MAC address to access media
1	Physical	Deals with bits, voltage, cabling

Now that we have seen the OSI model, for certification purposes, you must know each layer number and name, not to mention be able to recognize or define what job that layer is responsible for.

So, let's break down the OSI model into two parts: the upper layers and the lower layers.

The upper layers

Looking at the following three upper layers, we can understand that these layers work closest with user interaction, and how it will communicate with other end devices.

So, let's start defining each layer, starting from the top and working our way down:

Layer number	Layer name	Brief description
7	Application	Works closest to the user, data
6	Presentation	Deals with the format of the data
5	Session	Keeps different applications' data separate

The Application layer

This layer is the closest to the user, because it is the interface between an actual application and the next layer down.

People get confused with this layer because of its name. It does not mean that an application lives at that layer, such as IE or MS Word; it is the interface that allows the user to interact with it.

Any time we use any browser or Office application, the Application layer is involved, but that is not the only thing the Application layer does, it makes sure that the receiving end is ready to communicate and accept your incoming data.

So, for certification purposes, we need to remember the protocols that work on this layer: HTTP, HTTPS, FTP, TFTP, SNMP, DNS, POP, IMAP, TELNET, and any network service looking for communication across a large network.

The Presentation layer

This layer's function is very simple to remember: it is responsible for data translation and code formatting. When devices transmit information, it is coded in a certain format; an example used everywhere is ASCII, so when the data gets to its destination, it needs to understand this format, it should be able decode the ASCII, and present it to the Application layer so the user will be able to read it. A simpler example would be an Excel spreadsheet, or a picture taken with a proprietary software that you don't have. If you do not have the software installed on your computer and someone sends you a file with an extension of .xls, .doc, .ppt, and so on, your operating system will not understand it and simply place a generic icon wherever you save it, and if you try to open it you will get a dialogue box asking which program you would like to use to open the file with.

The Presentation layer is also responsible for key functions, such as data compression, decompression, encryption, and decryption.

The Session layer

The common definition for this layer is setting up, managing, and breaking down sessions between Presentation layer objects, and keeps user data separate. So, basically, it is like having a dialogue control while monitoring the type of mode the client/server communication has, such as full-duplex or half-duplex communication.

Full-duplex communication is pretty much like a conversation you would have with a person, or over the phone – it is two-way communication. Whereas, half-duplex is like a walkie-talkie; you talk, then you listen. So, you can either send or receive at any given time.

The lower layers

Simply stated, the following layers define how information will be transmitted from the source to the destination:

4	Transport	Provides reliable or unreliable delivery of information, segmentation
3	Network	Provides logical addressing, which routers use to route traffic, packets
2	Data Link	Deals with frames, error correction, and uses a MAC address to access media
1	Physical	Deals with bits, voltage, cabling

We now have a better understanding of the OSI model. By breaking them up into two parts, we can see the overall picture of what they are trying to achieve. But we must go in deeper and break down the OSI into its individual layers.

The Transport layer

This is the layer that segments and reassembles data. Services that live on this layer take all data coming from the Application layer and combine it into a succinct data stream.

This layer holds two very important protocols: the **Transmission Control Protocol (TCP)** and the **User Datagram Protocol (UDP)**.

The TCP is known as the connection-oriented protocol, which means it will provide reliable transmission, compared to UDP, which does not.

Let's define what exactly Connection-Oriented Communication is. In reliable transmission, we have something called a three-way handshake. The process consists of the source sending a SYN packet to the receiver. If the receiver is ready, it will reply with a SYN/ACK, and then the sender replies with an ACK, then communication can occur and transfer data.

Let's see a visual:

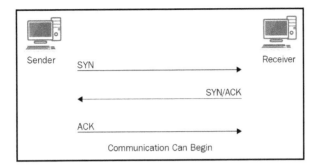

Remember that your topologies and your internetworking devices have a lot do with it as well. In a Star topology, everyone is connected to a central device. If you use a hub, you are in a shared collision domain, running at half-duplex and it's Ethernet, which uses the CSMA/CD access method.

Your network will burn to the ground in no time. That is why the internetworking device you use, the cables you run, and the protocols you use play a very important role in your network.

Luckily for us, we have a fail-safe solution called flow control and windowing.

Flow control prevents the sending device from overflowing the buffers on the receiving side.

The protocols that are involved with reliable communications make sure the following happens:

- Segments are acknowledged back to the sender
- Segments that do not get acknowledged are retransmitted

Services that are considered to be connection oriented have the following characteristics:

- Three-way handshake
- Uses sequencing
- Uses ACKs
- Uses flow control

Windowing

Windowing is the process to check how much information the receiver can handle in one segment.

This window is adjustable, based on how much information is coming in.

Imagine two people are unloading a truck full of boxes. You've got the sender, the guy on the truck you have the receiver, the guy on the warehouse floor. So, the unloading begins, one box at a time. After a while, the receiver says, *Hey! Send two boxes at a time.* The window got bigger so the receiver sends two boxes at a time and, if something happens along the way, the receiver will let the sender know, *Hey I did not get that box, send it again.*

The same principle is applied when using reliable networking, ACKs, NACKs, sequencing, and windowing.

The Network layer

The Network layer is my favorite layer. This layer is where all the routing of the packets that take place in your segment or remote segments. The Network layer works with routed protocols, such as IPv4 or IPv6, routing protocols, such as RIPv2, RIPng, EIGRP, EIGRP for IPv6 and OSPF, and OSPFv3. I will be explaining these protocols in more depth later in the book.

The Network layer creates a routing table that stores all the routes it learns from the routing protocols or static routes that one enters manually. By default, all routers know who they are connected to. So, when a source decides to send a packet to a destination not within its own segment, it will need a layer three device, such as a router, to send the information to the proper destination.

If a router receives a packet with a network destination that is not in the routing table, the router will simply drop the packet and send you an error statement: `Destination host unreachable` or you could get `Request Timeout`. These two errors have different meanings, the first is that an entry for that network was never found, and the second is that the destination router has no entry or path to get back.

So, clearly, when we configure routers or any layer-three device, we must be very careful when inputting the IP addresses and subnet mask on their interface. When you configure any routing protocol, make sure you input the network addresses you are directly connected to. Routers will always choose the shortest path to a destination based on its metric; this will determine the path the packet will take to the destination.

Let's define some of the terms used:

- **Routed protocols**: These are the protocols that sit on an interface, such as IPv4 and IPv6. These protocols will have a subnetted scheme, so data can be routed by a routing protocol that chooses the appropriate network.
- **Routing protocols**: These are the components that create the routing table based on their algorithm, which will use the routed protocol's IP information to obtain the network address, and then route protocols to the correct destination.
- **Metric**: This is a measurement of how far the destination is from the source; depending on the routing protocol in use, it will use the shortest metric to get to the destination.

Let's continue to the next layer.

The Data Link layer

This layer provides the physical transmission of information, and handles flow control, physical network topology, and error notification. At the Data Link layer, each message is translated into a data frame and this frame will have customized information in it, such as the source and destination hardware address.

The Data Link layer does not perform any routing at layer two. It simply uses these physical addresses of the end devices to get from source to destination within the same segment.

Routers do not care about layer-two addressing, they are more concerned with layer-three addressing.

Be careful with that statement, because if you're using Ethernet technology, at this point layer-two addressing becomes very important to the router.

The Data Link layer is divided into two sublayers.

Media Access Control layer

In this sub layer, packets are placed on the media, depending on the technology used, such as Contention-Based or Token-Passing. As you know, physical addressing, that is, the MAC address or burned-in address of an NIC card, is used through the physical topology as well as the logical topology.

Logical Link Control (LLC)

Here, the responsibilities change to identifying network protocols and then passing them on to encapsulate them. The LLC header will always tell the Data-Link layer what to do with a packet once the frame is received.

The Physical layer

This layer is responsible for sending bits from the source to the destination on whatever media it is using.

Remember, even though in theory we say 0's and 1's, it is really electrical impulses that are generated and sent through the air as a Carrier Wave; or through cabling, that might need specific encoding and decoding, such as serial cables. In this layer, you'll find devices such as hubs, repeaters, amplifiers, cabling, even a modem at the client side, known as a channel service unit/data service unit.

As far as your certification is concerned, you only need to know IEEE basic information where the OSI is concerned.

One last thing I would like to leave you with before we move on to more exciting and adventurous topics is **encapsulation** and **Protocol Data Units** (**PDUs**). But a visual will be much better:

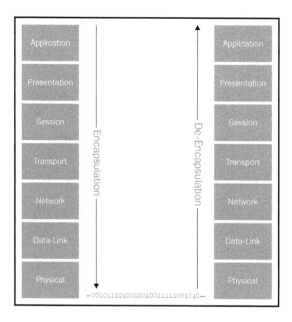

As packets flow down the OSI model, they will get encapsulated with the proper protocols, error corrections, and any other information they need to get to reach destination. Once they reach the destination, they will be de-encapsulated back into the original data format.

The process of encapsulation is a called data, segments, packets, frames, and bits or you could think of it as *Don't, Stop, Pouring, Free, Beer.*

These are called the PDUs, which communicates with their peer layer to make sure everything is in order.

Summary

We have learned quite a bit. We looked at basic topology types and devices on a network. Then we covered the OSI model. Finally, we looked at the different layers of the OSI model in detail.

In the next chapter, we will learn about fundamentals of Ethernet networking and data encapsulation.

Ethernet Networking and Data Encapsulations

2

Before we start our journey into the exciting world of Ethernet technologies, we really need to understand how important Ethernet is in today's networking. We will be learning not only about collision domains and broadcast domains, but also about half duplex versus full duplex, cabling, and the Cisco three layer model. Understanding all these concepts and technologies will help you become a more efficient network engineer.

In this chapter, you will not only learn the concepts of Ethernet but also, through diagrams, you will get a visual picture of setting up a network and why you are using the equipment you use.

We will be covering the following topics in this chapter:

- A brief overview of Ethernet networks
- Cabling in Ethernet networks
- The Cisco three-layer model

A brief overview of Ethernet networks

Ethernet is considered a contention-based or *first come, first served* access method. This will allow all nodes on a network to share the same link's bandwidth. It is the most popular and widely used type of networking in the world today. I know you may be thinking: *wait a minute, shared media*? Doesn't that slow everything down? The great thing about Ethernet is that you have options for configurations, scalability, and inter-operability, and it is also quite simple to implement.

Now, Ethernet takes advantage of both the data link and physical link layers of the OSI model, which means we will be gathering information from both of those layers, IP addresses, and the MAC address. So, we will need to effectively and vigilantly maintain an Ethernet network.

Collision domain

This Ethernet term simply means that in a network when one device sends a frame out onto the media of its network segment, it will force every other device on that same segment to hear or pay attention to the noise that is generated, which causes a slow down on the segment. That can cause major issues. Imagine yourself in the busiest intersection in the world, no stop signs, no traffic cops, no lights, and you are in the middle of rush hour with hundreds if not thousands of vehicles trying to get to their destination and at 100 MPH. Do you think a collision will occur? Oh, yeah! Let's look into the following diagram for more clarification:

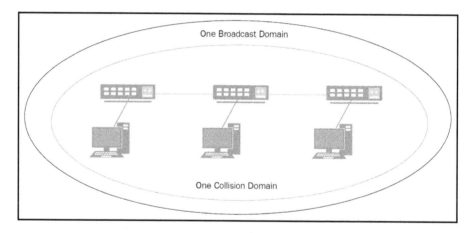

Looking at the preceding diagram, we can see that if one of those computers transmits any data on the wire, it will be heard by all, because it is a shared collision domain. So, imagine if these were hundreds of computers or even thousands. But even worse is the fact that using a hub for a network will also create one broadcast domain, so it is one big pile-up on the road! So, how do we fix this? Look at the following diagram:

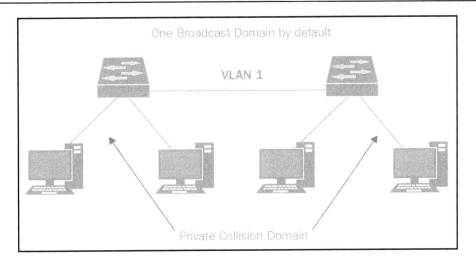

The main difference here is that we are using switches instead of hubs. This creates multiple private collision domains, which will increase the bandwidth and be able to run at full duplex unlike in a shared collision domain which runs at half duplex. I will explain half duplex and full duplex later in the chapter.

But we still have the issue of only one broadcast domain. Any end device that connects to this network will be part of VLAN 1, which is the native VLAN and all the noise will be heard across the network.

So, you fix the issue of the collision domains by substituting the hub for a switch. This will allow you to have multiple private collision domains, but you still have one broadcast domain. To truly fix that issue, you could use a router or logically segment the network by putting each switch in its own VLAN. Once you start using VLANs, you are creating multiple broadcast domains, which will contain that noise within its own segment.

CSMA/CD

Before we go any further, let's define the access method of Ethernet once again to make sure we understand how it works and give a formal definition to the broadcast domain.

Carrier Sense Multiple Access Collision Detection (**CSMA/CD**) is the access method used by Ethernet networks, which, simply stated, is a first come, first served type of access to the media; it's a race to see who can transmit first.

If multiple packets access the wire at the same time, a collision will occur and they will be dropped. At that moment, a jamming signal will be transmitted and no one will be able to send anything until the timer runs out, and then all nodes will be allowed to transmit once more.

So, you can see why hubs are not used anymore and, even if you use switches to minimize the effect of CSMA/CD, you would use VLANs, which will be explained later in the book. Let's put this process into steps:

1. A jamming signal tells all nodes on the network that a collision has been detected
2. Because of the collision, it invokes a back-off algorithm
3. During this period, no one can transmit onto the media
4. Once the timer ends, all nodes will have the opportunity to transmit again

Broadcast domain

Let's look at a better design for your infrastructure, and then I will give you the definition of a broadcast domain:

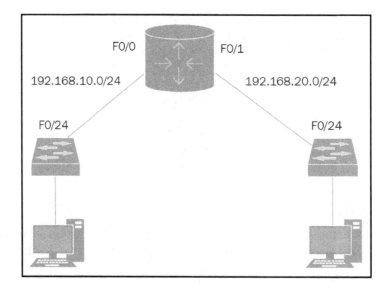

In the preceding diagram, we created a second broadcast domain by putting a router in the middle and physically creating that second broadcast domain. This means that what happens in the 192.168.10.0 network will stay within that network and the 192.168.20.0 network will not hear any noise. Therefore, it will not slow down that network.

Even though we made the network more efficient by increasing the bandwidth and also improving security and manageability, it's not very realistic. Imagine if you had hundreds of segments; are you going to physically segment them all? Nope.

Let's look at a more realistic approach and one that you will be most likely to be asked about when taking your CCNA certification. It is called a router on a stick design:

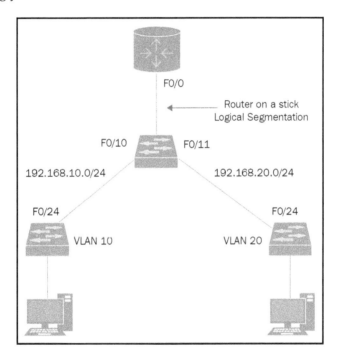

Using this design, all you need is one router and you can create multiple sub-interfaces to represent the gateway for each segment or subnet. There is no need to buy hundreds of routers or a router with hundreds of physical interfaces; you simply create sub-interfaces for each VLAN, segment, or subnet. They all mean the same thing: different broadcast domains; hence, making your network more efficient.

Half-duplex versus full-duplex

We are going to make this simple and straight to the point. The IEEE 802.3 standard for Ethernet explains it one way, while Cisco has somewhat of their own definition. So, I will give you the *Laz simplified method* of understanding this. If your internet-working devices, such as a switch or router are configured to run half-duplex on their ports, then you can only send or receive; you cannot do both.

This is defeating the purpose of creating multiple collision or broadcast domains. If you configure your internet-working devices to use full-duplex, then you can send and receive at the same time. This will allow you to take advantage of the 100 Mbps bandwidth available to you, if you are running STP CAT 5e cabling.

To make the event simpler than that, keep in mind what we described previously. In half-duplex, you only use one pair of wires, where as in full-duplex, you would be using two pairs of wires:

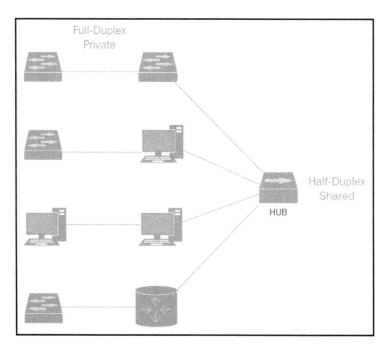

As you can see on the left side of the preceding diagram, those connections would be full-duplex, but be warned, always check the state of the ports to make sure they are set to full-duplex. When you use a hub, which you never will, it will always be a shared collision domain and therefore it will always run at half-duplex.

The following list is something I want you to keep in mind, for your certification and it is also good to know for your IT database of knowledge:

- There are no collisions in full-duplex mode (always monitor your network)
- Always check your ports on your internet-working devices to make sure they are indeed running at full-duplex
- A dedicated switch port is required for each full-duplex connection
- Please verify that your NIC cards can run in full-duplex

Ethernet at layer 2 of the OSI

We have discussed Ethernet networks and their access methods, and how to physically or logically segment the network. But now, we need to know how Ethernet works at the Data-Link layer.

Ethernet is responsible for addressing at the Data-Link layer, which is called the MAC address or hardware addressing. Ethernet also handles the framing when it receives a packet from the network layer, which is layer 3 of the OSI model. It takes those addresses and prepares them for transmission to your local segment.

If we don't know already, a MAC address, hardware address, or burned-in address is 48 bits long and it's in hexadecimal format. Let's look at how the MAC address is divided:

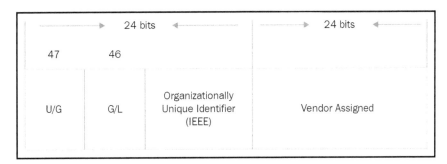

As you can see from the preceding diagram, a MAC address is broken into two parts: the OUI and the vendor-assigned portion. The MAC address, like an IP address, is unique to each host, or it should be.

The other bits you see there are U/G and G/L. These are three bytes in length. The *U* represents universal bit and the *G* represents global. So, what does that mean? Well, if the bit is set to 0, it becomes globally administered and the IEEE assigned it; if the bit is set to 1, it represents a locally administered or manufactured assigned code.

Just for your knowledge, and to help you out when subnetting or looking at IPv6 addresses, commit the following tables to memory. Believe me, this is going to save your life!

Bit	Decimal
10000000	128
11000000	192
11100000	224
11110000	240
11111000	248
11111100	252
11111110	254
11111111	255

In this table, as you can see, as you turn on bit values left to right the decimal increases.

The bit values that you are adding from left to right are as follows:

128·64·32·16·8·4·2·1

This next table is the hex table, which you should also commit to memory:

Hex number	Value
1	1
2	2
3	3
4	4
5	5
6	6
7	7
8	8
9	9
A	10

B	11
C	12
D	13
E	14
F	15

Also keep in mind that each hex number is four bits long. We use hex as a shortcut to writing binary numbers.

Let's see the following example:

Hex number: E6

Binary: 1110|0110 Result: 11100110

Decimal: 128 64 32 16 8 4 2 1

1 1 0 0 1 1 0 = 230 is the decimal

The function of Ethernet nodes is to forward frames between each other using MAC addressing. One the perks that this provides is error detection from a component called **Cyclic Redundancy Check (CRC)**. Let me give you a visual of a common Ethernet frame used in today's networking:

			Ethernet_II			
Preamble 7 bytes	5FD 1 byte	Destination 6 bytes	Source 6 bytes	Type 2 bytes	Data and Pad 46-1500 bytes	FCS 4 bytes
					Packet	

Unfortunately, we need to know exactly what each part of the Ethernet frame means. We have to give a definition so you can understand why it is needed, so before you start reading this, get some coffee, wash your face, but stay awake. I know we can make it through. Let's go through the following table:

Component	Definition
Preamble	It's a pattern of 1,0 that alternates. It has a 5 MHz clock at the beginning of each packet that will allow the receiving devices to home in to the incoming bit stream.
Start of Frame Delimiter (SFD)	The purpose of the SFD is to sync up to detect the beginning of the data. Keep in mind the SFD is 10101011 and it uses the last pair of 1's to do this.
Destination Address (DA)	This transmits a 48-bit value sync, the least significant bit first. It is used by the receiving node to determine if an incoming packet is addressed to a certain node.
Source Address (SA)	This identifies the host that is transmitting using the 48-bit address.
Length or type	This is an 802.3 length field or type for Ethernet II, to identify Layer 3 protocols.,
Data	This is the actual packet that is carrying the data and it can vary from 46 to 1500 bytes.
Frame Check Sequence (FCS)	This stores the CRC answer, so when a receiving host gets the frame and runs the CRC, it should be the same answer.

Enough of that; let's move on to our next topic.

Ethernet at layer 1 of the OSI

We have been talking a lot about Ethernet, and rightfully so. Ethernet is a standard that is implemented by a group of companies: Digital, Intel, and Xerox. This group was called DIX. They were the ones who implemented the Ethernet LAN standards first, which in turn helped the IEEE to create the 802.3 Committee.

The original LAN standard was lightening fast at 10 Mbps and ran over coaxial cable, until finally twisted pairs came into the picture, and now it even runs through fiber.

So you can see that Ethernet goes back a long way and, in order to understand Ethernet fully, you should know how it began. The following will show you all the different IEEE 802.3 standards that we should be aware of.

The laundry list of 802.3 standards and their amendments is given in the following table:

IEEE 802.3 standard	1983	10BASE5 10 Mbit/s (1.25 MB/s) over thick coax. Same as Ethernet II except type field is replaced by length, and an 802.2 LLC header follows the 802.3 header. Based on the CSMA/CD process.
802.3a	1985	10BASE2 10 Mbit/s (1.25 MB/s) over thin coax (also thinnet or cheapernet).
802.3b	1985	10BROAD36.
802.3c	1985	10 Mbit/s (1.25 MB/s) repeater specs.
802.3d	1987	Fiber-optic inter-repeater link.
802.3e	1987	1BASE5 or StarLAN.
802.3i	1990	10BASE-T 10 Mbit/s (1.25 MB/s) over twisted pair.
802.3j	1993	10BASE-F 10 Mbit/s (1.25 MB/s) over fiber-optic.
802.3u	1995	100BASE-TX, 100BASE-T4, 100BASE-FX fast Ethernet at 100 Mbit/s (12.5 MB/s) with autonegotiation.
802.3x	1997	Full-duplex and flow control; also incorporates DIX framing, so there's no longer a DIX/802.3 split.
802.3y	1998	100BASE-T2 100 Mbit/s (12.5 MB/s) over low quality twisted pair.
802.3z	1998	1000BASE-X Gbit/s Ethernet over fiber-optic at 1 Gbit/s (125 MB/s).
802.3-1998	1998	A revision of base standard incorporating the preceding amendments and errata.
802.3ab	1999	1000BASE-T Gbit/s Ethernet over twisted pair at 1 Gbit/s (125 MB/s).
802.3ac	1998	Max frame size extended to 1,522 bytes (to allow *Q-tag*). The Q-tag includes 802.1Q VLAN information and 802.1p priority information.
802.3ad	2000	Link aggregation for parallel links, since moved to IEEE 802.1AX.
802.3-2002	2002	A revision of base standard, incorporating the three prior amendments and errata.

802.3ae	2002	10 gigabit Ethernet over fiber; 10GBASE-SR, 10GBASE-LR, 10GBASE-ER, 10GBASE-SW, 10GBASE-LW, 10GBASE-EW.
802.3af	2003	Power over Ethernet (15.4 W).
802.3ah	2004	Ethernet in the first mile.
802.3ak	2004	10GBASE-CX4 10 Gbit/s (1,250 MB/s) Ethernet over twin axial cables.
802.3-2005	2005	A revision of base standard incorporating the four prior amendments and errata.
802.3an	2006	10GBASE-T 10 Gbit/s (1,250 MB/s) Ethernet over unshielded twisted pair (UTP).
802.3ap	2007	Backplane Ethernet (1 and 10 Gbit/s (125 and 1,250 MB/s) over printed circuit boards).
802.3aq	2006	10GBASE-LRM 10 Gbit/s (1,250 MB/s) Ethernet over multimode fiber.
P802.3ar	Cancelled	Congestion management (withdrawn).
802.3as	2006	Frame expansion.
802.3at	2009	Power over Ethernet enhancements (25.5 W).
802.3aw	2007	Fixed an equation in the publication of 10GBASE-T (released as 802.3-2005/Cor 2).
802.3-2008	2008	A revision of base standard incorporating the 802.3an/ap/aq/as amendments, two corrigenda and errata. Link aggregation was moved to 802.1AX.
802.3az	2010	Energy-efficient Ethernet.
802.3ba	2010	40 Gbit/s and 100 Gbit/s Ethernet. 40 Gbit/s over 1 m backplane, 10 m Cu cable assembly (4×25 Gbit or 10×10 Gbit lanes) and 100 m of MMF and 100 Gbit/s up to 10 m of Cu cable assembly, 100 m of MMF or 40 km of SMF, respectively.
802.3-2008/Cor 1	2009	Increase pause/reaction/delay timings, which are insufficient for 10 Gbit/s (workgroup name was 802.3bb).
802.3bc	2009	Move and update Ethernet-related TLVs (type, length, values), previously specified in Annex F of IEEE 802.1AB (LLDP) to 802.3.
802.3bd	2010	Priority-based flow control. An amendment by the IEEE 802.1 Data Center Bridging Task Group (802.1Qbb) to develop an amendment to IEEE Std 802.3 to add a MAC control frame to support IEEE 802.1Qbb priority-based flow control.

802.3.1	2011	MIB definitions for Ethernet. It consolidates the Ethernet-related MIBs present in Annex 30A&B, various IETF RFCs, and 802.1AB annex F into one master document with a machine-readable extract. (Workgroup name was P802.3be).
802.3bf	2011	Provide an accurate indication of the transmission and reception initiation times of certain packets as required to support IEEE P802.1AS.
802.3bg	2011	Provide a 40 Gbit/s PMD, which is optically compatible with existing carrier SMF 40 Gbit/s client interfaces (OTU3/STM-256/OC-768/40G POS).
802.3bm	2015	100G/40G Ethernet for optical fiber.
802.3bt	2017	Power over Ethernet enhancements up to 100 W using all four pairs, balanced twisted-pair cabling, lower standby power, and specific enhancements to support IoT applications (lighting, sensors, building automation).

As I said, you do not have to memorize this huge laundry list. Be aware that it exists and know where to find the standards and see what the requirements are.

When you are designing your network, you really need to consider the type of media your data will be traveling on. I know we would all like to be running the latest and greatest. Could you imagine running fiber in a LAN. Wow! It would be awesome, but not realistic. Why? Because of your budget limitations, running fiber all over your LAN would be pretty expensive. If you have deep pockets, then you can do whatever you want but nine out ten times, that is not the case.

With all that said, we look toward another organization, the EIA/TIA, which stands for the Electronic Industries Alliance and the Telecommunications Industry Association. This is the standard that governs the specifications for the physical layer of the OSI.

The EIA/TIA will let you know how far twisted-pair cabling can be run, from node to node and from end to end. This is the reason designing and planning your network is so important. Understanding *who* you're building the network for. Are we playing Bingo or are we transferring architectural drawings? All this information will help you decide which standard you should use.

The following table shows the more common Ethernet standards you should know about:

Standard	Definition
10Base-T IEEE 802.3	10 Mbps, CAT3, UTP, 100 meters uses RJ45
100Base-TX IEEE 802.3u	100 Mbps, CAT5e, UTP, 100 meters uses RJ45
100Base-FX IEEE 802.3u	Fiber 62.5/125-micron, multi-mode, 412 meters, uses ST or SC connectors
1000Base-CX IEEE 802.3z	Twinax cable, 25 meters High Speed Serial Data Connector
1000Base-T IEEE 802.3ab	1 Gbps, CAT5, 100 meters, UTP 4 pair
1000Base-SX IEEE 802.3z	1 Gbps, MMF, 62.5 and 50-micron core, 220 - 550 meters
1000Base-LX IEEE 802.3z	1 Gbps, SMF, 9-micron core, 3 kilometers up to 10 Km
1000Base-ZX (Cisco standard)	1 Gbps, SMF, can reach up to 70 Km
10GBase-T 802.3an	10 Gbps, UTP, CAT5,6 or 7,100 meters, RJ45

Once again, for your certification, the preceding table is what you need to concentrate on, but in real-world scenarios, you have to use reference material to decide what standard you should be using.

One of the more important reasons for choosing the right standard is that it will dictate what type of cabling you will be using. This will allow you to reach not only the speed, but the distance it could travel with the least amount of interference and attenuation.

Let's look at a diagram to get a more complete picture:

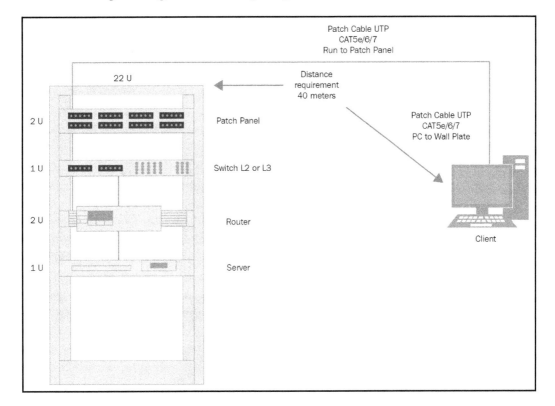

The preceding diagram gives you a more realistic view of what you would find in medium to large networks. You would run cables from the end device wall plate to the patch panel. That would be called your *horizontal cabling*. The cable that goes from the PC to the wall plate is your *patch cabling*.

Within the rack itself, those connections would be called *cross connects*, connecting the end devices to the switch, which in turn connects the switch to the router and server or other equipment.

The point to all this is that when you have this scenario, you must choose your cables correctly and that's where the Ethernet and the EIA/TIA standards come into play.

Since cabling is so important, let's dive deeper into cabling in a network.

Cabling in Ethernet networks

OK, we talked about Ethernet at layer 2 and layer 1, which dealt with cabling, and we even looked at some IEEE 802.3 standards. Now that we have an idea about the cables used in different IEEE 802.3 standards, let's dive in to three main cables that we need to be extremely familiar with:

- Straight-through cable
- Crossover cable
- Rolled cable

These cables are all going to be created using UTP CAT5e cabling. This type of cabling will allow a full duplex environment to go at speeds of 100 Mbps and reach 100 meters.

The abbreviation UTP stands for **Unshielded Twisted Pair Cabling**. This type of cabling is the most commonly used in any real-world scenario and is what you will be tested on. This is also the most frugal way of networking, because all you have is the jacket that makes up the cable and the cable itself.

This type of cable is very susceptible to electromagnetic interference, which can create a problem for your data going across your network. So, let's look at this very popular cable:

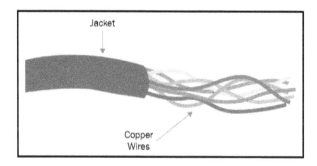

As you can plainly see, the copper wires have on protection from EMI, so interference is very likely to happen. That is why, when using UTP cabling, you must stay away from high-voltage devices.

Earlier in the chapter, we mentioned three types of cables you must know about, which are straight-through, cross over, and rolled. Let's first look at a diagram to show what devices are connected to what:

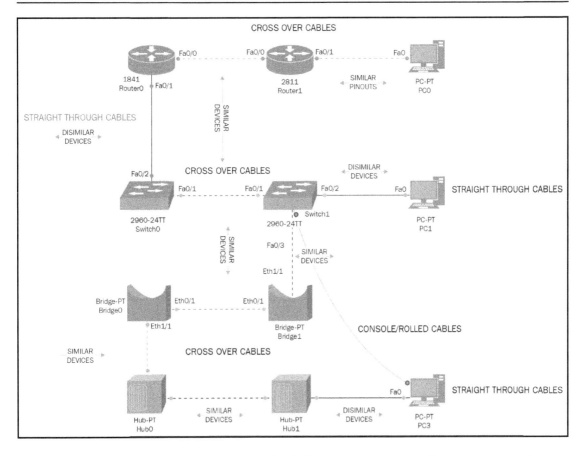

In the preceding diagram, there are a bunch of different internet-working devices and some PCs. Notice the lines that go from one device to another. The dashed lines are crossover cables and the solid lines are straight through cables. The blue line going from **PC3** to **Switch1** is called a console cable that you can purchase. When you do purchase any of the internet-working devices shown in the diagram, it will come with a console cable. If you do not have access to a console cable, one can be made using a CAT5e UTP cable.

Straight-through cables

How do you create or make a straight-through cable? Well, you follow the EIA/TIA 568B or EIA/TIA 586A standard.

If both ends of the cable have the same color code standard 568A or 568B, then you have a straight-through cable:

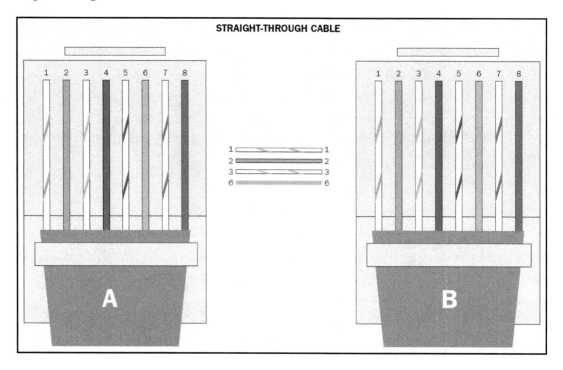

As shown in the preceding diagram, side A and side B both are using the 568B standard, which is the most common standard used in networking. You must know not only the color code but the pinouts as well. In this case, pins 1 and 2 transmit and pins 3 and 6 receive. Just keep in mind that this configuration will only give you 10/100 Mbps, not gigabit.

Straight-through cables are used to connect dissimilar devices, such as a router to a switch.

Crossover cable

How do you create or make a crossover cable? Well, you follow the EIA/TIA 568B or EIA/TIA 586A standard.

If both ends of the cable have the different color code standards 568A and 568B, then you have a crossover cable:

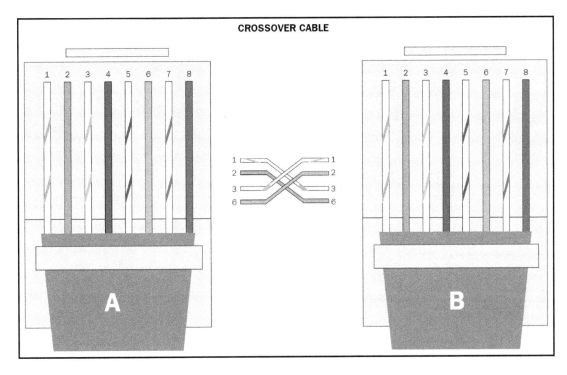

In this scenario, side A is using 568A and side B is using 568B. Since the standards differ on both ends of the cable, it becomes a crossover cable, with which you can connect similar devices, such as a router to a router.

In the cabling diagram showed previously, you have PC0 connecting to a Router1 using a crossover, so if dissimilar devices used a straight-through cable, what happened here? The pins on the NIC card of the PC are the same on the interface of a router, therefore making them similar devices, needing a crossover cable.

Rolled cable

This type of cable is used to connect from your PC to a console port of a router or switch, so you can gain access to the device that either has no configurations on it, or simple default configurations. But, you would also need a rolled-to-serial adapter to make this work:

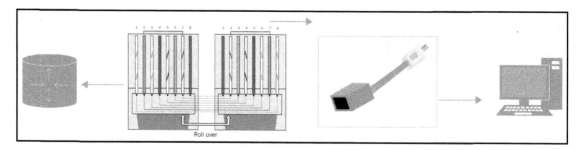

If you look closely at the actual rollover cable, it is using the 568B standard on the left and then it takes that same standard and reverses it on the other side. So, they are mirror images of each other.

Console cable

When you purchase your internet-working device, it should come with a console cable, so you do not have to create a rollover cable to connect to the console port of a switch or router. When using your console cable, there are some configurations you need to do to your Terminal emulator, such as PuTTY:

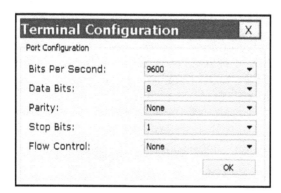

Notice the bit rate is set to **9600**. If you set it to anything else, all you will see on your screen is gibberish. **Data Bits** are set to **8**, **Parity** will be **None**, **Stop Bits** are set to **1** and **Flow Control** will be **None**.

Any deviation from this setting and you will not be able to gain access to your device, or it will be too slow, or cute characters will appear on your screen.

Fiber-optic cable

For you lucky ones that are able to acquire fiber for your network, there are some things you need to be aware of. Besides that, it allows for extremely fast transmission of data and nothing can interfere with it; no EMI or RFI.

On the downside, you are looking at a lot of $$$$$ to dish out for the cable and its installation of the cable. Not everyone can install fiber; you would need to be certified to do so.

Let's break down the cable into its main components, which are the core and the cladding. What happens is that the core will hold the light that goes through the cable and the cladding confines the light to the core. If the cladding that confines the light is tighter, the core will become smaller, which means faster and farther transmission for us:

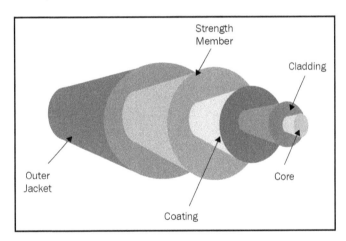

As you can see from the preceding diagram, fiber cables have a lot of protection from outside interference. There is the outer jacket, and then we have the strength member, the cladding, and finally the core, which is going to be emitting the light and transmitting our data.

Also, keep in mind that there are two types of connectors for fiber. Since you have multimode fiber and single-mode fiber, they must use different types of connectors.

The Cisco three-layer model

The Cisco three-layer model is simply a blueprint, just like the OSI model. This model creates a hierarchy that helps us to understand where our internet-working devices should be placed and what responsibilities they have at each one of the layers:

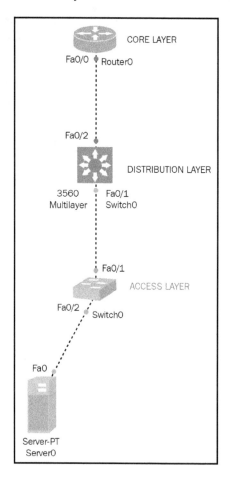

Core layer

This layer is responsible for sending large quantities of data that will generate lots of traffic, but it will be reliable and fast. Its only purpose in life is to route or switch traffic to its destination as quickly as possible. If something were to fail at the core layer, everyone below it will feel the impact and your network will be down.

Because of this, the core devices should steer away by performing the following at this layer:

- Make sure you are not going to configure anything at this level that may slow down its purpose.
- There is no work group access at this layer.
- If the core layer starts slowing down, look to upgrade your devices instead of adding on to the core. Adding or expanding to the core is not a very good idea.

Distribution layer

The distribution layer is often referred to as the work group layer. It is the communication point between the core and access layers. This layer provides the routing, filtering, WAN access, and determines how data packets can access the core.

This layer is where we want to implement policies for the network, due to the flexibility that is allowed at the distribution layer.

Things we must take into consideration when handling the distribution layer are as follows:

- Routing
- ACLs and packet filtering
- Security, network policies, NAT, and firewalls
- Inter-VLAN routing

Access layer

This layer controls users and work groups and access to the network resources. This layer is also known as the desktop layer. All resources that users need will be handled by this layer, since the distribution layer is concerned primarily with traffic.

Here is a list of some functions at the access layer:

- Continued use of ACL and policies
- Creating more collision and broadcast domains
- Connectivity to the distribution layer

Summary

We have learned quite a bit in this chapter. The topics covered are considered to be the fundamentals of Ethernet networking. We covered the access method of Ethernet, which is CSMA/CD, and the problems that can occur if running half-duplex or full-duplex. We know what half- or full-duplex mean, so we understand the pros and cons of running one or the other.

We discussed the standards that dealt with Ethernet cabling, such as the IEEE standard, 802.3. We also broke down each type of cable, such as straight-through, crossover, and rolled cables. We looked at what type of cable we should use when connecting internetworking devices together.

Finally, we covered Cisco's blueprint on how we should build a hierarchy in our network to make it more efficient by separating them into three distinct layers: core, distribution, and access.

Introducing the TCP/IP 3

In this chapter, we will focus our attention on the TCP/IP suite. It was created and implemented by the **Department of Defense (DoD)**, so in case of a calamitous event, our data and communications would be intact. I will cover protocols that use TCP/IP and, throughout this book, you will learn how to design solid, dependable, and secure networks using Cisco routers and switches.

We will begin by looking at the DoD's version of the TCP/IP model; there are two of them, and we will compare them both to the OSI model in how the layers map over to each other.

One very exciting topic we will also start covering in this chapter is the wonderful world of IPv4 addressing. We will cover the following topics:

- The TCP/IP model
- The host-to-host layer/transport layer
- The Internet layer
- Address types of IPv4

The TCP/IP model

Before we get into the details of the TCP/IP model, let's briefly go back in time. TCP was the first on the scene in 1973. In 1978, it got broken up into to two parts, TCP and IP, which replaced the **Network Control Protocol (NCP)** and was considered the official means to transport any data that would connect to ARPANET. Since 1983, ARPANET has been referred to as the internet.

TCP/IP became the foundation for the exponential growth and success of today's World Wide Web and the internal or private networks used by small to large businesses.

The TCP/IP model, or DoD model, is just a shortened version of the OSI model. Instead of having seven layers, it has four layers—or, at least, it did. For the new CCNA 200-125 certification, there is a new five-layer TCP/IP model.

Let's compare them:

	OSI		TCP/IP			TCP/IP
7	Application					Application
6	Presentation		Application	5-7		Application
5	Session					
4	Transport		Transport	4		Transport
3	Network		Internet	3		Network
2	Data Link		Link	2		Data Link
1	Physical			1		Physical

Comparing OSI and TCP/IP models

Looking at the preceding figure, we have four distinct layers in the TCP/IP model, which was the original model: Application, Transport, Internet, and Link (the Link layer used to be called Network Access); in the new TCP/IP model, we have five layers: Application, Transport, Network, Data-Link, and Physical.

Essentially, they broke up the Link or Network Access Layer of the original model into two distinct layers, but you can see that the mapping remains the same, which is as follows:

- The top three layers of the OSI still map over to the Application layer of both the TCP/IP models
- Transport maps directly over Transport layers of both the TCP/IP models
- Network on the OSI maps over to the Internet layer from the old TCP/IP model and the Network layer of the new TCP/IP model
- Layers 2 and 1 from the OSI map over the Link layer of the old TCP/IP model and over layers 2 and 1 of the new TCP/IP model

The mapping has not changed, they just broke up the Link layer to better explain what happens on each individual layer, and they changed the name of the Internet layer to the Network layer.

But other than that, the mapping remains the same. I guess the names were changed to protect the innocent.

Let's give a brief definition for each of the TCP/IP model layers:

Layer name	Definition
Application	Defines the protocols used to communicate between one node and another, and controls the user interface specifications.
Transport	Uses protocols to set up the level of transmission service for applications. Deals with reliable communications from end to end, and guarantees error-free delivery. Also keeps track of packet sequencing.
Network	Deals with the logical transmission of packets over the network, which means routing protocols and routed protocols, such as IP.
Data-Link	Deals with the physical addressing of the nodes, so switches come into play here. Prepares the frames for delivery to the physical layer.
Physical	Mainly deals with media, such as cables, connectors, voltage, and the information leaving this layer is in 0's and 1's.

We now know what each layer's responsibility is, so let's start looking at and defining the protocols that work on each of those layers.

Here is a list of the more common protocols that we use daily and that you will be tested on. These protocols belong to the Application or Process layer:

Telnet is used not only on the internet but on **local area networks** (**LANs**). It provides text-oriented communication using a virtual terminal connection. Telnet was developed in 1969 and standardized as an **Internet Engineering Task Force** (**IETF**) standard, one of the first internet standards. The name means **teletype network**.

It allows users to access internetworking devices or end devices remotely through the Command Prompt or through an application, such as PuTTY, to configure or take control of the remote device.

One downfall to Telnet is that it uses cleartext communication using port 23.

If you look at the following screenshot, you can see how someone can Telnet into a device:

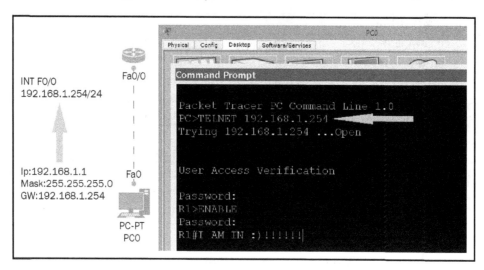

File Transfer Protocol (FTP)

The next protocol that we are going to look at is FTP, this protocol will allow you to transfer files from one machine to another, using less overhead than RDP or HTTP. FTP is also an application that allows us to designate users, passwords, encrypt transfers, assign different folders to clients, or even allow anonymous access, which I do not recommend.

Examples of applications that use FTP would be FileZilla, which is an open source FTP client, Cyberduck, which performs a lot of file-transfer needs, SFTP, WebDav, Amazon S3, Classic FTP, and WinSCP.

These applications will allow you to use FTP, but also be secure when you are transferring files. The FTP protocol uses two ports, 20 and 21. Port 20 is listening for incoming FTP traffic and port 21 does the transferring of data.

Let's look at the following screenshot, which uses a popular FTP application:

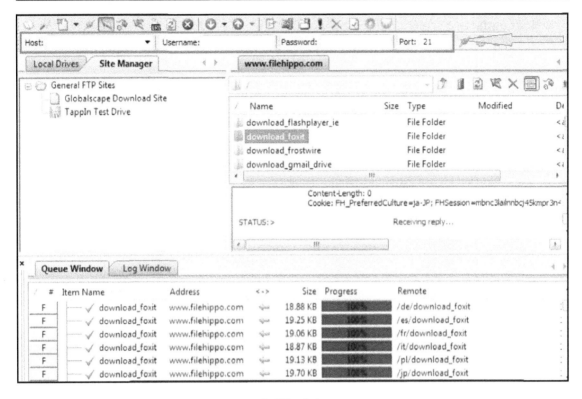

CuteFTP application

Look at the highlighted text boxes. They require you to fill in an IP address, username, password, and port number.

Trivial File Transfer Protocol (TFTP)

The next protocol at this layer is the TFTP, this is simply a broken-down version of FTP. This protocol does not have the same features as the complete version of FTP.

With TFTP, you cannot browse folders, create any usernames or passwords, and have no security whatsoever, but it is very fast at transferring files since it does not have all the overhead that FTP has.

Let's look at the two screenshots given here:

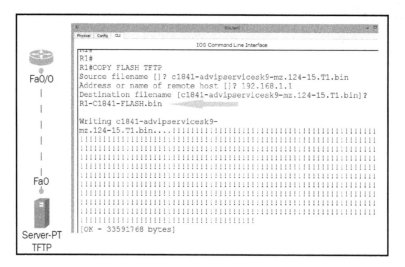

Common use of the TFTP protocol

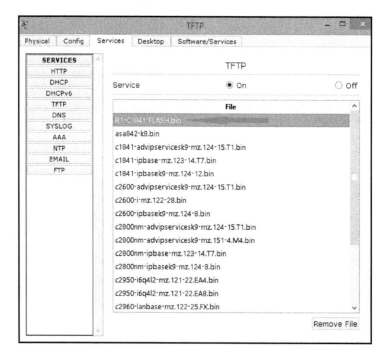

TFTP server with copied flash

As you can see from the preceding screenshot, TFTP is used with Cisco routers to copy the IOS to a server running TFTP to back up the IOS. It could be used to copy the startup configuration of a router or switch. The reason you would want to use TFTP is for its quick transfer of files; just keep in mind that this uses the UDP protocol, which is connectionless-oriented and does not guarantee packet delivery.

With that said, use TFTP for small, internal transfers; that is, those within your LAN.

Simple Network Management Protocol (SNMP)

Let's move on the next protocol that works at the Application layer, SNMP. This protocol collects and manipulates network information. SNMP acquires this data by polling all devices or designated devices, using a **Network Management Station** (**NMS**).

SNMP has the capability to gather this information at fixed or random intervals, demanding the end devices divulge information. An NMS can also be used to troubleshoot, we can gather network issues that any end device may be having.

If all is running as it should be in your network, SNMP will receive a message called a baseline, which is just a report stating the operational traits of a healthy network.

SNMP has three versions that we can use, so let's break them down:

- **SNMPv1**: Supports plaintext authentication with community strings, using only UDP.
- **SNMPv2c**: Supports plaintext authentication with community strings and with no encryption, but it does provide the GETBULK command. This command will allow you to get all the information at once, and minimize the GET requests. This version will offer a more detailed error-reporting method, called INFORM. SNMPv2 is more secure than SNMPv1, even though it uses no encryption. The default protocol is UDP, but you can configure it to use TCP.
- **SNMPv3**: Uses MD5 or SHA authentication, providing encryption and data integrity of messages through DES or DES-256 encryption between agents and managers. GETBULK is also a supported feature of SNMPv3 and, by default, it uses TCP.

SNMP also uses a database called the **Management Information Base** (**MIB**)—not *Men in Black*—which is a collection of information that is organized in a hierarchical fashion and can be accessed by SNMP.

SNMP has its own standards besides the RFCs. These standards are called **Organizational IDs (OIDs)** and are laid out on a tree with different levels assigned by different organizations, with top-level MIB OIDs belonging to various standards or organizations.

For certification purposes, and even in the real world, you do not have to remember OIDs. `.1.3.6.1.2.1.1.5.0` is what an OID looks like. So, don't worry, you don't have to memorize what the OID is for.

Let's look at a visual of what I am talking about:

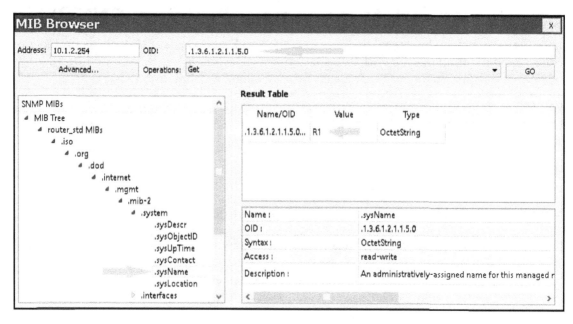

MIB browser on a PC

In the preceding screenshot, we are using SNMPv1. How would I know that? Well, I set it up—but let me show you exactly how you would do that. Take a look at the following screenshot:

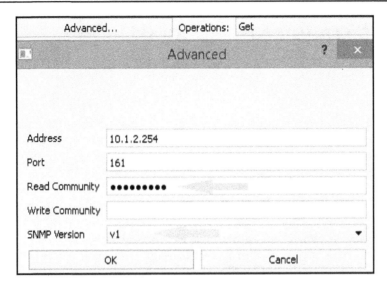

Configuring advanced configurations on SNMP MIB browser

Looking at the drop-down box SNMP version, here is where we can choose the version of SNMP we require. The most common is SNMPv2c, even though SNMPv3 is the one with the most security features and flexibility.

You also see the text fields called Community that are either read-only or write. You would want to choose read-only, so that no one can make changes to your MIB. Never give anyone write access unless ordered to do so by your superiors.

This field simply has a word or phrase that must be the same on the router. In our example, that word or phrase is really a name, Spartacus, it is case-sensitive so pay attention to detail.

Let me show you how you would enter that on a router:

```
R1#(config)#snmp-server community Spartacus ro
```

Voila! It's as simple as that, at least for certification purposes.

One final thing I want to mention: you do not have to be in the same subnet. If you are routing across your network and you have connectivity, you can get any SNMP messages across your network.

Hypertext Transfer Protocol (HTTP)

We have been using HTTP for years and some of us don't even know we are. Every time you go to a web page, it is the HTTP that makes it possible to reach those sites.

For us to use a browser to display a web page, it must find the correct server that is hosting that page, as well as the exact details that identify the information that you requested. When we type in the address bar of our browser, we usually just type `google.com` and, through the wonders of networking, we get to Google. But, if you looked at the address bar, it would really say `https://www.google.com/?gws_rd=ssl`.

This address is called a **Uniform Resource Locator** (**URL**). In this example, Google is using HTTPS, which is a secure version, which we will be talking about now, but you can see that by simply typing the `google.com` domain name, many DNS servers will search for that domain name and come back with a proper URL; that includes the types of Protocol, whether HTTP or HTTPS, a Fully-Qualified Domain Name, and the page for that site.

Now, let's use the secure version of the HTTP protocol, HTTPS. This is known as the Hypertext Transfer Protocol Secure, which uses the **Secure Socket Layer** (**SSL**). We could also refer to this protocol as SHTTP or even S-HTTP. There are minor changes between these protocols, but since the powers that be use HTTPS, this became the de facto standard for securing web communication.

HTTPS is what your browser needs in order to fill out forms, sign in, authenticate, and encrypt an HTTP message when you are online making all those vacation plans, such as purchasing cruise tickets and buying new clothes for the trip.

Network Time Protocol (NTP)

The next protocol on this layer we are going discuss is the NTP. The purpose of this protocol is to ensure synchronization between all devices and that they agree on a time. This is very crucial to a network, especially when dealing with database servers, domain controllers, and DNS servers.

The reason it's so important is because the mentioned servers must synchronize with each other to do transfers—if they are not in sync, no transfers will happen. Now that we are working with NTPv4, to look at the RFCs go to `http://www.ietf.org/rfc/rfc5907.txt`.

This is how you would look at the status of NTP on a router:

```
Router#sh ntp status
Clock is synchronized, stratum 2, reference is 192.168.1.1
nominal freq is 250.0000 Hz, actual freq is 249.9990 Hz, precision is 2**19
reference time is DD7F577F.00000175 (12:50:07.373 UTC Mon Nov 6 2017)
clock offset is 0.00 msec, root delay is 0.00 msec
root dispersion is 0.02 msec, peer dispersion is 0.02 msec.
```

NTP is a hierarchical protocol and is divided into strata that define the distance from the reference clock. A reference clock source that relays **Coordinated Universal Time** (**UTC**) and has little or no delay is known as a **stratum-0** device.

Domain Name Server (DNS)

Well, that's enough about NTP. Let's move on to the next protocol, and a very important protocol it is: DNS. This protocol will resolve a domain name to an IP address or the reverse. When we type a web address DNS is the one that is doing the resolution and finds the IP address for that web domain name.

As humans, we can't remember every IP address for every site on the internet, or objects in an Active Directory environment, so DNS comes to the rescue. DNS can also resolve IP addresses to FQDNs, but you would need to set this up yourself. Truth be told, an IT individual would have to set up a DNS server to handle all the requests. When doing so, you must set up forward-lookup zones, reverse-lookup zones, and pointer records. As in IT infrastructure, you will need multiple DNS servers to act as backup in case one server goes down to help other DNS servers with requests.

Before DNS came into the picture, we used LMHOST files, for which we needed to input manually a mapping of a name to an IP address manually. It was not very efficient and hard to keep up with. Then NetBIOS came into the picture, but it was a flat naming scheme, usually of 15 characters. To help NetBIOS's name resolution, they came up with WINS servers, or Windows Internet Name Servers, which created a database of these 15-character naming conventions, and WINS servers would talk to each other using a push/pull method.

Today, we use DNS, and if you are running Active Directory, it is a requirement that you have DNS servers so you can resolve FQDNs. The Fully-Qualified domain does not necessarily have to be `www.me.com`, it could be `laz.globed.net` or `PC1.thenetworkingdoctors.com`. You could have a public or private scheme, but a DNS or a group of DNS servers would find what you're looking for based on the domain structure.

Dynamic Host Configuration Protocol (DHCP)

The last protocol in the Application layer that we are going to discuss is DHCP. Be careful of the verbiage you use when defining this protocol. We are used to saying that the DHCP assigns IP addresses to end devices automatically, but that would be incorrect for certification purposes. Just change the word *assigns* to *allocates* and you will be fine. It is silly, but it's a test, and even in the real world you will run into this vocabulary discussion.

DHCP is very important in a network simply because it will allocate an IP address, subnet mask, default gateway, DNS, and WINS addresses for you. I don't think you want to walk around thousands, hundreds, or several end devices manually inputting all that information.

DHCP could be an actual service running on a server, or you could configure DHCP on a router. No matter where you configure it, DHCP has a process/step for allocating addresses to end devices:

1. **Discover**: It is a broadcast address of a client and server

2. **Offer**: The DHCP will offer the client an IP address from the pool of addresses you configured

3. **Request**: Client requests that IP address

4. **Acknowledge**: DHCP server basically says, *OK, here is your IP address*

If you are using DHCP, which you will do. If you want to do so outside your own segment, meaning that you would need to leave your router, you would need either a proxy server or an IP Helper address. What is their function? Since the first part of the process of DHCP is a broadcast, routers will drop those packets. So instead, you configure a proxy to go in on your behalf using a unicast address and retrieve your addresses for you.

Let's look at an example of such a dilemma:

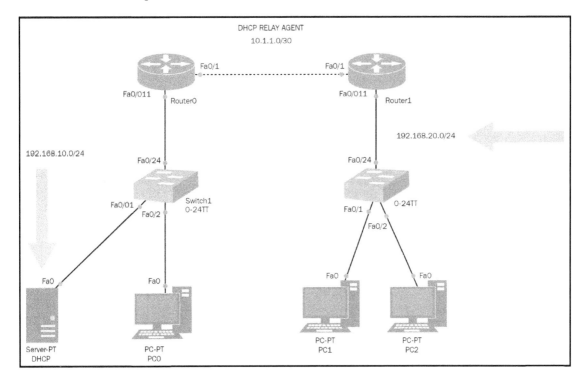

DHCP allocation topology across routers

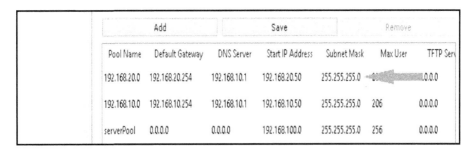

DHCP Pool

```
interface FastEthernet0/0
 ip address 192.168.20.254 255.255.255.0
 ip helper-address 192.168.10.1
```

Router configuration of an IP Helper address

As shown in the preceding three screenshots, the DHCP server exists only on the x.x.10.0 network, so anyone on that network will not have any issue in receiving an address from the server, but the x.x.20.0 network will not get an IP address from the DHCP server, due to the DORA process, so everyone on the x.x.20.0 network will receive an APIPA address, which is an Automatic Private IP Address. This is assigned by the OS of that PC and is a built-in feature. You could network with an APIPA within your network, but they are not routable addresses and you can't control the allocation of them.

So, how do you resolve that issue? As you can see in the router configuration, you use the IP Helper address that points to the DHCP server and it will act as a proxy for you. Also, it acquires an IP address from the DHCP server and allocates that to your end device.

We have reached the end of the Application layer of the TCP/IP model. Now, we must look at the other layers. Let's continue with the Host-to-Host, or Transport layer.

The host-to-host layer/transport layer

The main purpose of the Transport layer is to shield the upper-layer applications from the complexities of the network. In this layer, we will discuss the following topics:

- TCP
- UDP
- Key concepts to remember
- Port numbers

The Transmission Control Protocol is a connection-oriented protocol, meaning it makes sure that your data will get to the other side, using a series of checks and balances. TCP has in its arsenal things such as sequencing, windowing, acknowledgement, and negative acknowledgement.

Transmission Control Protocol (TCP)

TCP creates a virtual circuit or connection-oriented connection with the devices' TCP stacks to see whether they are ready to receive information. Once the other device *acknowledges* that it is ready, they will agree on how much information can travel back and forth; once this handshake is complete and both sides know what to expect, the transmission can continue.

You still may encounter errors on the way to Grandma's PC, but that is why TCP has NACKs also; if the receiver did not get the complete frame it will send a message to the sender, to resend the last transmission.

Thank heavens that TCP is full-duplex, because it does have a lot of overhead—it even has error checking. TCP has a cousin named UDP, which is connectionless. It really does not do any type of variation based on whether the message got there or not, but we know someone like that, don't we?

Amazingly enough, UDP is used in real-time video and VOIP. It works better due to less overhead:

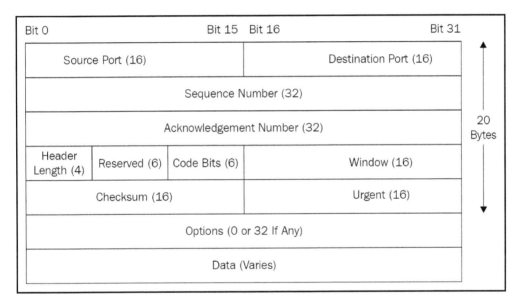

Table for TCP segment header

The preceding table shows us the TCP header, which we need to commit to memory for certification purposes and because an interviewer might ask you what the TCP header looks like. It's important to understand each field:

- **Source Port**: Port number of the sending application. Source port numbers are usually greater than 1,024.
- **Destination Port**: Port number of the destination application, such as FTP, Telnet, or SSH.
- **Sequence Number**: A number used by TCP that puts data back in the correct order. It could also retransmit damaged or missing data.

- **Acknowledgment Number**: The value that needs to be in that field.
- **Header Length**: The number of 32-bit words, which indicates where the data begins.
- **Reserved**: It is always set to zero.
- **Code bits/flags**: Sets up and terminates a session.
- **Window**: The amount of data the receiver can accept.
- **Checksum**: CRC is used due to lack of trust for the lower layers. It will check both the header and data fields.
- **Urgent**: If this is set, it will know where the segment of non-urgent data begins.
- **Options**: This field could be 0 or a multiple of 32 bits.
- **Data**: This is the actual data handed down from the upper layers.

The following screenshot shows a wireshark packet capture of a TCP segment:

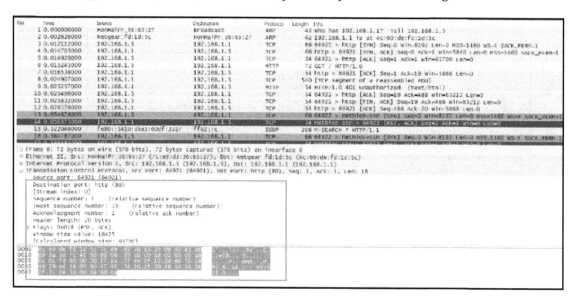

As you can see, the terminology we just defined can be found in the bottom portion of the image.

User Datagram Protocol (UDP)

This is basically a scaled-down version of the TCP protocol. This protocol has much less overhead than TCP because it does not use or offer all the *good stuff* that its big brother TCP uses. This protocol is dependent on the Application layer for reliability, meaning whoever designs an application, such as Outlook, will program in error checking, ACKS, and NACKS, so that UDP concerns itself only with the transportation of the data.

We still use UDP when we back up our internetworking devices—DNS will use UDP if the file size is 512 bytes or smaller, any file larger than 512 bytes will use TCP. But there are exceptions for some extensions the could use UDP up to 4,096 bytes.

UDP is concerned only with the fast transfer of files, end of discussion. Look at the following figure and compare the difference between headers with the TCP protocol:

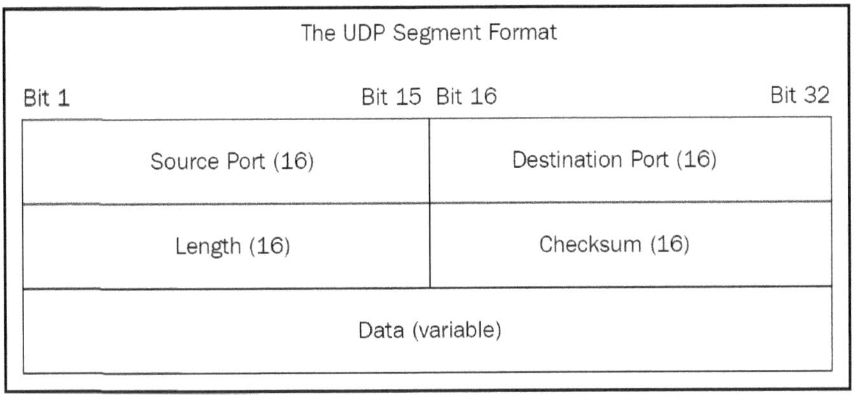

UDP segment

The Internet layers

In the TCP/IP model or DoD model, two main reasons exist for the Internet layer, which maps over to the OSI model's Network layer: routing and providing for a single network interface to the upper layers.

Without this layer, application programmers would need to write what are called **hooks** into every application for each different Network Access Protocol. If we think about it, that would mean a different version for each application—an example would be one for Ethernet and another for wireless, you get the picture. To cure this ineffective and unproductive method, we have the IP protocol, which is a single network interface for upper-layer protocols. The following is a list of the important protocols at the internet layer:

- **Internet Protocol (IP)**
- **Internet Control Message Protocol (ICMP)**
- **Address Resolution Protocol (ARP)**

Internet Protocol

The IP is essentially the Internet layer, and all the other protocols that exist at the Internet layer are to support the IP protocol. IP is the *see-all* protocol; that is, it is aware of all the interconnected networks. You may be asking yourself right now, *How does IP do this?*

It does this because it's assigned an IP address, but we will get to IP addressing soon. For now, understand that IP looks at each packet's address, uses a routing table, and decides in which direction a packet needs to go, choosing the best path. FYI, the best path depends on the type of routing you are using and on the routing protocol—patience, Grasshopper. We'll get there.

Identifying devices on a network requires knowing two different things: first, what network is it on? And second, who are you on that network? The answer to both of those questions is your Logical Address or IP address, which will provide you the information based accordingly on your subnet mask.

Let me take what I just stated a step further: to network, you really need four pieces of information:

- Source and Destination address (layer 3 logical addressing)
- Source and Destination address (layer 2 hardware address)
- Default Gateway Address (layer 3 logical addressing)
- Port number (Destination port number 80,25,21,23,22, and 3389)

Let's have a look at the IP header in the following diagram:

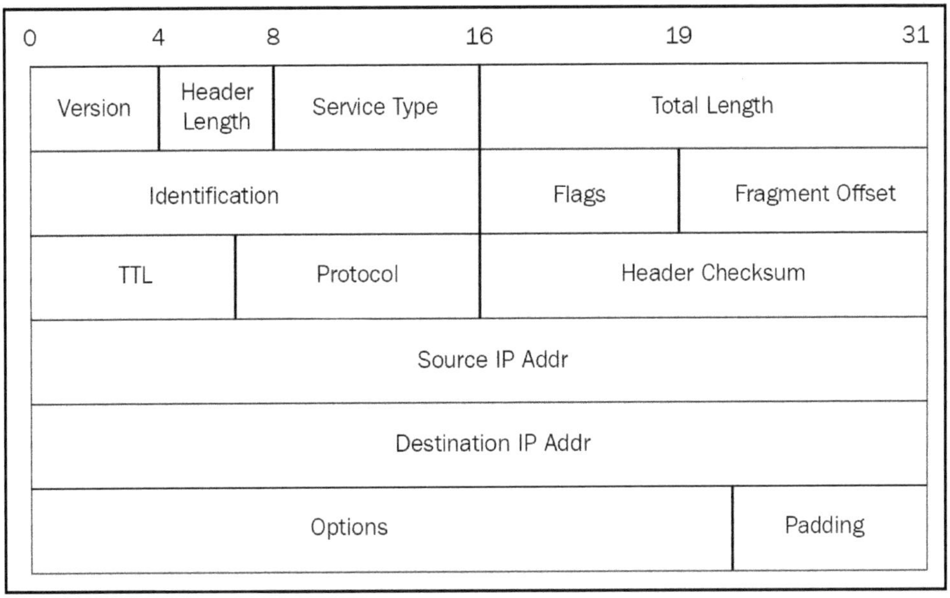

Let's define each of the IP header fields:

- **Version**: IP version number.
- **Header Length**: The length of the header in a 32-bit word.
- **Priority and Service Type**: The first three bits are what's called the differentiated service bits. It tells you how the datagram should be handled.
- **Total Length**: The length of a packet to include the header and data.
- **Identification**: It's a unique IP packet value used to differentiate fragmented packets from other packets.
- **Flags**: Specifies whether fragmentation should occur.
- **Fragment Offset**: It allows for max MTUs on the internet, and also provides fragmentation and reassembly if the packet is too large to put in a frame.
- **TTL**: The TTL is set inside a packet at the source. If the packet does not reach the destination before the TTL expires, this is when you start getting your unreachable destination or errors of that nature.
- **Protocol**: It can also be referred to as the type field in some analyzers. The port of the upper layer protocol such as, TCP is port 6 and UDP is port 17.
- **Header Checksum**: CRC on the header only.
- **Source IP**: 32-bit IP address of the sending device.

- **Destination IP**: 32-bit IP address the device is trying to get to.
- **Options**: User for network testing.
- **Data**: After the IP options field, will be the upper layer data.

We have defined each field of the IP header, which you should be familiar with, but the following table you need to commit to memory:

Protocol	Protocol number
ICMP	1
IP in IP tunneling	4
TCP	6
UDP	17
EIGRP	88
OSPF	89
IPV6	41
GRE	47
Layer 2 tunnel	115

The preceding table reflects the protocol field and the IP header along with the protocol numbers.

Internet Control Message Protocol (ICMP)

We are now going to discuss ICMP. This is basically a messaging protocol that will give us the following information:

- Provides hosts with information about network problems
- It is encapsulated within an IP datagram

When we test for connectivity, one of the most basic ways of doing that is using the `ping` command, which essentially is using ICMP to send an *echo request* and hopefully an *echo reply*.

If we reach the destination we are trying to ping, we will get four replies using the *Bang symbol !!!!* and if we can't reach our destination, we could get two different types of responses:

- **Destination unreachable**: Means you never left your own segment.
- **Request timeout**: Means the packet got to its destination, but it could not find its way back. It also has to do with the TTL on each packet sent:

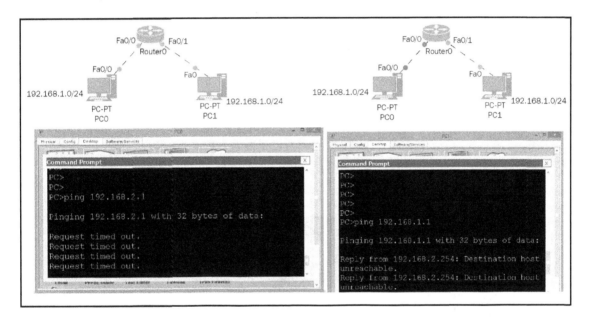

If you want to see more information about the ICMP echo request, you could use a network analyzer:

```
⊞ Frame 5: 114 bytes on wire (912 bits), 114 bytes captured (912 bits) on interface 0
⊞ Ethernet II, Src: c2:01:1a:18:00:00 (c2:01:1a:18:00:00), Dst: c2:02:09:58:00:00 (c2:02:09:58:00:00)
⊞ Internet Protocol Version 4, Src: 192.168.12.1 (192.168.12.1), Dst: 192.168.12.2 (192.168.12.2)
⊟ Internet Control Message Protocol
    Type: 8 (Echo (ping) request)
    Code: 0
    Checksum: 0x6c78 [correct]
    Identifier (BE): 0 (0x0000)
    Identifier (LE): 0 (0x0000)
    Sequence number (BE): 1 (0x0001)
    Sequence number (LE): 256 (0x0100)
    [Response frame: 6]
⊟ Data (72 bytes)
    Data: 00000000000111d0abcdabcdabcdabcdabcdabcdabcdabcd...
    [Length: 72]
```

Address Resolution Protocol (ARP)

The last protocol we need to understand is ARP.

On Ethernet networks, to include wireless you will find ARP at work. What this protocol does it sends out a broadcast to the entire *broadcast domain* saying hey who is the owner of this IP address, and the end device with that address will respond to that ARP request by sending back its hardware address.

ARP only happens the first time a source device communicates with a destination device. Once both devices know their source layer 2 and 3 addresses, destination layer 2 and 3 addresses, it will keep them in the ARP cache and will hold them for four hours in Cisco devices, before the ARP cache clears its tale.

This is important, because if you have a large network and you are all under the native VLAN, this could cause a problem. You do not want ARP broadcast to bring down your network. This is the reason we VLAN out or logically segment our network. Simply put, *what happens in your segment, stays in your segment.*

Let's look at the ARP cache table:

```
PC>arp -a
  Internet Address       Physical Address       Type
  192.168.1.254          0001.9735.c101         dynamic

PC>arp -d
PC>arp -a
No ARP Entries Found
PC>
```

The preceding table is showing you how you would look at the ARP table by typing the `arp -a` command. You see your default gateway IP address and MAC address which were learned dynamically. The second command is deleting all ARP entries and we verified that by using the `arp -a` command one more time.

Now that we have a deeper understanding of the TCP/IP suite and its protocols, let's discuss all IT professionals' favorite topic: **IP addressing**. Let's define some terminology first:

Term	Definition
Bit	One digit, either 0 or 1.
Byte	8 bits long, which creates a character.
Octet	Consists of 8 bits, with each bit having a specific value.
Network address	The address that tells you where your host is living. Routing tables use network addresses to get to the destinations.
Broadcast Address	A send-to-all address, in layer 3, it looks like 255.255.255.255, in layer 2, FF:FF:FF:FF:FF:FF.

What exactly is an IP address? An IP address is a logical address that is required for all devices connected to a network. This is the address that routers look at to send information across a network.

So, what does an IP address look like:

- **Dotted decimal numbering**: 192.224.240.252
- **Binary format**: 11000000.11100000.11110000.11111100
- **Hex format**: C0:E0: F0:FC

If you look at the binary format and IP address, it is 32 bits long. That is just too many 1's and 0's for us to remember the different combinations, so we use the DDN or dotted decimal format version, which is kinder to human eyes and minds.

You can also see that an IP address is 4 octets separated by decimals, each octet has 8 bits, and each of those bits have values. Turning the bits on or off is how you create those decimal numbers you see.

The following table will show you the octets' numbers and the binary format that each octet is in:

192	224	240	252
1st octet	2nd octet	3rd octet	4th octet
11000000	11100000	11110000	11111100

This next table will show the values of those bits:

128	64	32	16	8	4	2	1
0	0	0	0	0	0	0	0

The preceding table shows you that each octet has 8 bits and that each one of those bits has the same value in each octet. The way you get your DDN is by turning on those bits. The maximum value of each octet is 255, meaning that all of the bits are set to 1.

Refer to the bit-to-decimal table for more understanding:

Bit	Decimal
10000000	128
11000000	192
11100000	224
11110000	240
11111000	248
11111100	252
11111110	254
11111111	255

You MUST commit the preceding table to memory. This table will save your life when you're subnetting or converting numbers from hex to binary to decimal, or the reverse.

In IPv4, there are different classes of addresses that hold different numbers of host addresses.

What determines how many addresses there are per class is the subnet mask. When you look at an IPv4 address, it will always be accompanied by a subnet mask. This subnet mask can be a default mask for that class of address or it can be a customized mask that will allot the number of IP addresses needed for that network.

Here are some examples of subnet masks:

```
255.0.0.0
255.255.0.0
255.255.255.0
255.192.0.0
255.255.255.252
```

From the preceding examples, the first three are considered the default mask, and the last two are customized masks used in subnetting, which we will be getting into shortly.

So, let's look at the classes of IP addresses that exist, along with their ranges, default masks, and numbers of hosts based on those default masks:

Class	Range	Default mask in DDN	Default host
A	1 - 126	255.0.0.0	16,777,512
B	128 - 191	255.255.0.0	65,534
C	192 - 223	255.255.255.0	254
D	224 -239	N/A	N/A
E	240 - 255	N/A	N/A

Don't worry, I am going to explain each column. The first column is simply the classification of the address. It's very important to remember that when you are classifying an IPv4 address, you look at the first octet, that is why in the second column *Range*, that is the range of the first octet. This means if you see an IP address that starts with a number that starts from 1 - 16, it is classified as an *A* address and it uses the default mask as shown. This means the first octet is your network; you cannot change that octet, you can only change the last three octets, which are known as host bits. Using a Class *A* address with its default mask, you could have up to 16,000,000 hosts, and that is a lot of hosts, my friends.

With a Class *B* address, it's the same thing; any number that starts with 128 - 191 is considered a Class *B* address and uses the DDN of 255.255.0.0. Now, the first two octets are your network and the last two octets are host bits. Using the default mask, you could have 65,000 hosts, which is still a lot. I am saying this for a reason.

Then we have our Class *C* addresses, which begins with 192 - 223; the default mask is 255.255.255.0, so now the first three octets are your network and the last octet is your host bit. Using its default mask, you could only have 254 hosts.

We then move on to our Class *D* range, which is a very specific type of address. This type of address is used for multicasting purposes, meaning you would only allow a specific number of devices on this network, such as video conferencing. But more importantly, these addresses are used for routing protocols to send updates to their neighboring routers, and you must commit the following addressing to memory (for certification purposes):

    RIPv2 = 224.0.0.9 EIGRP = 224.0.0.10 OSPF = 224.0.0.5 and 224.0.0.6

They do not have a default mask, because it can use any mask, depending on the number of hosts you want on the multicast.

Finally, we have our Class *E* addresses, for which it searches high and low, and these are considered to be experimental addresses. I guess they are used by Ghost Recon and are highly classified. They are not defined, they are reserved. Just know the range.

In this table, you may have noticed we do not see the 127 number 127 or range; that is because it is reserved for loopback. What in the world is that? If you were to ping 127.0.0.1, you would hopefully get a reply from the TCP/IP protocol stack, NOT YOUR NIC CARD!

Also, you do not see the 0 number either, that is because it is a reserved address for 0.0.0.0, which is your universal IP address, or gateway of last resort addresses.

An address we need to be familiar with when you are troubleshooting an IP problem is the APIPA, so if you go the command prompt and type ipconfig/all you see the following:

```
169.254.13.58 is an APIPA or Automatic Private IP Address.
```

The operating system has a feature whereby if you do not receive an IP from a DHCP server or statically assign one, it will use an APIPA.

This is a problem simply because you have no power over the assignment of this address and they are not routable.

There are some IPv4 addresses, such as the loopback, which are special-purpose so let's create a table for that:

Name	IP	Purpose
Loopback (local host)	127.0.0.1 -127.255.255.254	Test TCP/IP stack
Layer 2 broadcast	FF:FF:FF:FF:FF:FF	All nodes on a LAN
Layer 3 broadcast	255.255.255.255	All nodes on a network
Unicast	X.X.X.X	Sent to one destination node
Multicast	X.X.X.X - X.X.X.X	Sent to a group of nodes or routing protocol to update messages

Now that we are familiar with the concept of IP addresses, that they are a logical address and all nodes connected to the network must have an IP address, let's talk about Private IP addresses. So far, you know the overall range for each class.

There is a portion of the address that the powers that be chose to remove and allotted them for internal use only; *they are not routable* on the internet. We use them simply for internal networks. Let's create a table for these networks, which you must commit to memory as well. I know I keep repeating that, but that is the nature of the test. Refer to the following private IP address table:

Class	Range	Mask
A	10.0.0.1 - 10.255.255.254	255.0.0.0
B	172.16.0.1 - 172.31.255.254	255.255.0.0
C	192.168.0.1 - 192.168.255.254	255.255.255.0

Private IP addresses are used for internal LANs by a company to assign IP addresses based on their network needs. They have complete control over what IP and mask they use internally. Keep in mind these are addresses that are not routable on the internet, so they cannot be assigned to an interface that faces the public network or internet.

Address types for IPv4

Before we move on, it's important that we review the special types of addresses mentioned. We need to have a good understanding of these addresses and the concepts behind them.

Layer 2 broadcast addresses

Let's start with layer 2 broadcast addresses. One of the first things we must understand about these addresses is that they are hardware broadcast addresses; they are specific to the segment you are in. They would never leave your LAN, so they would never leave the boundary of your router.

Typically, a hardware address is 48 bits in length. If you were to look at your MAC address on your computer by typing the `ipconfig/all` command in your command prompt, you would see this 48-bit hardware address: `00:12:34:56:78:9A`.

What you are looking at is your hardware address to your PC or device, and this is the address you would use when you are doing MAC filtering in your wireless network. A layer 2 broadcast address would have all its binary bits set to 1 or the on position. That address would look like this: `FF:FF:FF:FF:FF:FF`, this type of address sends a message to all nodes on its local segment. VLAN would receive this address, but the router would never forward this address anywhere.

To begin with, routers do not accept layer 2 or 3 broadcasts, nor do they deal with layer 2 addressing.

Layer 3 broadcast addresses

Now let's look at the layer 3 broadcast address. These addresses are meant to send a message to everyone in your broadcast domain or VLAN. We have already seen layer 3 addresses, such as 192.168.1.1; this is your typical address used in a network. This address would most commonly be used as a unique address. Just like layer 2, layer 3 broadcasts addresses and would have all their bits set to 1 or on. So the address would look like 255.255.255.255. All devices on the LAN would receive this address to include the router, but by default, routers would drop any broadcast address that they receive.

One way you could send layer 3 broadcast addresses is using an IP Directed Broadcast Address. As an example, let's say we have a source address of 192.168.1.1 and a destination network of 10.1.0.0/16. The broadcast of this network can be sent out, because it will only be sent out to the interface that has the 10.1.x.x on its interface, instead of to all interfaces, which would cause a broadcast storm. The command for this would be ip directed-broadcast under the interface of choice.

Unicast addresses

The unicast address is a very straightforward address, simply defined as a single IP address that is assigned to a single device. This address would appear in the destination IP address in a packet header. Its purpose is to send a message to a single device on the network, all would see the address but only the destination address would accept it.

Multicast addresses

Lastly, we will look at multicast addresses, which allow point-to-multi point communication. You may wonder, is that a broadcast? No, quite the opposite, it will send a unique set of addresses from the multicast range of addresses. It will not flood the entire network, like a broadcast address, since that would cause catastrophic effects on your network. Multicast addresses are sent to a particular group of addresses only.

As I mentioned earlier, there exist several unique multicast addresses for your routing protocols:

Routing protocol	Multicast address
RIPv2	224.0.0.9
EIGRP	224.0.0.10
OSPF	224.0.0.5 or 224.0.0.6

These multicast addresses are what forwards the request to the neighboring router. OSPF has two distinct multicast addresses and each one has a distinct purpose: 224.0.0.5 is for all routers to see; 224.0.0.6 is for designated routers only. We will be discussing all this further on in book.

Summary

We made it to the end of this chapter! We covered the TCP/IP model and all its protocols, and broke down each protocol and how we would use them. We compared the original TCP/IP model to the OSI model and to the new TCP/IP model. We also learned the anatomy of IP addresses, their classes, hosts, default masks, and we even looked at special types of addresses and reserved addresses.

I can't stress enough how important IP addressing is, not only for your certification but in the real world as well. You need to know IP addressing like you know your alphabet. In this chapter, we simply scratched the surface with IP addresses. In the next chapter, we will dive deep into the world of IP addressing.

Subnetting in IPv4
4

Well, I hope you're ready. As we learned in the previous chapter, there is a bunch of different IPv4 addresses, and they are divided into classes, even into public and private addresses.

I never told you, exactly, how many IPv4 addresses there are in total. But, so you know, there are 2.4 million addresses. That is quite a lot of addresses, is it not? But, I did keep saying, based on the default mask of the address, especially a Class A address, we have millions of addresses. That's where the problem begins.

The powers that do not create things for a good reason now. When they saw that the IPv4 addresses were slowly being used up, they were very surprised and scared. Nobody expected that the internet was going to grow exponentially. Everyone had not one but two or more devices that needed IP addresses, and a greater number of companies had a presence on the internet as well.

Just think of all the social media sites that were created: Myspace, Facebook, Twitter, LinkedIn, and so on. And also, there is all the online gaming, including *WOW*, *Halo*, *Call of Duty*, and so on, just to mention a few. If you think about it, even kids were creating their own websites.

Simply stated, we were caught with our proverbial pants down and we had to come up with mechanisms to slow down the demise of IPv4 addresses.

With private IP addresses, everyone can now use whatever they want within the company, but how do they reach the outside world, since private IP addresses are not routable on the internet?

That takes us to another mechanism: **Network Address Translation** (**NAT**). Its purpose is to translate private to public IPs or vice versa. But for NAT to be efficient, you would use NAT Overload, where you can use one public address to translate 65,000-plus private IPs.

But that was not enough, so we created **Variable Length Subnet Masking (VLSM)**. This means you could adjust the length of the prefix or subnet mask to meet your needs on each network.

So, as you can see, there is more to IP addressing than just putting an IP address and mask on your device. You must have a plan; you must design your IP scheme, so it will make sense and not waste IP addresses.

Subnetting

How does this come into play in our networks? Why would we want to subnet our network? And what in the world does that mean? Well, it is basically taking a huge network, and dividing the network into smaller, more manageable segments or parts.

Keep in mind what we have learned about how devices act; hubs do not have broadcast domains. They are basically a multiport repeater, so the more hubs you connect to each other, the more you are just creating a huge collision domain, waiting for that crash to happen.

Switches are better than hubs, because they create private collision domains. This allows for full-duplex, whereas a hub is a shared collision domain and can only go half-duplex. Switches, by default, are only using VLAN 1, which is the native VLAN where everyone exists. But, you do have the options to create more VLANs, therefore increasing the amount of broadcast domains, and decreasing the amount of broadcasts on each network.

Each VLAN would be its own subnet. So, what happens on that VLAN stays on that VLAN, unless you need to go outside the VLAN. If that happens, then we would have to configure inter-VLAN communications.

So, how exactly do you subnet? Well, from this point on, we will be using private IP addresses to do so, just to make it easier on the eye.

Let's start with the basics:

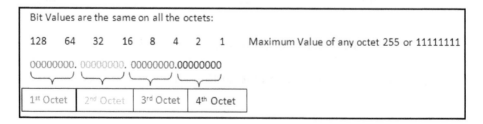

The subnet mask is the key to all subnetting problems. Up to now, you already know about DDN, but we also use something called **Classless Inter-Domain Routing (CIDR)**, denoted by this symbol: /.

An example would be /26. This means there there are 26 bits from left to right. In dotted decimals, that would equal to 255.255.255.192, or in binary it would look like this:

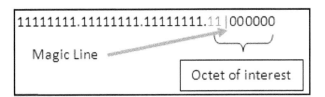

So, what does CIDR do for us? Well, it will tell us where to draw that magical line so you can get the answers to everything you need to know. Let's look at an example.

The original network is 192.168.1.0/24 (using the default mask, we have 254 hosts).

We need to subnet this into eight different subnets. So, how do we start?

You know we are going to be working on the last octet, simply because it is a Class C address:

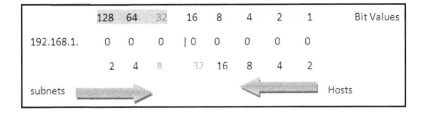

When counting for subnets you start from left to right, starting at **2** and doubling up as you go.

Okay, all I did was the following. I was instructed that I need to subnet the original network into eight different subnets. I knew I was going to be working on the last octet, so I wrote out the 8 bits for that octet, and then I counted by 2, starting from the left until I reached 8, and drew the magical line between the 32 and 16 bits.

Be careful when given a scenario like this. The only reason I stopped at that point is because we are using the zero network and we don't have to subtract 2 from the network side.

If we are not using the zero network, we would have to move the line, between bit 16 and 8, because we would need to subtract 2 from the network side. But, we will talk about the zero network soon.

What do we see here? Well, the bit value to the left is 32; this is how your network will increment starting with zero:

192.168.1.0
192.168.1.32
192.168.1.64
192.168.1.96   the highlighted address would be considered using the zero network
192.168.1.128   All these addresses are network ID's.
192.168.1.160
192.168.1.192
192.168.1.224

The highlighted bits on the top to the right is what you are going to use to calculate for broadcast addresses. You would take all those bits and add them together, getting 31. You then add that number to the network ID to get your broadcast address. Whatever is between the network ID and the broadcast ID are the usable addresses you can assign to your devices:

Network ID	Range of usable addresses	Broadcast address
192.168.1.0	192.168.1.1-192.168.1.30	192.168.1.31

How many usable hosts do we have? We count from right to left and we get 32, but we must subtract 2 from that number, to account for the network ID and the broadcast, so you have 30 host addresses that you can assign. But, we are missing something; what is the new mask? If you add the bit values to the left, which is highlighted, you would get your new mask, which would be /27 or 255.255.255.224.

So, let's complete the table on top to see what all the networks would look like:

Network ID	Range of usable addresses	Broadcast address	CIDR or mask
192.168.1.0	192.168.1.1–192.168.1.30	192.168.1.31	/27 or255.255.255.224
192.168.1.32	192.168.1.33–192.168.1.62	192.168.1.63	/27 or255.255.255.224
192.168.1.64	192.168.1.65–192.168.1.94	192.168.1.95	/27 or255.255.255.224
192.168.1.96	192.168.1.97–192.168.1.128	192.168.1.127	/27 or255.255.255.224
192.168.1.128	192.168.1.129–192.168.1.158	192.168.1.159	/27 or255.255.255.224
192.168.1.160	192.168.1.161–192.168.1.190	192.168.1.191	/27 or255.255.255.224
192.168.1.192	192.168.1.193–192.168.1.222	192.168.1.223	/27 or255.255.255.224
192.168.1.224	192.168.1.225–192.168.1.254	192.168.1.255	/27 or255.255.255.224

Once you find the magical line, you know how your network increments. It is the bit value immediately to the left of that line. Then you would add the bit values to the right, and the sum would be the number you add to all your network IDs, giving you the broadcast address (make sure you are working in the correct octet). Then, whatever is in between the network ID and the broadcast address will be the usable addresses to assign, allot, and give to your end devices. The reason I stated three different words is due to certification purposes. I refer to the word *allot* or *assigned* often. This is when dealing with DHCP handing out IP addresses. Real world the lingo is assigned, but for certification purposes is allot.

Did you notice in the previous table what did not change? The subnet mask remained the same for each of the different subnets. This is called class-full routing. Remember, you need to subnet to the needs of your network. Obviously, you always leave room to grow. But think of a point-to-point connection; you would be wasting 28 IP addresses. Let us look at an example:

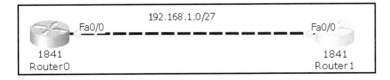

In the preceding diagram, you are using a CIDR of /27. This will allow you to have 30 host addresses, but you can clearly see here that all you would need is a /30. This would give you only two IP addresses. How did we come up with that number? Let me show you.

```
             128  64  32  16  8   4    2   1

192.168.1.    1   1   1   1   1   1|   0   0

The mask would be 255.255.255.252 (6 bits on in the last octet 252)
```

You need to remember your bit-to-decimal number table, so you can do this quickly.

But you need to understand that your subnet is based on the needs of the network. Always leave yourself room to grow. But, for the certification, do not worry about growth, just answer the question. They are testing you on concepts and procedures.

Learn to use the magical line and concern yourself with what exactly they are asking you. Let's use a Class B address and subnet that. You have the following address: 172.16.0.0/16.

We need to have **40** subnets. How do we begin? Focus on the highlighted part of the question.

With a Class B address, we have the third and fourth octet that we work with. Let's break it down:

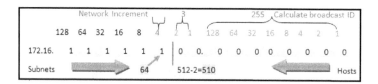

Remember, regardless of whether we are looking for subnets or hosts, we count by 2 and double as we go along.

So, let us create a table better to look at the new networks. I am not going to use all 64, but you will get the idea:

Network ID	Usable range	Broadcast ID	CIDR
172.16.0.0	172.16.0.1 - 172.16.3.254	172.16.3.255	/22
172.16.4.0	172.16.0.1 - 172.16.3.254	172.16.7.255	/22
172.16.8.0	172.16.0.1 - 172.16.3.254	172.16.11.255	/22
172.16.12.0	172.16.0.1 - 172.16.3.254	172.16.15.255	/22
172.16.16.0	172.16.0.1 - 172.16.3.254	172.16.19.255	/22
172.16.20.0	172.16.0.1 - 172.16.3.254	172.16.23.255	/22
172.16.24.0	172.16.0.1 - 172.16.3.254	172.16.27.255	/22
172.16.28.0	172.16.0.1 - 172.16.3.254	172.16.31.255	/22

See, that was not so bad. We use the same procedure; count for subnets and draw your line. The bit to the left is your network increments, the bits to the right are summed up to calculate for the broadcast address, and whatever is in between is your assignable IP address.

Please make sure you are incrementing or adding in the correct octet.

Let's look at a Class A example. Just for your knowledge, you will not get this type of question in the CCNA exam, but hey, while we are here, why not?

10.0.0.0/8 is your network ID. We need 20 subnets:

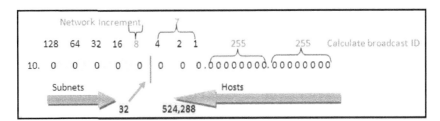

The following table will show you the Network ID, Usable Range, Broadcast ID and CIDR, based on the preceding diagram.

Network ID	Usable Range	Broadcast ID	CIDR
10.0.0.0	172.16.0.1 - 172.16.3.254	10.7.255.255	/13
10.8.0.0	172.16.0.1 - 172.16.3.254	10.15.255.255	/13
10.16.0.0	172.16.0.1 - 172.16.3.254	10.23.255.255	/13
10.24.0.0	172.16.0.1 - 172.16.3.254	10.31.255.255	/13
10.32.0.0	172.16.0.1 - 172.16.3.254	10.39.255.255	/13
10.40.0.0	172.16.0.1 - 172.16.3.254	10.47.255.255	/13
10.48.0.0	172.16.0.1 - 172.16.3.254	10.55.255.255	/13
10.56.0.0	172.16.0.1 - 172.16.3.254	10.63.255.255	/13

You can see that it is the same process. You simply need to be careful what octet you are incrementing and by how much. Also, make sure your math is correct. I highly doubt that you will be doing Class A subnetting, but in case you do, now you know.

Let me show you a visual of how this would look:

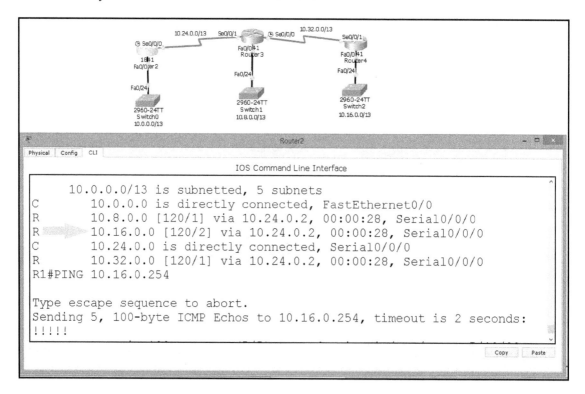

[88]

As you can see from the preceding diagram, we used a Class A scheme for our routers' interfaces and then configured the routing protocol RIPv2 and, were able to ping across the network, that is two hops away.

The interesting thing here, which we will cover at great length, is that we are using class-full routing, but we are using a subnetted Class A address. This means that when configuring a distance vector routing protocol, you must use the `no auto-summary` command, so it will not summarize the updates to the class boundary of its address. If you forget to use the `no auto-summary` command, the packets might get lost and not know which destination to go to, since it will summarize all the addresses to a `10.0.0.0`.

But never fear, we will be going over a lot of configurations later in the book.

I would like to clarify the zero network a bit more. Back in the beginning of time, when we subnetted, we subtracted 2 from the network side and the host side. The reason for subtracting from the network side was simply because the IOS did not understand how the zero network would get confused. But in today's technology, that is not the case; we can and will use the zero network so we don't waste any IP addresses at all. I will give you a very simple example of using or not using the zero network.

Look at the following table, `192.168.1.0/28 255.255.255.192`:

Using the zero network	Not using the zero network
192.168.1.0	Considered as zero network
192.168.1.64	192.168.1.64
192.168.1.128	192.168.1.128
192.168.1.192	Considered as zero network

As you can plainly see, we do not use the first network, due to a zero in the address, and the last network, because in the last network it has `192` and that is the same number of the mask. So, older IOSs got confused. But in today's network that is not the case; we will always use the zero network.

The reason I am telling you this is that in your certification exam, there could be a question in the IP addressing part that might state something like *Use the zero network* or *Don't use the zero network*. You must be careful with those pitfalls.

One last thing I would like to leave you with is how to convert hex to binary to decimal or vice versa. This topic was taken out of the certification, but it will be helpful in understanding hex numbers, since we are now using IPv6.

First you must know your hexadecimal numbers:

0	1	2	3	4	5	6	7	8	9	A	B	C	D	E	F
										10	11	12	13	14	15

Each one of those hex numbers is equal to four bits long, so to create a character you would need two hex numbers; that would create 8 bits. Something you must remember is that binary is your middle ground. Let me demonstrate this:

HEX	Covert to binary	Decimal
	E 4	
E4	8421|8421 11100100	128 64 32 16 8 4 2 1 = 228

All I did was put the bit values underneath each hex number. I then turned on bit values that make up the hex value E, which would be a value of 14. I repeated the same procedure in the hex value 4, which is an actual value of 4.

Then, I used 1's for the bit values highlighted and 0's for the bit values that are not, and behold, you have your 8-bit binary number.

Finally, to convert it to decimal, I simply added the bit values that were on, and we got 228.

It can't get any simpler than this, unless you use a calculator, which is not allowed in testing sites.

Summary

This chapter provided you with an important understanding of subnetting in IPv4, the easy way. If you keep on practicing, you should be able to subnet any number in under 30 seconds. I presented the diagrams, broken down and color-coded, so you can see what each part of the diagram does. If you learn the bit-to-decimal table, and if you memorize it thoroughly, you are good to go. Also, we have an image of three routers configured with the Class A scheme we created, and I configured the routing protocol RIPv2, so you can visualize what we are trying to accomplish.

When answering questions on IPv4 addressing, be careful with the subnet zero pitfall. Remember, *use the zero, do not subtract 2 from the network side. Do not use zero, subtract 2 from the network side.*

Next up, we will study VLSM and route summarization.

5
Variable Length Subnet Mask and Route Summarization

Before we begin this chapter, let's just do a little review of subnetting. Do you remember what subnetting is? It is simply taking a large address space divided into smaller segments. The segment size must meet the needs or requirements of the network.

The information that you need to remember will help you not only with subnetting, but also for the following topics that we will cover in this chapter:

- Variable Subnet Masking
- Route summarization

Consider the following example:

Bit values: 128 64 32 16 8 4 2 1.

These values will always remain the same per octet and the maximum value, when the values are added together, is 255.

Here is a bit-to-decimal table:

Bit	Decimal
10000000	128
11000000	192
11100000	224
11110000	240
11111000	248
11111100	252
11111110	254
11111111	255

The bit-to-decimal table is invaluable when dealing with IP addressing, so please memorize it.

As you may have noticed, I did not use formulas of any kind. It is simple addition or subtraction. The following diagram will pertain to this chapter also:

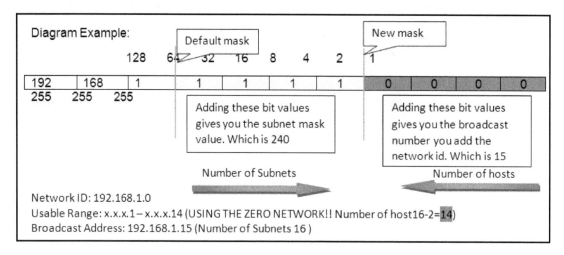

So, once you have practiced, this method of subnetting will allow you to subnet in less than 30 seconds. I guarantee it.

Variable Subnet Masking

Well, that is it for the quick review, so let's go ahead and start on **Variable Length Subnet Masking** (**VLSM**). It came into existence for the simple reason that IPv4 public addresses were running out. In the past, when companies purchased public IP addresses (let's say they only needed 1,000 IPs), they would give them a whole Class B address range, which can handle 65,534 IP addresses. They quickly found out that it was not the correct practice to follow.

So, what did the **Internet Assigned Numbers Authority** (**IANA**) and service providers do to fix this issue? VLSM. Now you can move the prefix line or subnet mask to the appropriate number of IP addresses needed for that segment. VLSM has some rules, which are as follows:

- You must start with highest number of IP addresses
- They should be in a continuous order
- The networks should start with an even number
- They should have an even number of networks

The reason for that is that your calculations would work out perfectly; you do not waste any IP addresses whatsoever. We had to start using VLSM on our public networks, or IPv4 would have died sooner than it did. Think about it; we have more than 7 billion people in this world, many of those people have some sort of a device that requires an IPv4 address, and IPv4 only holds 4.2 billion addresses.

The US is the lucky one; it got the greater portion of public IPv4 addresses than anywhere else in the world. VLSM is considered to be class-less routing and CIDR notation is class-less interdomain routing. You must subnet based on the needs of the network. So, let's look at some examples. However, before you start, you must set everything up.

You are given the following network: `172.16.0.0/16`. You have to break this down based on the following number of the network host: 2000, 1200, 500, 16, and 2. Here we go!

	128	64	32	16	8	4	2	1		128	64	32	16	8	4	2	1
172.16.	0	0	0	0	0	0	0	0	■	0	0	0	0	0	0	0	0

Number of host	Network ID	Range	Broadcast	CIDR
2000				
1200				
500				
16				
2				

The preceding diagram is what you must create; it really is simple. You were given a `172.16.0.0/16` network and you must come up with different networks for the amount of hosts given.

Each number of hosts is a different network, so you start counting for the host from the largest and work your way down, changing the mask each time to meet those needs. Remember, the point here is not to waste IP addresses:

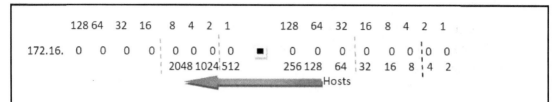

Number of host	Network ID	Range	Broadcast	CIDR
2000	172.16.0.0	x.x.0.1 – x.x15.254	172.16.15.255	/20
1200	172.16.16.0	x.x.16.1 – x.x.31.254	172.16.31.255	/20
500	172.16.32.0	x.x.32.1 – x.x.33.254	172.16.33.254	/23
16	172.16.34.0	x.x.34.1 – x.x.34.30	172.16.34.31	/27
2	172.16.34.32	x.x.34.33 – x.x.34.34	172.16.34.35	/30

 You must always start from the next available IP address, after the broadcast address.

As you can see, we have a CIDR that varies in length. At this point, with your newly created networks and masks, you would give that to the network administrator and he or she would resubnet that to segment the network as he/she sees fit.

Lucky for us that our routing protocols, RIPv2, EIGRP, and OSPF all support VLSM networks but let's look at a simple topology of what VLSM would look like:

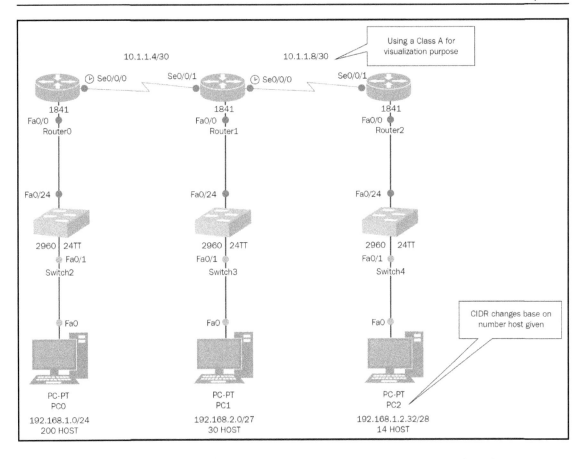

OK, this is the concept and calculation of using VLSM. After you practice for a bit, you won't even need a piece of paper; after doing it so many times, you will see the numbers in your head.

We are now going to move on to route summarization. Up to this point, we have learned how to make smaller networks out of one big network. We did it doing class-full subnetting, which means that we would have the same number of hosts on each network. That is OK for a LAN because you may want to expand your network and you do not need to resubmit the network. You also learned about VLSM, or class-less routing. What this allows you to do is adjust the subnet mask as needed by the network and not waste IP addressing, like you would in class-full subnetting, especially when using point-to-point links.

Route summarization

Route summarization is the opposite of subnetting. It takes a group of smaller networks and unites them as one big network or several bigger networks. The main purpose of route summarization is to reduce the amount of entries in the routing table of core routers.

This is essentially the problem we have on our internet backbone routers. There was no real thought to the design of the addressing scheme; the routing tables had entries that they really did not need to know. Internet backbone routers have thousands, if not hundreds of thousands, of entries in their routing tables.

This is most definitely a problem, since it could potentially crash your routers. Your core routers are meant to pass information quickly from one campus to another or from one company to another. They could also pass in information from one building to another, no matter the media. It could be twisted-pair cabling, coax cabling, fiber, wireless, or even a service provider.

Core routers should not be burdened with LAN segment information; they should simply get a summary of the networks that exist, so they can transfer the information quickly. Remember your Cisco three-layer model; core routers are meant for speed and the distribution and access layer routers are meant to not only route between local segments, but also handle, VLAN information, VTP, inter-VLAN communication, ACLs, policies, switchport security, and so forth.

Let's take a look at the topology and see what would be the result of *not* doing route summarization.

In the following topology, every PC is in its own VLAN and the inter-VLAN routing is configured. All the routers are running EIGRP with an AS of 51 and we have full connectivity across the network:

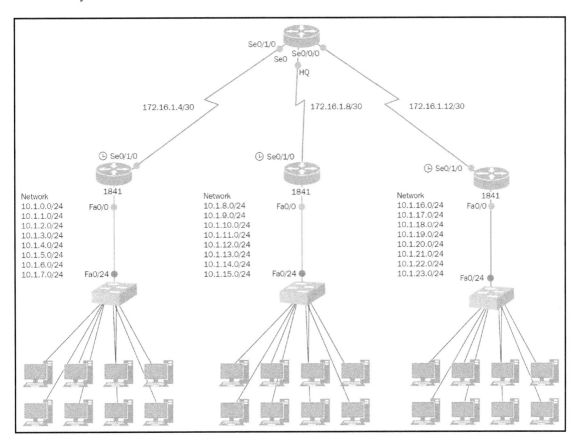

So, let's see what the routing table would look like on the core router with no route summarization:

```
       10.0.0.0/24 is subnetted, 24 subnets
D         10.1.0.0 [90/2172416] via 172.16.1.5, 00:05:18, Serial0/1/0
D         10.1.1.0 [90/2172416] via 172.16.1.5, 00:05:18, Serial0/1/0
D         10.1.2.0 [90/2172416] via 172.16.1.5, 00:05:18, Serial0/1/0
D         10.1.3.0 [90/2172416] via 172.16.1.5, 00:05:18, Serial0/1/0
D         10.1.4.0 [90/2172416] via 172.16.1.5, 00:05:18, Serial0/1/0
D         10.1.5.0 [90/2172416] via 172.16.1.5, 00:05:18, Serial0/1/0
D         10.1.6.0 [90/2172416] via 172.16.1.5, 00:05:18, Serial0/1/0
D         10.1.7.0 [90/2172416] via 172.16.1.5, 00:05:18, Serial0/1/0
D         10.1.8.0 [90/2172416] via 172.16.1.9, 00:05:17, Serial0/1/1
D         10.1.9.0 [90/2172416] via 172.16.1.9, 00:05:17, Serial0/1/1
D         10.1.10.0 [90/2172416] via 172.16.1.9, 00:05:17, Serial0/1/1
D         10.1.11.0 [90/2172416] via 172.16.1.9, 00:05:17, Serial0/1/1
D         10.1.12.0 [90/2172416] via 172.16.1.9, 00:05:17, Serial0/1/1
D         10.1.13.0 [90/2172416] via 172.16.1.9, 00:05:17, Serial0/1/1
D         10.1.14.0 [90/2172416] via 172.16.1.9, 00:05:17, Serial0/1/1
D         10.1.15.0 [90/2172416] via 172.16.1.9, 00:05:17, Serial0/1/1
D         10.1.16.0 [90/2172416] via 172.16.1.13, 00:05:16, Serial0/0/0
D         10.1.17.0 [90/2172416] via 172.16.1.13, 00:05:16, Serial0/0/0
D         10.1.18.0 [90/2172416] via 172.16.1.13, 00:05:16, Serial0/0/0
D         10.1.19.0 [90/2172416] via 172.16.1.13, 00:05:16, Serial0/0/0
D         10.1.20.0 [90/2172416] via 172.16.1.13, 00:05:16, Serial0/0/0
D         10.1.21.0 [90/2172416] via 172.16.1.13, 00:05:16, Serial0/0/0
D         10.1.22.0 [90/2172416] via 172.16.1.13, 00:05:16, Serial0/0/0
D         10.1.23.0 [90/2172416] via 172.16.1.13, 00:05:16, Serial0/0/0
       172.16.0.0/30 is subnetted, 3 subnets
C         172.16.1.4 is directly connected, Serial0/1/0
C         172.16.1.8 is directly connected, Serial0/1/1
```

As you can plainly see, the core router knows about each individual network, which creates a huge routing table. Our job, as IT professionals, is to minimize the routing table of the core router.

The way you would do this using EIGRP is to enter a summary route in the interface, facing the core router. You would do this in the following way:

```
Interface s0/1/0
IP summary-address EIGRP 51 10.1.0.0 255.255.248
```

You need to repeat this on every distribution router and the following would be the result on the core router's routing table:

```
Gateway of last resort is not set

     10.0.0.0/21 is subnetted, 3 subnets
D       10.1.0.0 [90/2172416] via 172.16.1.5, 00:00:11, Serial0/1/0
D       10.1.8.0 [90/2172416] via 172.16.1.9, 00:02:34, Serial0/1/1
D       10.1.16.0 [90/2172416] via 172.16.1.13, 00:01:57, Serial0/0/0
     172.16.0.0/30 is subnetted, 3 subnets
C       172.16.1.4 is directly connected, Serial0/1/0
C       172.16.1.8 is directly connected, Serial0/1/1
C       172.16.1.12 is directly connected, Serial0/0/0
HQ#
```

Wow! That shrunk the core router's routing table; you now have three entries instead of 24 entries.

This will allow for sending information a lot quicker to the destination, simply because it does not have to look at a telephone book of information. All the segment networks are within the summary address.

So, how is this magic trick done? There's no magic, my friends, but there is binary. Yes, binary is the truest way of getting the correct answer when summarizing addresses. By the way, the rule of summarization pretty much goes out the window in the real world and even in the test. But understand it, just in case it may be asked about in the test.

Let us look at some examples:

```
192.168.1.0
192.168.2.0
192.168.3.0
192.168.4.0
```

In the preceding network, assume that we are using the default mask and the octet of interest is the third octet, since it is one of the changes. Our goal is to bring all these networks together as one, by changing the subnet mask. How do we set this up so we can get our answer?

192.168.1.0	192	168	00000001	00000000
192.168.2.0	192	168	00000010	00000000
192.168.3.0	192	168	00000011	00000000
192.168.4.0	192	168	00000100	00000000

Original Mask /21   Original Mask /24

How did we get the new mask of 21 bits? Since the third octet is the interesting octet, we look for the column of uncommon values, meaning 0 and 1 from left to right, and we draw the line just before it.

So, what is the summary address? Well, the first two octets don't change, and everything in the third octet, left of the line, is zero and the fourth octet is also zero. The summary address is 192.168.0.0/21. Let us take a closer look at this summary address. It encompasses more networks than just the ones given. Let's do our subnetting:

	128 64 32 16	8	4	2	1		
192.168.	0 0 0 0	0	0	0	0.	00000000	(sum of all bits)

Network ID	Range	Broadcast
192.168.0.0	x.x.0.1 – x.x.7.254	192.168.7.255

So, we added the zero network and the 5, 6, and 7. Remember the rule: start with an even number and have an even number of networks.

Let's do another one:

			128 64 32 16 8 4	2 1	
192.168.100.0	192	168	0 11 0 0 1 0 0	0	00000000
192.168.101.0	192	168	0 11 0 0 1 0 1		00000000
192.168.102.0	192	168	0 11 0 0 1 1 0		00000000
192.168.103.0	192	168	0 11 0 0 1 1 1		00000000

So, what would be the summary address for these networks? Remember, the first two octets remain the same, the third octet has three bit values that are on 64, 32, and 4, and the fourth octet has all of the bits off.

With that said, the summary address is 192.168.100.0/22. Let's verify it:

Network ID	Range	Broadcast
192.168.100.0	x.x.100.1 - x.x.3.254	192.168.3.255

It works out perfectly; we do not add any network to these to the summary address.

So, based on the preceding topology, tell me the summary addresses for all three distribution routers:

10.1.0.0/24			
10.1.1.0/24			
10.1.2.0/24			
10.1.3.0/24			
10.1.4.0/24			
10.1.5.0/24			
10.1.6.0/24			
10.1.7.0/24			

10.1.8.0/24			
10.1.9.0/24			
10.1.10.0/24			
10.1.11.0/24			
10.1.12.0/24			
10.1.13.0/24			
10.1.14.0/24			
10.1.15.0/24			

10.1.16.0/24			
10.1.17.0/24			
10.1.18.0/24			
10.1.19.0/24			
10.1.20.0/24			
10.1.21.0/24			
10.1.22.0/24			
10.1.23.0/24			

Remember to verify your work, to see if only the networks are the ones given.

Summary

In this chapter, I provided that you learned about VLSM. You should be able not only to figure out a VLSM problem, but design your own. You also learned a very easy way of how to summarize and verify summary addresses, their purpose, and how you would apply them.

In the next chapter, we finally get to the IOS user interface. See you then!

6
The IOS User Interface

Finally, we start with the good stuff! In this chapter, I will introduce to you the **Internetworking Operating System (IOS)** that is in all Cisco routers and Catalyst switches. We will be going into the **CLI** or **Command Line Interface**, learning about its different modes has, learning how to navigate through the IOS, learning some editing commands (not on the CERT), and also learning some administrative commands that are important not only for your certification but for use in the real world also.

But, before we get into the CLI, how do we connect to a router or a switch to do our configurations? Let's define the IOS in a little more detail.

In this chapter, we will be covering the following topics:

- The IOS user interface
- Learning the CLI
- Giving some definitions to the terms we have used
- Editing commands that will help you configure faster
- Administrative configurations, or basic housekeeping commands

The Cisco IOS

The **Cisco IOS** is the proprietary kernel that provides routing, switching, internetworking, and telecommunication features. Here are a few of the features that the Cisco router IOS is responsible for:

- Scalability for network growth
- Security to control access or to stop unauthorized personnel
- Providing network protocols and its functions
- Connecting network resources

Each IOS is specific to the series of router or switch you are using. What exactly do I mean by that? Well, let's look at some routers and what IOS they are using:

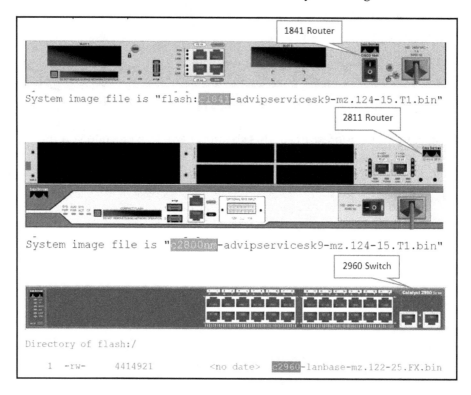

You can now see that it is important that the IOS matches the series of router or switch you're purchasing. You cannot put a 2,900 series router IOS in a 1,800 series router; it just won't work. This is not like purchasing a PC, in which you can put pretty much any Windows operating system you want if it meets the hardware requirements. Also, each IOS image brings different features you can use, so you need to know exactly what you need in your network to choose the correct Cisco device.

We have to connect to our Cisco devices to configure them, troubleshoot, or simply verify that all is working as it should. So, how do we exactly connect to a router or a switch to configure them?

Well, let's look at the Cisco **1,841 router** and the Cisco Catalyst **2,960 switch** a little closer. If you look at this diagram, you will see each slot or port depicted:

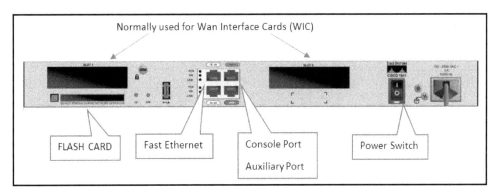

As you can see from the preceding diagram, we have several slots and ports, and of course a power switch to turn the router on and off. Slot 0 or Slot 1 can be used for many different types of connections. It can be Ethernet, serial, telephone RJ11, or even fiber connections. For certification purposes, we will be using WIC-1T or WIC-2T, which will be for our serial connections. It is important to remember that routers are *never turned off*, unless something goes wrong, which means you would do this during maintenance hours, meaning in the middle of the night. *Never ever turn off your router during the middle of the workday!!* However, if you need to do this for whatever reason, make sure that everybody from the janitor to the CEO knows exactly the date and time it will be switched off, the approximate length of time it will be off for, and the reason you are shutting it down.

If you purchase a router, normally it will come with some sort of basic configuration that will allow you to Telnet into the router or go in through a browser. If your router has zero configurations, you would use a console cable or create a rolled cable, to connect to the console port of the router.

The following photo is a console cable, using a serial-to-USB adapter:

Normally, you would need to install a driver for the adapter, for it to work. Make sure you verify in the device manager that it is present and working—plus, it should add a COM port, so you can use it.

Once you connect the cable from your computer to the router or switch's console port, you need to create a terminal session to the router. A lot of software exists, but the most common one is called **PuTTY**, which you can download from `http://www.putty.org/`.

You have to use a specific COM port, which is configured by the driver for the adapter you installed. You open the PuTTY application, go into settings and enter the following information:

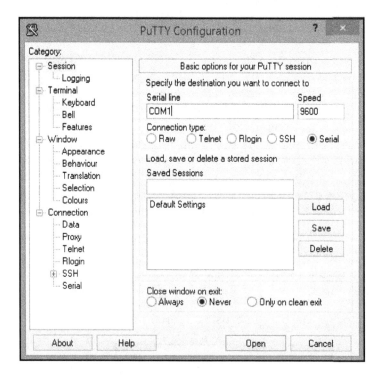

Under **Session** | **Logging**, choose the connection type, which is **Serial**, and then choose the correct COM port and speed, which is `9600`.

Remember, this is for a router or switch that has no configuration whatsoever. You can still use PuTTY afterward, but the connection type would be **Telnet** or **SSH** and you would put in the correct IP address and port number into the PuTTY software and any username or password required by the router or switch:

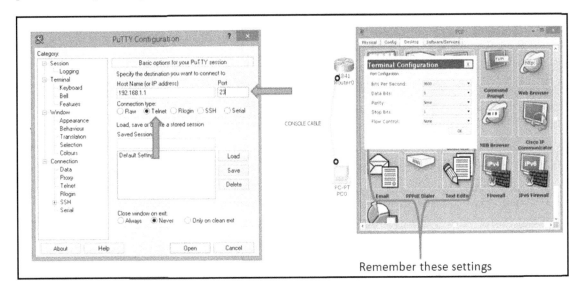

Remember these settings

Using a simulator, I created a terminal session, with the router using a console cable; I then selected from the desktop tab of the PC and clicked on the **Terminal** session. The settings that you see under the **Terminal Configuration** are exactly what you need to remember for testing or for real-world configurations.

Connecting to the router or switch is pretty straightforward. In the certification exam, since you will be using a simulator, you will do it as per the preceding diagram. In the real world, it would be the same, but it could vary from router to router. The 1,800, 1,900, 2,800, and 2,900 series routers are as shown. Once you get to the 9,000 or 10,000 series routers, these may vary. That is why they come with instructions on how to connect, or you can always Google or YouTube how to do it, or you could even visit the manufacturer's website.

Connecting to a switch would be the exact same procedure; the switches may come pre-configured, or you may have to use a console cable. Look at the following diagram:

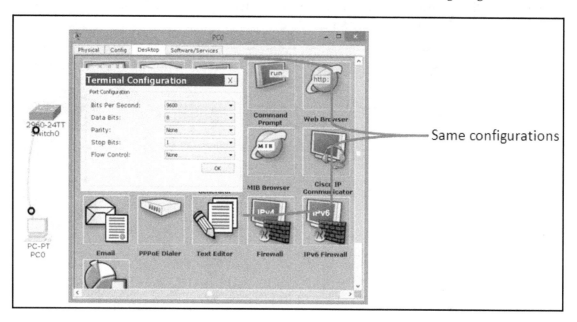

The switch shown is a Cisco Catalyst 2,960 switch. This switch has no configurations, so we must make a terminal connection as we would on a router. Once you console into a switch or a router, you can configure an IP address on the LAN interface, configure **Telnet** using the VTY lines, and use a password to get into privilege mode. Then, you can simply use the PuTTY software, and you could go Telnet into your router through the network and make any configuration changes you desire. We will talk about these configurations soon.

Booting up a Cisco switch or router

When you bring up a Cisco IOS device, just like a computer, it will go through a boot-up process. Let me give you just a brief heads up regarding what happens to a Cisco IOS device that has not been configured upon bootup:

1. It goes through a **Power-On Self-Test** (**POST**), once the machine goes through this step.

2. It will then look for the IOS in flash memory and it expands the IOS into RAM and, yes, the IOS is compressed. Don't worry about how it's compressed; just know it is. This is very important, because you need enough RAM on the router for it to be able to expand.

3. Then, the IOS needs to decide whether this device has any configurations—where does it look for this information? The answer to that is **Non-Volatile Random-Access Memory** (**NVRAM**); it is looking for the `startup-configuration` file. Once found, it will load any configurations that it may contain into RAM, and if no configuration exists in the `startup-configuration` file, then you will be prompted with a configuration dialogue box, so you can run through a step-by-step wizard. This mode is considered setup mode. At this point, you can choose to use setup mode or not, by typing `yes` or `no` at the prompt.

The following is setup mode:

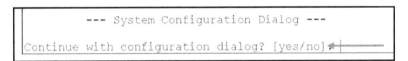

```
        --- System Configuration Dialog ---
Continue with configuration dialog? [yes/no]
```

Notice the brackets; they have the options you can type, `[yes/no]`. You could type the letter *Y* or type out the complete `yes` if you wished to use the wizard-driven guide. But, more often than not, you will be typing out `no` and configuring the router or the switch from scratch. This means you will be in the CLI, and you will need to know what commands to type and how to navigate through the router or the switch.

Using the CLI

Once you make a connection to the Cisco IOS, and node configurations where found in the `startup-configuration` file, you are automatically taken to setup mode. Since you made the decision of manually configuring the Cisco device by typing (`no`) when prompted, you need to understand the prompts and modes you will be navigating to configure the device. Let's create a table so you can identify the prompts and modes you need to know for your certification and real-world use.

This table lists the most common prompts and modes you will be faced with:

Prompt	Mode	Brief definition
>	User mode	Basic commands, very low privileges
#	Privilege mode	Administrative privileges, you can delete IOS
(config)#	Global configuration mode	Commands that effect the router as a whole
(config-if)#	Interface configuration mode	IP addresses, descriptions, bandwidth commands
(config-subif)#	Sub-interface configuration mode	Inter-VLAN configuration or Frame Relay
(config-line)#	Line configuration mode	Console, Telnet, or AUX ports
(config-router)#	Router configuration mode	Routing protocols
(config-std-nacl)#	Standard named ACL mode	Create named access-list standard
(config-ext-nacl)#	Extended named ACL mode	Create named access-list extended

Do you need to know the details in the preceding table? Oh, yes! Not only do you need to know the prompts, you need to know the commands to type to get you to that mode. Are these the only prompts? Not by a long shot. The prompts that you see are the ones you need to know for your test, and they are used in the real world also. So, how do we navigate to these different prompts, and what can you do within each mode? Let's look at those commands now.

We are already inside the router and have typed no to set up the mode, which means let's configure from scratch. So, you will be confronted with the following prompt >. This is the very first prompt you get, and you really can't do much at this level. There are basic commands to look at certain things which are configured and these commands will not cause harm to the router. Type a ? at the prompt and you will get the available options. The question mark implies a help command and it will show you all the available commands.

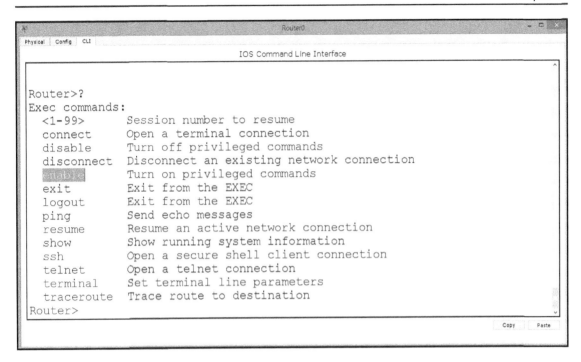

As you can see, you have various commands you can type with a brief description of what that command does. The command you are interested in is the one you see highlighted, which is the `enable` command. That command will take you to privilege mode, which will allow you to do more on the router, including deleting the IOS or the `startup-config` file where your configurations are saved in NVRAM. We will go into the components of the router and its bootup process later in the book. That is why to get into privilege mode you should always be prompted for a password or if configured, you could create usernames and passwords with the level privilege required to do your job instead of going straight into privilege mode. Creating a username and password should be the common practice.

So, let's look now at how it would look on the router when you go from user mode to privilege mode:

```
                              Router0                                    - □ x
Physical  Config  CLI
                        IOS Command Line Interface
   terminal    Set terminal line parameters
   traceroute  Trace route to destination
Router>enable
Router#?
Exec commands:
  <1-99>      Session number to resume
  auto        Exec level Automation
  clear       Reset functions
  clock       Manage the system clock
  configure   Enter configuration mode
  connect     Open a terminal connection
  copy        Copy from one file to another
  debug       Debugging functions (see also 'undebug')
  delete      Delete a file
  dir         List files on a filesystem
  disable     Turn off privileged commands
  disconnect  Disconnect an existing network connection
  enable      Turn on privileged commands
  erase       Erase a filesystem
  exit        Exit from the EXEC
  logout      Exit from the EXEC
  mkdir       Create new directory
  more        Display the contents of a file
  no          Disable debugging informations
  ping        Send echo messages
  reload      Halt and perform a cold restart
--More-- |
                                                              Copy    Paste
```

Once you type `enable` and hit the *Enter* key, you will be in privilege mode; now you type the question mark once again, and you get more commands you can use within privilege mode. Let's define the highlighted commands.

The `clear` command, as the brief definitions state, is to reset functions. What does that mean?

```
Router#clear ?  ←━━━━━━
  aaa                 Clear AAA values
  access-list         Clear access list statistical information
  arp-cache           Clear the entire ARP cache
  cdp                 Reset cdp information
  frame-relay         Clear Frame Relay information
  ip                  IP
  ipv6                IPv6
  line                Reset a terminal line
  mac-address-table   MAC forwarding table
  vtp                 Clear VTP items
Router#clear |
```

As you can see, the question mark comes to the rescue; here, you can see what subcommands are available to you. For the certification test, the one you need to familiarize yourself with is the following:

```
Router#clear ip ospf process
```

So, now we know not only how to get from user mode to privilege mode, but we can use the question mark to help us find which commands are available not only at the main prompt but also what sub commands are available with the clear command, shown in the preceding example.

The next command you need to know, without a doubt, is the configure command. This command will allow you to go into global configuration mode. Once you're in this mode, you can start configuring the router and go anywhere else. Let's see how that one looks:

```
Router#configure ?
  terminal  Configure from the terminal
  <cr>
```

Using the simulator, you only get the following option terminal, which is the most common way to configure the router, and once you type configure terminal and hit the *Enter* key, you will be in privilege mode. Other options would be network or memory, but for this exam, you do not need to worry about that. The full command from privilege mode that you would type would look as follows:

```
Router#configure terminal ←
Enter configuration commands, one per line.  End with CNTL/Z.
Router(config)#
```

Now we can start having some fun and begin configuring the router or the switch. Always remember: **when in doubt, use the question mark**. The *Tab* key is another way to help you finish typing a command if you type enough of that command. The IOS is smart enough to figure out what command you want to type if you type enough of that command:

```
Router#confi
Router#configure term
Router#configure terminal
```

You can see I typed `confi`, and then I pressed the *Tab* key and it finished the command for me, which is `configure`. I did the same thing for `term` and pressed the *Tab* key, and it typed the command for me—`terminal`. So, the question mark and the *Tab* key will be very helpful in your certification (*if allowed*) and in the real world, and you will be using it 99.9% of the time.

One last command that we highlighted while under privilege mode is `ping`. This command is used to test connectivity, and it uses the ICMP protocol to send an `echo request` and an `echo reply` to verify whether we have connectivity with destination devices, but we can also test our TCP/IP by pinging the loopback address of the end device:

```
Router#ping 10.1.1.1 ◄━━━━━━

Type escape sequence to abort.
Sending 5, 100-byte ICMP Echos to 10.1.1.1, timeout is 2 seconds:
.!!!!
Success rate is 80 percent (4/5), round-trip min/avg/max = 0/0/1 ms
```

The `ping` command is straight forward; all you're doing is checking for connectivity. What you want to see is the exclamation marks, which are also called **Bangs**; that means that your packet got to the destination and came back successfully. That one decimal point or period that you see always happens the first time on Ethernet networks, due to the ARP process.

The last thing we see highlighted is the **-More-** output; this is not a command, it is simply telling you there are more commands for you to see, and to do that, you could use your *Enter* key to look at those commands one at a time, or you could use the Spacebar to load a page at a time.

Let's look at what other commands we have available to us:

```
resume      Resume an active network connection
rmdir       Remove existing directory
send        Send a message to other tty lines
setup       Run the SETUP command facility
show        Show running system information
ssh         Open a secure shell client connection
telnet      Open a telnet connection
terminal    Set terminal line parameters
traceroute  Trace route to destination
undebug     Disable debugging functions (see also 'debug')
vlan        Configure VLAN parameters
write       Write running configuration to memory, network, or terminal
Router#
```

I hit the Spacebar key, so I can get one page at a time and find the rest of the commands that I can use also. The highlighted commands are what I want you to focus on, for the certification; as you gain experience configuring your routers in school using your simulators or actual routers or hopefully in the real world, you will begin to learn a plethora of commands.

The `setup` command just takes you back to the wizard-driven dialogue. If you remember, I told you to type `no` on the router and to quit setup mode.

You can only type the `show` command in privilege mode, and its purpose is to show us the output of what we want to see. There is a huge list of subcommands you can type, but the following table is what I need you to store in your NVRAM, meaning your brain:

Commands	Purpose
show running-configuration	Will show configuration in RAM
show startup-configuration	Will show configuration in NVRAM
show ip interface brief	Will show a summary of the interface, IP, and status
show ip route	Will show the routing table
show ip protocol	Will show routing protocols configured on the router
show ip dhcp binding	Will show which address you're binding with
show ip nat translation	Will show the translation from private to public address and ports
show access-list	Will show all access lists on the router that are configured

This is just the tip of the iceberg; there are a lot of `show` commands for you to use, and these are just a few to get you started. We will be going over more `show` commands in the other chapters. The only downside to the `show` command is that you must use it in privilege mode, so if you're in router configuration mode, or standard named access-list mode, you need to go back to privilege mode to do a `show` command. But that is what you must do for certification purposes.

In a real-world environment, you could use the do command in front of a command, and you do not have to go back to privilege mode. Look at the following output:

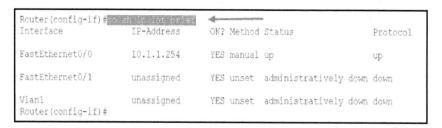

As you can plainly see, we are in interface configuration mode, and we are able to use a show command, if we type a do in front of the command first.

The ssh and telnet commands are used simply to configure access to the router through the network, but we will go into these two commands in more depth later.

The traceroute command is used to trace the path to a destination. Let's use the following topology as an example:

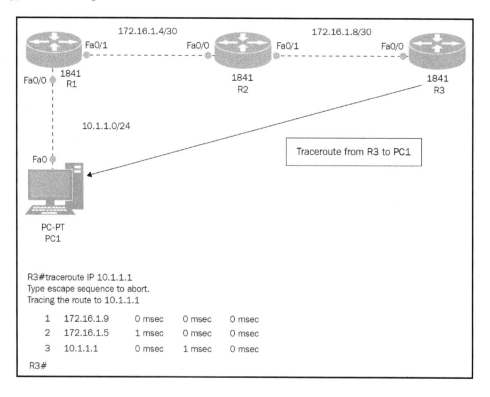

I did a `traceroute` from R3 to PC1 using the destination IP address of PC1. The `traceroute` command tells me the next hop address of R2 and then the next hop address of R1 and finally the destination IP of PC1. This is a very helpful troubleshooting tool, because you can pinpoint where the packet dropped or lost connectivity, and further troubleshoot from that point.

While we are here, another tool in our arsenal to look at things in a router or switch is called the **pipe** command. The pipe command is an output modifier (|); using this will allow you to take a more direct approach when looking at configurations on your router. The following would be an example of using the pipe command:

```
Router#sh run | begin interface
Router#sh ip route | include 10.1.1.4
```

In the certification exam, you won't be using it, but in your job, you will. It is essential that you learn how to use the pipe. Imagine this scenario. You type the command to look at the `running-config` file and hit *Enter*. If this is an enterprise company, there may be thousands of lines that make up your configuration, and you will overwhelm your router and maybe even crash it. At a minimum, you will go through excruciating pain wasting time scrolling through all those lines, not to mention the boss will be very upset.

Using the pipe (|) will allow you to see exactly what you want to see.

The following table will help you configure your Cisco devices faster; they are called **editing commands**:

Ctrl + A	Moves your cursor to the beginning of the line
Ctrl + E	Moves your cursor to the end of the line
Ctrl + B	Moves back one character
Ctrl + F	Moves forward one word
Ctrl + D	Deletes a single character (when the cursor is in front of that command)
Ctrl + R	Redisplays a line
Ctrl + U	Erases a line
Ctrl + W	Erases a word
Ctrl + Z	Takes you back to privilege mode, no matter what mode you are in in the router.
Tab	Finishes typing a command for you
Esc + B	Moves back one word
Esc + F	Moves forward one word
Backspace	Deletes a single character (when cursor is behind that command)

Global configuration commands

At this point, we have covered the basics of navigating through the CLI, show commands, verifying connectivity, and how you would connect to the router or switch. It is time to start the configuration. Even though we are going to focus on global configuration commands, I want to show you a guideline for your certification—what commands you should know. But bear in mind this order is not set in stone, it's a guideline which is provided in R1 configuration.

The following topology is what we are going to be using for our configurations for the majority of our configuration examples:

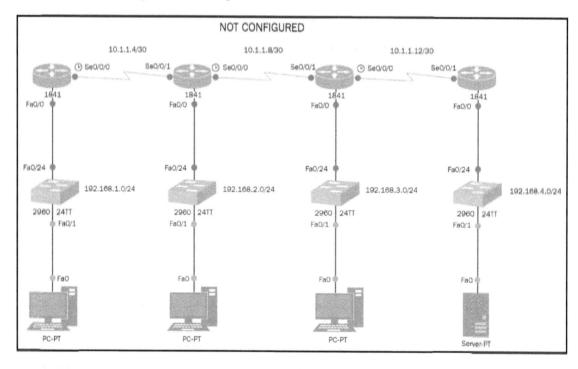

Here is the R1 configuration:

```
>ENABLE   (command to get to privilege mode)
#CONFIG T  (command to get to global configuration)
(CONFIG)#HOSTNAME R1 (command to give the router a hostname)
R1(CONFIG)#ENABLE PASSWORD CISCO (command to configure a Privilege
mode password plaint text)
R1(CONFIG)#ENABLE SECRET STUDENT (command to configure a Privilege
mode password encrypted)
R1(CONFIG)#SERVICE PASSWORD-ENCRYPTION (command to encrypt all
```

```
passwords)
R1(CONFIG)#BANNER MOTD $ WELCOME TO R1 $ (Message of the Day
banner)
R1(CONFIG)#IP DOMAIN-LOOKUP (Turning on Domain Name resolution)
R1(CONFIG)#IP DOMAIN-NAME CISCO.COM (creating a domain-name using
cisco.com)
R1(CONFIG)#IP NAME-SERVER 192.168.4.1 (Pointing to the DNS server
that resolves cisco.com)
...
```
The name for the keys will be: R1.CISCO.COM
Choose the size of the key modulus in the range of 360 to 2048
for your General Purpose Keys. Choosing a key modulus greater than
512
may take a few minutes.
How many bits in the modulus [512]: 512 (Using default size of key
in bits)
 % Generating 512 bit RSA keys, keys will be non-exportable...[OK]
R1(CONFIG)#LINE VTY 0 15 (command to go into Terminal lines)
***Mar 1 0:2:46.960: RSA key size needs to be at least 768 bits for
ssh
version 2**
*Mar 1 0:2:46.960: %SSH-5-ENABLED: SSH 1.5 has been enabled
R1(CONFIG)#TRANSPORT INPUT SSH (command to only allow SSH
sessions)
R1(CONFIG-LINE)#EXIT (command to return to previous prompt)
R1(CONFIG)#INT F0/0 (command to enter and interface)
R1(CONFIG-IF)#IP ADDRESS 192.168.1.254 255.255.255.0 (command to
put an IP address)
...
**Destination filename [startup-config]? HIT THE ENTER KEY (asking
you to save to default location)**
Building configuration...
```
[OK]
R1#
```

Wow! And that was only router one. They are the minimum commands you need to commit to memory. Make sure you understand what you have done. I will now highlight the more confusing or curious commands for you:

Complete command to type	Definition
ENABLE PASSWORD CISCO	It will allow you to configure a plain text password that users must type in when trying to gain access to privilege mode.
ENABLE SECRET STUDENT	It will allow you to configure an encrypted password that users must type in when trying to gain access to privilege mode.

`SERVICE PASSWORD-ENCRYPTION`	This will encrypt all passwords that have been written in the past, present, or future. It uses an MD5 hash, so it will create a very complex password that is more complex than the (`SECRET`) command.
`BANNER MOTD $ WELCOME TO R1 $`	This creates a banner that everyone will see when they try to access the router, locally or through the network. It is not a `Welcome` message; it is a warning for intruders to stay out or face the consequences. It could also be a message to tell your admins about an upgrade that needs to happen during maintenance hours. It is important to remember that whatever delimiter you start with it, you must end with. If you start with $, end the message with $. The symbols you can't use are " and %. You can have only 80 characters and 40 lines.
`IP DOMAIN-LOOKUP`	Turn on name resolution if you're going to use a DNS server.
`IP DOMAIN-NAME CISCO.COM`	Creates a domain name for name resolution if using a domain.
`IP NAME-SERVER 192.168.4.1`	Points the DNS server you are using for name resolution.
`USERNAME LDIAZ PRIVILEGE 15 PASSWORD 0 CISCO`	Creates a user level 15 privilege, which gives full administrative rights to the router, using a plain text password of Cisco.
`LINE CON 0`	Gets you into the line configuration mode for console 0.
`PASSWORD CISCO`	Configures the password CISCO for console 0.
`LOGIN`	Requires you to put in the password for console 0.
`LOGIN LOCAL`	This command is optional and won't be part of your certification, but you will use it in the real world. That is the purpose of creating users on the router. You will be prompted for a local username and a password.
`EXEC-TIMEOUT 0 0`	Think of this command as a screen saver; the first number is minutes and the next number is seconds. Your session will never time out, but you can do something such as 10 minutes and 0 seconds, so if you have not typed any command, your session will end in 10 minutes.

LOGGING SYNCHRONOUS	As you type, the router gives you feedback, and that is great, but it does interrupt your typing. So, if you type this command on whichever line you're configuring on, your typing will not be interrupted by the feedback.
LINE AUX 0	This is just another port you can access your router on, but you must have an external modem, and you must configure the router for this to work.
LINE VTY 0 15	This is to enter your virtual terminal lines; the default is 0 4; if you have more, you could type 0 100, for example, and make passwords and the login local, so individuals would have to type a username. These are your Telnet lines and SSH lines.
EXIT	This command just takes you one step back, meaning you could go from interface mode, to global config, then to privilege mode. You are backing out one step at a time. A shortcut to this is a keyboard command *Ctrl + Z*, so if you're in sub-interface mode, you could simply type *Ctrl + Z* and you would go straight to privilege mode.
IP SSH AUTHENTICATION-RETRIES 3	This command is to configure SSH, so you can set how many times you can type in a password before getting locked out.
IP SSH TIME-OUT 120	If you SSH into a router and do not type anything for 120 seconds, your session will time out.
CRYPTO KEY GENERATE RSA	This is the command to generate an RSA key. It's useful to to know that RSA stands for Rivest Adi Shamir. The initials of its co-founders.
How many bits in the modulus [512]: 512	This command will tell it how much encryption we are going to use. Keep in mind, the higher the encryption, the more overhead on the router.
TRANSPORT INPUT SSH	Instructs the router. If you are connecting through the network, you could only use SSH.
INT F0/0	This command lets you get into the Fast Ethernet 0/0 interface.
IP ADDRESS 192.168.1.254 255.255.255.0	This allows you to put an IP address on the router.

`DESCRIPTION CONNECTION TO LAN`	This is a courtesy command; when someone is doing any type of troubleshooting, it would be nice to know what interface is facing what and what type of interface it is. You could specify whatever you think is going to be useful for someone.
`NO SHUT`	Turns on an interface.
`CLOCK RATE 4000000`	This is the actual physical speed of that connection. You normally enter this on serial cables and on the DCE or Data Communication Equipment side of the cable.
`COPY RUN START`	This will copy all your configuration you have in RAM into NVRAM, which is the `startup-configuration` file or backup. This is the file that is used on boot up.
`Destination filename [startup-config]? HIT THE ENTER KEY`	This is the router asking you where you want to save the configuration. The default is in-between the brackets, so simply hit the *Enter* key. This is not so on all routers; for higher routers, you have to save the configuration.

All right, now that you have seen what commands you should type and at what prompt and what they do, from here it's all repetition of the same thing. So, let's look at the configurations for the rest of the routers.

These are the R2 configurations:

```
>ENABLE   (command to get to privilege mode)
#CONFIG T  (command to get to global configuration)
(CONFIG)#HOSTNAME R2 (command to give the router a hostname)
R2(CONFIG)#ENABLE PASSWORD CISCO (command to configure a Privilege
mode password plaint text)
R2(CONFIG)#ENABLE SECRET STUDENT (command to configure a Privilege
mode password encrypted)
R2(CONFIG)#SERVICE PASSWORD-ENCRYPTION ( command to encrypt all
passwords)
R2(CONFIG)#BANNER MOTD $ WELCOME TO R2 $ (Message of the Day
banner)
...
R2(CONFIG)#IP SSH AUTHENTICATION-RETRIES 3 (Command to enable SSH
retries)
R2(CONFIG)#IP SSH TIME-OUT 120 (command to set SSH session timeout
in seconds)
R2(CONFIG)#CRYPTO KEY GENERATE RSA (creating a key to generate for
ssh)
R2(CONFIG)#CRYPTO KEY GENERATE RSA
```

```
The name for the keys will be: R2.CISCO.COM
 Choose the size of the key modulus in the range of 360 to 2048 for
 your
 General Purpose Keys. Choosing a key modulus greater than 512 may
 take a few minutes.
 How many bits in the modulus [512]: 512 (Using default size of key
 in bits)
% Generating 512 bit RSA keys, keys will be non-exportable...[OK]
R2(CONFIG)#LINE VTY 0 15 (command to go into Terminal lines)
 *Mar 1 0:2:46.960:  RSA key size needs to be at least 768 bits for
 ssh
 version 2
 *Mar 1 0:2:46.960:  %SSH-5-ENABLED: SSH 1.5 has been enabled
R2(CONFIG-LINE)#TRANSPORT INPUT SSH (command to only allow SSH
sessions)
R2(CONFIG-LINE)#EXIT (command to return to previous prompt)
R2(CONFIG)#INT F0/0 (command to enter and interface)
R2(CONFIG-IF)#IP ADDRESS 192.168.2.254 255.255.255.0 (command to put
an IP address)
...
Destination filename [startup-config]? HIT THE ENTER KEY (asking you
to save to default location)
Building configuration...
[OK]
R2#
```

These are the R3 configurations:

```
>ENABLE   (command to get to privilege mode)
#CONFIG T   (command to get to global configuration)
(CONFIG)#HOSTNAME R3 (command to give the router a hostname)
R3(CONFIG)#ENABLE PASSWORD CISCO (command to configure a Privilege
mode password plaint text)
R3(CONFIG)#ENABLE SECRET STUDENT (command to configure a Privilege
mode password encrypted)
R3(CONFIG)#SERVICE PASSWORD-ENCRYPTION ( command to encrypt all
passwords)
R3(CONFIG)#BANNER MOTD $ WELCOME TO R3 $ (Message of the Day banner)
R3(CONFIG)#IP DOMAIN-LOOKUP (Turning on Domain Name resolution)
R3(CONFIG)#IP DOMAIN-NAME CISCO.COM (creating a domain-name using
cisco.com)
R3(CONFIG)#IP NAME-SERVER 192.168.4.1 (Pointing to the DNS server
that resolves cisco.com)
R3(CONFIG)#USERNAME LDIAZ PRIVILEGE 15 PASSWORD 0 CISCO (creating a
username with admin Writes and plaintext pwd)
...
The name for the keys will be: R3.CISCO.COM Choose the size of the key
modulus in the range of 360 to 2048 for
```

your General Purpose Keys. Choosing a key modulus greater than 512 may
take a few minutes.
 How many bits in the modulus [512]: 512 (Using default size of key in
bits)
% Generating 512 bit RSA keys, keys will be non-exportable...[OK]
R2(CONFIG)#LINE VTY 0 15 (command to go into Terminal lines)
*Mar 1 0:2:46.960: RSA key size needs to be at least 768 bits for
ssh
version 2
*Mar 1 0:2:46.960: %SSH-5-ENABLED: SSH 1.5 has been enabled
R3(CONFIG-LINE)#TRANSPORT INPUT SSH (command to only allow SSH
sessions)
R3(CONFIG-LINE)#EXIT (command to return to previous prompt)
R3(CONFIG)#INT F0/0 (command to enter and interface)
...
R3(CONFIG-IF)#EXIT (command to return to previous prompt)
R3(CONFIG)#EXIT (command to return to previous prompt)
R3#COPY RUN START (command to copy your config in RAM to NVRAM)
Destination filename [startup-config]? HIT THE ENTER KEY (asking you
to save to default location)
Building configuration...
[OK]
R3#

These are the R4 configurations:

>ENABLE   (command to get to privilege mode)
#CONFIG T   (command to get to global configuration)
(CONFIG)#HOSTNAME R4 (command to give the router a hostname)
R4(CONFIG)#ENABLE PASSWORD **CISCO** (command to configure a Privilege
mode password plaint text)
R4(CONFIG)#ENABLE SECRET **STUDENT** (command to configure a Privilege
mode password encrypted)
R4(CONFIG)#SERVICE PASSWORD-ENCRYPTION (command to encrypt all
passwords)
R4(CONFIG)#BANNER MOTD **$** WELCOME TO R4 **$** (Message of the Day
banner)
R4(CONFIG)#IP DOMAIN-LOOKUP (Turning on Domain Name resolution)
R4(CONFIG)#IP DOMAIN-NAME CISCO.COM (creating a domain-name using
cisco.com)
R4(CONFIG)#IP NAME-SERVER 192.168.4.1 (Pointing to the DNS server
that resolves cisco.com)
R4(CONFIG)#USERNAME LDIAZ PRIVILEGE 15 PASSWORD 0 CISCO (creating a
username with admin Writes and plaintext pwd)
The name for the keys will be: R4.CISCO.COMChoose the size of the
key modulus in the range of 360 to 2048 for your
    General Purpose Keys. Choosing a key modulus greater than 512 may
take a few minutes.

```
How many bits in the modulus [512]: 512 (Using default size of key
in bits)
% Generating 512 bit RSA keys, keys will be non-exportable...[OK]
R4(CONFIG)#LINE VTY 0 15 (command to go into Terminal lines)
*Mar 1 0:2:46.960:  RSA key size needs to be at least 768 bits for
ssh version 2
*Mar 1 0:2:46.960:  %SSH-5-ENABLED: SSH 1.5 has been enabled
R4(CONFIG-LINE)#TRANSPORT INPUT SSH (command to only allow SSH
sessions)
R4(CONFIG-LINE)#EXIT (command to return to previous prompt)
R4(CONFIG)#INT F0/0 (command to enter and interface)
R4(CONFIG-IF)#IP ADDRESS 192.168.4.254 255.255.255.0 (command to
put an IP address)
Destination filename [startup-config]? HIT THE ENTER KEY (asking
you to save to default location)
Building configuration...
[OK]
R4#
```

Well, you can see that after you do the first router, the rest are the same; the only thing that changes are the hostnames, IP addresses, descriptions, and the interfaces that you must configure. So, the more you configure, the more it will become second nature. Remember: *Repetition Breeds Retention*—the more you do it, the easier it becomes.

But not only that, you will run into issues, such as the wrong subnet mask, the wrong IP address, forgot to turn on an interface, but welcome them because if you never make a mistake, you won't learn how to fix it.

There is one thing I would like to clarify about the commands we just did. I know someone out there is wondering, *Why are we doing two privilege mode passwords?*

The plain text command `enable password cisco` gets overridden by the `enable secret student`.

So, why both? Well, we want encryption, but back in the Fred Flintstone age, routers did not understand or support the `enable secret` command, so you had no choice but to use plain text.

We do this, in case your flash, which is where your IOS resides, takes a dump; you can always put an older IOS, and you would have at least a plain text password to secure your router in the meantime.

Do we do this in real-world scenarios? Nope! This is just for certification purposes.

Now, there are still commands that you may be asked about but are not configured for your certification, so take a look at some of the ones I think may pop up:

Command	Purpose
`Router#clock set 12:00:00 December 25 2017`	Yes, the new 200-125. They want you to know how to set the clock on the router.
`Router(config)#clock timezone florida -4 5`	You also need to set the time zone for your location.
`Router(config)#Ntp update-calendar`	Configure NTP to update the calendar.

This is not too difficult at all, but it's very important; think about devices trying to synchronize with your routers.

Don't let the `clock` command confuse you. Make sure that it's done in two different prompts. In privilege mode, you simply set the time and date, and global configuration is where you set the time zone.

Viewing, saving, and erasing configurations

When you want to save your configurations, you will be typing the following:

```
R1#COPY RUN START
Destination filename [startup-config]?
Building configuration...
[OK]
R1#
```

After typing the `copy run start` command, just hit the *Enter* key twice and your configurations will be saved to NVRAM.

If you want to erase the entire `startup-config` file, which is in NVRAM, you would need to perform the following steps:

```
R1#erase start  ←
Erasing the nvram filesystem will remove all configuration files! Continue? [confirm]
[OK]
Erase of nvram: complete
%SYS-7-NV_BLOCK_INIT: Initialized the geometry of nvram
R1#Reload  ←
```

As shown in the preceding screenshot, you would have to type out `erase start`, which is short for startup-configuration; hit the *Enter* key to confirm this decision and then reload the router. You have just erased all your configurations on your router.

To view your existing configurations type `show run`; to view what is already saved type `show start`.

Summary

This was an interesting and fun chapter, because you got to learn not only how to connect to the routers CLI, but you got all the commands you would need to configure the basics and you got a router up and running. You also learned some show commands that will help you look at different parts of the router for you to troubleshoot. We also learned about some tools such as `ping` and `traceroute`, so we can verify connectivity and see exactly where the problem could be.

With the commands you typed, even though you may have green lights going across, you still can't network across the entire topology. We have not done any type of routing, but we will soon. Make sure you have these basic or administrative commands down and that you really understand their purpose.

Next, we will be getting into managing the Cisco network, so we are going to get into more details about the components of the router and bootup process and more. See you there!

7
Managing the Cisco Internetwork

In this chapter, we will be discussing LAN switching and Cisco routers in your network. I will be showing you how you can manage your internetworking devices through the network. You will learn the main components of Cisco's routers, and we will look at the boot sequence. Also, I will be showing how you can manage the switch or the router using TFTP, and you will be learning how to configure the router as a DHCP server and an NTP. Plus, we will be looking into the **Cisco Discovery Protocol** (**CDP**).

- Internal components of a Cisco router and switch
- The router boot sequence
- Backing up Cisco configurations
- Configuring DHCP on to a Cisco router
- Configuring DHCP relay
- Networking time protocol or NTP
- Configuring and verifying syslog
- Using Telnet and configuring Telnet

Internal components of Cisco router and switch

It's always good to be aware of the major components of your routers and switches and what they do, and how they all work together to create and maintain the network. Once you have a good understanding of this, you will become much better at your troubleshooting skills and will be able to minimize the errors.

I like to put this in the order of what components you will use more frequently:

Component	Description
RAM	Once the router decompresses the IOS into RAM, all your work will be done in RAM. This is the reason it's important to copy your configurations to NVRAM, which is your HDD of your router. RAM is responsible for holding routing table information, ARP cache, and packet buffers. The data structures of RAM allow the router to function properly. Something else to keep in mind with RAM is the amount of RAM you require for the size of the IOS. Just like a computer, you need to have enough RAM so it does not get overwhelmed by the amount of processes it is running. In today's networking world, anything less than 64 MB would not function effectively.
ROM	This component is vital for starting and maintaining the router. Within ROM, you will find the power on self-test or post, bootstrap, and the mini-IOS that you would use to bring up the router with minimal configurations to allow you to troubleshoot.
NVRAM	This is your non-volatile RAM; it is the location where the startup-configuration file is saved. All configurations done in RAM must be saved to NVRAM; otherwise, you run the risk of losing your work. Just as you would save your work in Windows Word to your hard drive, in a Cisco router or switch, you would save your configurations to NVRAM.
FLASH	Flash memory is where Cisco holds its IOS. On some routers, the flash memory is built into the motherboard as an EEPROM, which you can update to the latest version of the IOS. On other routers, it is a **Compact Flash Card** or **PMCIA** that fits into a specific slot on the back of the router. The size can be from 16 MB to 512 MB or greater, depending on your needs.
Configuration Register	This component controls the boot sequence of the router. By changing the settings of the register, you can make the router bypass the configuration file in NVRAM and just load the IOS into RAM. You can also configure it to boot into the mini-IOS in ROM. The way you make this possible is by changing hexadecimal numbers such as 0x2102, 0x2142, or 0x2101. By no means are these the only numbers you can change, but they are the most common.
POST	The power on self-test is a component that is stored in ROM. Just as in a Windows operating system, it checks the router's hardware to make sure it knows what it has to work with and also its functionality.

ROMMON	It's not where you want to be early in the morning. ROMMON is used because you are having issues when booting into your IOS. Using this component, you can troubleshoot the router, reload a new IOS using `tftpdnld` command, or even change the registry setting to control the boot sequence of your router.
Mini-IOS	The mini-IOS is another component that you can use for testing and troubleshooting your router. It is also held in ROM, but it is more flexible than working in ROMMON.
Bootstrap	This component is also held in ROM, and it is used at the very beginning of the router boot sequence to get things rolling, and once the router boots, it will assist in finding the IOS of the router.

Now that you are aware of the components of the router, let's look at the router boot sequence:

1. When you turn your router on, the very first thing it does is run a POST, which, just like a computer, is testing whether all the hardware of the device is present and working. During the POST, it will also look at all the different interfaces available to us, and it stores it and runs from ROM.

2. The next step is for the bootstrap in ROM to locate the IOS and load it into RAM. By default, the IOS is compressed, so it has to decompress the IOS into RAM, and it is also located in flash by default.

3. At this point, it is the IOS's responsibility to locate for a valid configuration file located in NVRAM. If any configuration is found, it is loaded into RAM, but if no configurations are found in the startup-configuration file, you will automatically enter setup mode.

4. Also, if no configuration is found, it will broadcast out all interfaces looking for configurations. But this will only happen if your router is plugged into your LAN or WAN. You could configure the router to always look for a TFTP or FTP server for the configurations needed, but you would need to set it up using the `boot` command, not to mention connectivity. Most of the time, you don't even know this is happening, but if you find yourself staring at the screen with some broadcast message stating `looking for configuration file 255.255.255.255` and nothing ever happens, you must use the `break` command: *Ctrl + C* or *Ctrl + Shift + 6* to escape from this annoying message.

Backing up your Cisco configurations

Once again, just as you would back up the state of your computer on a router or switch, you must back up your startup-configuration file. When you are configuring your router or switch, you should save your configurations by using the `copy run start` command from privilege mode to NVRAM; since RAM is volatile, it does not retain any information if the power is lost; it simply uses the information at that moment, while the router is running. With that said, once again, your first backup is NVRAM, executing the following command: `copy run start`, which saves everything you have configured in RAM to NVRAM.

Your second backup is to a TFTP or FTP server. It will save it as a `.bin` file, but if you ever need to restore it, you can, using those servers. Let's see how you would backup to NVRAM.

This is your first backup:

```
R1#COPY RUN START
Destination filename [startup-config]?
Building configuration...
[OK]
R1#
```

The preceding screenshot simply shows you how you copy from your running-configuration, that is in RAM, to the startup-configuration file, which is in your NVRAM, so you don't lose any work that has been done so far. You could just simply type `copy run start` or in real-world applications, you simply type `wr`, which means `write` and it will do so to the default location, which is the `startup-config` file.

The following diagram shows you the steps needed to copy or back up your `start` to a TFTP server. First, you need to verify you have connectivity, and then you would use the `copy start to tftp` command and follow the steps:

```
R1#ping 192.168.4.1  ◄──────────────   Verify connectivity

Type escape sequence to abort.
Sending 5, 100-byte ICMP Echos to 192.168.4.1, timeout is 2 seconds:
!!!!!
Success rate is 100 percent (5/5), round-trip min/avg/max = 4/10/18 ms

R1#copy start tftp   ◄──────────────   Command used
Address or name of remote host []? 192.168.4.1
Destination filename [R1-confg]?                IP address of TFTP

Writing startup-config...!!
[OK - 1058 bytes]                               Hit ENTER for default

1058 bytes copied in 0.012 secs (88166 bytes/sec)
R1#
```

Just as important as backing up your configuration is verifying your configuration. There are two commands you could use, the startup-config and the running-config, and they could be the same or different, it all depends on how often you save. Let me give you an example of the sh start, which looks at NVRAM:

```
R1#sh start
Using 1058 bytes
!
version 12.4
no service timestamps log datetime msec
no service timestamps debug datetime msec
service password-encryption
!
hostname R1
!
!
!
enable secret 5 $1$mERr$/8NQictp9.m0ns.z98EQq1
enable password 7 0802657D2A36
!
!
!
!
!
!
no ip cef
no ipv6 cef
!
!
!
username LDIAZ privilege 15 password 7 0802657D2A36
```

The sh run command shows you what you are running currently in your RAM:

```
R1#sh run
Building configuration...

Current configuration : 1107 bytes
!
version 12.4
no service timestamps log datetime msec
no service timestamps debug datetime msec
service password-encryption
!
hostname R1
!
!
!
enable secret 5 $1$mERr$/8NQictp9.mOns.z98EQq1
enable password 7 0802657D2A36
!
!
!
!
!
!
no ip cef
no ipv6 cef
!
!
!
username LDIAZ privilege 15 password 7 0802657D2A36
username bob privilege 7 password 7 08205C5E051C
```

The preceding screenshot shows the startup-config in comparison to the running-config and you can see that the running-config file has a username bob while the startup-config does not. The reason for that is when you are configuring your router, you are working within RAM, and once you save it using the copy run start command from privilege mode, then it will be in NVRAM.

I have always been asked in the classroom or online, *How often should we save? That* is up to you.

Think about this: if you are creating the resume for your dream job, are you going to save once you finish it or as you write it? There is no standard or guideline, just simple common sense.

So now we know how to backup to a TFTP server or simply to our NVRAM, but how do you restore a configuration or even an IOS file if it becomes corrupt. Simply do the opposite. Let's look at how it is done!

```
R1#COPY TFTP START
Address or name of remote host []? 192.168.4.1        Case sensitive
Source filename []? R1-confg ◄─────────────
Destination filename [startup-config]? ◄────          Hit enter key

Accessing tftp://192.168.4.1/R1-confg...
Loading R1-confg from 192.168.4.1: !
[OK - 1058 bytes]

1058 bytes copied in 0.006 secs (176333 bytes/sec)
R1#
```

The first thing you need to verify is the connectivity to the TFTP server, as before. Then you have access to save files on that server and you need to determine whether there is space to save the file. Once you have done that, as shown in the preceding diagram, you will first type the command, and then it will ask you for the destination IP address of the TFTP; hit *Enter* if you're just going to save it to the default location; type a different name if you want to have configurations present.

Tread lightly. Here, in the real world, there may be some people who have more than one configuration file, but for testing purposes, stick to what you see in the diagram. Hopefully, you'll get the result you want.

Let's say you get a router that has some configurations on it and you want to start from scratch; you want to make sure that no configuration is present that can cause you a problem. Scorch the earth and start over. This is how you would do that on a router:

```
R1#ERASE START
Erasing the nvram filesystem will remove all configuration files!
Continue? [confirm] ◄───────    Hit enter key
[OK]
Erase of nvram: complete
%SYS-7-NV_BLOCK_INIT: Initialized the geometry of nvram
R1#
```

After you execute the command and it successfully completes, you need to reload the router:

```
Erase of nvram: complete
%SYS-7-NV_BLOCK_INIT: Initialized the geometry of nvram
R1#reload
Proceed with reload? [confirm] ◄───────    Hit enter key
```

Configuring DHCP on a Cisco router

Dynamic Host Configuration Protocol (**DHCP**) is used when we turn on our laptops, phones, and client desktop PCs. We normally use a Microsoft DHCP server, where we create a **scope**. We give it a name such as `ACCT_LAN` and we identify it with a network ID such as `192.168.1.0/24`, and within that scope we have the usable addresses that will be assigned to the client machines. Using the example `NetID`, the range would be `192.168.1.1 − 192.168.1.254`, but we need to take into consideration things such as servers, switches, routers, and even printers. These devices cannot afford for IP addresses to change every time.

So, what do we do? We create something called **exclusions**, and we exclude the address or addresses that will be assigned statically to the internetworking devices, so they do not fall into the **pool of addresses** to be allocated. Once you create your exclusions, we also need to put some **scope options** such as the DNS server address, the gateway address, and for how long these leased addresses are going to last.

Just like renting a home, the lease must stipulate whether it is a month-to-month lease, a three-month lease, a six-month lease, or an annual lease, and how long before the lease expires the landlord needs to be notified that the lease will be renewed.

When configuring a DHCP server, all these things must be thought of before hand. Let's go ahead and see how you would do this on a router, not an actual DHCP server:

```
R3(config)#ip dhcp ?
  excluded-address  Prevent DHCP from assigning certain addresses
  pool              Configure DHCP address pools
  relay             DHCP relay agent parameters
R3(config)#ip dhcp
```

Question mark to the rescue—what do we do first? It really does not matter, so we will configure the pool of addresses first; let's see how that looks:

```
R3(config)#ip dhcp pool ACCT_LAN
R3(dhcp-config)#?
  default-router  Default routers
  dns-server      Set name server
  exit            Exit from DHCP pool configuration mode
  network         Network number and mask
  no              Negate a command or set its defaults
  option          Raw DHCP options
R3(dhcp-config)#
```

So, we created the pool for the ACCT_LAN, but now we have other subcommands that we need to configure; let's do that:

```
R3(dhcp-config)#?
  default-router   Default routers
  dns-server       Set name server
  exit             Exit from DHCP pool configuration mode
  network          Network number and mask
  no               Negate a command or set its defaults
  option           Raw DHCP options
R3(dhcp-config)#default-router 192.168.3.254
R3(dhcp-config)#dns-server 192.168.4.1
R3(dhcp-config)#network 192.168.3.0   ◄──── Needs a
% Incomplete command.                        subnetmask
R3(dhcp-config)#network 192.168.3.0 255.255.255.0
R3(dhcp-config)#
```

Now we have our gateway, DNS server, and the network we are using, so it knows the range of IPs we need in the network.

Now let's create the exclusions, so the IP addresses of your servers, routers, switches, and printers do not conflict with the IP addresses being allotted to end devices, such as your PCs:

```
R3(config)#ip dhcp excluded-address ?
  A.B.C.D   Low IP address
R3(config)#ip dhcp excluded-address 192.168.3.200 ?
  A.B.C.D   High IP address
  <cr>
R3(config)#ip dhcp excluded-address 192.168.3.200 192.168.3.254 ?
  <cr>
R3(config)#ip dhcp excluded-address 192.168.3.200 192.168.3.254
R3(config)#
```

The router will not allocate or assign any IP address between x.x.x.200 and x.x.x.254; those addresses will be used for servers, routers, and switches. Depending on the router you have and its IOS, the lease time may vary according to how you can configure it. Normally, it is days, hours, and minutes, so it is really up to you and your network. The reason I say this is an IP address renews its address at 25%, 50%, and then 100%, so short-term leases do not work so well in most environments, and you may want to have at least a five-day lease period; it also reduces the amount of bandwidth being taken up.

DHCP relay

A DHCP relay agent is used to allocate IP addresses to end devices that are outside the LAN. This is not common practice; it simply does not make sense to assign an IP address to a device across a wide area network. But there may be a situation where a relay agent is needed.

Routers by default do not accept broadcast addresses, and that is exactly what happens when a device wakes up on the LAN and requests an IP address.

We must keep in mind the process of DORA, the letter *D* stands for **Discover**, and it's broadcasting that it needs an IP address.

Since no local DHCP exists, the request is directed to the gateway, which is your router, and when it sees a broadcast coming its way, it will drop that packet. This only happens if you are in a different LAN segment; if you are in the same LAN, then you don't have to worry about that.

So, in a router you would configure something called the `ip helper-address`, which points to the DHCP server, and you would do this in the interface that faces the LAN, and the command you would type looks something like the following:

```
R3(config-if)#ip helper-address 190.168.4.1
```

Since you have configured an `ip helper-address` on your router, it will act as your proxy and will go on your behalf to the DHCP server and acquire an IP address from the correct scope, since it knows what network it is coming from, and assigns the address to the end devices on the correct LANs.

You always need to keep in mind the process of DHCP, which is DORA, and that it uses broadcast to request an IP address.

Using IPv4, that is a huge problem, and also you do not want to assign IP addresses across a WAN, due to bandwidth issues.

Everyone should have their own DHCP server locally on their LAN, or the router to that segment should be configured as a DHCP.

You can verify your DHCP configuration in four different ways:

- `show ip dhcp bindings`: This will show you IP addresses that are assigned.

- `show ip dhcp pool [poolname]`: This will show you IP addresses allotted, additional information for those IP addresses and the last available address that can be assigned for that network.
- `show ip dhcp server statistics`: This archives all DHCP indicators.
- `show ip dhcp conflict`: It will alarm you, if anyone in your network is using an IP address from your pool, without it being assigned..

The Network Time Protocol or NTP

In a network, it is extremely important that all devices that participate in it be in sync with one another.

By this I mean, their clocks should all be the same down to the second, heck, to a millisecond if you ask me; if they aren't, you could run into trouble. Just think about DC replication, DNS replication, intersite or intrasite replication, and the list does not stop there. And that's just Microsoft. The routers and switches that you are using must be in sync with one another as well, or updates will come in late or not at all. This in turn will hurt all your Microsoft devices as well.

Something else to think about is troubleshooting. You must have a timestamp when things go wrong, so you can have documentation as to when it all went bonkers, or if you are doing an update to your hardware or software, we should all be in sync so everyone can update properly. But as in IT, something always happens, so you must have the date and time of the incident for documentation purposes.

It is very easy to overlook this configuration, but it is vital to ensure the proper functioning of your network. I will give you three important bullet points that you really need to keep in mind:

- Correct time allows the tracking of events in the proper order
- Clock synchronization is critical for the correct interpretation of events within the syslog data
- Clock synchronization is critical for the digital certificates you create

Making sure all your devices have the correct time is especially helpful for your routers and switches for looking at logs regarding security issues. As an example, if an interface or a routing protocol goes down, syslog messages will be created that include the date and time it happened.

Configuring and verifying syslog

You must have a syslog server saving all the console messages and of course be able to have a time stamp on it, so you can investigate the incident more precisely. So, how would you configure logging on a router? Here it is:

```
Router(config)#logging host 192.168.4.1
Router(config)# service timestamp log datetime msec
```

Once you configure the preceding command, all console messages will be stored in one location that you can view at your leisure. Even though we configured the timestamp command, that does not mean that you are getting the correct time. You must make sure that all devices on the network are synchronized appropriately to a central server.

```
R3#clock set 12:00:00 1 January 2018
R3#config T
R3(config)#clock timezone florida -4
R3(config)#ntp server 192.168.4.1 key 1234
R3(config)#logging host 192.168.4.1
R3(config)#service timestamps log datetime msec
```

You would need to have the same key on the sever for the NTP to work. This is an example of the output you would get on the server:

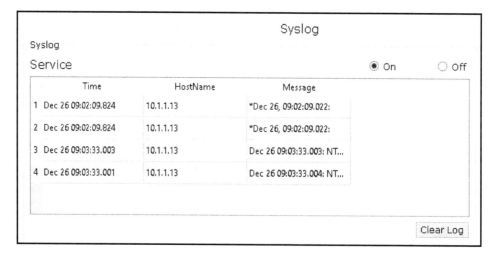

Obviously, this is a simulator; on a real router, running the full version of the IOS, you would have more features allotted to you. This would allow you to create more concise information as to what, when, where, and how. But if I am going to be honest with you, 99% of the time in the real world, you will be using third-party software that will give a more descriptive and easy-to-look-at output, but for your test, this is what you must know.

Either way, here are some `show` commands at your disposal:

```
R3#sh ntp status
Clock is synchronized, stratum 2, reference is 192.168.4.1
nominal freq is 250.0000 Hz, actual freq is 249.9990 Hz, precision is 2**19
reference time is DDC10E91.0000021E (09:08:33.542 UTC Tue Dec 26 2017)
clock offset is 0.00 msec, root delay is 0.00 msec
root dispersion is 0.02 msec, peer dispersion is 0.02 msec.
```

```
NTP-Master-Cisco#
NTP-Master-Cisco#sh ntp associations  <===

  address          ref clock      st   when   poll reach  delay  offset   disp
~127.127.1.1       .LOCL.          1      4     16   377  0.000   0.000  0.225
*~204.9.54.119     .CDMA.          1     35     64   377  0.000 -80.968  3.040
 * sys.peer, # selected, + candidate, - outlyer, x falseticker, ~ configured
NTP-Master-Cisco#
```

Being a network engineer, you need to know your network to make sure you can troubleshoot it or enhance it if anything is missing or improve upon it. I'm sure you know there are a million third-party tools that exist today that can monitor and maintain your network, but also it can give us information on how the network is running and what it is connected to; some even build a map for us.

We are now going to talk about two protocols that are really tools that can help us map out our network. We are going to assume you are an administrator and you just got handed off a network and you were not given any documentation or diagrams, or anything on this network. Your boss just said, *Take care of any issues that we have and make our network better; I have faith in you.* OK then...

Well, luckily for us, we have CDP and now LLDP at our disposal. CDP is the Cisco Discovery Protocol. This is a Cisco proprietary protocol designed by Cisco, as the name suggests. This protocol will tell you who you are connected to directly.

Cisco Discovery Protocol (CDP)

Let's look at exactly what CDP is looking at and we will use the following topology to test:

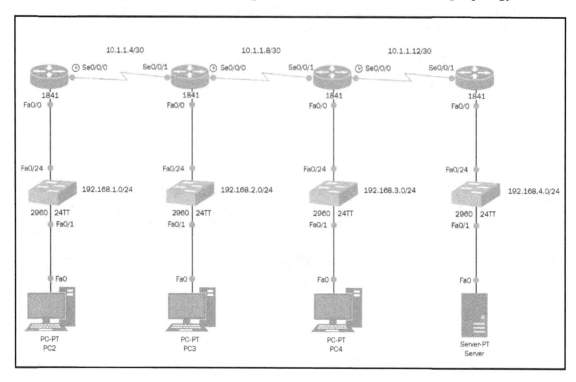

We are going to use this topology to use the CDP protocol, but before we can use CDP, it must be turned on globally and under each interface. Within global configuration, we would type cdp run, and under each interface, we would type cdp enable:

```
R2#config t
Enter configuration commands, one per line.  End with CNTL/Z.
R2(config)#cdp run ◄─────────────────┐
R2(config)#int f0/0              │  Turn cdp on globally
R2(config-if)#cdp enable
R2(config-if)#int s0/0/0
R2(config-if)#cdp enable
R2(config-if)#int s0/0/1
R2(config-if)#cdp enable ◄───── Turn cdp on within an interface
R2(config-if)#
```

Once we have turned on CDP on all routers and their interfaces, we can now see who our neighbors are. The two commands we are going to look at are show cdp neighbor and show cdp neighbor detail:

```
R3#SH CDP NEIGHBOR
Capability Codes: R - Router, T - Trans Bridge, B - Source
Route Bridge
                    S - Switch, H - Host, I - IGMP, r -
Repeater, P - Phone
Device ID      Local Intrfce    Holdtme     Capability    Platform
Port ID
Switch         Fas 0/0            159            S           2960
Fas 0/24
R2             Ser 0/0/1          164            R           C1841
Ser 0/0/0
R4             Ser 0/0/0          165            R           C1841
Ser 0/0/1
R3#
```

The show cdp neighbor command only shows us layer 2 information:

- Who are we connected to?
- Are they a switch or a router?
- The type of switch or router it is.
- The interface that we are learning it on.
- The interface that is sending the information.
- How long we will retain that information.

That's not so bad; we can create a simple network design and it gives us a basic look at our network. But as I said before, third-party applications have a lot more tools and are designed to give so much detail, not only about your network but the equipment on it, down to the end devices driver.

Once again, you need to know this for your certification, and, yes, for real-world use also, as you never know when you'll be in an interview, where they are asking you questions they don't themselves know the answer to.

But anyway here are the CDP fields with brief description:

Field	Definition
Device ID	Name of the device you are *directly* connected to.
Local Interface	This is your interface, where you are receiving the CDP packets.
Holdtime	How long the information will stay in the router before trashing it, if no more CDP packets are received.
Capability	Relates to your neighbor: are you a router, switch, or repeater.
Platform	The series of Cisco device you're connected to.
Port ID	The neighbor's device's port or interface on which the CDP packets are multicast.

The `show cdp neighbor detail` command will show you more information, such as the IP address of your neighbor, IOS version, and the port where the CDP packets are coming from. Both of these commands are crucial for your certification and in the real world. Here is an example of the `sh cdp neighbor detail`:

```
R3#sh cdp neighbor detail

Device ID: Switch
Entry address(es):
Platform: cisco 2960, Capabilities: Switch
Interface: FastEthernet0/0, Port ID (outgoing port):
FastEthernet0/24
Holdtime: 162

Version :
Cisco IOS Software, C2960 Software (C2960-LANBASE-M), Version
12.2(25)FX, RELEASE SOFTWARE (fc1)
Copyright (c) 1986-2005 by Cisco Systems, Inc.
Compiled Wed 12-Oct-05 22:05 by pt_team

advertisement version: 2
Duplex: full
-----------------------------

Device ID: R2
Entry address(es):
   IP address : 10.1.1.9
Platform: cisco C1841, Capabilities: Router
Interface: Serial0/0/1, Port ID (outgoing port): Serial0/0/0
Holdtime: 168
```

I say *real world* because if you are that individual who has no documentation, you can use these two commands to start building a map of your network. This is fine for your certification and if you work for a company that is too frugal to dish out the money to get some third-party software to do the same thing, if not better.

Here is a word to the wise: if you do not want to have CDP enabled on an interface that faces the public network or internet, you would do the following under the appropriate interface to disable CDP:

```
R1(config)#INT S0/0/1
R1(config-if)#NO CDP ENABLE
R1(config-if)#
```

One last command you should now use is the show cdp entry *:

```
R2#sh cdp entry *

Device ID: Switch
Entry address(es):
Platform: cisco 2960, Capabilities: Switch
Interface: FastEthernet0/0, Port ID (outgoing port): FastEthernet0/24
Holdtime: 136

Version :
Cisco IOS Software, C2960 Software (C2960-LANBASE-M), Version 12.2(25)FX, RELEASE SOFTWARE (fc1)
Copyright (c) 1986-2005 by Cisco Systems, Inc.
Compiled Wed 12-Oct-05 22:05 by pt_team

advertisement version: 2
Duplex: full
--------------------------

Device ID: R3
Entry address(es):
  IP address : 10.1.1.10
Platform: cisco C1841, Capabilities: Router
Interface: Serial0/0/0, Port ID (outgoing port): Serial0/0/1
Holdtime: 142
```

This command shows you the same thing as the `show cdp neighbor detail` with one difference at the end of it; the command uses an asterisk that is called a **wildcard**, showing all the CDP neighbors. The following table shows you all the switches you can use with the `show cdp entry` command:

Syntax Description	
*	Wildcard showing all the CDP neighbors.
entry-name	Name of the neighbor.
	You can enter an asterisk (*) at the end of an *entry-name*, such as `show cdp entry dev*`, which would show information about the neighbor, device.cisco.com.
protocol	(Optional) Limits the display to information about the protocols enabled on a router.
version	(Optional) Limits the display to information about the version of software running on the router.

Link Layer Data Protocol (LLDP)

Link Layer Data Protocol (LLDP) is a newer command that works just like CDP. So, what's the big deal if it does the same thing? It is not the property of Cisco and anyone can use it. For you, IEEE aficionados are the 802.1AB for station and Media Access Control Connectivity Discovery.

LLDP has all the bells and whistles that CDP does and is enhanced to specifically address the voice application, and this version is called **LLDP-MED (Media Endpoint Discovery)**.

But we must see how to turn on LLDP and do the show commands to see what it looks like:

```
CORE#SH LLDP NEighbors
Capability codes:
    (R) Router, (B) Bridge, (T) Telephone, (C) DOCSIS Cable Device
    (W) WLAN Access Point, (P) Repeater, (S) Station, (O) Other
Device ID          Local Intf      Hold-time   Capability      Port ID
STUDENT2           Fa0/23          120         R               Fa0/23
STUDENT            Fa0/24          120         R               Vlan
STUDENT2           Fa0/23          120         R               Vlan
STUDENT            Fa0/24          120         R               Fa0/24

Total entries displayed: 4
```

As you can see, it differs when it comes to the code; we now have Telephone, Docsis Cable Device, Station, WLAN AP, and in the fields, it has Port ID instead of Platform.

For me, what is cool about LLDP details is that I can see the Chassis ID number; believe me, I was asked this question quite often in Telecom. But you can see that there is more detailed information if you use LLDP, which I can almost guarantee it will be in the CCNA-200-125:

```
CORE#SH LLDP NEighbors DETAIL
-------------------------------------------------
Chassis id: 0001.960E.7917 ◄━━━━━━━━━━━━━━━━━━━━
Port id: Fa0/23
Port Description: FastEthernet0/23
System Name: STUDENT2
System Description:
Cisco IOS Software, C3560 Software (C3560-ADVIPSERVICESK9-M), Version 12.2(37)SE1, RELEASE SOFTWARE (fc1)
Copyright (c) 1986-2007 by Cisco Systems, Inc.
Compiled Thu 05-Jul-07 22:22 by pt_team
Time remaining: 90 seconds
System Capabilities: R
Enabled Capabilities: R
Management Addresses - not advertised
Auto Negotiation - supported, enabled
Physical media capabilities:
    100baseT(HD)
    100baseT(FD)
    1000baseT(HD)
Media Attachment Unit type: 10
Vlan ID: 1
```

Using and configuring Telnet

Telnet is one of the tools we discussed earlier, but let's get a little deeper into it. Telnet is part of the TCP/IP protocol suite; it's a virtual terminal protocol that allows you to make connections to remote sites or other devices attached to a network that has Telnet configured, and it is of course password protected.

In networking, we usually use Telnet to go inside a router or switch to do `show` commands, re-configure some setting, or add a brand-new configuration, or to simply troubleshoot the device. It need not be said that you can Telnet from anywhere to anywhere if you have the privileges to do so. But let's look again at how, the configuration and telnetting into another device is done:

```
R3(config)#line vty 0 15
R3(config-line)#password cisco
R3(config-line)#login local
R3(config-line)#exit
R3(config)#username ldiaz privilege 15 password 0 cisco
R3(config)#do wr
```

The preceding example is how you configure Telnet lines through the VTY terminal lines. You will always use a password, but in this example, we are also using the `login local` command, so you will need to input a username and their local password, instead of just the password on the line. Using this method will allow a certain amount of access that you as the administrator would determine.

The following is an example of how you would Telnet into a router securely:

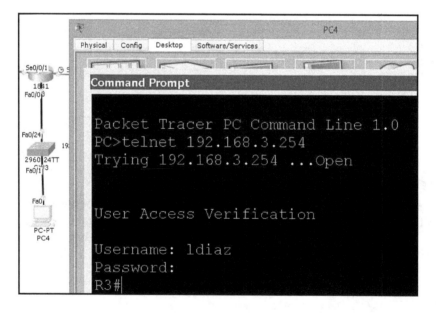

You will be prompted for a username and password, and once you give your username and hit the *Enter* key, you will then be prompted for the local username password, which is *Cisco*, in this scenario. Don't freak out, the password will not show up on the screen, not even dots, but it was typed.

Once you're in, you can then Telnet into other routers or switches right from that same router, unless you just want to quit the Telnet session, then simply type exit and you're back at your originating point.

The way Cisco wants you to do multiple Telnet sessions is by using the *Ctrl + Shift + 6* and then release *X* and it will take you back to the router you started telnetting through; let's take a peek:

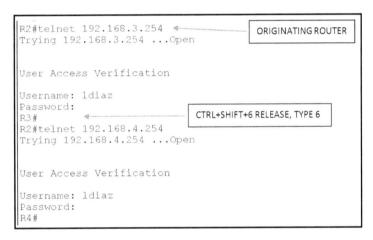

The purpose of *Ctrl + Shift + 6* release and then press *6*, is so you can keep all those Telnet sessions open, so if you type exit you could always go back to those Telnet sessions.

You could always check the Telnet connections; if you want to view the connections from your router or switch to a remote device, just use the show sessions command, which will show all the Telnet connections you have made, and the one that has an asterisk by it is the current connection. You could return to any session by typing the number of the connection and then hitting *Enter* or exit your way back.

You could also reveal all active consoles and VTY ports in use on the router with the show users command. It will show your console connection and however many routers or switches you are connected to:

```
R2#sh users
     Line       User      Host(s)            Idle         Location
*   0 con 0               idle               00:00:00
  196 vty 0    ldiaz      10.1.1.10          00:00:31 10.1.1.5
  197 vty 1    ldiaz      idle               00:04:19 10.1.1.10
```

We already mentioned how we can use the IP DOMAIN-LOOKUP command to resolve hostnames, which will allow us to ping or Telnet by name instead of IP. Let's take a quick peek back to that configuration:

R1(CONFIG)#IP DOMAIN-LOOKUP
R1(CONFIG)#IP DOMAIN-NAME CISCO.COM
R1(CONFIG)#IP NAME-SERVER 192.168.4.1

Obviously, you must have the DNS server configured with the correct host records for this to work.

You could also build your own host table using the ip host host_name ip address command, so let's see that in action:

```
R3(config)#ip host R2 10.1.1.9 10.1.1.6 192.168.2.254
R3(config)#exit
R3#
*Jan 01, 10:27:54.2727: *Jan 01, 10:27:54.2727: %SYS-5-
CONFIG_I: Configured from console by console
R3#ping R2 ←————————

Type escape sequence to abort.
Sending 5, 100-byte ICMP Echos to 10.1.1.9, timeout is 2
seconds:
!!!!!
Success rate is 100 percent (5/5), round-trip min/avg/max
= 7/9/16 ms

R3#
```

As you can see, we were able to ping by name instead of using the IP address. We used multiple IP addresses for redundancy, so if one fails, it could try the other IPs.

A network engineer not only must have the knowledge to type commands in a router, they should also be able to understand what they are typing, meaning what those commands are supposed to do, so they can troubleshoot network problems efficiently.

The tools in your arsenal are the following:

- **Ping**: ICMP protocol, just test connectivity end to end.
- **Traceroute**: This command will show you where in the path the problem exits.
- **Debugging**: Lets you see what is going on behind the scenes. You can debug almost anything; be careful, if you start debugging too many things, you will overwhelm your device. Here is an example of the things you can debug:

```
R4#debug ?
  aaa             AAA Authentication, Authorization and Accounting
  crypto          Cryptographic subsystem
  custom-queue    Custom output queueing
  eigrp           EIGRP Protocol information
  ephone          ethernet phone skinny protocol
  frame-relay     Frame Relay
  ip              IP information
  ipv6            IPv6 information
  ntp             NTP information
  ppp             PPP (Point to Point Protocol) information
R4#debug
```

This is a simulator, so it is a very small list of what you can debug, but here is an example of the following debug command debug ip rip:

```
  ppp             PPP (Point to Point Protocol) information
R4#debug ip rip
RIP protocol debugging is on
R4#RIP: received v2 update from 10.1.1.13 on Serial0/0/1
        10.1.1.4/30 via 0.0.0.0 in 2 hops
        10.1.1.8/30 via 0.0.0.0 in 1 hops
        192.168.1.0/24 via 0.0.0.0 in 3 hops
        192.168.2.0/24 via 0.0.0.0 in 2 hops
        192.168.3.0/24 via 0.0.0.0 in 1 hops
RIP: sending  v2 update to 224.0.0.9 via FastEthernet0/0 (192.168.4.254)
RIP: build update entries
        10.1.1.4/30 via 0.0.0.0, metric 3, tag 0
        10.1.1.8/30 via 0.0.0.0, metric 2, tag 0
        10.1.1.12/30 via 0.0.0.0, metric 1, tag 0
        192.168.1.0/24 via 0.0.0.0, metric 4, tag 0
        192.168.2.0/24 via 0.0.0.0, metric 3, tag 0
        192.168.3.0/24 via 0.0.0.0, metric 2, tag 0
RIP: sending  v2 update to 224.0.0.9 via Serial0/0/1 (10.1.1.14)
RIP: build update entries
        192.168.4.0/24 via 0.0.0.0, metric 1, tag 0
```

The preceding output is from the debug ip rip command; what is underlined is what you need to pay attention to: am I sending and receiving version 2 updates and the multicast address 224.0.0.9? This will let you know very quickly why maybe one router is not receiving the updates from another router.

One last show command I would put in my arsenal of tools is the Show processes command. This tool is very good for determining the routers CPU utilization, and it will give you a list of active processes, along with their corresponding ID, priority, scheduler test (status), CPU time used, number of times invoked, and much more.

Let's see an example of this command:

```
R4#sh processes
CPU utilization for five seconds: 0%/0%; one minute: 0%; five minutes: 0%
 PID QTy        PC Runtime (ms)     Invoked  uSecs      Stacks TTY Process
   1 Csp  602F3AF0          0          1627      0  2600/3000    0 Load Meter
   2 Lwe  60C5BE00          4           136     29  5572/6000    0 CEF Scanner
   3 Lst  602D90F8       1676           837   2002  5740/6000    0 Check heaps
   4 Cwe  602D08F8          0             1      0  5568/6000    0 Chunk
Manager
   5 Cwe  602DF0E8          0             1      0  5592/6000    0 Pool
Manager
   6 Mst  60251E38          0             2      0  5560/6000    0 Timers
   7 Mwe  600D4940          0             2      0  5568/6000    0 Serial
Backgrou
   8 Mwe  6034B718          0             1      0  2584/3000    0 OIR Handler
   9 Mwe  603FA3C8          0             1      0  5612/6000    0 IPC Zone
Manage
  10 Mwe  603FA1A0          0          8124      0  5488/6000    0 IPC
Periodic Ti
  11 Mwe  603FA220          0             9      0  4884/6000    0 IPC Seat
Manage
  12 Lwe  60406818        124          2003     61  5300/6000    0 ARP Input
  13 Mwe  60581638          0             1      0  5760/6000    0 HC Counter
Time
  14 Mwe  605E3D00          0             2      0  5564/6000    0 DDR Timers
  15 Msp  80164A38          0         79543      0  5608/6000    0 GraphIt
  16 Mwe  802DB0FC          0             2         011576/12000 0 Dialer
```

What this basically shows is that the router is not really utilizing any CPU processing power now. You see that in the first line it states that for five seconds: 0%; one minute: 0%; and five minutes: 0% processing used.

The following table will give you a brief description as to what the fields of this output mean. I can tell you with much certainty that in a real-world example you will see this command quite often. When you are on-call, you must generate reports on your routers in the morning and in the evening.

The `show processes` command is one of the outputs you must look at to make sure the routers are not being overloaded, and you must take a snippet of it and email it to the appropriate person:

Field	Description
X	Average total utilization during last five seconds (interrupts + processes)
Y	Average utilization due to interrupts, during the last five seconds
Z	Average total utilization during last minute
W	Average total utilization during last five minutes
PID	Process ID
Runtime	CPU time the process has used (in milliseconds)
Invoked	Number of times a process has been called
uSecs	Microseconds of CPU time for each invocation
5Sec	CPU utilization by task in the last five seconds
1Min	CPU utilization by task in the last minute
5Min	CPU utilization by task in the last five minutes
TTY	Terminal that controls the process
Process	Name of process

Summary

In this chapter, we covered the internal components of a router and how to back up and restore your configurations using TFTP. We also learned how to use CDP and LLDP, so we can build our map of the network if we have to, or simple troubleshooting tools. We then saw how we can Telnet into a router or multiple routers and even configure DNS or create an IP host table manually, so we can ping or Telnet using host names instead of IP addresses.

We talked briefly about three troubleshooting commands at your disposal, PING, TRACEROUTE, and DEBUG and how to look at CPU usage on a router. These commands, among many more to come, will allow you to efficiently correct your network quicker. That was awesome! Let's go to the next topics.

8
Managing Cisco Devices

In this chapter, we will learn how to manage a Cisco router. We will be going over several topics such as the registry, backing up, and restoring of Cisco IOS, licensing, and much more. We will be getting into these topics in great depth so you can have a better understanding of how you can efficiently manage your router or switch.

In this chapter, we are going to cover the following topics:

- Managing the Cisco configuration register:
    - Software configuration bit meaning
    - Checking the current configuration register value
- Boot system commands
- Recovering passwords
- Interrupting the router boot sequence
- Changing the configuration register
- Backing up and restoring the Cisco IOS
- How to use the Cisco **Integrated File System (IFS)**
- Licensing:
    - Right-to-use licensing (eval)
    - Backing up and uninstalling the license

Let's start with the internal components of a Cisco router; make sure you are familiar with these components and what they do, as this will enable you to troubleshoot problems in the future:

Component	Description
Bootstrap	Stored in the microcode of the ROM. The bootstrap will boot the router and then load the IOS.
POST	Also stored in the microcode of ROM. Checks functionality of the router hardware and verifies which interfaces are present (power on self test).
ROM monitor	Again, stored in the microcode of ROM. It is used for manufacturing testing and troubleshooting. Back in the day, it was called the mini-IOS.
RAM	Its purpose is to hold packet buffers, ARP caches, routing tables, and the software that allows the router to function. Most importantly, the running configuration file is stored in RAM, and the IOS is decompressed into RAM. Always keep in mind that RAM is volatile, which means you don't save it to NVRAM, as your configuration is gone like the wind.
ROM	This is used to start and maintain the router. It holds the POST and bootstrap and mini-IOS (ROM).
Flash memory	Holds the Cisco IOS by default. The good thing about flash is that it is not erased if the router is turned off, but it can be upgraded.
NVRAM	Non-volatile RAM is used to hold the startup configuration, which is your configuration that you copied from RAM. So, NVRAM is like the hard drive for the router.
Configuration register	This component controls how the router boots up; the values are a series of hex numbers. The one you need to be very familiar with is 0x2102, which is the default setting and all it does is to instruct the router upon boot up to look at NVRAM for the startup configuration and if any configurations are present, to load them. The other side of that coin is 0x2142 instructs the router to ignore NVRAM and just loads the IOS in setup mode.

Well, now that you have become more familiar with the router components, let's become even more familiar with how the router boots up. Just like a PC, there is a sequence that must be followed to see your operating system on the desktop, and the same goes for routers and switches, so let's get a better understanding of that sequence.

Understanding router boot sequence

Please go through the following steps to understand the router boot sequence:

1. The POST is performed; it will test the hardware to verify that all the components of the device are working and present. The POST checks for the different interfaces that exist. As we know already, POST exists in ROM:

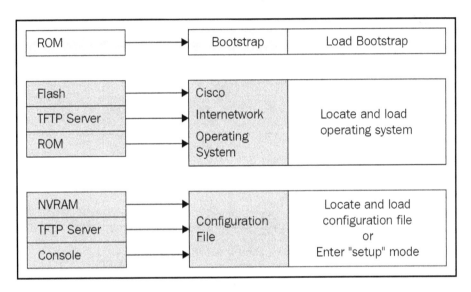

Main phases of the router boot sequence

2. Bootstrap will then search for and load the Cisco IOS. Bootstrap is a program in ROM that is used to execute programs. It is responsible for finding where each IOS program is located and then loading the file. As said previously, the IOS by default is stored in flash in all Cisco routers, but only after the configuration register is read and NVRAM is checked for the boot sequence.

3. After the IOS is decompressed into RAM, the IOS looks for a valid configuration file in NVRAM.

4. If a startup configuration file is found in NVRAM and it has configurations in it, then that configuration will be copied into RAM, but now it's called as running-configuration. If the startup configuration file is not found in NVRAM, the router will attempt to broadcast its interfaces if it detects CSMA/CD for a TFTP server in the hope of finding a startup configuration file. If this also fails, then when the router boots up, you will find yourself in setup mode.

So, if you had doubts about the bootup sequence before, you now should not. But, just like a PC, we can control how the router boots up. There are many reasons why you may want to change the boot sequence, troubleshooting is the most common, or you can re-direct it to find the startup config somewhere else. Let's get a better understanding about the Cisco register.

The Cisco register

Every Cisco router has a 16-bit software register written into its NVRAM. The default settings are set to load the Cisco IOS from flash memory and to look and load the startup config file from NVRAM. But, as I have said, you can change those settings.

Let's simplify the math, but first let's look at what hex numbers are:

Hex table		
HEX	**DECIMAL**	The table to the left is our Hexadecimal table. It lets us know the decimal value of each Hex number. Each Hex number represents four bits and each one of those bits has a specific value.
0	0	
1	1	
2	2	
3	3	An example of that would be the following:
4	4	
5	5	Default Cisco Registry value in Hex: 0x2102
6	6	The binary equivalent to that would be the following
7	7	0010 0001 0000 0010
8	8	
9	9	
A	10	Changed Cisco Registry value in Hex: 0x2142
B	11	The binary equivalent to that would be the following
C	12	0010 0001 0100 0010
D	13	
E	14	
F	15	

The binary bit that changes is what instructs the router on the boot up process to look at NVRAM for the startup configuration file (0x2102) or not to look or ignore the startup configuration in NVRAM (2,142) and just load the IOS into RAM.

Here is how you do the math manually:

```
Just turn the bits that are on
   2  |  1  |  0  |  2
 ____|____|____|____   0010 0001 0000 0010 Bit value is off
 8421   8421   8421   8421


Just turn the bits that are on
   2  |  1  |  4  |  2
 ____|____|____|        0010 0001 0100 0010 Bit value is on
 8421   8421   8421   8421
```

These are not the only settings you could change the registry to; the following table shows you the bit and hex values, along with a brief description of what they do:

Bit	Hex	Description
7	0x0080	OEM bit enabled
8	0x101	Break disabled
13	0x2000	Boot default ROM software if network boot fails

Once again, there are many more registry settings, but for certification purposes, this is more than you need, even for real-world use.

Checking the setting of your registry

So, how can we check to see what value our registry on our router or switch is set to? Well, simply type in the command `show version` in privilege mode and you will see the following:

```
R3#show version
Cisco IOS Software, 1841 Software (C1841-ADVIPSERVICESK9-M), Version 12.4(15)T1, RELEASE SOFTWARE (fc2)
Technical Support: http://www.cisco.com/techsupport
Copyright (c) 1986-2007 by Cisco Systems, Inc.
Compiled Wed 18-Jul-07 04:52 by pt_team

ROM: System Bootstrap, Version 12.3(8r)T8, RELEASE SOFTWARE (fc1)

System returned to ROM by power-on
System image file is "flash:c1841-advipservicesk9-mz.124-15.T1.bin"
```

So when you type the `show version` command you get a lot of information. Therefore, I have omitted output which is irrelevant to what I am explaining. Now, let's see what's relevant the

```
Cisco 1841 (revision 5.0) with 114688K/16384K bytes of memory.
Processor board ID FTX0947Z18E
M860 processor: part number 0, mask 49
2 FastEthernet/IEEE 802.3 interface(s)
2 Low-speed serial(sync/async) network interface(s)
191K bytes of NVRAM.
63488K bytes of ATA CompactFlash (Read/Write)

Configuration register is 0x2102  ◄━━━━━━━━━
```

This simple command shows you quite a bit of information: right at the very beginning, it is giving you information about the Cisco IOS on your system, but at the very bottom, it shows you the registry setting, as shown in the previous screenshot, but it also shows on your RAM, NVRAM, flash, interfaces, and processor board ID.

But, at the moment, we are simply focusing on that registry setting, 0x2102, that instructs the router when you boot up. Look at NVRAM, locate the startup configuration file, and if there are any configurations on it, load them into RAM.

We could change the registry setting by simply going into the global configuration and typing the following:

```
R1(config)#config-register 0x2142
R1(config)#exit
R1#copy run start
R1# Reload
```

Not until you reload will changes take effect, as shown in the following screenshot:

```
R3(config)#
R3(config)#config-register 0x2142
R3(config)#exit
R3#
*May 22, 11:06:30.066: *May 22, 11:06:30.066: %SYS-5-CONFIG_I: Configured from console by console
R3#copy run start
Destination filename [startup-config]?
Building configuration...
[OK]
```

So, when you type `show version` command, you will see lot of information in it. Therefore, I have omitted the output which was irrelevant to what I am explaining. Now, let's look to the information which is relevant.

```
Configuration register is 0x2102 (will be 0x2142 at next reload)
```

Boot system commands

Boot system commands are just another tool you can use to manipulate your router. Using this command, you can configure your router to boot from a different IOS in flash, or have it boot from a TFTP server, even though that is not practised anymore; TFTP servers are mainly used for back-up purposes.

So, let's look what we can do with the boot command and all of its sub-commands:

```
R2(config)#boot ?
  system  System image file
R2(config)#boot system ?
  WORD   TFTP filename or URL
  flash  Boot from flash memory
  tftp   Boot from a tftp server
R2(config)#boot system
```

Since this is a simulator, when you type the question mark to see what sub-commands are available underneath the command boot, you only get the system sub-command since this is what the certification calls for. Also, when you type the command boot system with the question, you get some more options such as word, flash, and TFTP. These sub-commands are specific to the certification, and there a lot more options than you see here, but again you could always question mark your way through any commands that may be available.

If you did want your system to boot from a specific flash file, you would first need to know the name of the flash file name.

So, these are the steps you would take to get this accomplished:

1. You need to see the IOS filename:

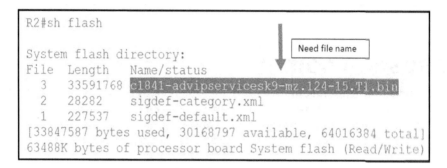

2. You also need to know how to configure the router using the boot system command:

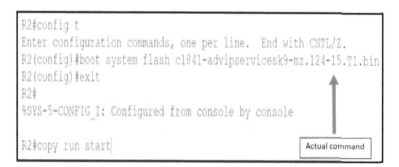

The preceding command will tell the router to boot from flash using the filename we entered. But as I mentioned earlier, we could do it from a TFTP server, even though this is not common practice:

```
R2(config)#boot system tftp ?
  WORD  System image filename
R2(config)#boot system tftp c1841-advipservicesk9-mz.124-15.T1.bin ?
  A.B.C.D  Address from which to download the file
  <cr>
R2(config)#boot system tftp c1841-advipservicesk9-mz.124-15.T1.bin 192.168.100.1 ?
  <cr>
R2(config)#boot system tftp c1841-advipservicesk9-mz.124-15.T1.bin 192.168.100.1
R2(config)#
```

As you can plainly see, we can question mark our way through it, until we finally have no more options.

The <cr> sub-command means *enter* or *no more options, buddy*.

On actual production routers and some simulators, you can use an actual Cisco IOS so you would have more options. The reason I mention this is if, for whatever reason, your router will not boot from flash or TFTP, your last option would be to boot from ROM, which is booting into a mini-IOS after six failed attempts at the TFTP server:

```
R2(config)#boot system rom
R2(config)#
R2(config)#
```

Recovering passwords

I hope this does not happen to anyone, but we are only human. So, if you did forget your password over the weekend because you partied too hard, you have no choice but to reboot the router and interrupt the boot sequence by using some keyboard break command, just so you know there is more than one.

Once your do whichever break command that works, you will find yourself in a deep and dirty dungeon called ROMMON and you must change the register setting to use 0x2142, so it won't look at NVRAM and just lets you in the router, and finally reboot your router by typing reset. At which point, you will be inside your router with no configurations, and you can then make any changes you want, in this case, it would be putting in a new password. I suggest you change all your passwords.

 You need to remember, when you booted into your router, there were no configurations in RAM, only the changes you made, *so do not save your changes yet*, first copy what you have in NVRAM to RAM and verify that all your configurations are there; you also need to look at your interfaces using the following command: show ip int brief. You will notice your interfaces are administratively down so you must do a no shut to turn them on. Finally, you can do a copy run start to save everything that is in RAM to your NVRAM using the same filename startup-config file.

The best practice for this is **do not lose or forget your password!**

This is how it would look inside:

```
Self decompressing the image :       INTERRUPT BOOT SEQUENCE USING
###############    ◄───────           CTRL+C KEYBOARD COMMAND
monitor: command "boot" aborted due to user interrupt
rommon 1 > CONFREG 0X2142 ◄─────────  CHANGING REGISTAR
rommon 2 > reset ◄──────  REBOOT ROUTER
```

One more thing: after you we made all your changes and copied everything to your `startup-config` file, one thing I did not mention, that should be part of your changes also, is changing the registry back to what it should be *look at NVRAM* that way it will load your configurations.

This is what that will look like within your IOS:

```
R1(config)#config-register 0x2102
R1(config)#
```

The reason we want to change the register back to the default `0x2102` is if there is any power failure or brownout, when your router reboots, it will always look at your NVRAM and load the configurations.

If you don't do this and leave it at `0x2142`, if your router reboots for any reason, it will not load any configuration and no one in your company will be able to network with anything.

Backing up and restoring your IOS

You should know by now that before you perform any kind of change to your internetworking devices or end devices, you need to back up your configurations and your IOS. It does not matter whether it's a hardware or a software update, especially if you're upgrading your IOS, you better be sure that you have a back up of the existing IOS and configurations.

This is IT, ladies and gentlemen: if something can go wrong, it will. So, back everything up.

With that disclaimer said, I will show how you would back up your IOS to a TFTP server:

1. Make sure you are connected to the server:

```
R4#ping 192.168.4.1

Type escape sequence to abort.
Sending 5, 100-byte ICMP Echos to 192.168.4.1, timeout is 2 seconds:
!!!!!
Success rate is 100 percent (5/5), round-trip min/avg/max = 0/0/2 ms
```

2. You need to know the source file name you are backing up:

```
R4#sh flash

System flash directory:
File  Length    Name/status
   3  33591768  c1841-advipservicesk9-mz.124-15.T1.bin
   2  28282     sigdef-category.xml
   1  227537    sigdef-default.xml
[33847587 bytes used, 30168797 available, 64016384 total]
63488K bytes of processor board System flash (Read/Write)
```

3. Start the back up process:

```
R4#copy flash tftp          ◄──────  Actual Command
Source filename []? c1841-advipservicesk9-mz.124-15.T1.bin
Address or name of remote host []? 192.168.4.1
Destination filename [c1841-advipservicesk9-mz.124-15.T1.bin]? c1841-R4-
IOS.BIN

Writing c1841-advipservicesk9-
mz.124-15.T1.bin...!!!!!!!!!!!!!!!!!!!!!!!!!!!!!!!!!!!!!!!!!!!!!!!!!!!!!!!!!!!
!!!!!!!!!!!!!!!!!!!!!!!!!!!!!!!!!!!!!!!!!!!!!!!!!!!!!!!!!!!!!!!!!!!!!!!!!!!!!!!
!!!!!!!!!!!!!!!!!!!!!!!!!!!!!!!!!!!!!!!!!!!!!!!!!!!!!!!!!!!!!!!!!!!!!!!!!!!!!!!
!!!!!!!!!!!!!!!!!!!!!!!!!!!!!!!!!!!!!!!!!!!!!!!!!!!!!!!!!!!!!!!!!!!!!!!!!!!!!!!
!!!!!!!!!!!!!!!!!!!!!!!!!!!!!!!!!!!!!!!!!!!!!!!!!!!!!!!!!!!!!!!!!!!!!!!!!!!!!!!
!!!!!!!!!!!!!!!!!!!!!!!!!!!!!!!!!!!!!!!!!!!!!!!!!!!!!!!!!!!!!!!!!!!!!!!!!!!!!!!
!!!!!!!!!!!!!!!!!!!!!!!!!!!!!!!!!!!!!!!!!!!!!!!!!!!!!!!!!!!!!!!!!!!!!!!!!!!!!!!
!!!!!!!!!!!!!!!!!!!!!!!!!!!!!!!!!!!!!!!!!!!!!!!!!!!!!!!!!!!!!!!!!!!!!!!!!!!!!!!
!!!!!!!!!!!!!!!!!!!!!!!!!!!!!!!!!!!!!!!!!!!!!!!!!!!!!!!!!!!!!!!!!!!!!!!!!!!!!!!
!!
[OK - 33591768 bytes]

33591768 bytes copied in 0.922 secs (3825376 bytes/sec)
```

4. Verify that the file was copied to the TFTP server:

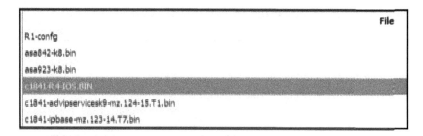

For certification purposes, they want you to know three steps:

1. Verify connectivity.
2. Does the TFTP sever have enough space?
3. The naming convention and any path requirements.

In today's technological world where we deal with terabytes or higher, I don't think that space is going to be an issue. You can name the file whatever you want, and if you are using TFTP, then wherever you're set up for the TFTP server, that is where the file is going to go.

So, know the three bullets for certification, but if you are really going to do it, the images explain it all.

If you wanted to restore the IOS from a TFTP server, then it would be just the opposite. Simply type the opposite command:

```
R4#copy tftp flash
Address or name of remote host []? 192.168.4.1
Source filename []? c1841-R4-IOS.BIN
Destination filename [c1841-R4-IOS.BIN]? c1841-advipservicesk9-mz.124-15.T1.bin
%Warning:There is a file already existing with this name
Do you want to over write? [confirm]

Accessing tftp://192.168.4.1/c1841-R4-IOS.BIN...
Loading c1841-R4-IOS.BIN from 192.168.4.1:
!!!!!!!!!!!!!!!!!!!!!!!!!!!!!!!!!!!!!!!!!!!!!!!!!!!!!!!!!!!!!!!!!!!!!!!!!!!!!!!!!!!!!!
!!!!!!!!!!!!!!!!!!!!!!!!!!!!!!!!!!!!!!!!!!!!!!!!!!!!!!!!!!!!!!!!!!!!!!!!!!!!!!!!!!!!!!
!!!!!!!!!!!!!!!!!!!!!!!!!!!!!!!!!!!!!!!!!!!!!!!!!!!!!!!!!!!!!!!!!!!!!!!!!!!!!!!!!!!!!!
!!!!!!!!!!!!!!!!!!!!!!!!!!!!!!!!!!!!!!!!!!!!!!!!!!!!!!!!!!!!!!!!!!!!!!!!!!!!!!!!!!!!!!
!!!!!!!!!!!!!!!!!!!!!!!!!!!!!!!!!!!!!!!!!!!!!!!!!!!!!!!!!!!!!!!!!!!!!!!!!!!!!!!!!!!!!!
!!!!!!!!!!!!!!!!!!!!!!!!!!!!!!!!!!!!!!!!!!!!!!!!!!!!!!!!!!!!!!!!!!!!!!!!!!!!!!!!!!!!!!
[OK - 33591768 bytes]

33591768 bytes copied in 0.929 secs (3796552 bytes/sec)
```

As you can see from the preceding screenshot, I wrote `copy tftp flash`. You will then be asked which TFTP server you want to copy it from. If you noticed, the source filename was the same one I backed up, and the destination filename is the same as the one that already exists on the router. That is why the router asked you, *Do you want to overwrite?* All you do is hit *Enter* to confirm.

This is where you really need to be careful, as you could give it another destination name, and if you have enough space in flash, you will have two Cisco IOSes, but if you know it's the same IOS, you could simply overwrite the existing one, as we did.

To verify, simply use the `show flash` and the `show version` commands.

Backing up your configurations

Well, you have just learned how to back up and restore your IOS, but what about your configurations?

You could use the same steps, but the command will be slightly different, and remember, we are still backing it up to a TFTP server; let's have a peek:

```
R4#copy start tftp
Address or name of remote host []? 192.168.4.1
Destination filename [R4-config]? ←
Writing startup-config...!!
[OK - 888 bytes]

888 bytes copied in 0.001 secs (888000 bytes/sec)
R4#
```

The preceding screenshot shows the command `copy start tftp`, which is going to copy your startup configuration file to the TFTP server. But the difference is it does not ask you for a source file.

It simply asks for a destination server and a filename. I simply hit *Enter* and accept the default.

You are still not done, as you must always verify that the file name copied; let's have a look:

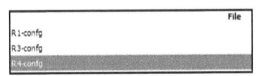

As you can see, we not only have the configurations of router four, but also R1 and R3.

The Cisco File System and its purpose

The Cisco IOS File System allows you to work with files and directories just like you would have done back in the day of DOS, or should I say MSDOS. The following table gives the commands and a brief description of each command:

Command	Brief description
dir	As in Windows or DOS, this will give you a list of directories that exist.
copy	The copies your run, start, flash even used to upgrade. Just make sure to be careful what you're copying into your router.
more	As with Unix, this will let you look at a text file on a card.
show file	This command will give you more detailed information on your file or file systems.
delete	Avoid this command; it has a level 15 privilege, and you could accidentally delete your IOS or configurations—OUCH!!
erase/format	If you want to erase all configurations, type *erase* to start bye-bye configs.
mkdir/rmdir	Create a directory or delete a directory.

All these commands depend on your Cisco IOS version. Let's see some visual representations of these commands.

The copy command

The copy run start command copies your current configurations to the startup config file:

```
R4>
R4>en
R4#copy run start
Destination filename [startup-config]?
Building configuration...
[OK]
R4#
```

The dir command

This command shows your existing directories on your router:

```
R4#dir
Directory of flash:/

    5   drw-            0        <no date>   backup
    3   -rw-     33591768        <no date>   c1841-advipservicesk9-
mz.124-15.T1.bin
    2   -rw-        28282        <no date>   sigdef-category.xml
    1   -rw-       227537        <no date>   sigdef-default.xml

64016384 bytes total (30168797 bytes free)
R4#
```

The mkdir command

This command creates a directory on your router:

```
R1#dir
Directory of flash:/

    3   -rw-     33591768        <no date>   c1841-advipservicesk9-
mz.124-15.T1.bin
    2   -rw-        28282        <no date>   sigdef-category.xml
    1   -rw-       227537        <no date>   sigdef-default.xml

64016384 bytes total (30168797 bytes free)
R1#mkdir laz
Create directory filename [laz]?
Created dir flash:laz

R1#dir
Directory of flash:/

    3   -rw-     33591768        <no date>   c1841-advipservicesk9-
mz.124-15.T1.bin
    4   drw-            0        <no date>   laz
    2   -rw-        28282        <no date>   sigdef-category.xml
    1   -rw-       227537        <no date>   sigdef-default.xml

64016384 bytes total (30168797 bytes free)
```

These were just a couple of examples of the plethora of commands you can use, and these commands *will not* be on your certification, but you may run into them in a real-world scenario. I can tell you from my personal experience that I have never used these commands.

Rommon or ROM monitor mode

I have already explained how we could get into rommon by using a break command to interrupt the boot sequence and that would take us to ROM's monitor mode. But we only used it to change register settings, and that was very simple.

But what would you do if you come into work on Monday and found the following screen staring you in the face, telling you that it could not find a bootable device.

Look at this screenshot:

```
System Bootstrap, Version 12.3(8r)T8, RELEASE SOFTWARE (fc1)
Initializing memory for ECC
..
c2811 processor with 524288 Kbytes of main memory
Main memory is configured to 64 bit mode with ECC enabled

Readonly ROMMON initialized

Boot process failed...

The system is unable to boot automatically.  The BOOT
environment variable needs to be set to a bootable
image.
rommon 1 >
```

You would be like, *what in the world?* At this moment, you need to take a breath and think, *OK, when I left, all was well and everything was copied to NVRAM and backed up to a TFTP server.* It could be possible that you changed the registry to boot to rommon by fat finger the keyboard.

So, what you first try is changing the registry to 0x2102 and resetting to see whether it boots fine, and it does not.

What is happening is your IOS got corrupted and you must replace it, from rommon—OUCH!

So, here is how it's done:

1. Type the `tftpdnld` command in lowercase:

```
rommon 1 > tftpdnld

Missing or illegal ip address for variable IP_ADDRESS
Illegal IP address.

usage: tftpdnld
  Use this command for disaster recovery only to recover an image via TFTP.
  Monitor variables are used to set up parameters for the transfer.
  (Syntax: "VARIABLE_NAME=value" and use "set" to show current variables.)
  "ctrl-c" or "break" stops the transfer before flash erase begins.

  The following variables are REQUIRED to be set for tftpdnld:
           IP_ADDRESS: The IP address for this unit
       IP_SUBNET_MASK: The subnet mask for this unit
      DEFAULT_GATEWAY: The default gateway for this unit
          TFTP_SERVER: The IP address of the server to fetch from
            TFTP_FILE: The filename to fetch

  The following variables are OPTIONAL:
         TFTP_VERBOSE: Print setting. 0=quiet, 1=progress(default), 2=verbose
     TFTP_RETRY_COUNT: Retry count for ARP and TFTP (default=7)
         TFTP_TIMEOUT: Overall timeout of operation in seconds (default=7200)
        TFTP_CHECKSUM: Perform checksum test on image, 0=no, 1=yes (default=1)
        FE_SPEED_MODE: 0=10/hdx, 1=10/fdx, 2=100/hdx, 3=100/fdx, 4=Auto(deflt)

rommon 2 >
```

You must follow the `variables are REQUIRED` to the letter for this process to work correctly:

2. Enter the commands it's asking for:

```
rommon 7 > IP_ADDRESS=10.1.3.253
rommon 8 > IP_SUBNET_MASK=255.255.255.0
rommon 9 > DEFAULT_GATEWAY=10.1.3.254
rommon 10 > TFTP_SERVER=10.1.3.1
rommon 11 > TFTP_FILE=c1841-advipservicesk9-mz.124.15.T1.bin
```

3. Once you type exactly what you see in this screenshot, you could type the `set` command, and this will show you what configurations you have done. Finally, all you have to do is type `tftpdnld` once more and it will start doing the upgrade. Since you have an IOS that exists already, you will be prompted to delete the existing IOS and replace it with the new one.

This process does not always work the first time around, and it may take several tries. So, it is best to avoid the situation to begin with. **Do not delete your flash**, and keep your routers and switches physically locked in a secure location.

Licensing

If you work in any branch of IT, you are going to run into licensing issues. By that, I mean every piece of software you have needs to be licensed, and Cisco is no exception.

If we look back several years, the Cisco IOS 15.0 had no licensing; it was based on an honor code. That may have worked back in the time of Camelot, but those days are gone. So, that means when you order your router or switch, you are also paying for the IOS that comes with it. But you need to choose wisely which IOS you purchase, as not all IOSes have the same features. So, you need to analyze your network requirements and choose an IOS that will meet those needs.

You might be wondering why Cisco is putting this topic into its certification. The answer is simple. A lot of people were on the **honor system** and, believe it or not, they did not honor it. But not only that, we have so called Cisco engineers who don't even know how to install a license or even back it up.

Cisco does give out evaluations of its IOS, but that only last for 60 days, which means if you want all the bells and whistles that come with that version of the IOS, you need to purchase the license for it.

There are three distinct technology packages that Cisco has available that you can purchase. These packages can be installed as an addition to the prerequisite of the IP base, which only provides basic functionality. Let me briefly describe them to you:

Name	Features
Data	MPLS, ATM, and multi-protocol support
Unified Communication	VoIP and IP Telephony
Security	Cisco IOS firewall, IPS, IPSec, 3DES, and VPN

For you to acquire a license, you will need a unique number called the **Unique Device Identifier** (**UDI**). This UDI is made up of two different components: the product ID and the serial number of the device. So, how can we find these numbers? We can simply type in privilege mode and show the `license udi` command:

```
Router#sh license udi
Device#    PID                   SN               UDI
--------------------------------------------------------------------------------
*1         CISCO1941/K9          FTX152425DY      CISCO1941/K9:FTX152425DY
Router#
```

When you purchase the software package with the features that you want to install, you need to permanently activate the software package using your specific UDI and the **Product Authorization Key** (**PAK**), which will be sent to you along with your purchase. But, first, we must look at the features that the IOS has to offer:

```
Router#sh license feature
Feature name     Enforcement   Evaluation   Subscription   Enabled
ipbasek9         no            no           no             yes
securityk9       yes           yes          no             no
datak9           yes           no           no             no
```

As you can see from the preceding screenshot, the only feature that is active is the default ipbasek9, so the other two need to be activated. You could look at more detailed information about the license using the following:

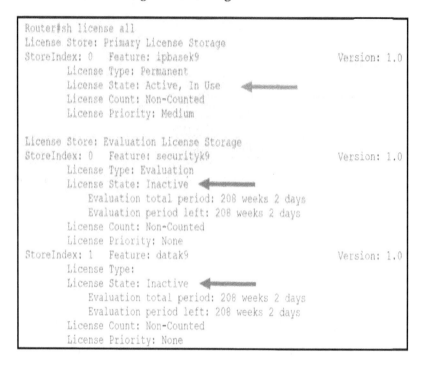

Using the show license all command, you can see which package is activated and the total evaluation period.

Let's say we want to activate the securityk9 package; we would go to privilege mode and do the following:

```
Router(config)#license boot module c1900 technology-package securityk9
```

After hitting the *Enter* key, you will be confronted with the license agreement.

After reading it, you would type yes. After accepting the license agreement, you would get the following information:

```
ACCEPT? [yes/no]: yes
% use 'write' command to make license boot config take effect on next boot

Router(config)#: %IOS_LICENSE_IMAGE_APPLICATION-6-LICENSE_LEVEL: Module
name = C1900 Next reboot level = securityk9 and License = securityk9

Router(config)#
```

At this point, you can go back to privilege mode and do a copy run start or wr, but for certification purposes, copy run start is what you need to type, and then you reboot the router, log back in, and verify that the package is active:

```
Router#sh license all
License Store: Primary License Storage
StoreIndex: 0    Feature: ipbasek9                              Version: 1.0
        License Type: Permanent
        License State: Active, In Use
        License Count: Non-Counted
        License Priority: Medium

License Store: Evaluation License Storage
StoreIndex: 0    Feature: securityk9                            Version: 1.0
        License Type: Evaluation
        License State: Active, In Use
            Evaluation total period: 208 weeks 2 days
            Evaluation period left: 208 weeks 2 days
        License Count: Non-Counted
        License Priority: None
StoreIndex: 1    Feature: datak9                                Version: 1.0
        License Type:
        License State: Active, Not in Use, EULA accepted
            Evaluation total period: 208 weeks 2 days
            Evaluation period left: 208 weeks 2 days
        License Count: Non-Counted
        License Priority: None

Router#
```

As you can see, now the feature securityk9 is activated and in use.

Summary

Well, all good things must come to an end. We have covered how Cisco routers are configured and, more importantly, how to manage the configurations.

The chapter covered the main components of the router such as RAM, NVRAM, ROM, and flash.

Also, we dived deeper into the register and the different settings it could have to control the router on bootup. We looked at ROMMON, that holds a mini-IOS and you can also reload your IOS through a TFTP server, but we don't want to do that.

We navigated through the CLI and touched on the IFS, which Cisco now has. The last topic that we covered was the licensing with the router. Just remember, the series of router you choose for IOS will be specific to that series, and the IOS must meet the needs of your network. So, before purchasing any internetworking device, know your network design and its needs and calculate the potential growth of your network so you can not only correct purchase the device but the proper IOS with its features and, most definitely, purchase the license with Cisco so you can get all the bells and whistles.

See you in the next chapter, where we will begin to discuss the meat and potatoes of Cisco, which are the basics of routing.

The IP Routing Process

9

In this chapter, we finally get to the meat and potatoes of what Cisco is known for, and that is **routing**.

When we speak of routing, we are talking about layer 3 devices, and their function is to route data from source to destination, across WANs or multiple LANs.

Before we begin, let's get something straight. I know that a lot of you are already in the IT field and use layer 3 switches; well, I am not going to be talking about that in this book. Layer 3 switches have the capabilities of routing, but they do not even come close to the functionality of a router. So, use the appropriate equipment for the job intended.

In this chapter, we will be discussing the following topics:

- Routing concepts:
    - Packet switching
    - Routing table
- Breaking down the routing table:
    - Network mask
    - Next hop address
    - Administrative distance
    - Metrics
    - Gateway of last resort
- How the routing table gets built, by using multiple routing sources
- Configuring IPv4 and IPv6 static routing
    - Default routes
    - Network routes
    - Host routes
    - Floating static routes
    - Configuring RIPv2

One thing to remember, before we begin our journey into the wonderful world of routing, is we will be understanding the difference between **routing protocols** and **routed protocols**.

Routing protocols, such as RIPv2, EIGRP, and OSPF, are used to determine the best path from source to destination, based on their particular algorithms.

For routed protocols, once the path is determined and all the routers have converged, the protocols will send packets found in the routing table through the path that has been already been laid out by the routing protocols. Examples of routed protocols are IPv4, IPv6, AppleTalk, and IPX. Obviously, the most used routed protocol would be IPv4, followed by IPv6, but this is due to a syndrome called *resistance to change*, but soon enough IPv6 will be more dominant in the force. Still, IPv4 will always exist somewhere, so you must know it.

As I mentioned before, we will be discussing the fundamentals of routing such as the following:

- The routing basics—as tedious as this may be, this is an invaluable lesson you must undergo
- The IP routing process
- Default routing
- Static routing
- Dynamic routing

Routing basics

As I have mentioned, routing is the act of sending source packets to a different destination; they could go across a WAN or a different VLAN, but some sort of routing must take place, by using a router. If you do not have multiple VLANs or must go across the internet to reach a branch office, well, then there is no routing needed. If that's the case, you must be on a small network or a bogged-down network.

Think about the scenario in the following screenshot:

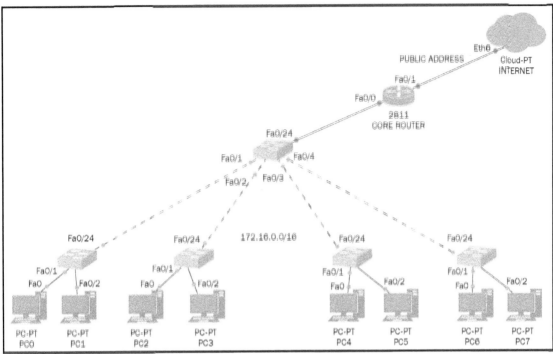

The preceding screenshot shows a very common configuration used by schools: they have switches in their classrooms, all in the native VLAN, connected to a core switch, which then gets connected to a router. At this point we are all still on the same network, but with different IP addresses; however, once it goes to the public side of the router, we use a public IP address so we can access the internet.

Does anyone see a problem with this? We are all on the same network; this could be hundreds of computers! What would happen if someone in IT wanted to throw an image to a classroom or a PC? It would slow down the network to a crawl.

The simple fact is that when every student comes to class and starts working on their respective projects, it will bog down the network. We know this is not true, the priority is, we must check our social media, watch YouTube video, or find some way around the firewall.

The point of all this is that the preceding diagram is not the ideal configuration for a network, and we must VLAN everything out, meaning that every department and classroom should be on their own VLAN. That means it would be a different subnetwork for which we need to create inter-VLAN routing on the router and sub-interfaces with a gateway for each VLAN with the correct encapsulation, so everyone can communicate. But any packets that flow through a specific VLAN will not be heard by other VLANs, increasing the overall bandwidth.

So, there are five requirements or factors that a router must know to send packets across a network:

- Destination addresses
- Its neighbor's router so it can learn about other networks, using routing protocols
- Based on the routing protocol, all possible routes to remote networks
- Based on the routing protocol, the best route to remote networks
- Based on the routing protocol, maintain and verify routing information

The router must learn about remote networks in two different ways statically, meaning you are the one creating the routing table entries, and dynamically, using a routing protocols such as RIP; through the updates sent by neighboring routers, it will create the routing table. I said *remote networks* because routers know who they are directly connected to, so using routing protocols, they learn about remote networks beyond their directly connected networks. We could also do it statically, which means the IT person in charge of the router would manually have to input all the routes to the remote networks. In a small network, that is fine, but if it's a large network, then that could be very time consuming, not to mention mind numbing.

So, let's discuss the differences between static routing and dynamic routing. In dynamic routing, the routing protocols algorithm does all the work, and it actually *snitches you out*. Using a multicast address specific to that routing protocol, it will send updates to their neighboring router about the network it knows, and all the other routers would do the same thing. So, when all the routers have learned about the networks that are remote to them, it would be called **fully converged**. So, the routing protocol does all the heavy lifting for us, but it means more burden on the router and not us.

If we use static routing, we need to input all the remote networks manually, and if a network goes down or is taken down, you must remove that network from the routing table manually also. Static routing is used mainly for backups or small networks. It opens the door for lots of human error, and, as I said previously, it will put you to sleep, but you free up resources on your router, because you are the one creating the routing table manually.

The default routing basically tells the router that there is no match in the routing table for that destination network, uses the default route, and sends to the next router. So, default routing is really a mechanism, so the router does not drop packets if there is no match on the routing table.

Also, default routes are only placed on stub routers, since you can only point them in one direction. Let us look at the following topology:

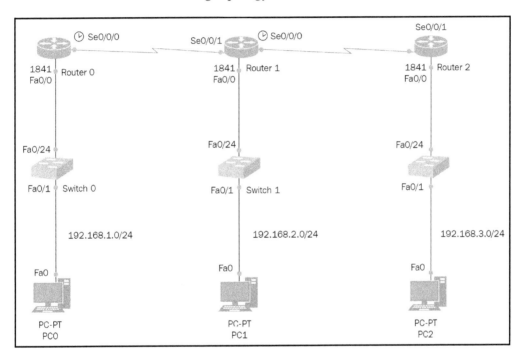

In the preceding topology, the routers only know who they are directly connected to because there is no routing protocol or static routing configured. But you can see that the router in the middle knows about the networks it's connected to by looking at its routing table:

```
R2#sh ip route
Codes: C = connected, S = static, I = IGRP, R = RIP, M = mobile, B - BGP
       D = EIGRP, EX = EIGRP external, O = OSPF, IA = OSPF inter area
       N1 = OSPF NSSA external type 1, N2 = OSPF NSSA external type 2
       E1 = OSPF external type 1, E2 = OSPF external type 2, E = EGP
       i = IS-IS, L1 = IS-IS level-1, L2 = IS-IS level-2, ia = IS-IS inter area
       * = candidate default, U = per-user static route, o = ODR
       P = periodic downloaded static route

Gateway of last resort is not set

     10.0.0.0/30 is subnetted, 3 subnets
C       10.1.1.4 is directly connected, Serial0/0/1
C       10.1.1.8 is directly connected, Serial0/0/0
C    192.168.2.0/24 is directly connected, FastEthernet0/0
R2#
```

CONNECTED TO THE THREE NETWORKS

As you can see, this router already knows about the three networks it is directly connected to. If you look at the left side of the routing table, you will see three letters C that represent directly connected to. So, this proves the point that a router builds its own routing table by simply using the routed protocol placed on the interfaces.

Please note that the interfaces had to be up and working for this to happen.

So, now we know that the router builds its own routing table with its neighbor, we need to route, but first let's see what happens when we are using static default routes. We will be configuring static default routes on R1 and R3, since these are the stub routers:

```
R1(config)#ip route 0.0.0.0 0.0.0.0 s0/0/0   ◄────
R1(config)#do wr
Building configuration...
[OK]
R1(config)#do sh ip route
Codes: C - connected, S - static, I - IGRP, R - RIP, M - mobile, B - BGP
       D - EIGRP, EX - EIGRP external, O - OSPF, IA - OSPF inter area
       N1 - OSPF NSSA external type 1, N2 - OSPF NSSA external type 2
       E1 - OSPF external type 1, E2 - OSPF external type 2, E - EGP
       i - IS-IS, L1 - IS-IS level-1, L2 - IS-IS level-2, ia - IS-IS inter area
       * - candidate default, U - per-user static route, o - ODR
       P - periodic downloaded static route

Gateway of last resort is 0.0.0.0 to network 0.0.0.0 ◄────

     10.0.0.0/30 is subnetted, 1 subnets
C       10.1.1.4 is directly connected, Serial0/0/0
C    192.168.1.0/24 is directly connected, FastEthernet0/0
S*   0.0.0.0/0 is directly connected, Serial0/0/0    ◄────
```

Static route configuration using exit interface.

Gateway of last resort set

Notice the S*

```
R3#CONFIG T
Enter configuration commands, one per line.  End with
R3(config)#IP ROUTE 0.0.0.0 0.0.0.0 S0/0/1   ◄────
R3(config)#DO SH IP ROUTE
Codes: C - connected, S - static, I - IGRP, R - RIP, M - mobile, B - BGP
       D - EIGRP, EX - EIGRP external, O - OSPF, IA - OSPF inter area
       N1 - OSPF NSSA external type 1, N2 - OSPF NSSA external type 2
       E1 - OSPF external type 1, E2 - OSPF external type 2, E - EGP
       i - IS-IS, L1 - IS-IS level-1, L2 - IS-IS level-2, ia - IS-IS inter area
       * - candidate default, U - per-user static route, o - ODR
       P - periodic downloaded static route

Gateway of last resort is 0.0.0.0 to network 0.0.0.0 ◄────

     10.0.0.0/30 is subnetted, 1 subnets
C       10.1.1.8 is directly connected, Serial0/0/1
C    192.168.3.0/24 is directly connected, FastEthernet0/0
S*   0.0.0.0/0 is directly connected, Serial0/0/1    ◄────
```

Static route configuration using exit interface.

Gateway of last resort set

Notice the S*

Once we configure a default static route, it creates the gateway of last resort, which means if the router does not find a match for the destination network in its routing table, then it will use the gateway of last resort and sends out its exit interface to the neighbor router to see whether that router knows where that network is. So, let's see if we can ping from PC0 to PC2:

```
Packet Tracer PC Command Line 1.0
C:\>ping 192.168.3.1

Pinging 192.168.3.1 with 32 bytes of data:

Request timed out.
Request timed out.
Request timed out.
Request timed out.

Ping statistics for 192.168.3.1:
      Packets: Sent = 4, Received = 0, Lost = 4
(100% loss),

C:\>|
```

It isn't working, but why? Because the routing process is not complete, even though R1 did send the destination network to the middle router and R3 sent its destination to the middle router. The router in the middle has no idea about these networks because no one told it about those networks, and since we have not configured a routing protocol, it has not learned about that either. Let's have a look at R2's routing table:

```
R2#sh ip route
Codes: C - connected, S - static, I - IGRP, R - RIP, M - mobile, B - BGP
       D - EIGRP, EX - EIGRP external, O - OSPF, IA - OSPF inter area
       N1 - OSPF NSSA external type 1, N2 - OSPF NSSA external type 2
       E1 - OSPF external type 1, E2 - OSPF external type 2, E - EGP
       i - IS-IS, L1 - IS-IS level-1, L2 - IS-IS level-2, ia - IS-IS inter area
       * - candidate default, U - per-user static route, o - ODR
       P - periodic downloaded static route

Gateway of last resort is not set

     10.0.0.0/30 is subnetted, 2 subnets
C       10.1.1.4 is directly connected, Serial0/0/1
C       10.1.1.8 is directly connected, Serial0/0/0
C    192.168.2.0/24 is directly connected, FastEthernet0/0
```

As you can see, the X.X.3.0 network or the X.X.1.0 network do not exist in this, which is why we can't ping.

This is where we must understand the IP routing process.

The IP routing process

The routing process is simple; it does not matter how small or large your network is. With that said, we are speaking of IPv4. Because in IPv4 we have ARP that must happen in the first time around and in IPv6 that does not exist. But we will talk about that later in the book.

So, using the same three-router topology, we get the following diagram:

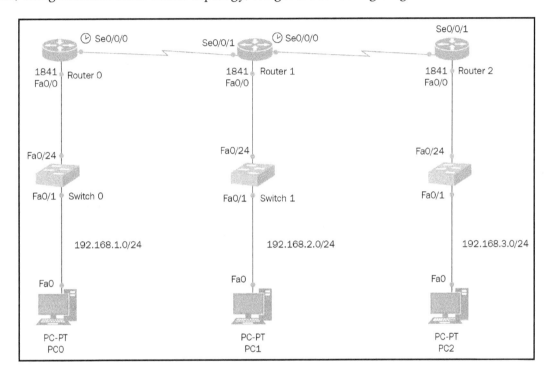

If PC0 wants to communicate with any PC outside its own network, it must go through the default gateway. There are a couple of things that need to be known to the network:

- Layer 3 source address
- Layer 3 destination address
- Layer 2 source address
- Layer 2 destination address
- Source port number (chosen randomly, ports above 1024)
- Destination port number (depends on the protocol you are using—Telnet, SSH, HTTP, and so on)

Once this information is known, the packet can go to the router and be forwarded to its desired destination.

Let's put the routing process into steps:

1. **PC0**: I know the source L3 address, destination L3 address, and source L2 address, but I don't know the L2 destination address. This is where ARP comes into play, and, remember, ARP happens only the first time you need to communicate with any device, and then it holds it in the ARP Cache. On Cisco devices, the default hold time is four hours; after that, it tries to refresh itself. In Windows, the ARP cache hold time could be 15 seconds to 45 seconds; this is called the **reachable time**. If no entries are registered before the reachable time, another ARP must happen:

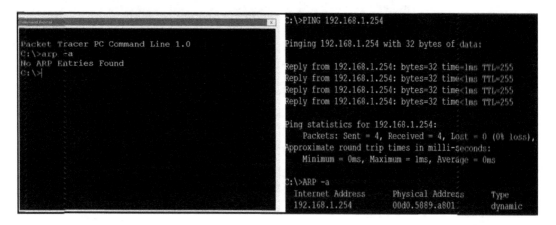

   Preceding is a side-by-side comparison. Before you try to reach your gateway, there are no ARP entries; once you ping the gateway and then do an ARP -a, you will see one entry, and the focus is to get the physical address of the routers F0/0, which is your gateway to the outside world. Once we have the physical address of your gateway, you have completed the requirements of what is needed to network and the data can now move to the router.

2. Once the information reaches the router, it removes any layer 2 information. Remember, routers are interested in L3 information, so it gets the destination layer 3 address and matches it against its routing table. If there is an entry, it will forward it out of the exit interface to the neighboring router. Since this topology is using serial cables to connect to one another, no ARP is needed; this is where the clocking comes in and the DCE and DTE cables take charge. The cables themselves will synchronize and encapsulate the packet so it can be forwarded to the neighbor router.

3. Keep in mind, we are trying to reach the 192.168.3.0/24 network, so the router will take that destination layer 3 address, and if it finds an entry in the routing table, it will have forwarded out the exit interface to go across the next router. Also keep in mind, if no matches are made in non-stub routers where you cannot configure a Gateway of last resort, the packet will be dropped and a request timeout will be returned to the originating device.

4. If the packet reaches R3, it will do the same thing: take the destination network and attempt to find a match in its routing table. When it does make a match, it sees that the exit interface is a Fast Ethernet interface, which requires an ARP, because you need to know that layer 2 address to meet the requirements or networking. The router at this point will send an ARP request to PC2, in which PC2 will reply with its physical address, completing the requirements, and the data can be sent down to PC2.

5. If the packet needs to return an acknowledgement back to the originating device, the process is reversed, only this time it is much faster, since everyone knows their layer 2 address.

If you recall, when we tried to ping the first time from PC0 to PC2, we got a request timeout, because R1 or the middle router had no clue those networks existed; it was not part of their routing table. So, let's fix that by adding those networks manually using static addresses:

```
R2#config t
Enter configuration commands, one per line.  End with CNTL/Z.
R2(config)#ip route 192.168.1.0 255.255.255.0 s0/0/1 150
R2(config)#ip route 192.168.3.0 255.255.255.0 s0/0/0 150
R2(config)#do wr
Building configuration...
[OK]
R2(config)#
```

This is the AD

Now that we have added the routes, let's take a look at our routing table and see whether those entries exist:

```
R2#sh ip route
Codes: C - connected, S - static, I - IGRP, R - RIP, M - mobile, B - BGP
       D - EIGRP, EX - EIGRP external, O - OSPF, IA - OSPF inter area
       N1 - OSPF NSSA external type 1, N2 - OSPF NSSA external type 2
       E1 - OSPF external type 1, E2 - OSPF external type 2, E - EGP
       i - IS-IS, L1 - IS-IS level-1, L2 - IS-IS level-2, ia - IS-IS inter area
       * - candidate default, U - per-user static route, o - ODR
       P - periodic downloaded static route

Gateway of last resort is not set

     10.0.0.0/30 is subnetted, 2 subnets
C       10.1.1.4 is directly connected, Serial0/0/1
C       10.1.1.8 is directly connected, Serial0/0/0
S    192.168.1.0/24 is directly connected, Serial0/0/1
C    192.168.2.0/24 is directly connected, FastEthernet0/0
S    192.168.3.0/24 is directly connected, Serial0/0/0

R2#
```

Network Entries

OK, now that we have verified that the network entries for the destination networks exist on R2's routing table and we have default routes on R1 and R3, which are the stub routers, let's see if we can now ping across our network:

```
C:\>ping 192.168.3.1

Pinging 192.168.3.1 with 32 bytes of data:

Request timed out.      Lost packet due to ARP request
Reply from 192.168.3.1: bytes=32 time=2ms TTL=125
Reply from 192.168.3.1: bytes=32 time=2ms TTL=125
Reply from 192.168.3.1: bytes=32 time=2ms TTL=125

Ping statistics for 192.168.3.1:
    Packets: Sent = 4, Received = 3, Lost = 1 (25% loss),
Approximate round trip times in milli-seconds:
    Minimum = 2ms, Maximum = 2ms, Average = 2ms

C:\>ping 192.168.3.1

Pinging 192.168.3.1 with 32 bytes of data:

Reply from 192.168.3.1: bytes=32 time=3ms TTL=125
Reply from 192.168.3.1: bytes=32 time=2ms TTL=125
Reply from 192.168.3.1: bytes=32 time=6ms TTL=125
Reply from 192.168.3.1: bytes=32 time=6ms TTL=125

Ping statistics for 192.168.3.1:
    Packets: Sent = 4, Received = 4, Lost = 0 (0% loss),
Approximate round trip times in milli-seconds:
    Minimum = 2ms, Maximum = 6ms, Average = 4ms
```

You can see that the first time we ping, we lose a packet, which is due to ARP, but the second time we ping, we get all four replies, since everyone knows their layer 2 addresses.

Let's assess your routing comprehension

Now that you have read and seen examples of what is needed for a packet to reach its destination, let's see if you can figure out the following problems. It is extremely important that you do understand the routing process, so you can troubleshoot efficiently and get to the root of any problem quickly, especially if you are taking your certification, so you don't waste precious minutes.

Problem 1

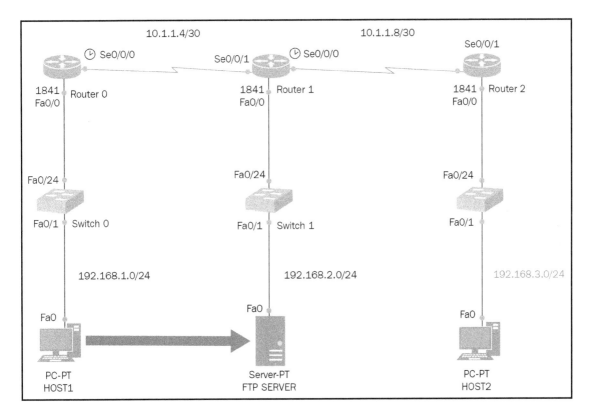

Try not to look at the answer.

Host1 is trying to reach the FTP Server. Answer the following:

- What would be the destination L2 address based on Host1?

  Answer: Default Gateway interface physical address

- What would be the destination L3 address based on Host1?

  Answer: IP address of the FTP server

- What would be the source L3 address based on Host1?

  Answer: IP address of Host1

- What would be the source L2 address based on Host1?

  Answer: Physical address of Host1

- What would be the destination port number?

  Answer: Port 21

One of the important things that you need to remember is that the layer 2 address never leaves the segment they belong too. Only layer 3 addresses go across the network, with the help of the router and the type of routing you perform.

In the topology that we are using ,we have layer 2 switches, and they are not configured at all. Their purpose is a pass through, meaning they just send the information throughout all their ports, to find the owner of the IP address and gain the MAC address to map it to a port. In both topologies, we have eight collision domains and five broadcast domains. We do not have any VLANs configured, so really the routers are the ones creating the broadcast domains, as the switches do not play a part in the routing at all. They do create a MAC address table, but that is just simply for reducing the ARP broadcast.

Problem 2

```
R2#sh ip route
Codes: C - connected, S - static, I - IGRP, R - RIP, M - mobile, B - BGP
       D - EIGRP, EX - EIGRP external, O - OSPF, IA - OSPF inter area
       N1 - OSPF NSSA external type 1, N2 - OSPF NSSA external type 2
       E1 - OSPF external type 1, E2 - OSPF external type 2, E - EGP
       i - IS-IS, L1 - IS-IS level-1, L2 - IS-IS level-2, ia - IS-IS inter area
       * - candidate default, U - per-user static route, o - ODR
       P - periodic downloaded static route

Gateway of last resort is not set

     10.0.0.0/30 is subnetted, 2 subnets
C       10.1.1.4 is directly connected, Serial0/0/1
C       10.1.1.8 is directly connected, Serial0/0/0
R    192.168.1.0/24 [120/1] via 10.1.1.5, 00:00:15, Serial0/0/1
C    192.168.2.0/24 is directly connected, FastEthernet0/0
R    192.168.3.0/24 [120/1] via 10.1.1.10, 00:00:07, Serial0/0/0

R2#
```

OK, you are confronted with the output of a routing table that is running an RIP routing protocol.

- What would happen if the router receives a source address of 192.168.2.15 and a destination address of 172.16.30.0?
    - **Answer:** The source address is connected directly to my F0/0, and the destination network is not an entry on my routing table and I have no default route setup, so the router would drop the packet and send a Destination Unreachable message back to the originating device.

If you did not peak at the answer, and you got it right, not necessarily verbatim, but the gist of it, then that is *awesome*!! If you had some problems understanding, go back and re-read the chapter and try again. But next we are going to IP routing, and there will be a lot of examples, so you will get enough practice.

IP routing configuration

It's time to show the configuration for each router to include the administrative commands, so you can follow along with your simulator or live equipment.

The topology you know already is three routers connected through serial cables or **smart serials**, since we are using WIC2T as the WAN side. Also, we will be using three L2 switches of 2960-s, two PCs, and one server acting as an FTP server for now. The following is the IP scheme of the network:

- **R1**
    - **S0/0/0**: 10.1.1.5/30
    - **F0/0**: 192.168.1.254/24
- **R2**
    - **S0/0/1**: 10.1.1.6/30
    - **S0/0/0**: 10.1.1.9/30
    - **F0/0**: 192.168.2.0/24
- **R3**
    - **S0/0/1**: 10.1.1.10/30
    - **F0/0**: 192.168.3.254

When you are configuring this interface with the IP addresses, the clock rate will always go on the S0/0/0 and you could also add a description to the interface, that way you know who your router is connecting to.

Let's start configuring R1 with its full configuration:

```
>ENABLE
#CONFIG T
(CONFIG)#HOSTNAME R1
R1(CONFIG)#ENABLE PASSWORD CISCO
R1(CONFIG)#ENABLE SECRET STUDENT
R1(CONFIG)#SERVICE PASSWORD-ENCRYPTION
R1(CONFIG)#BANNER MOTD $ WELCOME TO R1 $
R1(CONFIG)#IP DOMAIN-LOOKUP
R1(CONFIG)#IP DOMAIN-NAME CISCO.COM
R1(CONFIG)#IP NAME-SERVER 192.168.2.1
R1(CONFIG)#USERNAME LDIAZ PRIVILEGE 15 PASSWORD 0 CISCO
R1(CONFIG)#LINE CON 0
...
R1(CONFIG-LINE)#EXIT
R1(CONFIG)#IP SSH AUTHENTICATION-RETRIES 3
R1(CONFIG)#IP SSH TIME-OUT 120
```

```
R1(CONFIG)#CRYPTO KEY GENERATE RSA
R1(CONFIG)#CRYPTO KEY GENERATE RSA
The name for the keys will be: R1.CISCO.COM
```
Choose the size of the key modulus in the range of 360 to 2048 for your General Purpose Keys. Choosing a key modulus greater than 512 may take a few minutes.
```
How many bits in the modulus [512]: 512
```
% Generating 512 bit RSA keys, keys will be non-exportable...[OK]
```
R1(CONFIG)#LINE VTY 0 15
```
*Mar 1 0:2:46.960: RSA key size needs to be at least 768 bits for ssh version 2
*Mar 1 0:2:46.960: %SSH-5-ENABLED: SSH 1.5 has been enabled
```
R1(CONFIG-LINE)#TRANSPORT INPUT SSH
R1(CONFIG-LINE)#EXIT
R1(CONFIG)#INT F0/0
R1(CONFIG-IF)#IP ADDRESS 192.168.1.254 255.255.255.0
R1(CONFIG-IF)#DESCRIPTION CONNECTION TO LAN
R1(CONFIG-IF)#NO SHUT
R1(CONFIG-IF)#INT S0/0/0
R1(CONFIG-IF)#IP ADDRESS 10.1.1.5 255.255.255.252
R1(CONFIG-IF)#CLOCK RATE 4000000
R1(CONFIG-IF)#DESCRIPTION CONNECTION TO R2
R1(CONFIG-IF)#NO SHUT
R1(CONFIG-IF)#EXIT
R1(CONFIG)#EXIT
R1#COPY RUN START
Destination filename [startup-config]? HIT THE ENTER KEY
Building configuration...
[OK]
```

The configuration of R1 has the complete administrative commands to include enabling SSH communication through the Telnet lines. In some networks, the IP domain-lookup is turned off, so if you fat finger the keyboard, the router won't try to look for a DNS server to resolve what you just typed, and you would be spinning your wheels. I configured the DNS name resolution, created a domain name, `cisco.com`, and pointed to the `192.168.2.1` that can act as a DNS server. Why? Because you need to know it for your certification, and you will be using it in the *real world*.

The commands you see underneath each of the lines, such as `logging synchronous` and `exec-timeout 0 0`, are important but not required. The `logging synchronous` is, simply, seen when the router gives you feedback, and it won't interrupt your typing, and the `exec-timeout 0 0` means how long your session will last in minutes and seconds.

In a lab environment, you usually put zero minutes and zero seconds, so your session will never timeout, but in the real world, you would put something like 20 minutes, 30 seconds. It is completely up to the administrator what they want to do.

Let's move on to R2 configurations:

```
>ENABLE
#CONFIG T
(CONFIG)#HOSTNAME R2
R2(CONFIG)#ENABLE PASSWORD CISCO
R2(CONFIG)#ENABLE SECRET STUDENT
R2(CONFIG)#SERVICE PASSWORD-ENCRYPTION
R2(CONFIG)#BANNER MOTD $ WELCOME TO R2 $
R2(CONFIG)#IP DOMAIN-LOOKUP
R2(CONFIG)#IP DOMAIN-NAME CISCO.COM
R2(CONFIG)#IP NAME-SERVER 192.168.2.1
R2 (CONFIG)#USERNAME LDIAZ PRIVILEGE 15 PASSWORD 0 CISCO
...
R2(CONFIG-LINE)#EXIT
R2(CONFIG)#IP SSH AUTHENTICATION-RETRIES 3
R2(CONFIG)#IP SSH TIME-OUT 120
R2(CONFIG)#CRYPTO KEY GENERATE RSA
R2(CONFIG)#CRYPTO KEY GENERATE RSA
      The name for the keys will be: R2.CISCO.COM
  Choose the size of the key modulus in the range of 360 to 2048 for your
General Purpose Keys. Choosing a key modulus greater than 512 may take a
few minutes.
How many bits in the modulus [512]: 512
% Generating 512 bit RSA keys, keys will be non-exportable...[OK]
R2(CONFIG)#LINE VTY 0 15
*Mar 1 0:2:46.960:  RSA key size needs to be at least 768 bits for ssh
version 2
  *Mar 1 0:2:46.960:  %SSH-5-ENABLED: SSH 1.5 has been enabled
    R2(CONFIG-LINE)#TRANSPORT INPUT SSH
    R2(CONFIG-LINE)#EXIT
    R2(CONFIG)#INT F0/0
    R2(CONFIG-IF)#IP ADDRESS 192.168.2.254 255.255.255.0
    R2(CONFIG-IF)#DESCRIPTION CONNECTION TO LAN
    R2(CONFIG-IF)#NO SHUT
    R2(CONFIG-IF)#INT S0/0/1
    R2(CONFIG-IF)#IP ADDRESS 10.1.1.6 255.255.255.252
    R2(CONFIG-IF)#DESCRIPTION CONNECTION TO R1
    R2(CONFIG-IF)#NO SHUT
    R2(CONFIG-IF)#INT S0/0/0
    R2(CONFIG-IF)#IP ADDRESS 10.1.1.9 255.255.255.252
    R2(CONFIG-IF)#CLOCK RATE 4000000
    R2(CONFIG-IF)#DESCRIPTION CONNECTION TO R3
    R2(CONFIG-IF)#NO SHUT
```

```
R2 (CONFIG-IF)#EXIT
R2(CONFIG)#EXIT
R2#COPY RUN START
Destination filename [startup-config]? HIT THE ENTER KEY
Building configuration...
[OK]
```

The configuration of R2 is the same, except that we added more interfaces and the hostname changed. So, just some minor but important changes; one wrong IP address and you will not be able to route, so *pay attention to detail*.

If you want to make sure that you have a blank slate to start with, before you start configuring, you may want to **erase start** and **reload**, and that will make sure you do not have any other configuration on that router that may interfere with your configuration.

Once you have configured, you obviously want to verify that all you typed got saved, so there are several show commands you could use:

- show start: It will show you all the configurations stored in NVRAM, which means commands are saved.
- show run: It will show your current configurations in RAM, commands that are not saved yet.
- show ip int brief: It will give you a summary of your interfaces, IP addresses, and whether the interface is working.
- show protocols: It is like showing ip int brief, but this gives you the mask as well.
- show ip protocols: It will show you whether any routing protocol is configured, with other details also.
- show history: It will show by default the last 10 commands you typed.
- show ip route: It will show you the routing table of the router, which is very helpful in letting you know whether you are connecting to your networks.
- show controllers S0/0/0: When you use this command, be specific as to what interface you want to look at. If not, you will be looking through hundreds of hardware information on all your interfaces.

Try to use commands that are more specific, so you can get quickly where you need to go. Do not make a habit of typing show start or show run, especially on a production router. This is mainly because you may overwhelm the router, and you may have to look through a bunch of information you don't need.

The following are some examples of the pre-mentioned commands:

```
R1#sh controllers s0/0/0          ◄─────────────
Interface Serial0/0/0
Hardware is PowerQUICC MPC860     ◄────────
DCE V.35, clock rate 4000000
idb at 0x81081AC4, driver data structure at
SCC Registers:
General [GSMR]=0x2:0x00000000, Protocol-specific [PSMR]=0x8
Events [SCCE]=0x0000, Mask [SCCM]=0x0000, Status [SCCS]=0x00
Transmit on Demand [TODR]=0x0, Data Sync [DSR]=0x7E7E
Interrupt Registers:
Config [CICR]=0x00367F80, Pending [CIPR]=0x0000C000
Mask   [CIMR]=0x00200000, In-srv  [CISR]=0x00000000
Command register [CR]=0x580
Port A [PADIR]=0x1030, [PAPAR]=0xFFFF
       [PAODR]=0x0010, [PADAT]=0xCBFF
Port B [PBDIR]=0x09C0F, [PBPAR]=0x0800E
       [PBODR]=0x00000, [PBDAT]=0x3FFFD
Port C [PCDIR]=0x00C, [PCPAR]=0x200
       [PCSO]=0xC20,  [PCDAT]=0xDF2, [PCINT]=0x00F
Receive Ring
       rmd(68012830): status 9000 length 60C address 3B6DAC4
       rmd(68012838): status B000 length 60C address 3B6D444
Transmit Ring
 --More--

R1#sh ip protocols          ◄────────────────
Routing Protocol is "rip"
Sending updates every 30 seconds, next due in 19 seconds
Invalid after 180 seconds, hold down 180, flushed after 240
Outgoing update filter list for all interfaces is not set
Incoming update filter list for all interfaces is not set
Redistributing: rip
Default version control: send version 2, receive 2
   Interface              Send  Recv  Triggered RIP  Key-chain
   FastEthernet0/0         2     2
   Serial0/0/0             2     2
Automatic network summarization is not in effect
Maximum path: 4
Routing for Networks:
     10.0.0.0
     192.168.1.0
Passive Interface(s):
Routing Information Sources:
   Gateway           Distance      Last Update
     10.1.1.6              120      00:00:05
Distance: (default is 120)
```

> Main reason, is it DTE or DCE so you can put a clock rate on the interface.

In the topology that we are using, the three routers have a DCE on one of their interfaces, so each router would need a clock rate to set the synchronization, and encapsulation to be able to communicate with its neighbor router. In the simulator, it's easy to see which side is the DCE since the cable has a clock on it.

This is strictly for certification purposes; it is rare to see companies using serial cables to connect their WAN infrastructure, and it would normally be Ethernet connections.

Finally, we move on to R3 configuration:

```
>ENABLE
#CONFIG T
 (CONFIG)#HOSTNAME R3
R3(CONFIG)#ENABLE PASSWORD CISCO
R3(CONFIG)#ENABLE SECRET STUDENT
R3(CONFIG)#SERVICE PASSWORD-ENCRYPTION
R3(CONFIG)#BANNER MOTD $ WELCOME TO R3 $
R3(CONFIG)#IP DOMAIN-LOOKUP
R3(CONFIG)#IP DOMAIN-NAME CISCO.COM
R3(CONFIG)#IP NAME-SERVER 192.168.2.1
R3(CONFIG)#USERNAME LDIAZ PRIVILEGE 15 PASSWORD 0 CISCO
 ...
R3(CONFIG)#IP SSH AUTHENTICATION-RETRIES 3
R3(CONFIG)#IP SSH TIME-OUT 120
R3(CONFIG)#CRYPTO KEY GENERATE RSA
R3(CONFIG)#CRYPTO KEY GENERATE RSA
The name for the keys will be: R3.CISCO.COM
Choose the size of the key modulus in the range of 360 to 2048 for your
General Purpose Keys. Choosing a key modulus greater than 512 may take a
few minutes.
How many bits in the modulus [512]: 512
% Generating 512 bit RSA keys, keys will be non-exportable...[OK]
R1(CONFIG)#LINE VTY 0 15
*Mar 1 0:2:46.960:  RSA key size needs to be at least 768 bits for ssh
version 2
*Mar 1 0:2:46.960:  %SSH-5-ENABLED: SSH 1.5 has been enabled
R3(CONFIG-LINE)#TRANSPORT INPUT SSH
R3(CONFIG-LINE)#EXIT
R3(CONFIG)#INT F0/0
R3(CONFIG-IF)#IP ADDRESS 192.168.3.254 255.255.255.0
R3(CONFIG-IF)#DESCRIPTION CONNECTION TO LAN
R3(CONFIG-IF)#NO SHUT
R3(CONFIG-IF)#INT S0/0/1
R3(CONFIG-IF)#IP ADDRESS 10.1.1.10 255.255.255.252
```

```
R3(CONFIG-IF)#DESCRIPTION CONNECTION TO R2
R3(CONFIG-IF)#NO SHUT
R3(CONFIG-IF)#EXIT
R3(CONFIG)#EXIT
R3#COPY RUN START
Destination filename [startup-config]? HIT THE ENTER KEY
Building configuration...
[OK]
```

We have configured all three routers with administrative commands and given descriptions to interfaces, and we have even enabled SSH communication, so we can securely connect to our routers remotely.

Next, we need to decide about our end devices. Are we going to assign them static IP address, subnet mask, default-gateway, and DNS address? Or are we going to dynamically assign them through DHCP? My money is on DHCP; you could configure a Microsoft DHCP server or just let the router be a DHCP server for you.

On the Enterprise network, it would be an administrator's nightmare to assign static IP addresses to all your end devices. If it is a router, a printer, or a server, I can see why you would assign them static IP addresses but not for your PCs.

So, let's see how we configure DHCP on a router. But, before we do, we will choose PC0 to be configured to acquire an IP address from a DHCP server, and R1 will serve as the DHCP:

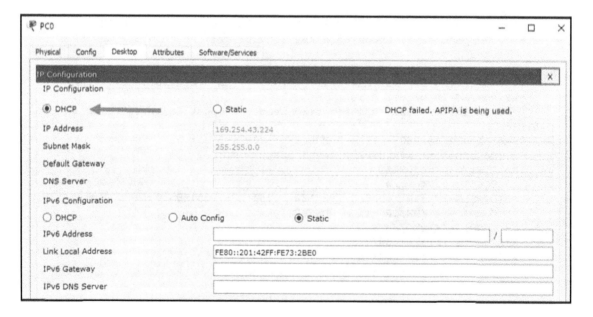

As you can see from the IPv4 settings of PC0, is set for **DHCP** and since at the moment there is no DHCP configured, the TCP/IP protocol assigned an APIPA address, which by the way is not routable.

Let's configure DHCP on R1:

```
R1(config)#ip dhcp ?
  excluded-address  Prevent DHCP from assigning certain addresses
  pool              Configure DHCP address pools
  relay             DHCP relay agent parameters
R1(config)#ip dhcp pool ?
  WORD  Pool name
R1(config)#ip dhcp pool R1_LAN          ◄————  Must have a Pool Name
R1(dhcp-config)#?
  default-router  Default routers
  dns-server      Set name server
  exit            Exit from DHCP pool configuration mode
  network         Network number and mask
  no              Negate a command or set its defaults
  option          Raw DHCP options
R1(dhcp-config)#default-router 192.168.1.254
R1(dhcp-config)#dns-server 192.168.2.1
R1(dhcp-config)#network 192.168.1.0 255.255.255.0
R1(dhcp-config)#exit
R1(config)#ip dhcp excluded-address 192.168.1.254
```

Must exclude any IP address for that pool, which you will assign statically. If not, you will run into an IP conflict.

OK, I know what some of you are thinking: *why didn't he do the exclusions first?* The answer to that is simple: *I did not want to;* it makes no difference when you do it—just make sure it gets done. Also, I have been using the word *assign* when it comes to the IP addresses, for certification purposes. Cisco does not like that word; it would prefer *allocate* IP addresses, and this is something to keep in mind.

Now we must save our configuration, by using the `copy run start` from `privilege mode`, and then verify that the configuration was saved. There are two ways we can do this:

```
R1#sh start
Using 901 bytes
!
version 12.4
no service timestamps log datetime msec
no service timestamps debug datetime msec
no service password-encryption
!
hostname R1
!
!
!
!
ip dhcp excluded-address 192.168.1.254
!
ip dhcp pool R1_LAN
  network 192.168.1.0 255.255.255.0
  default-router 192.168.1.254
  dns-server 192.168.2.1
```

Here is a more direct approach:

```
R1#sh ip dhcp pool

Pool R1_LAN :
 Utilization mark (high/low)    : 100 / 0
 Subnet size (first/next)       : 0 / 0
 Total addresses                : 254
 Leased addresses               : 1
 Excluded addresses             : 1
 Pending event                  : none

 1 subnet is currently in the pool
 Current index        IP address range
Leased/Excluded/Total
 192.168.1.1          192.168.1.1    - 192.168.1.254   1   / 1   /
254
```

The reason I showed the `show start` command is the DHCP configuration is right at the top of the page. The `show ip dhcp pool` is a more direct and efficient way to look at the scope you created. Remember, you could be the DHCP server for multiple scopes, so if you have hundreds or thousands of scopes, using the `show start` would not be feasible at all, if anything, it would be confusing.

If asked about the certification, to show the pool for X.X.X.X, use the `show ip dhcp pool` command.

But let's verify whether our PC0 is actually being *allocated* an IP address configuration:

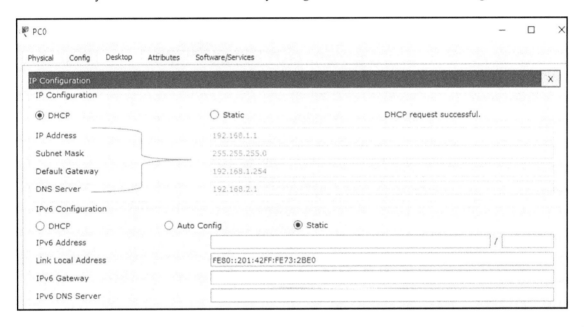

Indeed, we are receiving our IP addressing information, so it worked like a charm. But just keep in mind all this takes planning beforehand, and you just can't be shooting from the hip. It takes methodical planning for everything in your network to work properly.

Now, I am hoping, someone is thinking or is somewhat intrigued about **multiple scopes**. How is someone going to get an IP address allocated from R1 if they're in another broadcast domain?

The rule of DHCP is DORA, the **D** is for Discover, which is a broadcast, and routers by default will drop those broadcast packets. So, how do we get around this conundrum?

Well, we configure an IP helper address that will work on your network's behalf to retrieve an IP address for you and allocate that to your end devices. So, let's give this a try.

The **Offer**, means the DHCP server is giving the host device a choice of IP settings. The **Request** comes from the host accepting the **Offer** from the DHCP, and finally the **Acknowledgement** comes from the DHCP stating; it has acknowledged your offer and will send you the IP settings:

```
hostname R1
!
!
!
!
ip dhcp excluded-address 192.168.1.254
ip dhcp excluded-address 192.168.2.254
ip dhcp excluded-address 192.168.3.254
!
ip dhcp pool R1_LAN  ◄──────
 network 192.168.1.0 255.255.255.0
 default-router 192.168.1.254
 dns-server 192.168.2.1
ip dhcp pool R2_LAN  ◄──────
 network 192.168.2.0 255.255.255.0
 default-router 192.168.2.254
 dns-server 192.168.2.1
ip dhcp pool R3_LAN  ◄──────
 network 192.168.3.0 255.255.255.0
 default-router 192.168.3.254
 dns-server 192.168.2.1
```

So, we created three different scopes and their exclusions, and now we must configure the end devices to receive an IP address from the DHCP server. But for that to work, we must put the `ip helper-address` that points to that DHCP server.

Let's have a look:

```
R2#config t
Enter configuration commands, one per line.  End with CNTL/Z.
R2(config)#int f0/0
R2(config-if)#ip helper-address 10.1.1.5
```

You would do the same thing on R3: you would put the IP helper address on the LAN's interface, since it's the end devices you want to allocate the IP addresses to. The address `10.1.1.5` is the `S0/0/0` of R1, which is the first IP address you encounter when reaching the router.

Let's now verify that we did get an IP address assigned to our PCs:

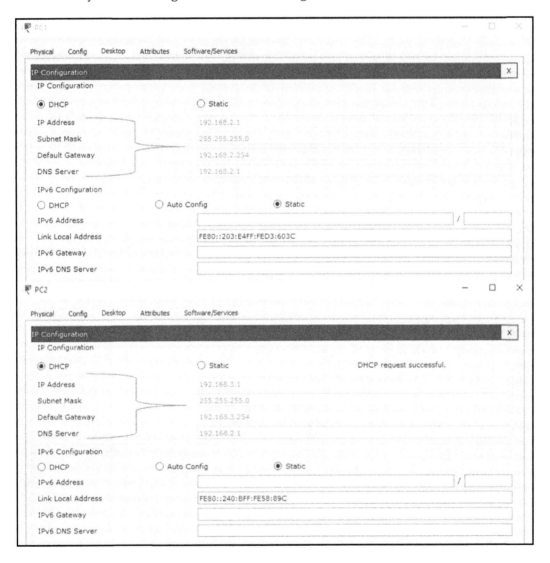

The `IP helper-address` command worked really well! Just keep in mind what interface I am putting the command in and that I am pointed to the correct DHCP server.

Configuring IP routing in our network

We configured our routers with administrative commands and we are able to manage them if we are on the same subnet. We have connectivity within our subnet, and routers can talk with their directly connected neighbors. But the point to networking is to be able to talk to devices beyond our own LAN; businesses would not be able to function if they did not have connectivity across the world.

I have already given you a glimpse of how important routing is, as we used default routes and static routes to build the routing table. But now we are going to discuss the three types of routing in more detail, which are the following:

- Static routing
- Default routing
- Dynamic routing

Don't think you only have to use one or the other; you can combine all three to make a very robust, redundant and dependable network.

Static routing

If you remember, static routing is adding the destination networks manually, which means that you are building the routing table.

Benefits of using static routes

- You are not putting less burden on the CPU, which in turn may allow you to purchase a more inexpensive router. That does not mean you should buy cheap IT equipment.

- Since you are not going to use a dynamic routing protocol, the router will not be sending updates across your WAN, which in turn means less bandwidth usage, and you pay less.
- Since you are building the routing table from scratch, you are in complete control of who can access what network and where they can go on the network. So, a layer of security does exist by using static routes.

Disadvantages of using static routes

- You, as the administrator, must have a detailed understanding of how your topology looks. What is connected to what? What devices are running? Your knowledge of your network and networking skills better be on point. Think about overhead, putting in routes, taking out routes—you must keep track of every node on that network.
- The fact that you must manually add and remove networks is simply not feasible on large networks. Especially when you are dealing with branch offices with different IP schemes and policies—a web of problems can occur.

Regardless of the nightmarish points of static routes, you still need to know how to configure them. Static routes are useful, and they can be used in unison with routing protocols and act as back-up routes.

This is the syntax for a static route:

```
IP ROUTE 192.168.3.0 255.255.255.0 S0/0/0 150
(Using exit interface and using an AD of 150)
IP ROUTE 192.168.3.0 255.255.255.0 10.1.1.6 150
(Using next routers hop address an AD of 150)
```

So, let's break each part down, so you can get a clearer picture:

Syntax	Description
IP ROUTE	The command to start creating a static route.
Destination Network	This would be the destination network you want to reach.
Destination Mask	The mask that the destination network is using.
Exit interface	If you use the name of the exit interface, such as s0/0/0, it would show up as directly connected. Only on lookup of the routing table.
Next Hop Address	If you use the IP address of your neighbor router, it would show with an AD as *1* or the administrative distance you gave it.

Administrative Distance	This is the believability of a route; the lower the number, the more trustworthy the route. They range from 1-255.
Permanent	This command keeps the route in the routing table, even if the interface goes down.

OK, now that you have seen the syntax and what each part of it means, let's go ahead and use the following topology and configure static routes on all the routers:

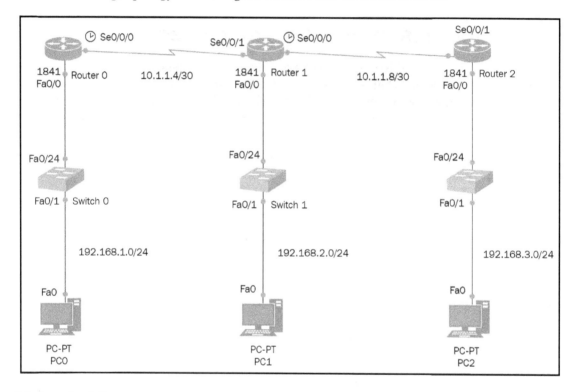

R1 does the following:

```
R1#CONFIG T
Enter configuration commands, one per line.  End with CNTL/Z.
R1(config)#IP ROUTE 10.1.1.8 255.255.255.252 S0/0/0 150
R1(config)#IP ROUTE 192.168.2.0 255.255.255.0 S0/0/0 150
R1(config)#IP ROUTE 192.168.3.0 255.255.255.0 S0/0/0 150
R1(config)#
```

As you can see, we are using the exit interface of R1 with an AD of 150 because when we configure a routing protocol, the static route will act as a backup route and the routing protocol will take over in the routing table since the administrative distance of the routing protocols such as RIP, EIGRP and OSPF will be lower than 150.

For R2, do the following:

```
R2#CONFIG T
Enter configuration commands, one per line.  End with CNTL/Z.
R2(config)#IP ROUTE 192.168.1.0 255.255.255.0 S0/0/1 150
R2(config)#IP ROUTE 192.168.3.0 255.255.255.0 S0/0/0 150
R2(config)#
```

When we are configuring static routes on routers that have more than one direction they could go, you must be very careful when inputting the exit interface. As you can see, the 192.168.1.0 network has an exit interface of s0/0/1 and the network 192.168.3.0 has an exit interface of s0/0/0. It is very easy to make a mistake here, so pay attention to the detail.

For R3, do the following:

```
R3#CONFIG T
Enter configuration commands, one per line.  End with CNTL/Z.
R3(config)#IP ROUTE 10.1.1.4 255.255.255.252 S0/0/1 150
R3(config)#IP ROUTE 192.168.2.0 255.255.255.0 S0/0/1 150
R3(config)#IP ROUTE 192.168.1.0 255.255.255.0 S0/0/1 150
R3(config)#
```

This router is an inverse of R1, and one thing you need to note is that we need to include the networks between the routers if the router is not touching that network directly. You must remember routers only know about networks they are directly connected to.

Now we must verify that the static routes we entered work, and the way we do that is to ping across the network. But we also need to verify the routing table to make sure those routes are in there:

```
R1#sh ip route
Codes: C - connected, S - static, I - IGRP, R - RIP, M - mobile, B - BGP
       D - EIGRP, EX - EIGRP external, O - OSPF, IA - OSPF inter area
       N1 - OSPF NSSA external type 1, N2 - OSPF NSSA external type 2
       E1 - OSPF external type 1, E2 - OSPF external type 2, E - EGP
       i - IS-IS, L1 - IS-IS level-1, L2 - IS-IS level-2, ia - IS-IS inter
area
       * - candidate default, U - per-user static route, o - ODR
       P - periodic downloaded static route

Gateway of last resort is 0.0.0.0 to network 0.0.0.0

     10.0.0.0/30 is subnetted, 2 subnets
C       10.1.1.4 is directly connected, Serial0/0/0
S       10.1.1.8 is directly connected, Serial0/0/0
C    192.168.1.0/24 is directly connected, FastEthernet0/0
S    192.168.2.0/24 is directly connected, Serial0/0/0
S    192.168.3.0/24 is directly connected, Serial0/0/0
S*   0.0.0.0/0 is directly connected, Serial0/0/0
```

Looking at R1's routing table, we see connected routes, static routes, and default routes, so everything seems to be in order. Let's ping:

```
R1#ping 192.168.3.1

Type escape sequence to abort.
Sending 5, 100-byte ICMP Echos to 192.168.3.1, timeout is 2 seconds:
!!!!!
Success rate is 100 percent (5/5), round-trip min/avg/max = 4/6/14 ms

R1#
```

Success! We were able to ping all the way to PC2. When we ping, we send an echo request and an echo reply, so we know how to get to the destination and back.

Dynamic routing

Now the fun begins; we are now moving into the realm of routing protocols, so no longer will we have to manually input the static route for each network; we have a beefy router and we have the bandwidth, so it is time to automate the routing process.

There are many variables that you need to consider when you are deciding to use a routing protocol; first, there are two types of routing protocols: **Interior Gateway Protocols** (**IGPs**); these protocols are RIP, EIGRP, and OSPF; they exchange information within an **autonomous system** or **AS**. There are also **EGP** or **Exterior Gateway Routing Protocols**, which are used to exchange information between different autonomous systems.

Other things you need to keep in mind are the size of the network. Each routing protocol has its limitations regarding how many routers it can handle, how scalable it is, whether we can grow our network with the existing routing protocol, and how fast the routing protocol can converge so all routers are able to communicate with one another.

The truth is, you can use all routing protocols if needed, and you can always make the routing protocols talk to one another using route redistribution (but that is beyond the scope of this book). That is why you must have an intimate knowledge of your network and your business, so you can make an intelligent decision when it comes to the type of routing protocols you are going to use.

Administrative distances

As mentioned before, the **Administrative Distance** (**AD**) is the belief or trustworthiness of the route being advertised. The lower the AD, the more you can trust that route to be the best path to take; in the 0-255 range, 0 is the best and 255 cannot trusted at all. Routers will always choose the network with the lowest AD, but if a router receives the same route from two different locations and has the same AD, then it will use the metric, cost, or hop count to decide which would be the better route. It will always be the smallest number that would win.

Each routing protocol has an algorithm to calculate the best route to a network, and we will get into that later in the book. The following table gives the default AD to static and dynamic routes:

Route source	Administrative distance
Connected Interface	0
Static route	0 or 1
RIP	120
EIGRP	90
OSPF	110
External EIGRP	170
External BGP	20
Internal BGP	200
Unknown	255 (Forget about it)

Let's say that we have RIP, EIGRP, and OSPF configured on all routers; which routing protocol will be placed in the routing table? EIGRP would be the correct answer because it has the lowest AD. Therefore, we used the AD of 150 when we created the static routes, so when we decide to configure a routing protocol, it will be placed on the routing table and the static routes will be used as back-up routes. Don't take out the static routes; yes, they are taking up space in your NVRAM, but I think the router can handle it.

Routing protocols

Just as there are two types of routing protocols, IGP and EGP, there are three different classes of routing protocols, and also we need to understand the differences, not only for the certification but for real-world solutions also.

Distance vector

These types of protocols are limited to distance, meaning every time a packet goes through a router, it's considered a hop, and RIP being a DV has a limit of 15 hops. So, if the network you're trying to reach is 16 routers away, it would be unreachable. The vector simply means the direction the packet is going. Also, DV protocols sends updates periodically, and with RIP, it would be every 30 seconds that the entire routing table gets sent to its neighboring router. You can tweak it, but it is still using up bandwidth.

Link state

If using a link state protocol such as OSPF, it is also considered a **Shortest Path First** or **SPF** protocol. Link state protocols will build three tables:

- **The topology table**: this learns the entire internetwork
- **The routing table**: this has routes learned by other OSPF protocols in the same area
- **The neighbor table**: this keeps track of directly connected neighbors

Link state protocols do not send periodic updates; they are triggered updates, meaning if you add or remove a subnet, that would trigger an update. They do send periodic keepalives in the form of hello messages, just to let neighbors know we are still here, and these messages are small, so it is an efficient method.

Advanced distance vector

These types of routing protocols are a mixture of link state and distance vector. The **Enhanced Interior Gateway Routing Protocol** (**EIGRP**) is a very good example of an ADV; it acts like a link state because it sends periodic hello messages to discover their neighbors and because it only sends partial updates when changes occur. Full updates only occur at the beginning when the routers are trying to converge.

They are still a distance vector routing protocol, because they rely on their neighbors to learn about the network. But EIGRP is a very good protocol to use in a medium or even an enterprise network, due to all the features and tables they create as well. But that will be discussed in the EIGRP chapter.

Routing Information Protocol (RIP)

Let's get down and dirty with RIP. This protocol has three versions: RIPv1, RIPv2, and RIPng. Version 1 of this protocol is not used anymore, but you should know that RIPv1 is a **class-full routing protocol**, which means you need to use the same mask across your network and the same class of address. It also will not receive any updates from RIPv2 unless you specifically go into the interface and tell it to, but, again, *it is not used any more*. Oh, and the updates are sent as broadcast.

RIPv2 is a classless routing protocol that allows you to have different classes of addresses and different masks that would meet the needs of the network, allowing you not to waste IP addresses. This is possible due to the command `no auto-summary`. It does send periodic updates, but now it's using the multicast address `224.0.0.9`, which is a lot easier on your network.

Both RIPv1 and RIPv2 have a 15-hop count limit, and annoying periodic updates, but you can tweak it.

RIPng will be discussed in the IPv6 chapter. It is easier to configure but still has all the same limitations as its predecessors.

Configuring RIPv2 routing

When configuring any dynamic routing protocol, you will be advertising the networks you are connected to. You do not enter any destination network. Basically, you are snitching yourself out; you are telling your neighboring routers what networks you are connected to.

Let's go ahead and configure RIP on our topology; keep in mind we already have static routes configured, but their AD is 150, so RIP should take over and the static routes will be used as back up routes. Let's look at our topology:

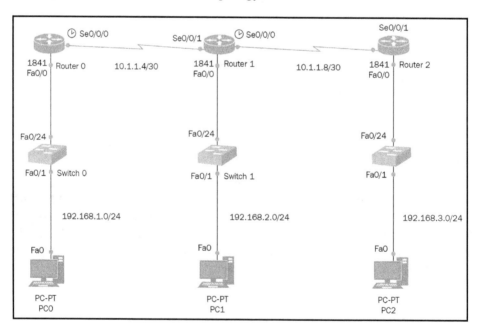

Let's configure R1:

```
R1#sh ip int brief
Interface              IP-Address      OK? Method Status
Protocol
FastEthernet0/0        192.168.1.254   YES manual up                        up
FastEthernet0/1        unassigned      YES unset  administratively down
down
Serial0/0/0            10.1.1.5        YES manual up                        up
Serial0/0/1            unassigned      YES unset  administratively down
down
Vlan1                  unassigned      YES unset  administratively down
down
R1#
```

I like to do the `show IP int brief` command so I know the networks that I need to advertise:

```
R1#config t
Enter configuration commands, one per line.  End with CNTL/Z.
R1(config)#router rip          ◄──────  Starts the config of RIP
R1(config-router)#ver 2
R1(config-router)#net 10.0.0.0  ◄──────  Class-full boundary address
R1(config-router)#net 192.168.1.0
R1(config-router)#no auto-summary  ◄──────  DO NOT FORGET FOR DV
R1(config-router)#
```

RIP is simple to configure: you start with the command `router rip`, then the version, and then the networks you're attached to. You may be thinking, should the `10.0.0.0` be `10.1.1.4`? It really does not matter because RIP will summarize the address to its class-full boundary, so I always put the class-full boundary. Here is an example:

```
Class A: X.0.0.0 Class B: X.X.0.0 Class C: X.X.X.0
```

Let's configure R2:

```
R2#SH IP INT BRIEF
Interface              IP-Address      OK? Method Status
Protocol
FastEthernet0/0        192.168.2.254   YES manual up                        up
FastEthernet0/1        unassigned      YES unset  administratively down
down
Serial0/0/0            10.1.1.9        YES manual up                        up
Serial0/0/1            10.1.1.6        YES manual up                        up
Vlan1                  unassigned      YES unset  administratively down
down
R2#
```

Now we know our networks:

```
R2(config)#router rip
R2(config-router)#ver 2
R2(config-router)#net 10.0.0.0
R2(config-router)#net 192.168.2.0
R2(config-router)#no auto-summary
R2(config-router)#
```

There is the same configuration here, but this router is attached to both 10.1.1.4 and 10.1.1.8; it does not matter that it will be summarized into one class-full *A* address. Just don't forget to put the no auto-summary command, as that command is the one that tells RIP to please send the mask out on the updates.

Let's configure R3:

```
R3#sh ip int brief
Interface              IP-Address      OK? Method Status
Protocol
FastEthernet0/0        192.168.3.254   YES manual up                            up
FastEthernet0/1        unassigned      YES unset  administratively down
down
Serial0/0/0            unassigned      YES unset  administratively down
down
Serial0/0/1            10.1.1.10       YES manual up                            up
Vlan1                  unassigned      YES unset  administratively down
down
R3#
```

Again, now we know the networks to advertise:

```
R3(config)#router rip
R3(config-router)#ver 2
R3(config-router)#net 10.0.0.0
R3(config-router)#net 192.168.3.0
R3(config-router)#no auto-summary
R3(config-router)#
```

This is no different; it is the same configuration all the way through. Now we need to verify each router's routing table to see whether RIP made it to the routing table and they are talking to one another.

Here is the R1 routing table:

```
R1#SH IP ROUTE
Codes: C - connected, S - static, I - IGRP, R - RIP, M - mobile, B - BGP
       D - EIGRP, EX - EIGRP external, O - OSPF, IA - OSPF inter area
       N1 - OSPF NSSA external type 1, N2 - OSPF NSSA external type 2
       E1 - OSPF external type 1, E2 - OSPF external type 2, E - EGP
       i - IS-IS, L1 - IS-IS level-1, L2 - IS-IS level-2, ia - IS-IS inter
area
       * - candidate default, U - per-user static route, o - ODR
       P - periodic downloaded static route

Gateway of last resort is 0.0.0.0 to network 0.0.0.0

     10.0.0.0/30 is subnetted, 2 subnets
C       10.1.1.4 is directly connected, Serial0/0/0
R  ←--- 10.1.1.8 [120/1] via 10.1.1.6, 00:00:02, Serial0/0/0
C    192.168.1.0/24 is directly connected, FastEthernet0/0
R ←- 192.168.2.0/24 [120/1] via 10.1.1.6, 00:00:02, Serial0/0/0
R ←- 192.168.3.0/24 [120/2] via 10.1.1.6, 00:00:02, Serial0/0/0
S*   0.0.0.0/0 is directly connected, Serial0/0/0
```

As you can see, we are learning about the remote networks, and you can see that the 192.168.3.0 network is two hops away.

Here is the R2 routing table:

```
R2#SH IP ROUTE
Codes: C - connected, S - static, I - IGRP, R - RIP, M - mobile, B - BGP
       D - EIGRP, EX - EIGRP external, O - OSPF, IA - OSPF inter area
       N1 - OSPF NSSA external type 1, N2 - OSPF NSSA external type 2
       E1 - OSPF external type 1, E2 - OSPF external type 2, E - EGP
       i - IS-IS, L1 - IS-IS level-1, L2 - IS-IS level-2, ia - IS-IS inter
area
       * - candidate default, U - per-user static route, o - ODR
       P - periodic downloaded static route

Gateway of last resort is not set

     10.0.0.0/30 is subnetted, 2 subnets
C       10.1.1.4 is directly connected, Serial0/0/1
C       10.1.1.8 is directly connected, Serial0/0/0
R  ←_ 192.168.1.0/24 [120/1] via 10.1.1.5, 00:00:16, Serial0/0/1
C    192.168.2.0/24 is directly connected, FastEthernet0/0
R  ←_ 192.168.3.0/24 [120/1] via 10.1.1.10, 00:00:04, Serial0/0/0

R2#
```

Once again, you can see we are learning about our remote networks.

Here is the R3 routing table:

```
R3#sh ip route
Codes: C - connected, S - static, I - IGRP, R - RIP, M - mobile, B - BGP
       D - EIGRP, EX - EIGRP external, O - OSPF, IA - OSPF inter area
       N1 - OSPF NSSA external type 1, N2 - OSPF NSSA external type 2
       E1 - OSPF external type 1, E2 - OSPF external type 2, E - EGP
       i - IS-IS, L1 - IS-IS level-1, L2 - IS-IS level-2, ia - IS-IS inter
area
       * - candidate default, U - per-user static route, o - ODR
       P - periodic downloaded static route

Gateway of last resort is 0.0.0.0 to network 0.0.0.0

     10.0.0.0/30 is subnetted, 2 subnets
R        10.1.1.4 [120/1] via 10.1.1.9, 00:00:12, Serial0/0/1
C        10.1.1.8 is directly connected, Serial0/0/1
R     192.168.1.0/24 [120/2] via 10.1.1.9, 00:00:12, Serial0/0/1
R     192.168.2.0/24 [120/1] via 10.1.1.9, 00:00:12, Serial0/0/1
C     192.168.3.0/24 is directly connected, FastEthernet0/0
S*    0.0.0.0/0 is directly connected, Serial0/0/1
```

OK, looks like we have fully converged the routers, so let's verify by pinging:

```
R3#ping 192.168.1.254

Type escape sequence to abort.
Sending 5, 100-byte ICMP Echos to 192.168.1.254, timeout is 2 seconds:
!!!!!
Success rate is 100 percent (5/5), round-trip min/avg/max = 5/9/14 ms

R3#
```

OK, we can ping, but a real test to see whether RIP is working is to do a debug IP RIP:

```
 ppp              PPP (Point to Point Protocol) information
R4#debug ip rip    ◄────────────
RIP protocol debugging is on
R4#RIP: received v2 update from 10.1.1.13 on Serial0/0/1  ◄──────────
        10.1.1.4/30 via 0.0.0.0 in 2 hops
        10.1.1.8/30 via 0.0.0.0 in 1 hops
        192.168.1.0/24 via 0.0.0.0 in 3 hops
        192.168.2.0/24 via 0.0.0.0 in 2 hops
        192.168.3.0/24 via 0.0.0.0 in 1 hops
RIP: sending  v2 update to 224.0.0.9 via FastEthernet0/0 (192.168.4.254) ◄──
RIP: build update entries
        10.1.1.4/30 via 0.0.0.0, metric 3, tag 0
        10.1.1.8/30 via 0.0.0.0, metric 2, tag 0
        10.1.1.12/30 via 0.0.0.0, metric 1, tag 0
        192.168.1.0/24 via 0.0.0.0, metric 4, tag 0
        192.168.2.0/24 via 0.0.0.0, metric 3, tag 0
        192.168.3.0/24 via 0.0.0.0, metric 2, tag 0
RIP: sending  v2 update to 224.0.0.9 via Serial0/0/1 (10.1.1.14) ◄──────────
RIP: build update entries
        192.168.4.0/24 via 0.0.0.0, metric 1, tag 0
|
```

When we debug, we go behind the scenes, as you can see how RIP is sending and receiving version 2 updates via the multicast address 224.0.0.9. Also remember our static routes are not on the routing table but they are still configured on the router, so if something goes wrong with the RIP protocol, the static route will take over.

Holding down RIP propagations

When you configure a dynamic routing protocol in IPv4, it will send out updates on all interfaces, but you may not want that. What you can do to stop some interface from sending out updates on their interfaces is use the passive-interface s0/0/0 sub-command:

```
R1(config)#router rip
R1(config-router)#ver 2
R1(config-router)#passive-interface s0/0/0
R1(config-router)#
```

Now this interface will be able to receive updates, but you should not send updates out of its interface.

Default routes using RIP

We have configured default routes on our stub routers, so the router won't drop a packet if it does not find a match on the routing table. How about using RIP to tell all the routers the way out of your own autonomous system or network, and get to the internet in this way. So, how would you configure something such as this?

```
R3(config)#router rip
R3(config-router)#ver 2
R3(config-router)#default-information originate
R3(config-router)#
```

The default-information originate is what does the magic. I already had a default route, so it was just a matter of going into RIP and typing the command. Let's see what that did:

```
R2#sh ip route
Codes: C - connected, S - static, I - IGRP, R - RIP, M - mobile, B - BGP
       D - EIGRP, EX - EIGRP external, O - OSPF, IA - OSPF inter area
       N1 - OSPF NSSA external type 1, N2 - OSPF NSSA external type 2
       E1 - OSPF external type 1, E2 - OSPF external type 2, E - EGP
       i - IS-IS, L1 - IS-IS level-1, L2 - IS-IS level-2, ia - IS-IS inter
area
       * - candidate default, U - per-user static route, o - ODR
       P - periodic downloaded static route

Gateway of last resort is 10.1.1.10 to network 0.0.0.0

     10.0.0.0/30 is subnetted, 2 subnets
C       10.1.1.4 is directly connected, Serial0/0/1
C       10.1.1.8 is directly connected, Serial0/0/0
S    192.168.1.0/24 is directly connected, Serial0/0/1
C    192.168.2.0/24 is directly connected, FastEthernet0/0
R    192.168.3.0/24 [120/1] via 10.1.1.10, 00:00:11, Serial0/0/0
R*   0.0.0.0/0 [120/1] via 10.1.1.10, 00:00:11, Serial0/0/0  ◄━━━━━━━
```

RIP is now updating all the routers, telling them where they need to go if they want to get out of their network.

Summary

In this chapter, we covered the IP routing process in detail and gave quite a few examples and tested you. I can't say this enough: **you must understand how packets get from their start point source to their destination**. Remember, there are a lot of variables, cables, routing protocols, algorithms, and much more, which we will discuss further in the following chapters. But if you understood how to create static routes, default routes, how to configure RIPv2, and how to verify that all this is working, you have a solid foundation to work from.

10
The IPv6 Protocol

In this chapter, we will be learning about the benefits of using IPv6 in your network. We will be breaking down the different components of an IPv6 address, to gain a better understanding of the IPv6 address. We will look at different ways of writing an IPv6 address and the rules or guidelines to properly write an IPv6 address. We will also look at the three main IPv6 routing protocols: RIPng, EIGRPv6, and OSPFv3. This and much more will give us an understanding of how IPv6 works on an internet-working device.

In this chapter, we will be discussing the following topics that deal with IPv6:

- The importance of why we need to know about IPv6 concepts and features
- Understanding the benefits of IPv6 versus the IPv4 routed protocol
- Breaking down the IPv6 address and how we can express IPv6
- Different address types and how they are broken down
- Special type of addresses that you need to know about for your certification
- How IPv6 works on a network, including:
    - Manually assigning IPv6 addresses to our devices
    - Stateless autoconfiguration, which in this case is the `eui-64` command
    - Using DHCPv6 for stateful configurations
- Breaking down the IPv6 header
- Understanding that ICMPv6 is extremely important, looking at:
    - **Neighbor Discovery (ND)**
    - **Router Solicitation (RS)**
    - **Router Advertisements (RA)**
    - **Neighbor Solicitation (NS)**
    - **Neighbor Advertisements (NA)**
    - **Duplicate Address Detection (DAD)**
- Routing using the IPv6 routing with default static addressing and RIPng

The history of IP

The history of the IP protocol is very interesting; its roots are within the ARPANET Project. The very first nodes that were actually networked together was back in 1969 using the Interface Message Processor. It connected four devices from Los Angeles, California to Santa Barbara, California and the University of Utah.

It was not until 1970-1979 that the *Key Internet Protocols* were implemented. Professor Peter Kirstein of University College London was the first to start the European ARPANET device using IP transatlantic connectivity .

It wasn't until 1973 that the TCP/IP protocol began its development. This new protocol allowed the elements of a very diverse network to be able to interconnect and have communications with each other. It was not for another year, 1974, that the term *internet* was used for the first time, in Vint Cerf and Robert Kahn, *A Protocol for Packet Network interconnection*, which defined the design of TCP in minute details.

To jump further ahead, in 1983 ARPANET made the change to TCP/IP and in April of 2005 YouTube came on the scene. Incredibly enough, the WWW became public to the world in 1991.

So, you can see that IP has been around for a long time. To be more specific, the IPv4 protocol was first developed in the 1970s. It uses the RFC 791 that governs IPv4 functionality, but that RFC was published in 1981, a decade later.

The reason I want you to know about the history of this protocol is for your own knowledge and understanding. You will not be tested on this, but you will gain some foundation knowledge about how we are now in IPv6.

With that said, IPv4 addresses were not assigned equally across the globe, and the addresses I speak about are the public routable addresses on the *internet*. The United States got the bigger chunk of addresses and other countries got the short end of the stick. That is why China moved to IPv6 before the US. If you remember, in the 2008 summer Olympics, which was held in Beijing, all of it was done in IPv6; they had no choice.

China had already run out of IPv4 addresses by that time. The US, on the other hand, did not run out of public addresses until 2011.

This was put out by the APNIC Internet Registry. But if you look at the following table, you will see the exact date of IPv4 exhaustion:

Regional internet registry	Date of exhaustion for IPv4
AFRINIC	N/A

APNIC	April 15, 2011
ARIN	September 24, 2015
LACNIC	June 10, 2014
RIPE NCC	September 14, 2012

But as we know, people do not like change, so we came up with a bunch of methods or tricks to avoid changing over.

The demise of IPv4 was noticed by the **Internet Engineering Task Force** (**IETF**), and they came up with a clever method to slow that down. So, they implemented some technologies that could help us with this growing shortage. The first was **Network Address Translation**, (**NAT**), where we could use one public IPv4 address to translate 65,536 private addresses. We know this as NAT Overload or PAT, which stands for **Port Address Translation**. The other technology that came on board was the use of CIDR, which is short for Classless Inter-Domain Routing. Both technologies were put in place in 1993.

The damage was done. Nobody could have expected that the growth of the internet and the number of devices that required public addresses would reach the number it did. We were warned by the IETF to start the transition to IPv6, but it has been a very painful process.

Just so you know, there was an IPv5 that they also worked on, but it never came to light. There were too many issues and confusion, so IETF decided on the name IPv6.

So, now that you know a good amount about the history of IP, let us start talking about why we need IPv6.

Need for IPv6

If you read about the history of IP, then definitely you would know the need for IPv6. We have run out of public IPv4 addresses, and the technologies that were created to reduce the death of IPv4 were just a band aid to a problem that was inevitable. NAT, CIDR, and subnetting worked well for a while; it lent us a couple of years.

But the time has come for us to embrace IPv6 in all its glory. Why? Well, just the fact that IPv6 has 340 undecillion addresses. What in the world is that? This is the exact number of IPv6 addresses that exist: 340,282,366,920,938,463,463,374,607,431,768,211,456.

Let me give you an analogy by Diwakar Tundlam; *we could assign an IPV6 address to EVERY ATOM ON THE SURFACE OF THE EARTH, and still have enough addresses left to do another 100+ earths.*

I think Mr. Tundlam puts that into perspective. We will never run out of IPv6 addresses. If you compare that to IPv4's 2.4 billion addresses, it falls short of the mark. But that is irrelevant now, since we do not have any IPv4 public addresses to allocate to everyone.

Obviously, we cannot just replace all the addresses at once. This has to be done in a very calculated way and designed properly or we will suffer the consequences. But just to think that one IPv6 network can hold 15 quintillion addresses, it is truly amazing. If your company reaches that size, I fear you would be rubbing elbows with someone on the other side of the world and you would be filthy rich.

So, to answer the question, *do we need IPv6?*, yes we do, no matter how scary it looks. If we want to be able to communicate globally, it needs to happen. So embrace the pain and you will see that it was not that hard.

What are the benefits of using IPv6?

When we rolled out IPv4 and started allocating IPv4 addresses to routers, switches, and PCs, we really did not take into consideration any hierarchy. We simply just assigned addresses as they came. That is why now our backbone routers are struggling to stay up and those routing tables are huge!

 You can get this table at the following link for the latest updates: `https://www.cidr-report.org/as2.0/#General_Status`:

Status Summary

Table History

Date	Prefixes	CIDR Aggregated
14-06-18	725855	392829
15-06-18	725348	394132
16-06-18	725645	394096
17-06-18	725260	390829
18-06-18	725555	390942
19-06-18	725678	391270
20-06-18	725642	390826
21-06-18	725355	391294

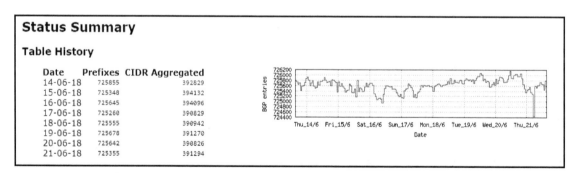

IPv6 was designed for efficiency, and even has built-in security, such as IPsec, for end-to-end security. But besides that, the protocols themselves have been trimmed down and are aligned for 64-bit processing, which will speed things up. If you look at the header of an IPv4 and IPv6 protocol, you will see how much smaller the IPv6 header is. Let's compare them in the following diagram:

Ver	IHL	Type of Service	Total Length	
Identification			Flags	Fragment Offset
Time to Live		Protocol	Header Checksum	
Source Address				
Destination Address				
Options + Padding				

Version	Traffic class	Flow label		
Payload length			Next header	Hop limit
Source address				
Destination address				

IPv4 and IPv6 headers

As you can see from the preceding diagram, the IPv4 header is larger than the IPv6 header. An IPv4 header is 20 octets, which equals to 480 bits, and an IPv6 header is built completely differently, so it's 40 octets but it equals to 320 bits. The header in IPv6 is now more efficient than that in IPv4, especially as there is no ARP or TTL. This information was moved to the **Next Header** field.

Another benefit of IPv6 is the new addresses, such as anycast. The anycast address is considered as *the one to nearest*, which means they have allowed us to assign this anycast address, the same exact address on all the devices. The reason for that is that when a device is looking for a specific service, based on the routing protocol, it will use the nearest anycast address to get to the destination.

We will be looking at more IPv6 addresses later in the chapter. But regarding the benefits seen here, why are you not on IPv6 yet? I know the answer to that; because it is a long hexadecimal funky address.

But do not fear, Laz is here. I will break it down for you.

Addressing in IPv6 and expressions

IPv6 addresses are 128 bits long; the predecessor is 32 bits long. We have already spoken in length about the amount of IPv6 addresses that are available to us, which is exponentially larger than IPv4.

Now we must understand what the IPv6 address looks like and break it down. We also know that IPv6 addresses are hexadecimal numbers, and to be honest, in my humble opinion, this is the reason we hesitate to embrace IPv6.

So, let's start breaking down the format of the IPv6 address:

The IPv6 address is separated into two separate parts; the network prefix and the interface ID, which make up the 128-bit address. In IPv6, there is no subnet mask; it is called a prefix length and it could go all the way to /128 for some addresses, which we will be discussing later in this chapter.

In all honesty, the interface ID will not be the main concern. Remember, I said you could have 15 quintillion addresses with one IPv6 network. Our concern is the network prefix portion of the address. IPv6 was built with hierarchy in mind, so they actually allocated each one of those sections to entities, as shown in the following table:

Entities	Section	Description
Registry	2001/23	The first section will be your registry *ARIN*
ISP	2800/32	The second section will be your internet provider *AT&T*
Company	FACE/48	The third section will identify the company
LAN or Subnet	1000/64	The fourth section is left for the company to subnet the addresses, for their internal network

So, for companies around the world, it would now be easily identifiable and routers would have an easier time building the routing tables. Let me show you a theoretical example:

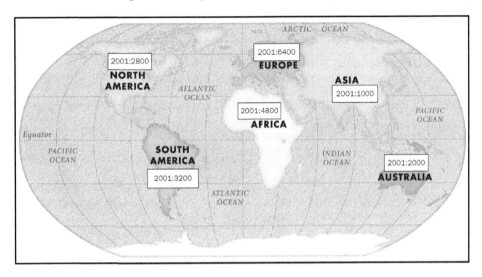

The IPv6 addresses that I designated to each continent are made up, but now routers will identify, by the first and second section/field, where the IP address is coming from, and build a hierarchy of networks, so building a routing table just became easier, more organized, and smaller.

You might be saying, *Laz, that is a huge address to be typing out*. I would agree; that is why we have the copy/paste option and, with IPv6, we have the option of shortening the address.

Shortened IPv6 expressions

To make life easier for all of us, we could express the 128-bit monster address in a shorter method, but as with everything, there are rules we must follow:

- The first rule is that you can drop any leading zero, meaning any zero in front of your address

- The second rule is that you can only drop consecutive blocks of zeros and replace them with a double colon
    - You can only have one double colon in the address:

Examples:

2001:0ABC:BADD:0020:0000:0DEF:0123:0008   Leading Zero Rule

2001:ABC:BADD:20::DEF:123:8 Much shorter and all I did was take out the zeros in the front "VALID"

2001:0000:0000:0ABC:BADD:0000:0000:0008   Double Colon Rule

2001::ABC:BADD::8 This is not a valid IPv6 address, because you two double colons in the address. "INVALID"

2001:0:0:ABC:BADD::8 This a valid IPv6 address, because we only one double colon and the other blocks we used one zero in each block. "VALID"

So, the powers that be gave a way for us to shorten the address. Notepad and copy/paste will be your best friend. For your CCNA certification, they don't dive too deep into IPv6, but it's not without tricky questions.

Let's consider the following example:

- Is the address 2001:3200:FADE:4000:0GH1:FDC1:FCCA:0658, a valid IPv6 address?

    INVALID. Hex numbers go up to the letter F.

    FE80::11FE:2E0A:9C35 INVALID. You need eight sections; here you only have six sections.

Now that we have got that out of the way, let's take a look at some IPv6 address types.

Address types

This information comes straight from https://www.ripe.net/:

Prefix	Designation and explanation	IPv4 equivalent
::/128	Unspecified. This address may only be used as a source address by an initializing host before it has learned its own address.	0.0.0.0

`::1/128`	Loopback.	`127.0.0.1`

`fc00::/7`	**Unique Local Addresses** (**ULAs**). These addresses are reserved for local use in home and enterprise environments and are not public-address spaces.	`10.0.0.0/8`
		`172.16.0.0/12`
		`192.168.0.0/16`

`fe80::/10`	Link-local addresses. These addresses are used on a single link or a non-routed common access network, such as an Ethernet LAN. They do not need to be unique outside of that link.	`169.254.0.0/16`
`2000::/3`	Global Unicast.	Equivalent to an IPv6 Address
`FF00::/8`	Multicast. These addresses are used to identify multicast groups. They should only be used as destination addresses, never as source addresses.	`224.0.0.0/4`

Special addresses

Address	Description
`0:0:0:0:0:0:0:0`	Can be expressed as `::`. This is the same as IPv4's `0.0.0.0` and is typically the source address of the host before the host receives an IP address when you are using DHCP stateful configuration.
`3FFF:FFFF::/32`	Reserved or examples and documentation.
`2001:0DB8::/32`	Also reserved for examples and documentation.
`2002::/16`	Used with 6-4 tunneling, which is a transition system in IPv6 that allows IPv6 packets to flow through an IPv4 network.

Working with IPv6 on your internetwork

In this section of the chapter, let's dive in and see how IPv6 works. I will discuss how to assign an IPv6 address on a PC and a router's interface. I will also discuss stateful and stateless configurations and I will explain ICMPv6, which has been totally revamped.

So, how do you start to configure IPv6 on your network? Well, you need to start assigning IPv6 addresses, but unlike your PCs, on the routers, you must type the following command: `ipv6-unicast routing`. This command will turn on the features you need to route in IPv6.

You could assign addresses manually, but if it is a large network; copy/paste, my friends. Let me show you an example:

```
interface FastEthernet0/0
 no ip address                    Interface ID
 duplex auto
 speed auto
 ipv6 address 2001:3200:BADD:1000::F/56
```

That address is not too bad to type out. If you look at the interface ID portion of the address, I got slick and used all zeros except for the last hex number. If I were to type that out, it would look like the following: `2001:3200:BADD:1000:0:0:0:F` or `2001:3200:BADD:1000:0000:0000:0000:000F`. The latter is not an option.

One of the new features for assigning the interface portion is that using `eui-64` allows you to use the MAC address of the interface to create the interface ID:

```
interface FastEthernet0/0
 no ip address
 duplex auto
 speed auto
 ipv6 address 2001:3200:1700:1000::/64 eui-64
```

The `eui-64` command at the end will create the interface ID, by using the MAC address of the interface and padding the MAC address using the FFFE, smack in the middle of the address:

```
R1#sh ipv6 route
IPv6 Routing Table - 3 entries
Codes: C - Connected, L - Local, S - Static, R - RIP, B - BGP
       U - Per-user Static route, M - MIPv6
       I1 - ISIS L1, I2 - ISIS L2, IA - ISIS interarea, IS - ISIS summary
       O - OSPF intra, OI - OSPF inter, OE1 - OSPF ext 1, OE2 - OSPF ext 2
       ON1 - OSPF NSSA ext 1, ON2 - OSPF NSSA ext 2
       D - EIGRP, EX - EIGRP external
C   2001:3200:1700:1000::/64 [0/0]
     via ::, FastEthernet0/0
L   2001:3200:1700:1000:2D0:FFFF:FE7D:9901/128 [0/0]  <-----
     via ::, FastEthernet0/0

                        The Padding
```

Stateless autoconfiguration using the EUI-64

Let me explain how the EUI-64 exactly created the interface ID address. It is a cool feature that a simple command typed after the network prefix and prefix length can generate an IP address.

The way the interface ID gets created is by using the 48 bit MAC address of the interface; but wait a minute, we said that the interface ID is 64 bits. If you are using the MAC address of the interface, you fall short by 16 bits. That is why EUI-64 pads the address with the FFFE to make up the 16 bits:

```
Actual MAC of the Interface:
R1#sh int f0/0
FastEthernet0/0 is up, line protocol is up (connected)
Hardware is Lance, address is 00d0.ff7d.9901
```

After the `eui-64` command is used, we get the following:

```
2001:3200:1700:1000:2D0:FFFF:FE7D:9901/128
```

Do you see where it padded the address? Now it becomes a 64-bit address that we can use on the interface.

But there is something funny about the generated address. The original address started with `00` and now after the `eui-64`, it starts with a `2`. Why was the number changed?

OK, get the coffee, Red Bull, whatever energy drink; you need time to do some math! Easy math though.

First of all we are going to focus our attention to the first two hex numbers of the MAC address we used, and we need to look at it in binary; don't go crazy; it will be OK, just stay with me. This is where your hex conversion knowledge will now come into play.

So the seventh bit of the MAC address, starting from left to right, is called the U/L bit, which will specify if the address is going to be a locally unique address or globally unique address. If it's going to be a global address, the seventh bit will be converted to a `1`; if not, it will be left alone.

Let's look at some examples:

MAC Address: **00**d0.ff7d.9901

Binary of first 2 hex numbers: 0000 00**0**0 The red bit is the 7th bit

After EUI-64 command: 0000:00**1**0 7th converted to a one, which the value is 2

Conclusion: **02**d0.ff7d.9901 (Remove the zero from the address) 2d0

MAC Address: **aa**812:bcbd:5678

Binary of first 2 hex numbers: 1010.10**1**0 The red bit is the 7th bit

After EUI-64 command: 1010.10**0**0   7th converted to a zero, which the value is 0

Conclusion: a**0**812 Remove the zero from the address) a812

MAC Address: **0b**0c:afed:deed

Binary of first 2 hex numbers: 0000.10**1**1 The red bit is the 7th bit

After EUI-64 command: 0000.10**0**1   7th bit converted to a zero, which the value is 0

Conclusion: **0**90c Remove the zero from the address) 90c

One of the main things you need to keep in mind here is your hex table and the values of each of the bits for each hex number:

Hex Table			Binary to decimal		
Letter	**Value**	**Binary**	**Binary**	**Value**	**Add Binary Bits ON**
A	10	1010	1010	8421	10
B	11	1011	1011	8421	11
C	12	1100	1100	8421	12
D	13	1101	1101	8421	13
E	14	1110	1110	8421	14
F	15	1111	1111	8421	15

Let's look at a diagram of this autoconfiguration feature:

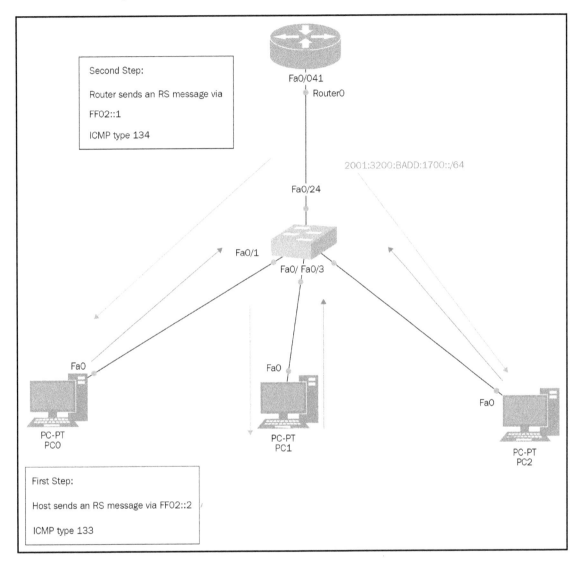

Let's look at the following table for the description of addresses:

Address	ICMP type	Description
FF02::2	133	Multicast address sent out to all routers. **Router Solicitation** (**RS**)
FF01::1	134	Message sent to all nodes. **Router Advertisement** (**RA**) (sent periodic basis)

So the autoconfiguration feature is really helpful, but there is still one more thing that it can do. You don't even have to type an IPv6 address at all; you could use the `ipv6 address autoconfiguration` command and it will configure a link-local address for you, which is globally significant.

Life just keeps getting better and better. Let's check it out:

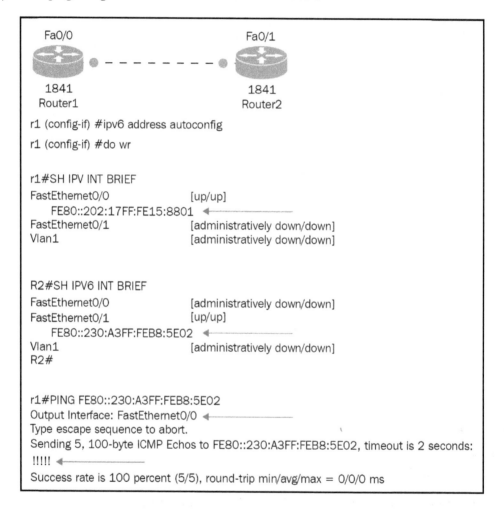

As you can see from the images, this type of configuration is extremely easy. It's known as **stateless autoconfiguration** because it does not contact to and receive any further information from the other device.

If you needed to route beyond the device you are connected to, you could always use a default route.

DHCPv6 stateful

DHCP servers have been around for a long time, and they're a pretty common practice in medium to large networks. The purpose for DHCP servers is to allocate IPv4 addresses, DSN addresses, gateway addresses, WINs, and a lot more options if needed. In DHCPv6 there is no difference; it works just like an IPv4 DHCP, but with obvious differences, such as the addresses and the way clients advertise to them.

In IPv4, clients send a discover message, which is in the form of a broadcast looking for a DHCP server to allocate an IP address. In IPv6, RA, and RS processes happens first, so if it finds a DHCP server for use, the RA will come back with the DHCP information to the client, but if does not find a DHCP server, all clients will respond with a DHCP solicit message, which is the following multicast address: ff02::1::2. This looks for all DHCP severs or relay agents on the network.

Although the autoconfiguration feature is a very simple and fast method to use, it lacks certain capabilities, such as assigning DNS servers, domain names, and pretty much most of the options that DHCP has to offer.

So DHCP is not going anywhere, for long time.

ICMPv6

This new version of the ICMP protocol is used for RS and RA and for NS and NA, which means it will be finding the MAC addresses for IPv6 neighbors and redirecting the host to the best router or default gateway.

ICMPv6 is not implemented as separate L3 protocol, but, it is an integrated part of IPv6 and is carried in an extension header, within the next header field of the IPv6 header.

By default, IPv6 is prevented from doing fragmentation through an ICMPv6 process called the MTU path:

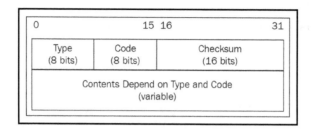

ICMPv6 types

Let's refer to the following table of ICMPv6 types and their descriptions:

ICMPv6 type	Description
1	Destination unreachable
128	Echo request
129	Echo reply
133	Router solicitation
134	Router advertisement
135	Neighbor solicitation
136	Neighbor advertisement

So how exactly does ICMPv6 work on the network? The source sends a packet that is equal to the MTU size of its local links. As it reaches the destination, for any link it finds with an MTU smaller than the originating source, it will send a `packet too big` message back to the source machine.

Neighbor Discovery Protocol (NDP)

As I mentioned before, ICMPv6 is used to find the address of other devices on the local link. Since IPv6, there is no ARP. We now have neighbor discovery inside ICMPv6. There is no more broadcast; it is now a multicast address called the **solicited-node address**.

The following are NDP-enabled functions:

- Determining the MAC address of neighbors

- Router Solicitation, or RS FF02::2
- Router Advertisements, or RA FF02::1
- Neighbor Solicitation, or NS
- Neighbor Advertisement
- Duplicate Address Detection, or DAD

In IPv6, the multicast address `FF02::1:FF/104` is referred to as a solicited node address, so when this address is used, the corresponding host will reply with its layer 2 address.

Also, the IGMP function that IPv4 used as multicast is now replaced by ICMPv6 and the new term is called **multicast listener discovery**. This is a really cool capability, with IPv6 having multiple gateways, without having to configure some redundancy protocol. Since now we have NDP, the host will send an RS to all routers using `FF02::2` and the routers on the same link will respond with a RA using `FF02::1`, so it can use whichever router that responds to it.

Look at the following diagram:

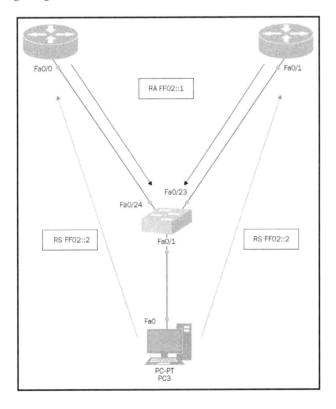

In the preceding diagram, the process would work as explained, but you cannot use stateless autoconfiguration, because you will be in the same FE80 network.

Let's look at the following example:

```
R1(config-if)#IPV6 ADDRESS AUTOCONFIG
R1#SH IPV6 INT BRIEF
FastEthernet0/0 [up/up]
FE80::2E0:B0FF:FEEC:9301
R2(config-if)#IPV6 ADDRESS AUTOCONFIG
R2#SH IPV6 INT BRIEF
FastEthernet0/0 [administratively down/down]
FastEthernet0/1 [up/up]
FE80::2E0:8FFF:FE0C:5102
C:\>IPCONFIG /ALL
FastEthernet0 Connection:(default port)
Connection-specific DNS Suffix..:
Physical Address.................: 00E0.A3E1.D093
Link-local IPv6 Address..........: FE80::2E0:A3FF:FEE1:D093
C:\>PING FE80::2E0:B0FF:FEEC:9301
Pinging FE80::2E0:B0FF:FEEC:9301 with 32 bytes of data:
Reply from FE80::2E0:B0FF:FEEC:9301: bytes=32 time<1ms TTL=255
Reply from FE80::2E0:B0FF:FEEC:9301: bytes=32 time<1ms TTL=255
Reply from FE80::2E0:B0FF:FEEC:9301: bytes=32 time<1ms TTL=255
Reply from FE80::2E0:B0FF:FEEC:9301: bytes=32 time<1ms TTL=255
C:\>PING FE80::2E0:8FFF:FE0C:5102
Pinging FE80::2E0:8FFF:FE0C:5102 with 32 bytes of data:
Reply from FE80::2E0:8FFF:FE0C:5102: bytes=32 time=1ms TTL=255
Reply from FE80::2E0:8FFF:FE0C:5102: bytes=32 time<1ms TTL=255
Reply from FE80::2E0:8FFF:FE0C:5102: bytes=32 time<1ms TTL=255
Reply from FE80::2E0:8FFF:FE0C:5102: bytes=32 time<1ms TTL=255
```

As you can see, you would get a reply to either one, because you are on the same link-local network.

Duplicate Address Detection (DAD)

OK, this is my favorite function of IPv6. When two end devices make up or receive an IPv6 address, they send DAD, using NDP NS to see if someone has the same address as they do. It is sent not once but three times. I'm all for troubleshooting, verifying, and so on, but when you have one IPv6 network that can hold 15 quintillion IPv6 addresses, the odds of duplicating the IP address are slim to non-existent.

But hey, we thank you for putting that functionality within IPv6.

Basic introduction to IPv6 routing

In this section, we will be discussing IPv6 static routing, default routes, and RIPng. They are pretty much the same thing except for the address and the way you would advertise the route.

When using static routes, you just simply use IPv6 addresses, and always remember to turn on the **IPv6 unicast-routing** so you can route in IPv6 and turn on the features on your router to support IPv6.

Let's look at an example of both static routing and default routing.

Topology

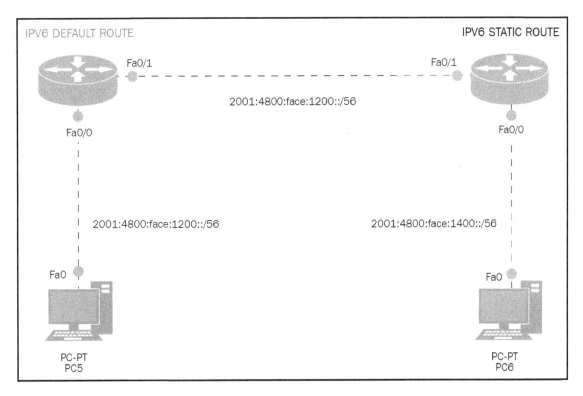

Router 1	Router 2
Interface fast Ethernet0/0	Interface fast Ethernet0/0
No IP address	No IP address
Duplex auto	Duplex auto
Speed auto	Speed auto
ipv6 address 2001:4800:FACE:1200::F/56	**ipv6 address 2001:4800:FACE:1400::F/56**
!	!
interface FastEthernet0/1	interface FastEthernet0/1
no ip address	no ip address
duplex auto	duplex auto
speed auto	speed auto
ipv6 address	ipv6 address
2001:4800:FACE:1000::1/56	**2001:4800:FACE:1000::2/56**

PC IP configurations

PC5	PC6
C:\>ipv6config	C:\>ipv6config
FastEthernet0 Connection:(default port)	FastEthernet0 Connection:(default port)
Link-local IPv6 Address.........: FE80::20A:41FF:FE72:8EC4	Link-local IPv6 Address.........: FE80::230:A3FF:FE11:4A
IPv6 Address...................: 2001:4800:FACE:1200::1/56	IPv6 Address...................: 2001:4800:FACE:1400::1/56
Default Gateway.................: **2001:4800:FACE:1200::F**	Default Gateway.................: **2001:4800:FACE:1400::F**

Before we even begin to route using default or static routes, we need to verify basic connectivity for PC to router and router to router, using the `ping` command:

```
R1#ping 2001:4800:face:1000::2
Type escape sequence to abort.
Sending 5, 100-byte ICMP Echos to 2001:4800:face:1000::2, timeout is 2
seconds:
!!!!!
Success rate is 100 percent (5/5), round-trip min/avg/max = 0/0/1 ms

PC5

C:\>ping 2001:4800:FACE:1200::F
```

```
Pinging 2001:4800:FACE:1200::F with 32 bytes of data:
Reply from 2001:4800:FACE:1200::F: bytes=32 time=1ms TTL=255
Reply from 2001:4800:FACE:1200::F: bytes=32 time<1ms TTL=255
Reply from 2001:4800:FACE:1200::F: bytes=32 time<1ms TTL=255
Reply from 2001:4800:FACE:1200::F: bytes=32 time<1ms TTL=255


PC6

C:\>PING 2001:4800:FACE:1400::F
Pinging 2001:4800:FACE:1400::F with 32 bytes of data:
Reply from 2001:4800:FACE:1400::F: bytes=32 time<1ms TTL=255
Reply from 2001:4800:FACE:1400::F: bytes=32 time<1ms TTL=255
Reply from 2001:4800:FACE:1400::F: bytes=32 time=4ms TTL=255
Reply from 2001:4800:FACE:1400::F: bytes=32 time<1ms TTL=255
```

Now that we have checked the basic connectivity, and all is good, we can begin with the routers that are going to have a default route. In IPv4, when creating a default route, you must use the following syntax: `ip route 0.0.0.0 0.0.0.0 f0/1`. But in IPv6, we express it the following way: `ipv6 route ::/0 f0/1`. This is much shorter thanks to the *leading zero* rule.

Let's go ahead and configure that on R1:

```
R1(config)#ipv6 route ?
X:X:X:X::X/<0-128>  IPv6 prefix
R1(config)#ipv6 route ::/0 2001:4800:FACE:1000::2
R1#sh ipv6 route
IPv6 Routing Table - 6 entries
Codes: C - Connected, L - Local, S - Static, R - RIP, B - BGP
U - Per-user Static route, M - MIPv6
I1 - ISIS L1, I2 - ISIS L2, IA - ISIS interarea, IS - ISIS summary
O - OSPF intra, OI - OSPF inter, OE1 - OSPF ext 1, OE2 - OSPF ext 2
ON1 - OSPF NSSA ext 1, ON2 - OSPF NSSA ext 2
D - EIGRP, EX - EIGRP external
S ::/0 [1/0]
via 2001:4800:FACE:1000::2
C 2001:4800:FACE:1000::/56 [0/0]
via ::, FastEthernet0/1
L 2001:4800:FACE:1000::1/128 [0/0]
via ::, FastEthernet0/1
C 2001:4800:FACE:1200::/56 [0/0]
via ::, FastEthernet0/0
L 2001:4800:FACE:1200::F/128 [0/0]
via ::, FastEthernet0/0
L FF00::/8 [0/0]
via ::, Null0
```

One thing to notice is that it does not say `Gateway of last resort`; it shows up as a normal static route. It does not even have an asterisk, but you are being specific as to where to send the packet.

Now let's go to R2 and configure a normal static route:

```
R2(config)#ipv6 route 2001:4800:face:1200::/56 2001:4800:face:1000::1
R2#sh ipv6 route
IPv6 Routing Table - 6 entries
Codes: C - Connected, L - Local, S - Static, R - RIP, B - BGP
U - Per-user Static route, M - MIPv6
I1 - ISIS L1, I2 - ISIS L2, IA - ISIS interarea, IS - ISIS summary
O - OSPF intra, OI - OSPF inter, OE1 - OSPF ext 1, OE2 - OSPF ext 2
ON1 - OSPF NSSA ext 1, ON2 - OSPF NSSA ext 2
D - EIGRP, EX - EIGRP external
C 2001:4800:FACE:1000::/56 [0/0]
via ::, FastEthernet0/1
L 2001:4800:FACE:1000::2/128 [0/0]
via ::, FastEthernet0/1
 S 2001:4800:FACE:1200::/56 [1/0]
 via 2001:4800:FACE:1000::1
C 2001:4800:FACE:1400::/56 [0/0]
via ::, FastEthernet0/0
L 2001:4800:FACE:1400::F/128 [0/0]
via ::, FastEthernet0/0
L FF00::/8 [0/0]
via ::, Null0
```

Now that we have our configurations, let's do a test to see if we can ping from PC6 to PC5:

```
C:\>PING 2001:4800:FACE:1200::1
Pinging 2001:4800:FACE:1200::1 with 32 bytes of data:
Reply from 2001:4800:FACE:1200::1: bytes=32 time<1ms TTL=126
Reply from 2001:4800:FACE:1200::1: bytes=32 time<1ms TTL=126
Reply from 2001:4800:FACE:1200::1: bytes=32 time<1ms TTL=126
Reply from 2001:4800:FACE:1200::1: bytes=32 time<1ms TTL=126
```

Since we are using Fast Ethernet connections, when creating the static routes or default routes, we must be very specific about which network and interface we are sending them to. If it would be serial, it would be a point-to-point connection, not a multi-point, and we could have used the exit interface.

Yes, even though your router will accept the command, your pings will never work.

Using RIPng

Using static routes is fine for small networks, especially if you're using IPv6. That is a big address to be typing repeatedly. Remember that in static routes, the burden is on you to put in or take out any static routes as they change, so dynamic routing is the way to go.

RIPng is the same as in IPv4, when it comes to its characteristics. It is still a distance vector routing protocol, which means it will send periodic updates every 30 seconds. It still has a 15-hop count limitation and the timers are still the same.

What has changed is the multicast address. It is FF02::9 instead of 224.0.0.9, and as far as the configuration of RIPng goes, to be honest, it is much easier. You do not have to be worried about the no auto-summary command and you can enable RIPng on the interface that you want to participate in the RIP routing process. RIPng has a process ID number, which it did not have before.

So, the only changes are really the addresses and how they are configured. So, let's go ahead and look at our topology and configure RIPng.

Topology for RIPng

The only difference from the static and default route topology is that we are using serial cables across our network instead of Fast Ethernet. The configurations are still the same as far as the IP address is concerned:

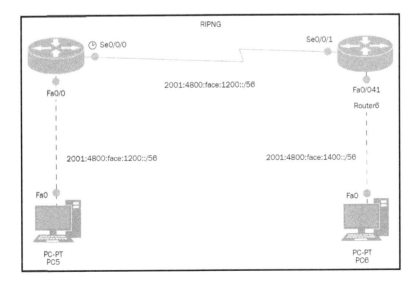

The default route and static routes have been removed, so we can configure our routing protocol:

```
R1(config)#int s0/0/0
R1(config-if)#ipv6 rip 1 enable
R1(config-if)#int f0/0
R1(config-if)#ipv6 rip 1 enable
```

That is all you really need to do, but if you check the startup-config, you will see what was created automatically by simply enabling RIPng on an interface. If you do a show start and scroll down toward the bottom, this is what you would see:

```
ipv6 router rip 1
```

We will configure the second router the longer way:

```
R2(config)#ipv6 router rip ?
WORD User selected string identifying this process
R2(config)#ipv6 router rip 1
R2(config-rtr)#?
distance Administrative distance
exit Exit from routing protocol configuration mode
no Negate a command or set its defaults
redistribute Redistribute IPv6 prefixes from another routing protocol
R2(config-rtr)#
```

If you create the process first, you no need to go to each interface and enable that RIP routing process. Notice that there is no network command and no need for a no auto-summary in IPv6:

```
R2(config)#int s0/0/1
R2(config-if)#ipv6 rip 1 enable
R2(config-if)#int f0/0
R2(config-if)#ipv6 rip 1 enable
```

After configuring both routers with RIPng, we want to verify that our routing table is being created by using RIP routes:

```
R2#sh ipv6 route
IPv6 Routing Table - 6 entries
Codes: C - Connected, L - Local, S - Static, R - RIP, B - BGP
U - Per-user Static route, M - MIPv6
I1 - ISIS L1, I2 - ISIS L2, IA - ISIS interarea, IS - ISIS summary
O - OSPF intra, OI - OSPF inter, OE1 - OSPF ext 1, OE2 - OSPF ext 2
ON1 - OSPF NSSA ext 1, ON2 - OSPF NSSA ext 2
D - EIGRP, EX - EIGRP external
C 2001:4800:FACE:1000::/56 [0/0]
via ::, Serial0/0/1
```

```
L 2001:4800:FACE:1000::2/128 [0/0]
via ::, Serial0/0/1
R 2001:4800:FACE:1200::/56 [120/2]
via FE80::2D0:97FF:FED7:A601, Serial0/0/1
C 2001:4800:FACE:1400::/56 [0/0]
via ::, FastEthernet0/0
L 2001:4800:FACE:1400::F/128 [0/0]
via ::, FastEthernet0/0
L FF00::/8 [0/0]
via ::, Null0
```

As you can see, we are learning about the 2001:4800:FACE:1200::/56 network. But can we ping?

```
R2#ping 2001:4800:FACE:1200::f
Type the escape sequence to abort.
Sending five, 100-byte ICMP echos to 2001:4800:FACE:1200::f, timeout is 2
seconds:
!!!!!
The success rate is 100 percent (5/5), round-trip min/avg/max = 3/7/25 ms:
R2#ping 2001:4800:FACE:1200::1
Type the escape sequence to abort.
Sending five, 100-byte ICMP echos to 2001:4800:FACE:1200::1, timeout is 2
seconds:
!!!!!
The success rate is 100 percent (5/5), round-trip min/avg/max = 1/5/15 ms.
```

So we can ping the gateway for the 1200 network and the end device as well. Finally, let's do a debug IPv6 ND so we can see neighbor discovery at work:

```
R2#debug ipv6 nd
ICMP Neighbor Discovery events debugging is on.
```

Ping from PC6 to PC5:

```
R2#*Mar 1 00:36:38.564: ICMPv6-ND: Received NS for 2001:4800:FACE:1400::F
on FastEthernet0/0 from 2001:4800:FACE:1400::1
*Mar 1 00:36:38.564: ICMPv6-ND: Sending NA for 2001:4800:FACE:1400::F on
FastEthernet0/0
```

Summary

In this chapter, we learned about the IPv6 routed protocol. We learned a little history about IP and how it benefits us, by creating a true hierarchy of IPv6 networks, which will allow our backbone or internet routers' routing table, to become more streamlined and efficient.

We also learned that IPv6 is a giant IP address, and that it is in hex format. But thanks to the powers that be, they gave us a way to express the IPv6 address in a lot shorter way by using the *leading zero* rule, but don't forget you can only have one double colon in an IPv6 address.

We also took the time to dive deep into the header of IPv6 and ICMPv6 and explain how important ICMPv6 is and the role that it plays in our network. We also delved into the `autoconfiguration` commands and saw how they work, if we want to be lazy with our configurations. Just keep in mind that with autoconfiguration, or stales configuration, you do not have the options you would have with DHCPv6, or V4, for that matter.

Finally, we configured our default, static, and dynamic routes. As usual, typing out those IPv6 addresses is a huge pain and even with a default route, since we were using Fast Ethernet ports, we had to be very specific when we created the routes. That is why you saw how simple it is to configure RIPng; all you really must do is enable it on the interface of your choosing.

Now, you just need to practice and keep practicing until it becomes second nature. See you in the next chapter.

Introduction to IPv6 Routing

11

In the previous chapter, we gained a good foundation regarding the IPv6 Protocol, its features, addressing, and the different ways we can route. We also discussed and configured default, static, and dynamic routing using RIPng.

We will be covering the following topics in this chapter:

- The benefits of using dynamic routing
- How to configure EIGRP for IPv6, including the topology
- How to configure OSPFv3, including the following:
    - The tables it forms
    - Manipulating the administrative distance

Benefits of dynamic routing

One thing about routing that we need to keep in mind when we are deciding to configure dynamic routing in our network, is the convergence time and how quickly our routers can learn about each other's networks. The reason for this is that we need to take in to account some factors such as the following:

- The limitations or the features that the routing protocol is offering.
- Our own network limitations, such as: bandwidth and how many routers are the packets going to traverse. Are our routers up for the job? Are the routers beefy? And what is the percentage of the traffic being used across wide area connections?

So, as you can see, it is not just about choosing the easiest or most popular routing protocol. You must choose a routing protocol that can meet the demands of your network. With that said, it could be a combination of protocols or types of routing.

You may decide to use default routes on your stub/edge routers, which creates the `Gateway of last resort` so that packets do not get dropped and then configure static routes with a higher AD than the routing protocol being used. They can then act as a backup route and you can configure a routing protocol based on your network needs. It could also be a combination of IPv4 and IPv6 because you are transitioning over to IPv6.

Routing must be an informed, intelligent, and a logical decision. Always keep in mind the needs of our network. Let's create a table of routing protocols that would give us a basic understanding of which routing protocols would best suit our network to run efficiently and with some redundancy:

Routing Protocol	Type of Routing	Size of Network	Advantages	Dis-advantages
RIP(IPv4)	Dynamic DV	Small	Easy to configure and uses multicast for updates	Limited to 15 hops and choose the most direct route, not considering Bandwidth or load of that line.
EIGRP(IPv4)	Dynamic DV	Medium/Large	Scalable for larger networks. Excellent for complex networks. Choose best path based on Bandwidth and delay	Limited to 100 hops by default but it can go up to 255. EIGRP use to be proprietary to Cisco Only but that has changed. http://www.cisco.com/go/eigrp
OSPF(IPv4)	Dynamic LS	Enterprise	Extremely scalable for enterprise networks. It is aware of its complete topology, so it can calculate routes much better. No limitations	Due to the algorithm that it uses to calculate routes, it is processor and memory intensive.
RIPng	Dynamic DV	Small	Same as IPv4, , except different configuration	Same as IPv4
EIGRP(IPv6)	Dynamic DV	Medium/Large	Same as IPv4, except different configuration	Same as IPv4
OSPFv3	Dynamic LS	Enterprise	Same as IPv4, except different configuration	Same as IPv4
S routes	Static	Small	Takes up no bandwidth, processing on the router and it is more secure, because you are complete control of the routing process.	Too much administrative overhead, so on a large scale, very hard to administer.

The preceding table is just a very basic guideline when you start routing in your company. Believe me, it gets a lot deeper than that, but luckily for us, this book is geared to CCNA topics; but look for those real-world issues also.

One last thing you should also ask yourself before you begin purchasing routers and start configuring routing is: do you need to route? Some companies just need an internet connection and that is that; they don't have branch offices or anything like that. That's something to think about.

Before I end this section, I would like to add one more thing: topologies. When referring to *network needs*, the topology is also a variable you need to consider. Take a look at the following topologies:

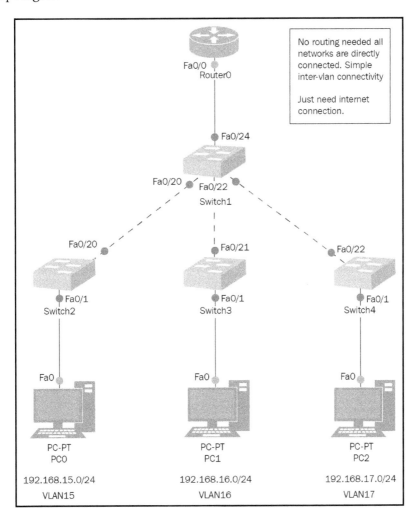

In the Dual Stack lab, you can put default routes at the end routers and static routes in the middle router, with a higher AD than the routing protocol you're going to use. Use static routes as backup routes. Use whichever routing protocol you prefer on all routers.

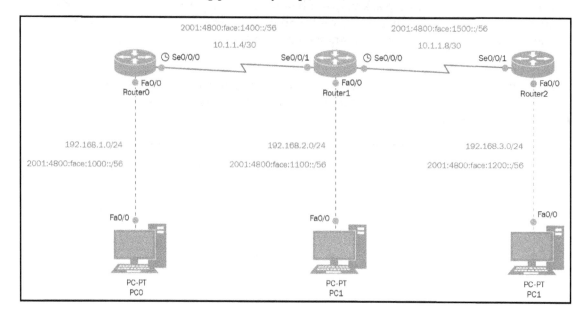

Configuring IPv6 routing

For the following IPv6 configurations, we will be using the following simple topology:

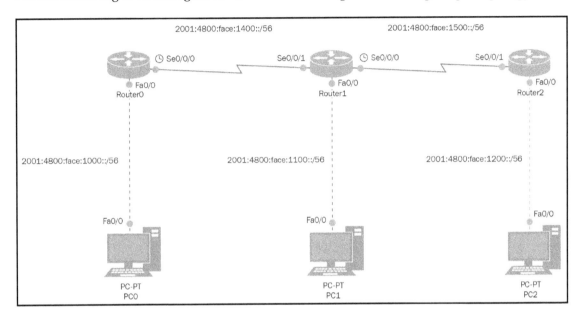

We have five networks, three LANs, and two WANs. You can see the IPv6 addressing scheme that we are using. The IPv6 addresses that you see are only the network prefix with the prefix length, so we are going to put those IPv6 addresses manually on the routers and PCs.

Let's start with the PCs and then move to the routers. I personally like to assign the IP addresses first, test for basic connectivity, and then dive deep and start the routing configurations:

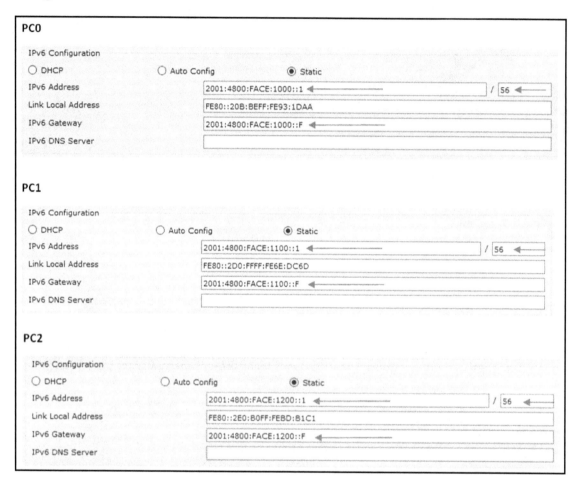

The IPv6 addresses that you see are the ones that I assigned. I am using the rule of zero. If we do not do that, then we would have to type the following:

    2001:4800:FACE:1000:0000:0000:0000:0001

Not happening! So, I took out all the leading zeros.

As mentioned in the previous chapter, the interface ID does not really matter. You could have a combination of hexadecimal numbers randomly chosen. If you remember, we can have 15 quintillion addresses per network.

The reason you see a /56 is because I subnetted the address. If I had made an error, it would not accept the address, just like for IPv4 addressing.

That took care of the PCs. Now, we must go into the routers and configure the interfaces with IPv6 addresses. But before you start doing anything to do with with IPv6 on a router, you must type the following command in the global configuration on all routers:

```
R1#config t
Enter configuration commands, one per line. End with CNTL/Z.
R1(config)#ipv6 unicast-routing
R2#conf t
Enter configuration commands, one per line. End with CNTL/Z.
R2(config)#ipv6 unicast-routing
R3#conf t
Enter configuration commands, one per line. End with CNTL/Z.
R3(config)#ipv6 unicast-routing
```

Now that we have turned on IPv6 routing and any feature that deals with IPv6, we can begin to type the IPv6 addresses on the routers' interfaces. One main difference with assigning IPv6 addresses on router interfaces is that a router can have multiple IPv6 addresses in the same interface. You cannot simply override the address; you must take the unwanted IPv6 address out and then put in a new one.

Please look at the following example:

```
Interface FastEthernet0/0
ipv6 address 2001:3200:BADD:1000::/64 eui-64 (generate an IPv6 address)
ipv6 address 2001:4800:FACE:1200::F/56    (statically assigned an address)
```

So, if you fat-finger the keyboard and assign the wrong IPv6 address, it still takes it; you will have to take it out manually using the no command. Let's begin the interface configuration:

```
R1(config)#INT F0/0
R1(config-if)# IPV6 ADDRESS 2001:4800:FACE:1000::F/56
R1(config-if)#NO SHUT
R1(config)#INT S0/0/0
R1(config-if)# IPV6 ADDRESS 2001:4800:FACE:1400::1/56
R1(config-if)#CLOCK RATE   4000000
R1(config-if)#NO SHUT
R2(config)#INT F0/0
R2(config-if)# IPV6 ADDRESS 2001:4800:FACE:1100::F/56
```

```
R2(config-if)#NO SHUT
R2(config)#INT S0/0/1
R2(config-if)# IPV6 ADDRESS 2001:4800:FACE:1400::2/56
R2(config-if)#NO SHUT
R2(config)#INT S0/0/0
R2(config-if)# IPV6 ADDRESS 2001:4800:FACE:1500::1/56
R2(config-if)#CLOCK RATE  4000000
R2(config-if)#NO SHUT
R3(config)#INT S0/0/1
R3(config-if)# IPV6 ADDRESS 2001:4800:FACE:1500::2/56
R3(config-if)#CLOCK RATE  4000000
R3(config-if)#NO SHUT
R3(config)#INT F0/0
R3(config-if)# IPV6 ADDRESS 2001:4800:FACE:1200::F/56
R3(config-if)#NO SHUT
```

Once we finish configuring the IPv6 address of all the router interfaces, you need to verify several ways using the following show commands:

```
Show ipv6 int brief
Show ipv6 route
Ping 2001:4800:FACE:1100::F (This address would be the farthest from where
you are)
```

Let's see what that would look like:

```
R1#SH IPV6 INT BRIEF
FastEthernet0/0 [up/up]          This is what you want to see UP/UP
FE80::206:2AFF:FEB3:C501         Link Local Address
2001:4800:FACE:1000::F           Actual Address Assigned to interface
FastEthernet0/1 [administratively down/down]
Serial0/0/0 [up/up]
FE80::206:2AFF:FEB3:C501         Link Local Address
2001:4800:FACE:1400::1           Actual Address Assigned to interface
Serial0/0/1 [administratively down/down]
R2#SH IPV6 INT BRIEF
FastEthernet0/0 [up/up]
FE80::290:CFF:FE36:2301
2001:4800:FACE:1100::F
FastEthernet0/1 [administratively down/down]
Serial0/0/0 [up/up]
FE80::290:CFF:FE36:2301
2001:4800:FACE:1500::1
Serial0/0/1 [up/up]
FE80::290:CFF:FE36:2301
2001:4800:FACE:1400::2
R3# SH IPV6 INT BRIEF
FastEthernet0/0 [up/up]
```

```
FE80::290:2BFF:FE18:8A01
2001:4800:FACE:1200::F
FastEthernet0/1 [administratively down/down]
FE80::290:2BFF:FE18:8A02
Serial0/0/0 [administratively down/down]
Serial0/0/1 [up/up]
FE80::290:2BFF:FE18:8A01
2001:4800:FACE:1500::2
Serial0/1/0 [down/down]
```

This shows us that the interfaces are up and working with the appropriate IPv6 address we assigned. Always remember that the link local address will exist on every interface. Let's move on to the next command:

```
R1#SH IPV6 ROUTE
C 2001:4800:FACE:1000::/56 [0/0]      (Network you are attached to)
via ::, FastEthernet0/0
L 2001:4800:FACE:1000::F/128 [0/0]   (IP of the connected interface)
via ::, FastEthernet0/0
C 2001:4800:FACE:1400::/56 [0/0]      (Network you are attached to)
via ::, Serial0/0/0
L 2001:4800:FACE:1400::1/128 [0/0]    (IP of the connected interface)
via ::, Serial0/0/0
R2#SH IPV6 ROUTE
C 2001:4800:FACE:1100::/56 [0/0]
via ::, FastEthernet0/0
L 2001:4800:FACE:1100::F/128 [0/0]
via ::, FastEthernet0/0
C 2001:4800:FACE:1400::/56 [0/0]
via ::, Serial0/0/1
L 2001:4800:FACE:1400::2/128 [0/0]
via ::, Serial0/0/1
C 2001:4800:FACE:1500::/56 [0/0]
via ::, Serial0/0/0
L 2001:4800:FACE:1500::1/128 [0/0]
via ::, Serial0/0/0
R3#SH IPV6 ROUTE
C 2001:3200:BADD:1000::/64 [0/0]
via ::, FastEthernet0/0
L 2001:3200:BADD:1000:290:2BFF:FE18:8A01/128 [0/0]
via ::, FastEthernet0/0
C 2001:4800:FACE:1200::/56 [0/0]
via ::, FastEthernet0/0
L 2001:4800:FACE:1200::F/128 [0/0]
via ::, FastEthernet0/0
```

We just verified that we do have an actual routing table, only to directly connected networks, but that is OK, as we have not configured any routing yet. We are creating the foundation where we are going to do our routing.

One last thing we want to verify is connectivity between directly connected devices. We will now use the `ping` command to verify connectivity:

```
PC0
C:\>PING 2001:4800:FACE:1000::F
Pinging 2001:4800:FACE:1000::F with 32 bytes of data:
Reply from 2001:4800:FACE:1000::F: bytes=32 time<1ms TTL=255
Reply from 2001:4800:FACE:1000::F: bytes=32 time<1ms TTL=255
Reply from 2001:4800:FACE:1000::F: bytes=32 time<1ms TTL=255
Reply from 2001:4800:FACE:1000::F: bytes=32 time<1ms TTL=255
PC1
C:\>PING 2001:4800:FACE:1100::F
Pinging 2001:4800:FACE:1100::F with 32 bytes of data:
Reply from 2001:4800:FACE:1100::F: bytes=32 time<1ms TTL=255
Reply from 2001:4800:FACE:1100::F: bytes=32 time<1ms TTL=255
Reply from 2001:4800:FACE:1100::F: bytes=32 time<1ms TTL=255
Reply from 2001:4800:FACE:1100::F: bytes=32 time<1ms TTL=255
PC2
C:\>PING 2001:4800:FACE:1200::F
Pinging 2001:4800:FACE:1200::F with 32 bytes of data:
Reply from 2001:4800:FACE:1200::F: bytes=32 time<1ms TTL=255
Reply from 2001:4800:FACE:1200::F: bytes=32 time<1ms TTL=255
Reply from 2001:4800:FACE:1200::F: bytes=32 time<1ms TTL=255
Reply from 2001:4800:FACE:1200::F: bytes=32 time<1ms TTL=255
```

We have connectivity to our gateway. Awesome! Now, we check the router-to-router connectivity:

```
R1#ping 2001:4800:face:1400::2
Type escape sequence to abort.
Sending 5, 100-byte ICMP Echos to 2001:4800:face:1400::2, timeout is 2
seconds:
!!!!!
Success rate is 100 percent (5/5), round-trip min/avg/max = 4/7/16 ms
R3#ping 2001:4800:face:1500::1
Type escape sequence to abort.
Sending 5, 100-byte ICMP Echos to 2001:4800:face:1500::1, timeout is 2
seconds:
!!!!!
Success rate is 100 percent (5/5), round-trip min/avg/max = 1/4/14 ms
```

OK, we have connectivity between our connected devices. Now, let's start routing. We will be configuring EIGRP for IPv6 and OSPFv3.

Configuring EIGRP for IPv6

The only difference between EIGRP and EIGRP for IPv6 is the configuration. But, it still has all the features that we normally use. One good thing that Cisco has done with EIGRP is that it is *not* proprietary to Cisco. It is now an open standard. Refer to the following page: http://www.cisco.com/go/eigrp.

```
R1(config)#ipv6 router eigrp 500
R1(config-rtr)#?
eigrp     EIGRP specific commands
exit       Exit from routing protocol configuration mode
metric    Modify EIGRP routing metrics and parameters
neighbor  Specify a neighbor router
no         Negate a command or set its defaults
passive-interface   Suppress routing updates on an interface
redistribute         Redistribute IPv6 prefixes from another routing
protocol
shutdown            Shutdown protocol
variance             Control load balancing variance
R1(config-rtr)#
```

When configuring any routing protocol in IPv6, you will always start with the IPv6 suffix. With this version of EIGRP, when you are in router configuration mode, all you are interested in are the two commands highlighted.

The shutdown command turns the protocol on and the eigrp subcommand makes you put in a router ID in IPv4 format:

```
R1(config-rtr)#no shutdown
R1(config-rtr)#eigrp router-id 10.10.10.10
R1(config-rtr)#
```

Once you have done those commands in the router configuration mode, all you have to do now is go into the interface you want to participate in the eigrp 500 autonomous system:

```
R1(config-rtr)#int f0/0
R1(config-if)#ipv6 eigrp 500
R1(config-if)#
```

You would repeat this process in every interface that you want to participate in the EIGRP autonomous system `500`.

But we must verify that EIGRP is working using the `sh ipv6 route` command:

```
R1#sh ipv6 route
IPv6 Routing Table - 9 entries
Codes: C - Connected, L - Local, S - Static, R - RIP, B - BGP
U - Per-user Static route, M - MIPv6
I1 - ISIS L1, I2 - ISIS L2, IA - ISIS interarea, IS - ISIS summary
O - OSPF intra, OI - OSPF inter, OE1 - OSPF ext 1, OE2 - OSPF ext 2
ON1 - OSPF NSSA ext 1, ON2 - OSPF NSSA ext 2
D - EIGRP, EX - EIGRP external
D 2001:3200:BADD:1000::/64 [90/2684416]
via FE80::290:CFF:FE36:2301, Serial0/0/0
C 2001:4800:FACE:1000::/56 [0/0]
via ::, FastEthernet0/0
L 2001:4800:FACE:1000::F/128 [0/0]
via ::, FastEthernet0/0
D 2001:4800:FACE:1100::/56 [90/2172416]
via FE80::290:CFF:FE36:2301, Serial0/0/0
D 2001:4800:FACE:1200::/56 [90/2684416]
via FE80::290:CFF:FE36:2301, Serial0/0/0
C 2001:4800:FACE:1400::/56 [0/0]
via ::, Serial0/0/0
L 2001:4800:FACE:1400::1/128 [0/0]
via ::, Serial0/0/0
D 2001:4800:FACE:1500::/56 [90/2681856]
via FE80::290:CFF:FE36:2301, Serial0/0/0
L FF00::/8 [0/0]
R2#sh ipv6 route
IPv6 Routing Table - 10 entries
Codes: C - Connected, L - Local, S - Static, R - RIP, B - BGP
U - Per-user Static route, M - MIPv6
I1 - ISIS L1, I2 - ISIS L2, IA - ISIS interarea, IS - ISIS summary
O - OSPF intra, OI - OSPF inter, OE1 - OSPF ext 1, OE2 - OSPF ext 2
ON1 - OSPF NSSA ext 1, ON2 - OSPF NSSA ext 2
D - EIGRP, EX - EIGRP external
D 2001:3200:BADD:1000::/64 [90/2172416]
via FE80::290:2BFF:FE18:8A01, Serial0/0/0
D 2001:4800:FACE:1000::/56 [90/2172416]
via FE80::206:2AFF:FEB3:C501, Serial0/0/1
C 2001:4800:FACE:1100::/56 [0/0]
via ::, FastEthernet0/0
L 2001:4800:FACE:1100::F/128 [0/0]
via ::, FastEthernet0/0
D 2001:4800:FACE:1200::/56 [90/2172416]
via FE80::290:2BFF:FE18:8A01, Serial0/0/0
```

```
C 2001:4800:FACE:1400::/56 [0/0]
via ::, Serial0/0/1
L 2001:4800:FACE:1400::2/128 [0/0]
via ::, Serial0/0/1
C 2001:4800:FACE:1500::/56 [0/0]
via ::, Serial0/0/0
L 2001:4800:FACE:1500::1/128 [0/0]
via ::, Serial0/0/0
L FF00::/8 [0/0]
R3#sh ipv6 route
IPv6 Routing Table - 10 entries
Codes: C - Connected, L - Local, S - Static, R - RIP, B - BGP
U - Per-user Static route, M - MIPv6
I1 - ISIS L1, I2 - ISIS L2, IA - ISIS interarea, IS - ISIS summary
O - OSPF intra, OI - OSPF inter, OE1 - OSPF ext 1, OE2 - OSPF ext 2
ON1 - OSPF NSSA ext 1, ON2 - OSPF NSSA ext 2
D - EIGRP, EX - EIGRP external
C 2001:3200:BADD:1000::/64 [0/0]
via ::, FastEthernet0/0
L 2001:3200:BADD:1000:290:2BFF:FE18:8A01/128 [0/0]
via ::, FastEthernet0/0
D 2001:4800:FACE:1000::/56 [90/2684416]
via FE80::290:CFF:FE36:2301, Serial0/0/1
D 2001:4800:FACE:1100::/56 [90/2172416]
via FE80::290:CFF:FE36:2301, Serial0/0/1
C 2001:4800:FACE:1200::/56 [0/0]
via ::, FastEthernet0/0
L 2001:4800:FACE:1200::F/128 [0/0]
via ::, FastEthernet0/0
D 2001:4800:FACE:1400::/56 [90/2681856]
via FE80::290:CFF:FE36:2301, Serial0/0/1
C 2001:4800:FACE:1500::/56 [0/0]
via ::, Serial0/0/1
L 2001:4800:FACE:1500::2/128 [0/0]
via ::, Serial0/0/1
L FF00::/8 [0/0]
```

Even though we verified that we are getting updates from destination networks through EIGRP, we still need to verify that we can get to the destination networks by simply pinging an IP address of a destination network:

```
R1#ping 2001:4800:FACE:1200::1
Type escape sequence to abort.
Sending 5, 100-byte ICMP Echos to 2001:4800:FACE:1200::1, timeout is 2
seconds:
!!!!!
Success rate is 100 percent (5/5), round-trip min/avg/max = 3/7/13 ms
R1#ping 2001:4800:FACE:1100::1
Type escape sequence to abort.
Sending 5, 100-byte ICMP Echos to 2001:4800:FACE:1100::1, timeout is 2
seconds:
!!!!!
Success rate is 100 percent (5/5), round-trip min/avg/max = 1/3/14 ms
```

I chose R1 to ping the destination PC's IP address and, as you can see, I have connectivity to both networks.

But EIGRP for both IPv4 and IPv6 has the same features, like the topology table, which you cannot ignore. Basically, the topology table holds all the routes learned, but based on the metrics, it designates a *successor route* and *a feasible successor route*. The feasible successor, which has a higher metric, will remain in the topology table as a backup route and the successor route will be placed in the routing table as the best and fastest path to the destination network, since it has a lower metric.

EIGRP uses what is called K values to determine this metric among other variables, which will be discussed in detail in a later chapter. These values are bandwidth, delay, reliability, load, and MTU. The latter is debatable; some believe it makes a difference, others do not. The main K values that you need to be concerned for the CCNA certification are bandwidth and delay.

Let's take a quick look at the topology table:

```
R2#sh ipv6 eigrp topology
IPv6-EIGRP Topology Table for AS 400/ID(2.2.2.2)
Codes: P - Passive, A - Active, U - Update, Q - Query, R - Reply,
r - Reply status
P 2001:4800:FACE:1000::/56, 1 successors, FD is 2172416
via FE80::206:2AFF:FEB3:C501 (2172416/28160), Serial0/0/1
P 2001:4800:FACE:1100::/56, 1 successors, FD is 28160
via Connected, FastEthernet0/0
P 2001:4800:FACE:1200::/56, 1 successors, FD is 2172416
```

```
via FE80::290:2BFF:FE18:8A01 (2172416/28160), Serial0/0/0
P 2001:4800:FACE:1400::/56, 1 successors, FD is 2169856
via Connected, Serial0/0/1
P 2001:4800:FACE:1500::/56, 1 successors, FD is 2169856
via Connected, Serial0/0/0
```

To give you a brief explanation as to what you are looking at, let me explain the two most important things to look at. The metrics in this topology to the destination networks, which are the `1000` and `1200`, are the same, so there is no feasible successor, since there is only one way you could go. The letter `P` stands for **passive**, which means, *Hey! I am done looking for destination networks*.

If you ever see the letter `A`, which stands for **active**, that is a problem, because it is still *actively* looking for the destination network.

OK, that is EIGRP in IPv6 for now. Let's move on to OSPF.

Configuring OSPFv3

Using the Topology shown, we will configure the Routing Protocol OSPFv3:

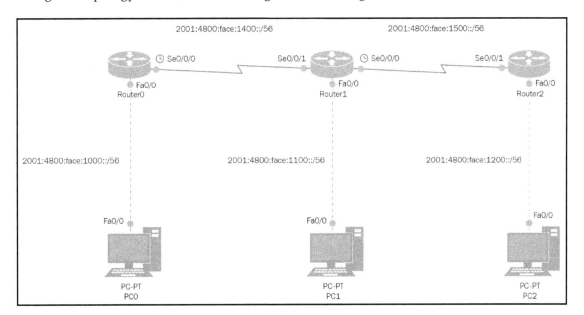

Once again, we will be using the same topology, since we already have the IPv6 addresses in place and we know we have connectivity throughout the network. We are simply going to change the routing protocol to OSPF.

This presents an interesting situation, not only for your certification but for real-world scenarios as well. Let's analyze this more closely. We already have EIGRP for IPv6 working fine, but your boss wants you to use OSPFv3, so what do you do?, so what is the issue? The issue is the **administrative distance (AD)** of the routing protocols. EIGRP has an AD of 90, while OSPF has an AD of 110, so that means if we don't change the AD of OSPF to something lower than EIGRP, OSPF will never make it to the routing table. Removing EIGRP completely before you have another routing protocol in place is not the solution, unless you have static routes configured as backups and you can prove that you would not lose connectivity in your network.

Something like this should never be done during normal working hours. You would do it between midnight and 6 a.m., and this time is called **maintenance hours**. If something goes wrong, you can fix it before anyone comes in to work, hopefully.

So, let's go ahead and configure OSPFv3:

```
R1(config)#ipv6 router ospf 2
R1(config-rtr)#?
area                OSPF area parameters
auto-cost           Calculate OSPF interface cost according to bandwidth
default-information Distribution of default information
distance            Administrative distance
exit                Exit from routing protocol configuration mode
log-adjacency-changes Log changes in adjacency state
no                  Negate a command or set its defaults
passive-interface   Suppress routing updates on an interface
redistribute        Redistribute information from another routing protocol
router-id           router-id for this OSPF process
```

Once you create the OSPF process, which in this case is the number 2, all you need to do is to give the router a router-id, which is the name of the router in IPv4 addressing format:

```
R1(config)#ipv6 router ospf 2 R1(config-rtr)#router-id 1.1.1.1
```

When you complete doing that, all you need to do now is enable OSPF in the interfaces you want to participate in the OSPF process and area. Yes, that is where you actually put the area command and area 0 is always the first area you will create. This is your backbone area and everyone must connect back to area 0:

```
R1(config-rtr)#int f0/0
R1(config-if)#ipv6 ospf 2 area 0
R1(config-if)#int s0/0/0
```

```
R1(config-if)#ipv6 ospf 2 area 0
R2(config)#ipv6 router ospf 2
R2(config-rtr)#router-id 2.2.2.2
R2(config-if)#int s0/0/0
R2(config-if)#ipv6 ospf 2 area 0
R2(config-if)#int f0/0
R2(config-if)#ipv6 ospf 2 area 0
R2(config-if)#int s0/0/1
R2(config-if)#ipv6 ospf 2 area 0
R2(config-if)#
19:55:20: %OSPFv3-5-ADJCHG: Process 2, Nbr 1.1.1.1 on Serial0/0/1 from
LOADING to FULL, Loading Done (This is what you want to see when
configuring OSPF)
R3(config)#ipv6 router ospf 2
R3(config-rtr)#router-id 3.3.3.3
R3(config-rtr)#int f0/0
R3(config-if)#ipv6 ospf 2 area 0
R3(config-if)#int s0/0/1
R3(config-if)#ipv6 ospf 2 area 0
R3(config-if)#
19:59:38: %OSPFv3-5-ADJCHG: Process 2, Nbr 2.2.2.2 on Serial0/0/1 from
LOADING to FULL, Loading Done
```

Now that we have configured OSPFv3 on all our routers and seen that OSPF did go through the process of discovering all its neighbors, because we saw the Full Loading Done feedback from the router, we must verify our routing table to make sure that OSPF made it to the routing table. At this moment, keep in mind the AD of OSPF is 110 by default:

```
R3#sh ipv6 route
IPv6 Routing Table - 10 entries
Codes: C - Connected, L - Local, S - Static, R - RIP, B - BGP
U - Per-user Static route, M - MIPv6
I1 - ISIS L1, I2 - ISIS L2, IA - ISIS interarea, IS - ISIS summary
O - OSPF intra, OI - OSPF inter, OE1 - OSPF ext 1, OE2 - OSPF ext 2
ON1 - OSPF NSSA ext 1, ON2 - OSPF NSSA ext 2
D - EIGRP, EX - EIGRP external
C 2001:3200:BADD:1000::/64 [0/0]
via ::, FastEthernet0/0
L 2001:3200:BADD:1000:290:2BFF:FE18:8A01/128 [0/0]
via ::, FastEthernet0/0
D 2001:4800:FACE:1000::/56 [90/2684416]
via FE80::290:CFF:FE36:2301, Serial0/0/1
D 2001:4800:FACE:1100::/56 [90/2172416]
via FE80::290:CFF:FE36:2301, Serial0/0/1
C 2001:4800:FACE:1200::/56 [0/0]
via ::, FastEthernet0/0
```

```
L 2001:4800:FACE:1200::F/128 [0/0]
via ::, FastEthernet0/0
D 2001:4800:FACE:1400::/56 [90/2681856]
via FE80::290:CFF:FE36:2301, Serial0/0/1
C 2001:4800:FACE:1500::/56 [0/0]
via ::, Serial0/0/1
L 2001:4800:FACE:1500::2/128 [0/0]
via ::, Serial0/0/1
L FF00::/8 [0/0]
```

As we look at the routing table, we notice that we are still routing with EIGRP because we see the letter D, which tells us that, and if you notice the AD is 90, then both values are highlighted.

So, how do we fix this without taking out EIGRP? We need to make sure that OSPF is working properly before we get rid of any routing protocol; we cannot afford to lose connectivity in our network.

Let us go back to OSPF and lower the administrative distance to a lower number than 90:

```
R1(config)#ipv6 router ospf 2
R1(config-rtr)#distance 85
R2(config)#ipv6 router ospf 2
R2(config-rtr)#distance 85
R3(config)#ipv6 router ospf 2
R3(config-rtr)#distance 85
```

Alright. Now, let's check the routing table again to make sure that what we did allowed OSPF to make it to the routing table. In this situation, you should verify all routing tables, to make sure that they are using OSPF to get across the network:

```
R3#sh ipv6 route
IPv6 Routing Table - 10 entries
Codes: C - Connected, L - Local, S - Static, R - RIP, B - BGP
U - Per-user Static route, M - MIPv6
I1 - ISIS L1, I2 - ISIS L2, IA - ISIS interarea, IS - ISIS summary
O - OSPF intra, OI - OSPF inter, OE1 - OSPF ext 1, OE2 - OSPF ext 2
ON1 - OSPF NSSA ext 1, ON2 - OSPF NSSA ext 2
D - EIGRP, EX - EIGRP external
C 2001:3200:BADD:1000::/64 [0/0]
via ::, FastEthernet0/0
L 2001:3200:BADD:1000:290:2BFF:FE18:8A01/128 [0/0]
via ::, FastEthernet0/0
O 2001:4800:FACE:1000::/56 [85/129]
via FE80::290:CFF:FE36:2301, Serial0/0/1
O 2001:4800:FACE:1100::/56 [85/65]
via FE80::290:CFF:FE36:2301, Serial0/0/1
```

```
C 2001:4800:FACE:1200::/56 [0/0]
via ::, FastEthernet0/0
L 2001:4800:FACE:1200::F/128 [0/0]
via ::, FastEthernet0/0
O 2001:4800:FACE:1400::/56 [85/128]
via FE80::290:CFF:FE36:2301, Serial0/0/1
C 2001:4800:FACE:1500::/56 [0/0]
via ::, Serial0/0/1
L 2001:4800:FACE:1500::2/128 [0/0]
via ::, Serial0/0/1
L FF00::/8 [0/0]
```

Looking good. We see the letter O, which means we are receiving updates from OSPF. Also take a look at the AD; it has now become 85. Let's continue:

```
R2#sh ipv6 route
IPv6 Routing Table - 10 entries
Codes: C - Connected, L - Local, S - Static, R - RIP, B - BGP
U - Per-user Static route, M - MIPv6
I1 - ISIS L1, I2 - ISIS L2, IA - ISIS interarea, IS - ISIS summary
O - OSPF intra, OI - OSPF inter, OE1 - OSPF ext 1, OE2 - OSPF ext 2
ON1 - OSPF NSSA ext 1, ON2 - OSPF NSSA ext 2
D - EIGRP, EX - EIGRP external
O 2001:3200:BADD:1000::/64 [85/65]
via FE80::290:2BFF:FE18:8A01, Serial0/0/0
O 2001:4800:FACE:1000::/56 [85/65]
via FE80::206:2AFF:FEB3:C501, Serial0/0/1
C 2001:4800:FACE:1100::/56 [0/0]
via ::, FastEthernet0/0
L 2001:4800:FACE:1100::F/128 [0/0]
via ::, FastEthernet0/0
O 2001:4800:FACE:1200::/56 [85/65]
via FE80::290:2BFF:FE18:8A01, Serial0/0/0
C 2001:4800:FACE:1400::/56 [0/0]
via ::, Serial0/0/1
L 2001:4800:FACE:1400::2/128 [0/0]
via ::, Serial0/0/1
C 2001:4800:FACE:1500::/56 [0/0]
via ::, Serial0/0/0
L 2001:4800:FACE:1500::1/128 [0/0]
via ::, Serial0/0/0
L FF00::/8 [0/0]
R1#sh ipv6 route
IPv6 Routing Table - 9 entries
Codes: C - Connected, L - Local, S - Static, R - RIP, B - BGP
U - Per-user Static route, M - MIPv6
I1 - ISIS L1, I2 - ISIS L2, IA - ISIS interarea, IS - ISIS summary
O - OSPF intra, OI - OSPF inter, OE1 - OSPF ext 1, OE2 - OSPF ext 2
```

```
ON1 - OSPF NSSA ext 1, ON2 - OSPF NSSA ext 2
D - EIGRP, EX - EIGRP external
O  2001:3200:BADD:1000::/64 [85/129]
via FE80::290:CFF:FE36:2301, Serial0/0/0
C 2001:4800:FACE:1000::/56 [0/0]
via ::, FastEthernet0/0
L 2001:4800:FACE:1000::F/128 [0/0]
via ::, FastEthernet0/0
O  2001:4800:FACE:1100::/56 [85/65]
via FE80::290:CFF:FE36:2301, Serial0/0/0
O  2001:4800:FACE:1200::/56 [85/129]
via FE80::290:CFF:FE36:2301, Serial0/0/0
C 2001:4800:FACE:1400::/56 [0/0]
via ::, Serial0/0/0
L 2001:4800:FACE:1400::1/128 [0/0]
via ::, Serial0/0/0
O  2001:4800:FACE:1500::/56 [85/128]
via FE80::290:CFF:FE36:2301, Serial0/0/0
L FF00::/8 [0/0]
```

OK, all the routers seem to be receiving updates from the destination networks, but we still need to verify connectivity, so from R1, we will use the `ping` command to test that connectivity to remote networks:

```
R1#ping 2001:4800:FACE:1200::1
Type escape sequence to abort.
Sending 5, 100-byte ICMP Echos to 2001:4800:FACE:1200::1, timeout is 2
seconds:
!!!!!
Success rate is 100 percent (5/5), round-trip min/avg/max = 4/7/13 ms
R1#ping 2001:4800:FACE:1100::1
Type escape sequence to abort.
Sending 5, 100-byte ICMP Echos to 2001:4800:FACE:1100::1, timeout is 2
seconds:
!!!!!
Success rate is 100 percent (5/5), round-trip min/avg/max = 1/6/16 ms
```

According to the `ping` command, we can reach our remote networks `1100` and `1200` without a problem.

So, OSPF was not so bad, but this is just the basics of configuring OSPF. It can be very complex in much larger networks, where you would have to consider a lot more variables to make OSPF more efficient.

Summary

In this chapter, we learned about the importance of choosing not only the type of routing you want to do, but also which routing protocol would be a best fit for your network. We found out that it all depends on your hardware and the size of your network and its design. We also learned how to configure EIGRPv6 and OSPFv3, which really was not as difficult as we thought it would be. But, you must always verify everything you do before you move on, step by step, and have a well-thought-out plan before you start making changes.

One very important command that we learned that we must configure, if you are going to be working in IPv6, is `ipv6 unicast-routing`. If you do not turn this on, you will *not* be able to route in IPv6 at all.

Next, get ready to attack Layer 2 switching.

12
Switching Services and Configurations

In this chapter, we will be taking a look at different layer 2 switching technologies, which will be crucial to the CCNA 200-125 certification and real-world scenarios you run into. The concepts of what type of addresses switches learn, and how they learn them, is extremely important, especially when troubleshooting layer 2 issues. We all know that security is a big issue in today's network, so learning how to use switchport security is going to be an essential tool that you will learn in this chapter as well.

This chapter will also show you the complete administrative commands for including IP addresses you would need to configure on your switch, and how to manage them. Finally, please pay close attention to all the `show` commands that are done in the labs. It is a must know for certification and definitely real-world applications.

We will be covering the following topics in this chapter:

- How networks evolved into using layer 2 switching
- Describing and verifying switching concepts, including:
  - MAC learning and aging
  - Frame switching
  - Frame flooding
  - MAC address tables

- Configuring, verifying, and troubleshooting port security, including:
  - Static
  - Dynamic
  - Sticky
  - Max number of MAC addresses
  - Violation actions
  - ERR-disable recovery

The evolution of networks

To be a professional network engineer, you need to know the differences between internetworking devices, such as repeaters, hubs, bridges, switches, and routers.

In the dawn of networks, we used a topology called a bus, which was simply one main cable, usually a coaxial cable, that every other node was connected to using vampire taps, and the PCs used NIC cards that had BNC connectors.

These networks served their purpose at the time when bus topologies and coaxial cable were used for networking, but it was extremely slow, and if there was a break in any part of the cable, the entire network would be down. That means no one could send or receive any information. Why? Because the broken part of the cable would send signals back onto the network called reflection, and all computers would hear noise on the network and not transmit.

But it did not have to be a break in the cable; you could have forgotten to terminate the network on either side. Here is a visualization of a bus topology.

Bus topology

Even though it was cheap to implement bus topologies, the speed of the network was just not enough. You need to keep in mind this is an Ethernet network that works on CSMA/CD. As it only has one collision domain and one broadcast domain, the more nodes you would put on this type of network, the more the bandwidth would suffer:

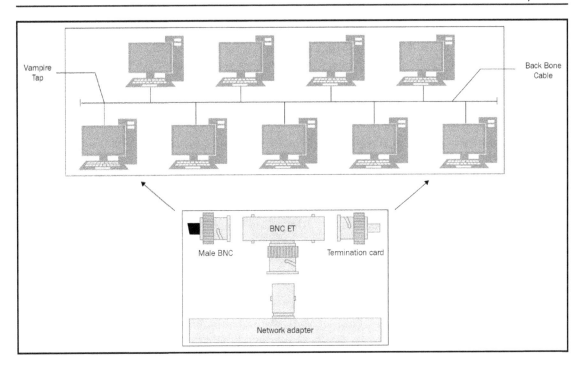

Not to mention that either a break anywhere on the cable, or you forgetting to terminate the cable on both ends, would cause the entire network to fail. The reason for that is that it would cause reflection or send electrical signals back into the network causing noise, so all nodes would think they could not transmit; hence the network would not function.

You would also have had to ground one side of the bus in case of a power surge so as not to fry all your end devices. Not a very scalable network; we could have used repeaters to make the network larger, but a repeater would basically clean up the signal and send out the signal that was *cleaned up* of any fragmentation, out the other side. Again, not a good idea.

Much later came the hub, and it became the central point of the network where we could plug in all our devices, and by this time we were using UTP cabling Ethernet. But there was a problem. Hubs are not intelligent devices; they are basically multiport repeaters and they reside at layer 1 of the OSI model.

We still had the issue of one collision domain and one broadcast domain because hubs do not break up collision domains or have the capability of creating new broadcast domains.

To make matters worse, this type of topology, named a STAR topology, uses the CSMA/CD access method, but the one collision domain it has is a *shared collision* domain, which means your 100 Mbps UTP cable is divided up into how many ports you have on your network. So, let's say you have a four-port hub; you divide the 100 Mbps into four ports and your bandwidth per port would be 25 Mbps or slower if you have traffic on your network.

Then we came up with bridges. Awesome! We can break up collision domains but not broadcast domains. They do all the work using built-in software, which will make it slower in making decisions, and it has limits on the number of ports. I believe the maximum number of ports is 12.

So, to fix all those issues, we now use switches, and we have multiple collision domains. By creating VLANs, we create more broadcast domains, which reduces the amount of broadcast on the network. We can tweak the switch, since it has lots of features, such as STP, VTP, switchport security, and *private collision domains*, which means we can send and receive at the same time.

So a switched network gives us a lot of features and flexibility on our network, not to mention scalability if done correctly. So, let's take a look at some of the services that switches give us.

Switching services

As we mentioned before, bridges used software to create the CAM table. With switches, we have **Application-Specific Integrated Circuits** (**ASICs**) that can build and maintain the MAC table. One thing you should keep in mind is that switches are faster than routers because they only concentrate on layer 2 addressing; they do not deal with any of the layer 3 protocols. That is true only for layer 2 switches; as we know, we have layer 3 switches that have routing capabilities if turned on.

Switches look at the frame's hardware address to see if it's going to forward, flood, or drop the frame. Let's take a look at four main important advantages that layer 2 switching gives us:

- Hardware-based bridging (ASICs)
- Wired speed
- Low latency
- Low cost

Using layer 2 switching is much faster and better for segmenting a network. It only reads the frame encapsulating the packet and errors are lessened at this layer. Using layer 2 switches, you can create a lot more segmentation than you can on a router. Think about it; a switch can have from 4 to 48 ports and each one of those ports are private collision domains.

Three main switch functions at layer 2

The three main switch functions that you need to commit to memory are the following:

- **Address learning**: Layer 2 switches use source MAC addresses and map them to the port the end device is connected to
- **Forward/filter decision**: The switch will look at the destination hardware address and send it out to the appropriate interface
- **Loop avoidance**: The nature of a switch is to forward frames. To prevent a broadcast storm due to a loop, it will use the **Spanning Tree Protocol** (**STP**)

Let's dive a little deeper into these functions.

Address learning

When you first power on a switch, the MAC address table is completely empty, as you can see in the following diagram:

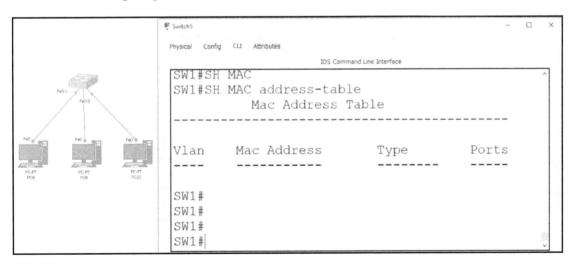

Once the devices start to communicate with each other, the switch will see a frame coming its way. It will take the source MAC address and map the port from the port the end device is connected on. It will then take the destination hardware address and will do an ARP and flood out of all the other ports to find the owner of that MAC address. Once that end device responds to the ARP, the switch will take the destination MAC address and map it to the port it learned it on.

This process continues until the switch learns about all the end devices on its segment and the MAC address table is filled up, as you can see in the following diagram:

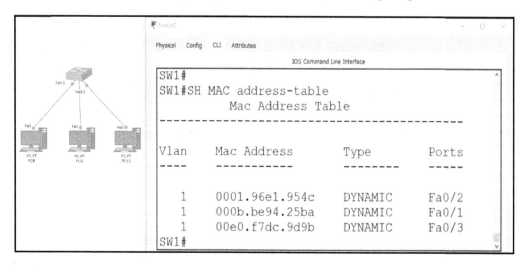

Just keep in mind that ARP only happens one time. Once the switch learns your MAC address and it's mapped to a port on the MAC table, it will hold that information for 5 minutes by default and then it will flush the MAC table. But, as long as there is constant communication between devices, the MAC addresses will never be flushed. You could change the default time using the following command:

```
mac address-table aging-time seconds [vlan vlan-id]
```

The range for aging is 0- 100,0000 seconds; the default is 300 seconds, and if you put 0, it will disable MAC addressing aging. vlan-id is optional; the purpose is to change the aging time per VLAN.

Forward/filter decisions

When a frame reaches the interface on a switch, it will query its forward/filter database to see if it can find that MAC address. If it finds a match, it will simply send it out to the appropriate interface. But, if the switch cannot make a match in its database, it will have to flood all active ports on the switch, except the interface it was received on.

Once the database is updated with the new MAC address, it will be mapped to the port, and from that moment onward, there would be no need to go through the entire process again. You must keep in mind that an ARP is a type of broadcast and switches by default have only one broadcast domain, so the ARP will flood that entire broadcast domain or segment.

So, if you had multiple VLANs, the ARP broadcast will stay within the VLAN, as layer 2 addresses do not leave their own segment. Let's look at a visual of this process.

The forward and filter table already knows about PCs 8, 9, and 10, but not PC 11. So, if PC9 wanted to communicate with PC11, the switch will have to do an ARP broadcast, flooding all ports until someone responds and it can map the PC 11 MAC address to port f0/4:

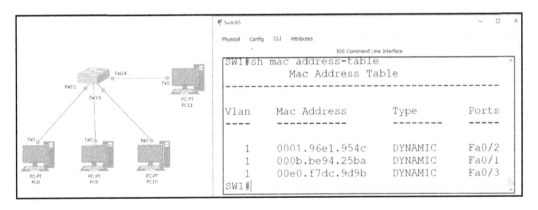

Once the ARP process finishes and the new MAC address is added to the forward and filter table, anyone can communicate with that PC. So, now, the MAC address table would look like the following:

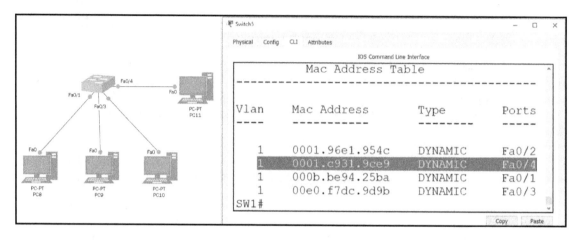

Now, you can see the PC 11 MAC address was added to the forward/filter table. This means that for anyone who wants to communicate with PC 11, there will be a direct communication and no ARP broadcast. I highlighted ARP because a lot of people are confused by this process.

By default, a switch has one broadcast domain, which is VLAN 1. The bigger this VLAN 1 gets, the bigger the broadcast domain gets. Everyone who is a member of a VLAN will hear all the chatter that is going on in that VLAN, so if you stay using VLAN 1 on a huge network, you will always hear chatter, and that will take up a bandwidth, and since we are on an Ethernet network, we are all fighting for access to the media.

The ARP broadcast only happens when the switch needs to find a destination MAC address. Layer 2 addresses never leave their own segment, as shown in the following diagram:

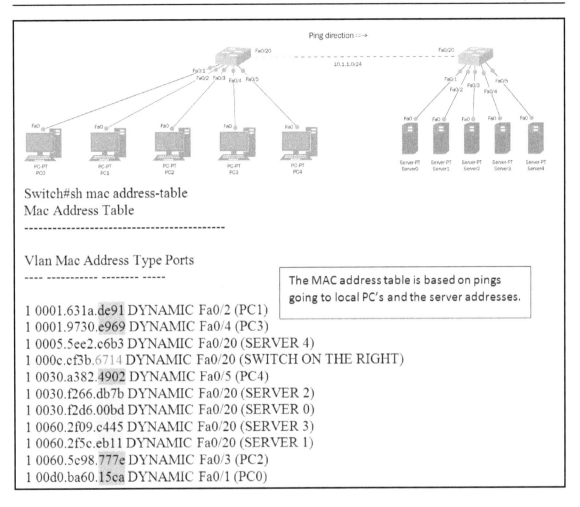

```
Switch#sh mac address-table
Mac Address Table
-------------------------------------------

Vlan Mac Address Type Ports
---- ----------- -------- -----

1 0001.631a.de91 DYNAMIC Fa0/2 (PC1)
1 0001.9730.e969 DYNAMIC Fa0/4 (PC3)
1 0005.5ee2.c6b3 DYNAMIC Fa0/20 (SERVER 4)
1 000c.cf3b.6714 DYNAMIC Fa0/20 (SWITCH ON THE RIGHT)
1 0030.a382.4902 DYNAMIC Fa0/5 (PC4)
1 0030.f266.db7b DYNAMIC Fa0/20 (SERVER 2)
1 0030.f2d6.00bd DYNAMIC Fa0/20 (SERVER 0)
1 0060.2f09.c445 DYNAMIC Fa0/20 (SERVER 3)
1 0060.2f5c.eb11 DYNAMIC Fa0/20 (SERVER 1)
1 0060.5c98.777e DYNAMIC Fa0/3 (PC2)
1 00d0.ba60.15ca DYNAMIC Fa0/1 (PC0)
```

The MAC address table is based on pings going to local PC's and the server addresses.

So, if you analyze the MAC address table on the left switch, you can see that when you ping any PC, you will see the interface that PC is connected to. But if you ping the server, you will only see the MAC address of the trunk port, which in this case is F0/20.

Also, the MAC addresses belong to the actual destination addresses to include port F0/20.

Port security

It goes without saying that securing your network is crucial. When we talk about security, the main topics that usually spring up are firewalls, policies, certificates, share permissions, and so on. Very few people actually think of the lonely layer 2 switch sitting in every department, classroom, and floor of your company.

Securing those ports is just as important as configuring policies on a firewall. Imagine this scenario; you walk into a hospital to visit someone and you are asked to wait in the lobby area. Being the IT guru you are, you have a laptop and CAT5 UTP straight through cable with you, so you find a wall plate and plug your laptop in, and guess what, you have the internet. But then curiosity sets in and you run a network protocol analyzer and you start seeing all these other computers on the network, so now you get even more curious and you try to access one of these computers, and you do so!

This sounds very close to home for me. Unfortunately, companies are not protecting their ports or even shutting them down. As per Cisco; we need to secure our ports and switchport security is a very easy way to do this in a small-to medium-sized network.

So, how would you do this. Let's take a look:

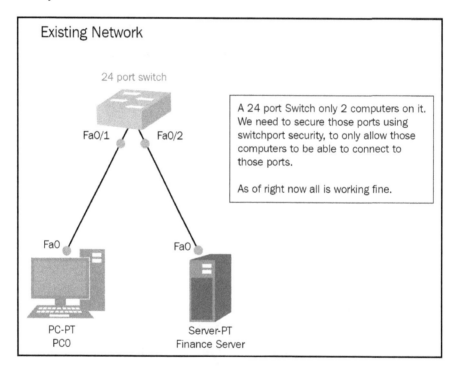

Let's secure the switch with the following commands:

```
Switch(config)#int range f0/1-15
Switch(config-if-range)#switchport mode access
Switch(config-if-range)#switchport port-security
Switch(config-if-range)#switchport port-security mac sticky
Switch(config-if-range)#switchport port-security max 1
Switch(config-if-range)#switchport port-security vio shut
```

Let's break down the configuration line by line. The first line is just to get you into the range of ports you want to secure. The second line is required in order to turn on `switchport port-security`. The ports by default are on dynamic-auto, so you must change the mode of the ports to `access`. The third line actually turns on port security on the range of ports you selected.

In the fourth line, you instruct the switch that when it learns a MAC address dynamically, it will be categorized as static, which is the purpose of the `sticky` command. The switch will never flush this MAC address out since it thinks it was statically assigned. The fifth line will only allow one MAC address to be learned on this port, so the first computer to be plugged into that port and the switch learns its MAC address; will be remembered forever, and no other MAC address will be allowed.

But for everyone who listens to the rules, some just don't get the memo, so the last line is the action the switch will take if someone *violates* the rule of only one MAC address, which in this scenario will be to *shut down* the port.

Let's take a look to see what happens when all of this is in play. First, let's verify that port security is enabled on the switch:

```
Switch#sh port-security
Secure Port    MaxSecureAddr    CurrentAddr    SecurityViolation    Security
Action
                  (Count)          (Count)         (Count)
----------------------------------------------------------------------------
----------------------------
Fa0/1             1                0               0
Shutdown
Fa0/2             1                0               0
Shutdown
Fa0/3             1                0               0
Shutdown
Fa0/4             1                0               0
Shutdown
Fa0/5             1                0               0
Shutdown
Fa0/6             1                0               0
Shutdown
Fa0/7             1                0               0
Shutdown
Fa0/8             1                0               0
Shutdown
Fa0/9             1                0               0
Shutdown
Fa0/10            1                0               0
Shutdown
```

Secure Port	MaxSecureAddr (Count)	CurrentAddr (Count)	SecurityViolation (Count)	Security Action
Fa0/11	1	0	0	Shutdown
Fa0/12	1	0	0	Shutdown
Fa0/13	1	0	0	Shutdown
Fa0/14	1	0	0	Shutdown
Fa0/15	1	0	0	Shutdown

We have `switchport-security` enabled and it shows a MAX value of 1 address per port. No current addresses are learned, so no violations have occurred. If a violation should occur, shut down the port.

So, let's go ahead and ping the other computer so we can populate the second column `CurrentAddr`:

```
Switch#sh port-security
```

Secure Port	MaxSecureAddr (Count)	CurrentAddr (Count)	SecurityViolation (Count)	Security Action
Fa0/1	1	1	0	Shutdown
Fa0/2	1	1	0	Shutdown
Fa0/3	1	0	0	Shutdown
Fa0/4	1	0	0	Shutdown
Fa0/5	1	0	0	Shutdown
Fa0/6	1	0	0	Shutdown
Fa0/7	1	0	0	Shutdown
Fa0/8	1	0	0	Shutdown
Fa0/9	1	0	0	Shutdown
Fa0/10	1	0	0	Shutdown
Fa0/11	1	0	0	Shutdown

Fa0/12	1	0	0
Shutdown			
Fa0/13	1	0	0
Shutdown			
Fa0/14	1	0	0
Shutdown			
Fa0/15	1	0	0
Shutdown			

Now, it has learned the MAC addresses of both computers, and only one is allowed per port. What happens if somebody else tries to plug into your port?

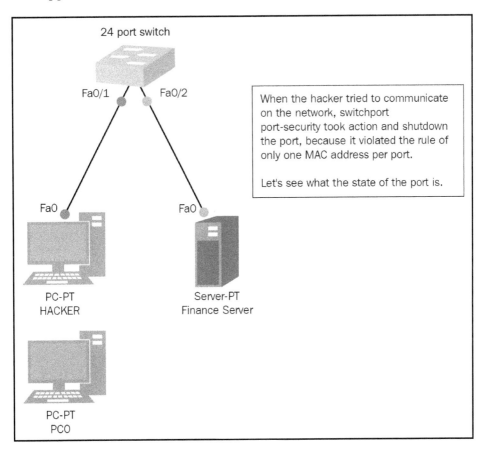

When the hacker tried to communicate on the network, switchport port-security took action and shutdown the port, because it violated the rule of only one MAC address per port.

Let's see what the state of the port is.

```
Switch#sh int f0/1
FastEthernet0/1 is down, line protocol is down (err-disabled)
Hardware is Lance, address is 0010.11cb.9201 (bia 0010.11cb.9201)
```

As you can see, the actual state of the port is err-disabled. The port is down completely; it is not working at all. You would need to manually turn it back on by doing the `shut not shut` command in *interface configuration mode* to bring it back. But let's take a look at the port-security output:

```
Switch#sh port-security
Secure Port    MaxSecureAddr    CurrentAddr    SecurityViolation    Security
Action
               (Count)          (Count)        (Count)
-------------------------------------------------------------------------------
--------------------------------
Fa0/1          1                1              1
Shutdown
Fa0/2          1                1              0
Shutdown
```

Now, in the `SecurityViolation` column, we have a violation count, and until you remove the hacker, put back the original PC and turn the port back on, it will stay that way.

There is a command that will clear the `port-security` table and reset everything back to zero:

```
Switch#clear port-security sticky
Secure Port    MaxSecureAddr    CurrentAddr    SecurityViolation    Security
Action
               (Count)          (Count)        (Count)
-------------------------------------------------------------------------------
--------------------------------
Fa0/1          1                0              0
Shutdown
Fa0/2          1                0              0
Shutdown
Fa0/3          1                0              0
Shutdown
```

Loop avoidance

Redundancy in a network is extremely important. We cannot have just one cable going from source to destination. In case that cable breaks, we should always have some redundancy to keep up our network. Let's clarify this with a simple scenario. Imagine a school. Each classroom has a switch.

In the classrooms, we have end devices that connect to the switch in the classroom, but then you run only one cable from the classroom to the main/core switch in the telecommunications closet. What happens if that one cable from the classroom to the main switch breaks? That entire classroom can only communicate with each other; they would not be able to access any other network outside the classroom they are in.

Switches forward by default, and if you have redundant links with other switches, you could run into problems such as broadcast storms or multiple copies of the same frame, and if you really think about it, the MAC address table would be confused about who is the source MAC address:

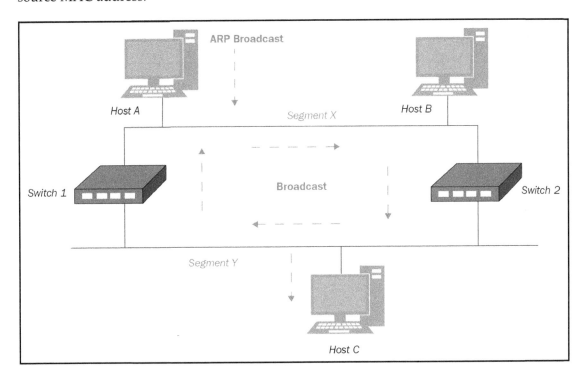

How can you tell whether you have a broadcast storm or simply way too much traffic on your network? Just look at the lights on your switches; they should be blinking all together like a Christmas tree, or just look at whatever monitoring software you have. That will tell exactly what is going on.

So, how do we avoid this situation but maintain our redundancy at layer 2? The answer is Spanning-Tree to the rescue. Spanning-Tree will run an election, which I will explain soon, that chooses a root bridge, non-root bridges, root ports, forwarding ports, and blocked ports.

Configuring switches

But before we get into the election process of STP, let's learn how to configure our switches with the following tasks:

- Administrative commands
- IP address and subnet mask
- IP default-gateway
- Switchport port-security
- As usual, verify all is working

The topology that we will be using for our layer 2 configurations is as follows:

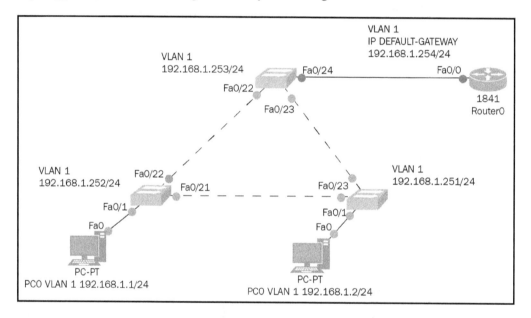

It is very important that you assign IP addresses to your management VLAN, whichever number it is. By default, it is VLAN 1 and that is what I am using in this example. The reason it is so important to have IP addresses is to be able to access the switch to configure it and make it more efficient.

The IP default-gateway is also very important. According to Cisco, you cannot gain access to the switch remotely if it does not have an IP default-gateway, which is your routers' LAN interface.

Let's look at each of the configurations for the switches:

SW1 administrative commands:

```
Switch>enable
Switch#clock set 01:15:30 21 august 2017
Switch#config t
Enter configuration commands, one per line. End with CNTL/Z.
Switch(config)#hostname SW1
SW1(config)#clock timezone florida -4
SW1(config)#enable password cisco
SW1(config)#enable secret student
SW1(config)#service password-encryption
SW1(config)#banner motd # Welcome all #
SW1(config)#lldp run
SW1(config)#ip domain-lookup
SW1(config)#ip domain-name laz.com
SW1(config)#ip name-server 192.168.1.200
SW1(config)#username ldiaz privilege 15 password 7 cisco
Invalid encrypted password: cisco
SW1(config)#crypto key generate rsa
The name for the keys will be: SW1.laz.com
Choose the size of the key modulus in the range of 360 to 2048 for your
General Purpose Keys. Choosing a key modulus greater than 512 may take
a few minutes.

How many bits in the modulus [512]: 512
% Generating 512 bit RSA keys, keys will be non-exportable...[OK]

SW1(config)#ip ssh authentication-retries 3
*Aug 20 21:15:30.91: RSA key size needs to be at least 768 bits for ssh
version 2
*Aug 20 21:15:30.91: %SSH-5-ENABLED: SSH 1.5 has been enabled
SW1(config)#ip ssh time-out 120
SW1(config)#line con 0
SW1(config-line)#password bob
SW1(config-line)#login local
SW1(config-line)#exec-timeout 0 0
SW1(config-line)#logging synchronous
SW1(config-line)#line vty 0 15
SW1(config-line)#password bob
SW1(config-line)#login local
SW1(config-line)#exec-timeout 0 0
SW1(config-line)#logging synchronous
SW1(config-line)#transport input ALL
SW1(config-line)#do wr
Building configuration...
[OK]
```

SW2 administrative commands:

```
Switch>enable
Switch#clock set 01:17:30 21 august 2017
Switch#config t
Enter configuration commands, one per line. End with CNTL/Z.
Switch(config)#hostname SW2
SW2(config)#clock timezone florida -4
SW2(config)#enable password cisco
SW2(config)#enable secret student
SW2(config)#service password-encryption
SW2(config)#banner motd # Welcome all #
SW2(config)#lldp run
SW2(config)#ip domain-lookup
SW2(config)#ip domain-name laz.com
SW2(config)#ip name-server 192.168.1.200
SW2(config)#username ldiaz privilege 15 password 7 cisco
Invalid encrypted password: cisco
SW2(config)#crypto key generate rsa
The name for the keys will be: SW2.laz.com
Choose the size of the key modulus in the range of 360 to 2048 for your
General Purpose Keys. Choosing a key modulus greater than 512 may take
a few minutes.

How many bits in the modulus [512]: 512
% Generating 512 bit RSA keys, keys will be non-exportable...[OK]

SW2(config)#ip ssh authentication-retries 3
*Aug 20 21:17:30.93: RSA key size needs to be at least 768 bits for ssh
version 2
*Aug 20 21:17:30.94: %SSH-5-ENABLED: SSH 1.5 has been enabled
SW2(config)#ip ssh time-out 120
SW2(config)#line con 0
SW2(config-line)#password bob
SW2(config-line)#login local
SW2(config-line)#exec-timeout 0 0
SW2(config-line)#logging synchronous
SW2(config-line)#line vty 0 15
SW2(config-line)#password bob
SW2(config-line)#login local
SW2(config-line)#exec-timeout 0 0
SW2(config-line)#logging synchronous
SW2(config-line)#transport input ALL
SW2(config-line)#do wr
Building configuration...
[OK]
```

SW3 administrative commands:

```
Switch>enable
Switch#clock set 01:19:30 21 august 2017
Switch#config t
Enter configuration commands, one per line. End with CNTL/Z.
Switch(config)#hostname SW3
SW3(config)#clock timezone florida -4
SW3(config)#enable password cisco
SW3(config)#enable secret student
SW3(config)#service password-encryption
SW3(config)#banner motd # Welcome all #
SW3(config)#lldp run
SW3(config)#ip domain-lookup
SW3(config)#ip domain-name laz.com
SW3(config)#ip name-server 192.168.1.200
SW3(config)#username ldiaz privilege 15 password 7 cisco
Invalid encrypted password: cisco
SW3(config)#crypto key generate rsa
The name for the keys will be: SW3.laz.com
Choose the size of the key modulus in the range of 360 to 2048 for your
General Purpose Keys. Choosing a key modulus greater than 512 may take
a few minutes.

How many bits in the modulus [512]: 512
% Generating 512 bit RSA keys, keys will be non-exportable...[OK]

SW3(config)#ip ssh authentication-retries 3
*Aug 20 21:19:30.107: RSA key size needs to be at least 768 bits for ssh
version 2
*Aug 20 21:19:30.107: %SSH-5-ENABLED: SSH 1.5 has been enabled
SW3(config)#ip ssh time-out 120
SW3(config)#line con 0
SW3(config-line)#password bob
SW3(config-line)#login local
SW3(config-line)#exec-timeout 0 0
SW3(config-line)#logging synchronous
SW3(config-line)#line vty 0 15
SW3(config-line)#password bob
SW3(config-line)#login local
SW3(config-line)#exec-timeout 0 0
SW3(config-line)#logging synchronous
SW3(config-line)#transport input ALL
SW3(config-line)#do wr
Building configuration...
[OK]
```

We have configured the administrative commands or the house keeping of the router. We have yet to put in the IP address of the switch or the IP default-gateway address, but we did configure the IP address of the DNS server, which is 192.168.1.200.

So, basically, if you were connected with a console cable or rolled cable to the console port of the switch, you get in using console zero. But that is not the reality of a real world or even the certification exam; you will have to either Telnet in or SSH in to the switch or router. So, we must put in the configuration for IP connectivity and then make sure it works.

We already configured Telnet and SSH in our house keeping commands. Now, let's configure the IP addressing on the switches for VLAN 1.

SW1 IP addressing configurations:

```
SW1(config)#ip default-gateway 192.168.1.254
SW1(config)#int vlan 1
SW1(config-if)#ip address 192.168.1.253 255.255.255.0
SW1(config-if)#no shut
SW2 IP addressing Configurations
SW2(config)#ip default-gateway 192.168.1.254
SW2(config)#int vlan 1
SW2(config-if)#ip address 192.168.1.252 255.255.255.0
SW2(config-if)#no shut
```

SW3 IP addressing configurations:

```
SW3(config)#ip default-gateway 192.168.1.254
SW3(config)#int vlan 1
SW3(config-if)#ip address 192.168.1.251 255.255.255.0
SW3(config-if)#no shut
```

OK, we should now have connectivity with our switches and the other PC. Let's verify that we can Telnet, SSH, or ping to our devices:

```
C:\>ping 192.168.1.252

Pinging 192.168.1.252 with 32 bytes of data:

Request timed out.
Reply from 192.168.1.252: bytes=32 time<1ms
TTL=255
Reply from 192.168.1.252: bytes=32 time<1ms
TTL=255
Reply from 192.168.1.252: bytes=32 time<1ms
TTL=255

Ping statistics for 192.168.1.252:
    Packets: Sent = 4, Received = 3, Lost = 1
(25% loss),
Approximate round trip times in milli-seconds:
    Minimum = 0ms, Maximum = 0ms, Average = 0ms

C:\>
```

```
C:\>
C:\>
C:\>
C:\>
C:\>
C:\>
C:\>
C:\>
C:\>
C:\>telnet 192.168.1.252
Trying 192.168.1.252 ...Open Welcome all


User Access Verification

Username: ldiaz

Password:
SW2#
```

```
SW2#
SW2#
SW2#
SW2#
SW2#
SW2#
SW2#
SW2#
SW2#
SW2#
SW2#
SW2#
SW2#ssh -l ldiaz 192.168.1.252
Open
Password:

 Welcome all

SW2#
```

Awesome! Our configuration is working and we can ping, Telnet, and SSH into our switch. That way, we can work from our office or if need be work from home; but obviously, for security purposes, we would take further steps to secure that remote connection with VPN and IPSec, but that is for another time.

Meanwhile, we could secure our ports using `switchport port-security` like I showed you earlier in the chapter. That would allow us to control what devices can or cannot be physically plugged into our network.

One last thing we must do, and you may find it redundant, is to verify our configurations on our switches using show commands. It is imperative that you know these commands, not only for the certification but for real-world scenarios also.

S2 verification of configurations:

```
SW2#sh int vlan 1
Vlan1 is up, line protocol is up
Hardware is CPU Interface, address is 00e0.a353.1e73 (bia 00e0.a353.1e73)
Internet address is 192.168.1.252/24
MTU 1500 bytes, BW 100000 Kbit, DLY 1000000 usec,
reliability 255/255, txload 1/255, rxload 1/255
Encapsulation ARPA, loopback not set
```

When you run this command, you are checking that the interface is up. By default, this interface is down. If we do not turn it on, then we cannot communicate with it:

```
SW2#sh mac address-table
Mac Address Table
-------------------------------

Vlan Mac Address Type Ports
---- ----------- -------- -----

1 0001.c994.3715 DYNAMIC Fa0/21
1 0060.5c04.220e DYNAMIC Fa0/21
1 00e0.a33c.1b89 STATIC Fa0/1
1 00e0.b00a.0628 DYNAMIC Fa0/22
1 00e0.b0a2.7d3e DYNAMIC Fa0/21
1 00e0.f7d6.c416 DYNAMIC Fa0/22
```

When you run this command, you are looking to see whose address the switch has learned and to what port they are mapped to.

But more importantly, the preceding output shows that on port `F0/0` the MAC address seems to have been statically assigned but it has not. The `sticky` command we configured actually takes the MAC address learned dynamically and categorizes it as `STATIC`, and it will never be flushed out of the MAC address table:

```
SW2#sh version
24 FastEthernet/IEEE 802.3 interface(s)
2 Gigabit Ethernet/IEEE 802.3 interface(s)

63488K bytes of flash-simulated non-volatile configuration memory.
Base ethernet MAC Address : 00E0.A353.1E73
Motherboard assembly number : 73-9832-06
Power supply part number : 341-0097-02
Motherboard serial number : FOC103248MJ
Power supply serial number : DCA102133JA
Model revision number : B0
Motherboard revision number : C0
Model number : WS-C2960-24TT
System serial number : FOC1033Z1EY
Top Assembly Part Number : 800-26671-02
Top Assembly Revision Number : B0
Version ID : V02
CLEI Code Number : COM3K00BRA
Hardware Board Revision Number : 0x01


Switch Ports Model SW Version SW Image
------ ----- ----- ---------- ----------
* 1 26 WS-C2960-24TT 12.2 C2960-LANBASE-M
```

This is also a very cool command to run, because it gives you the Ethernet address, model numbers, serial numbers, part numbers, and so on. If you need to replace a piece of hardware, you have the serial number at your fingertips.

Summary

Well, all good things must come to an end. You now should know how a switch differs from a bridge, not only in speed, but in the functionality the switch brings to the network. We also went over the configurations of each switch, the administrative commands, and the IP configuration commands, including the `ip default-gateway` command. We looked at the capability of creating VLANs, to increase the number of broadcast domains, which leads to less broadcast advertisements on your network.

By no means is this the last that we will be talking about switches. In the coming chapters, we will be talking about STP, VTP, VLANs, 802.1q, and much more. This was a foundation on switching so you can get a firm grasp before we move on to the more advanced topics. See you in the next chapter.

13
VLANs and Inter-VLAN Routing

This chapter is extremely important, not just because I said so, but because VLANs are crucial to your network's efficiency. I may sound somewhat repetitive, but you need to remember that switches break up collision domains, which is great, meaning you are in a private collision domain increasing your bandwidth. You can also configure your switch to run at full-duplex, send, and receive at the same time. Switches create MAC address tables, so they reduce the ARP broadcast.

You can create a **Virtual Local Area Network** (**VLAN**), which means you can also break up broadcast domains on your switch. When designing your VLAN network, you need to think it through carefully: How exactly am I going to create these virtual LANs? You could create a VLAN by department, by floor, or, in a school environment, by classroom; it is completely up to you.

The idea is to create VLANs so you, as the administrator, can better manage your network by having tighter security and not having any physical limitations when it comes to placing your users. An example of not having physical limitations would be placing a user that works in finance in the warehouse, but they are plugged into a port on the switch that belongs to the finance VLAN, so they would be able to access the same information as if they were sitting in the finance department.

In this chapter, we will cover the following topics:

- Configuring VLANs
- Naming VLANs
- Assigning VLANs
- Verifying VLANs
- Access ports versus trunk ports
- Changing the native VLAN (CAREFUL!)
- Inter-VLAN connectivity

The basics of VLANs

To understand the future, we first need to understand the past. Before switches, we had hubs where we would plug in all our devices; I am talking about a star topology using twisted-pair cabling.

The problem with using hubs is that they created one collision domain and one broadcast domain, there was no way of making it better, unless you physically segmented each network, which is insane.

Let's look at a star topology using hubs, so we can understand this concept better:

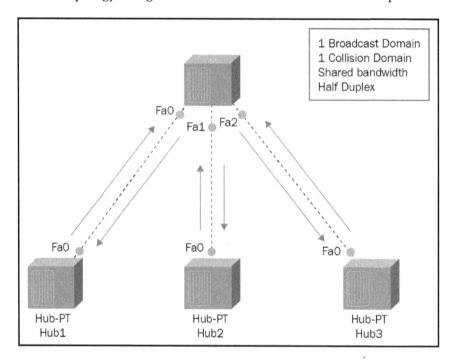

The star topology you see is using hubs. Every time someone transmits data, everyone is privileged to hear that noise on the network. This is considered to be a flat network structure, since it only has one broadcast domain.

To make matters worse, in an Ethernet network, the access method is CSMA/CD, meaning everyone is fighting for access to transmit, but since Ethernet uses the *first come, first served* method, you will see tons of broadcasts, dropped packets, and your bandwidth will suffer, because using hubs is considered a *shared collision domain* that divides your possible 100 Mbps bandwidth into all your ports.

In today's world, we use switches to bring functionality, efficiency, and security to our network.

Switches have the capability to create VLANs, which will create more broadcast domains. This is a good thing; the more broadcast domains we have, the more bandwidth we have, and it's considered a private collision domain, security and it allows for better administration of the network.

By default, all switches only have one VLAN, which is called the native VLAN and by default is VLAN 1.

This means all your devices or nodes will be on the same VLAN, therefore defeating the purpose or miss out on using what the switch is supposed to do.

As an administrator, it is your responsibility to configure VLANs in your network; it is vital to the health of your network and your peace of mind.

First, let's look at a star topology using switches with no VLANs, so we can understand the difference:

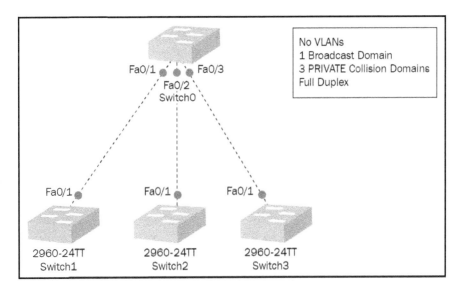

Now, let's look at a star topology using switches with VLANs:

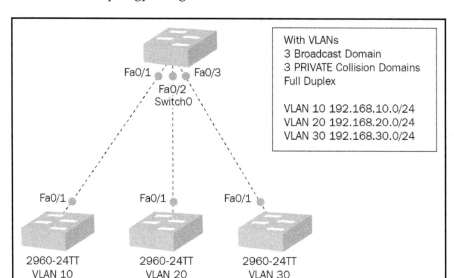

The star topology that is using the VLANs will be more efficient. Why? Because what happens on that VLAN stays on that VLAN, so if you're communicating within your own VLAN segment, no one else in your network hears the noise—the broadcast is contained within your own broadcast domain. Once you leave your network, all others will hear that noise. But, you have dramatically reduced the amount of noise on your network and made the administration of each VLAN segment much easier.

You may have noticed that each VLAN belongs to its own subnetwork. Keep in mind you are logically segmenting the network. What does that mean? It means you could have one network of 48 port switches and four VLANs each with 12 ports that represent a department.

Once again, let's look at a visual:

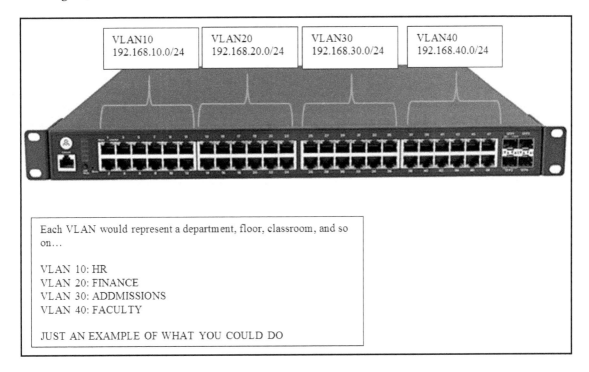

VLAN10	VLAN20	VLAN30	VLAN40
192.168.10.0/24	192.168.20.0/24	192.168.30.0/24	192.168.40.0/24

Each VLAN would represent a department, floor, classroom, and so on…

VLAN 10: HR
VLAN 20: FINANCE
VLAN 30: ADDMISSIONS
VLAN 40: FACULTY

JUST AN EXAMPLE OF WHAT YOU COULD DO

Even though you could logically segment one switch however you want, it must make sense and you must create a network that will be scalable. The preceding diagram in a medium network would not be feasible, and in an enterprise network would just be foolish.

In smaller networks, you could get away with logically segmenting one switch, but even in smaller networks you would at least have two or three switches and you could have the same VLANs on both switches. Remember, you have no physical limitation where the user must sit in the department they work for. If the user is part of the same VLAN, it's all good:

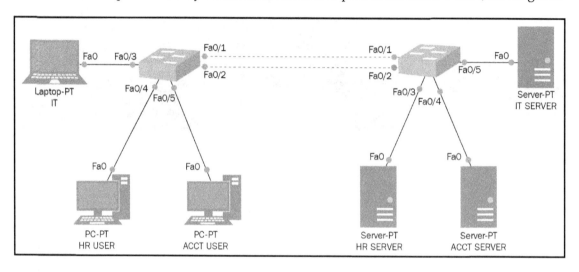

SWITCH 1:

PC name	VLAN#	Network	Department
Laptop_LJD	1	192.168.1.0/24	IT
PC1	10	192.168.10.0/24	HR
PC2	20	192.168.20.0/24	ACCT

SWITCH 2:

PC name	VLAN#	Network	Deparment
IT Server	1	192.168.1.0/24	IT
HR Server	10	192.168.10.0/24	HR
ACCT Server	20	192.168.20.0/24	ACCT

Broadcast control

Controlling broadcasts in your network is one of your top priorities, so by using switches, that uses private collision domains with full-duplex and that allows us to transmit and receive at the same time. You now know we can create VLANs that break up the broadcast domain into smaller logical segments.

We must still be wary of broadcasts on our network, or each VLAN. If you place too many nodes on one VLAN, that segment could get overwhelmed, so you must constantly monitor you network/VLANs to make sure that traffic is still flowing efficiently.

One thing IT personnel overlook is protocols—every protocol creates some type of broadcast. It depends on three basic things:

- The type of protocol
- The application running on the network
- How the services are being used

So, it is not just creating VLANs and forgetting about it; we could be our own worst enemy. We could be using an application for security purposes that is bandwidth-intensive. When we image our computers through the network, that takes up a lot of bandwidth, so you must make sure that you properly segment your network. Thus, if you are going to image a department or classroom, you won't slow down the rest of the network.

One thing you'd better be sure of is the policies on the firewall and what you are allowing your users to browse. At work, no one should be using a work computer for any kind of social media. These sites will eat your bandwidth up. They are one of the seven deadly sins, gluttony, so make sure you create policies that forbid social media sites. Yes, I am the bad guy, but my network is running at 100%, and that is my paycheck.

Security

So, how exactly do we create security by using VLANs? Well, no one can talk to each other because they are on a different network. If you want one VLAN to talk to another VLAN, you would implement inter-VLAN communication, so you can control communications between VLANs. There are other commands that we will be learning in the advanced switch technology chapter that will teach us how to control the device that is plugged in to your switch.

If you do have the need for inter-VLAN communication, you can simply create **access control lists (ACLs)**, which are policies on the server, firewall, or router, and control the type of traffic and the network you allow. If we do things correctly, our network can scale very easily from a medium to a large network, but as for any network, the designing of the network is the top priority.

This type of security was not possible when we used hubs; now, anyone can plug in a device and become part of your workgroup—you really had to jump through hoops to secure your network and then you made the network more difficult for your users to work in.

Using switches in our network has really enhanced the way we implement and manage all our devices.

How do VLANs get identified?

When we create VLANs, how does the switch know where to send the frame? Even in a small-to-medium sized network, the number of frames going through a switch is high. The switch has a protocol called the **Virtual Trunking Protocol (VTP)**, which tags all the frames that go through its trunk ports with the appropriate VLAN number and name.

VTP is a crucial switching protocol that we must understand, but we will be discussing that in the advanced switch technology chapter. Let's look at a simple example of the process of frame tagging:

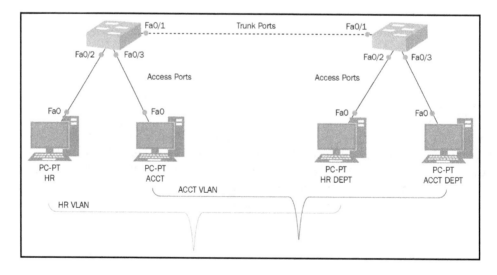

All VLANs need to be tagged by VTP to go across the trunk ports. The only one that does not need to be tagged is the native VLAN since it has a PVID, or port VLAN identifier, already in the frame.

But we will discuss that in the advanced switch chapter.

Types of ports

When working with VLANs, you will have to change the ports from their default setting of **dynamic auto** to either **trunk** and **voice**, or **access ports**. Let's define each of the ports:

- **Trunk ports**: This term was forged from the world of telecommunications, which carried multiple telephone communications at the same time. It only seemed proper to call point-to-point communications between switches or switches to routers trunks, since they carry multiple VLANs at the same time. Trunk ports can be 100, 1,000, or 10,000 Mbps and the range of VLANs that they carry is from 1 to 4,094.
- **Voice access ports**: Another type of access port, used for IP telephony, one port can have both data and voice, but you must configure the port deliberately for both data and voice. Doing this will allow you to use your PC and phone on the same port. The configuration would look something like the following:

```
SW2(config)#vlan 80
SW2(config-vlan)#name voice
SW2(config-vlan)#vlan 10
SW2(config-vlan)#name data
SW2(config-vlan)#int f0/19
SW2(config-if)#switchport mode access
SW2(config-if)#switchport access vlan 10
SW2(config-if)#switchport voice vlan 80
```

- If you were to do a show `vlan brief` command to verify, you would see the following:

`SW2(config-if)#do sh vlan brief`

VLAN	Name	Status	Ports
1	default	active	Fa0/1, Fa0/2, Fa0/3, Fa0/4
			Fa0/5, Fa0/6, Fa0/7, Fa0/8
			Fa0/9, Fa0/10, Fa0/11, Fa0/12
			Fa0/13, Fa0/14, Fa0/15, Fa0/16
			Fa0/17, Fa0/18, Fa0/20, Fa0/21
			Fa0/22, Fa0/23, Fa0/24, Gig0/1
			Gig0/2
10	HR	active	Fa0/19
80	voice	active	Fa0/19

- **Access ports**: This type of port is for the native VLAN. It does not need to be tagged by VTP since it assumes you are part of the native VLAN, which holds the PVID in its frame. Access ports only carry one VLAN at a time, so if your network has multiple VLANs, you must create trunk ports, so they would be able to be carried across those trunk ports. You must use a router to route between the different VLANs since each VLAN is in its own subnetwork.

Basics of frame-tagging

Since we now know that we can create thousands of VLANs and they can span across multiple switches, these could get confusing even for the switches. You must remember that by default, regular access ports remove any VLAN ID information. Hence, we trunk ports between switches and switches to routers, so ports can look at the frame and be able to identify or tag that port with a VLAN ID.

The other great thing about trunk ports is that they permit tagged or untagged VLANs to go through their ports.

Any VLAN that is **Not Tagged**, **Native**, or **Default** belongs to access ports and they already have a Port VLAN Identifier within the frame, so they could go across trunk ports or access ports.

Types of trunking

In the world of switching, when you are trunking ports, you have two options: **Inter-Switch Link (ISL)** or IEEE 802.1q. Using either of the following trunking methods identifies the VLAN as they go across switches in your network.

Inter-Switch Link (ISL)

This type of trunking is Cisco's proprietary trunking type; it is limited to only 1,000 VLANs, but still gets the job done. It will explicitly identify VLANs going across the trunk links, and has more overhead than the IEEE 802.1q trunking method since it tags the native VLAN and all other VLANs as well.

Today, some Cisco switches still support ISL trunking, but Cisco is moving away from ISL to the newer type of trunking; that is, 802.1q.

IEEE 802.1q trunking

This type of trunking inserts a field into the frame to identify the VLAN. It can be used across different types of vendors, not just Cisco equipment. Unlike the ISL form of trunking, that encapsulates the frame with control information. The IEEE 802.1q inserts an 802.1q field with tag control information.

The main thing you need to keep in mind is that we do not use ISL anymore, we use 802.1q. The Layer 2 switches, such as 2960, do not support ISL, but the Layer 3 switches do. But again, Cisco has moved away from that trunking method.

Routing between VLANs

OK, you have created your VLANs, which means you logically segmented your network at the data-link layer of the OSI model. You understand the reasons why you did this: better administration, more security, broadcast control, increased bandwidth, and it's much easier to administrate.

All those are excellent reasons to create VLANs, but now departments cannot communicate with each other. If you are in your own VLAN, you can talk to everyone in your VLAN, but that's it. What happens when you want to go out to the internet? Who is your default gateway? Think about it: you have four VLANs, which means four networks and your router may have one or two Ethernet ports on it. So, how do we accomplish communications with the outside world and between departments? The answer is inter-VLAN routing must be configured on a Layer 3 or network layer device.

Let's look at several examples:

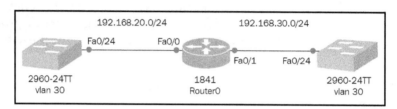

In the preceding example, we are using the two Fast Ethernet ports that exist on this router to connect our two VLANs or networks. This is fine if your network is going to stay this small, but that is not the reality.

The reality is that you're going to have dozens, hundreds, even thousands of VLANs to handle, so having a port per VLAN on your router is not the ultimate solution.

You could purchase a Layer 3 switch that will have routing capabilities, and then you can do a port per VLAN. Let's see what that would look like:

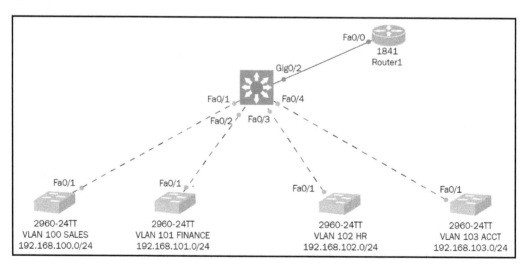

In the preceding scenario, using a Layer 3 switch, we could plug in multiple Layer 2 switches in each port of the core switch and they would represent different VLANs. Using this method, we could do inter-VLAN communications on the core switch and not have to bog down the router for this task.

If you are going to follow this type of topology using a Layer 3 switch, there is some upfront work that you would need to do. You will need to create, not assign, the VLANs on the core switch, create a VTP domain name for security purposes, and trunk the appropriate ports, which are F0/1-F0/4, and G0/2, which goes to the router. Since this a Layer 3 switch, to trunk the ports, you must set the encapsulation first and then set the mode to trunk.

Here is an example of trunking the ports on a Layer 3 switch:

```
Core(config)#INT RANGE F0/1 - 4
Core(config-if-range)#SWITCHPORT TRUNK ENCAPSULATION DOT1Q
Core(config-if-range)#SWITCHPORT MODE TRUNK
Core(config-if-range)#EXIT
Core(config)#INT G0/2
Core(config-if)#SWITCHPORT TRUNK ENCAPSULATION DOT1Q
Core(config-if)#SWITCHPORT MODE TRUNK
```

The highlighted command is the extra command that you would need to type on the Layer 3 switch. On the Layer 2 switches, all you need is the SWITCHPORT MODE TRUNK command.

Once the ports are trunked, you should verify they are trunked by typing the following command:

```
Core#SH INT TRUNK
Port    Mode    Encapsulation    Status      Native vlan
Fa0/1   on              802.1q          trunking        1
Fa0/2   on              802.1q          trunking        1
Fa0/3   on              802.1q          trunking        1
Fa0/4   on              802.1q          trunking        1
```

Don't worry if you don't see the G0/2 at this moment, this is because we have not configured anything on the router and the interface that faces the Layer 3 switch is administratively off.

So, you trunked the appropriate ports; let's go ahead and create the VLANs we need. Remember we are creating the VLANs on the core switch, but we are not going to assign them to any port. We are simply creating them here so they can propagate across the network to all other switches, and then, at the Layer 2 switch, you would assign them.

Let's go ahead and create the VLANs:

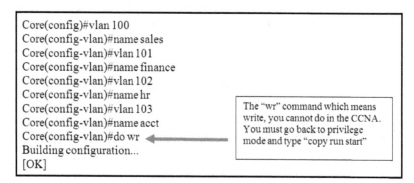

```
Core(config)#vlan 100
Core(config-vlan)#name sales
Core(config-vlan)#vlan 101
Core(config-vlan)#name finance
Core(config-vlan)#vlan 102
Core(config-vlan)#name hr
Core(config-vlan)#vlan 103
Core(config-vlan)#name acct
Core(config-vlan)#do wr   ◄━━━━━━━  The "wr" command which means write, you cannot do in the CCNA. You must go back to privilege mode and type "copy run start"
Building configuration...
[OK]
```

Next, you must verify that the VLANs you created work and they exist on the Layer 3 switch, using the following command:

```
Core#sh vlan
VLAN       Name                          Status         Ports
----   ------------------------------   ---------   -----------------------------
----
   1       default               active       Fa0/5,  Fa0/6,  Fa0/7,  Fa0/8
                                               Fa0/9,  Fa0/10, Fa0/11, Fa0/12
                                               Fa0/13, Fa0/14, Fa0/15, Fa0/16
                                               Fa0/17, Fa0/18, Fa0/19, Fa0/20
                                               Fa0/21, Fa0/22, Fa0/23, Fa0/24
                                               Gig0/1, Gig0/2
 100       sales                 active
 101       finance               active
 102       hr                    active
 103       acct                  active
1002       fddi-default          active
1003       token-ring-default    active
1004       fddinet-default       active
1005       trnet-default         active
```

Now, we need to create the VTP domain name, so only the switches in that domain communicate with each other and the VLANs can propagate down to the Layer 2 switches, which are our client switches. When I say client switches, I am talking about the VTP mode, in which, by default, all switches are in *server mode*. We will be configuring the VTP mode on the Layer 2 switches to *client mode*. We will be discussing VTP more in the *Advanced Switching* chapter.

But, I will still show you where you need to go to check for VTP configurations:

```
Core#sh vtp status
VTP Version : 2
Configuration Revision : 8
Maximum VLANs supported locally : 1005
Number of existing VLANs : 9
VTP Operating Mode : Server
VTP Domain Name :
VTP Pruning Mode : Disabled
VTP V2 Mode : Disabled
VTP Traps Generation : Disabled
MD5 digest : 0x00 0x11 0x18 0xA0 0xB0 0x23 0x16 0x38
Configuration last modified by 0.0.0.0 at 3-3-93 05:44:49
Local updater ID is 0.0.0.0 (no valid interface found)
```

By default, there is no VTP domain name, so let's create one:

```
Core#config t
Enter configuration commands, one per line. End with CNTL/Z.
Core(config)#vtp domain cisco
Changing VTP domain name from NULL to cisco
Core(config)#exit
Core#
```

As usual, we must verify what we did, so let's check whether there are any changes to effect:

```
Core#sh vtp status
VTP Version : 2
Configuration Revision : 0
Maximum VLANs supported locally : 1005
Number of existing VLANs : 9
VTP Operating Mode : Server
VTP Domain Name : cisco
VTP Pruning Mode : Disabled
VTP V2 Mode : Disabled
VTP Traps Generation : Disabled
MD5 digest : 0x98 0xC9 0x50 0xBA 0xAA 0x36 0x12 0x90
Configuration last modified by 0.0.0.0 at 3-3-93 05:44:49
Local updater ID is 0.0.0.0 (no valid interface found)
Core#
```

The changes are in place, so for the moment we are done with the core switch. Now, it is time to go to the client switches or Layer 2 switches and see whether the VLANs propagated down.

We'll start with the `192.168.100.0/24` network, which is on VLAN 100. We are looking for what happens if the VLANs propagated down from the core switch. But, before we check for that, we will change the operating mode of the switch to *client*. As per Cisco, there should be one server switch and the rest should be client switches.

This is a suggestion and for CCNA purposes it fits just fine, but for real-world scenarios, you may have more than one server switch—it all depends on the size and complexity of the network.

For the moment we are OK, so let's see how we change the VTP mode on the Layer 2 switch:

```
Switch#config t
Enter configuration commands, one per line. End with CNTL/Z.
Switch(config)#vtp mode client
Setting device to VTP CLIENT mode.
Switch(config)#
```

Now that we have done that, let's verify that the VLANs from the core switch were sent down:

```
Switch#sh vlan brief
VLAN    Name                 Status          Ports
----    --------------------------------     ---------   ----------------------------
----
 1      default              active          Fa0/2, Fa0/3, Fa0/4, Fa0/5
                                             Fa0/6, Fa0/7, Fa0/8, Fa0/9
                                             Fa0/10, Fa0/11, Fa0/12, Fa0/13
                                             Fa0/14, Fa0/15, Fa0/16,
                                             Fa0/17 Fa0/18, Fa0/19, Fa0/20,
                                             Fa0/21 Fa0/22, Fa0/23, Fa0/24,
                                             Gig0/1 Gig0/2
 100    sales                active
 101    finance              active
 102    hr                   active
 103    acct                 active
```

Awesome! Now, we can assign whichever VLAN we want to this switch, but follow the order, so this first switch will be the sale switch. Let's name the switch and assign the VLAN to a range of ports:

```
Switch(config)#hostname Sales
Sales(config)#int range f0/2-10
Sales(config-if-range)#switchport mode access
Sales(config-if-range)#switchport access vlan 100
Sales(config-if-range)#exit
Sales(config)#exit
Sales#
%SYS-5-CONFIG_I: Configured from console by console
Sales#copy run start
Destination filename [startup-config]?
Building configuration...
[OK]
Sales#
```

If, in your certification, you need to configure a hostname, assign VLANs, and make sure you save the configurations to the NVRAM or `startup-configuration` file, the preceding commands are how you would do it.

Once again, let's verify our configuration of the VLAN that was assigned:

```
Sales#sh vlan
VLAN    Name                             Status      Ports
----    -------------------------------- ---------   ---------------------------
----
1       default                          active      Fa0/11, Fa0/12, Fa0/13, Fa0/14
                                                     Fa0/15, Fa0/16, Fa0/17, Fa0/18
                                                     Fa0/19, Fa0/20, Fa0/21, Fa0/22
                                                     Fa0/23, Fa0/24, Gig0/1, Gig0/2
100     sales                            active      Fa0/2, Fa0/3, Fa0/4, Fa0/5
                                                     Fa0/6, Fa0/7, Fa0/8, Fa0/9
                                                     Fa0/10
101     finance                          active
102     hr                               active
103     acct                             active
```

All is well; VLAN 100 is assigned to ports F0/2 - 10, so we got that accomplished. Now, let's do the same thing to the next three switches: give them a hostname and assign the VLAN to the switches.

The Finance Switch configuration:

```
Switch(config)#hostname Finance
Finance(config)#vtp mode client
Setting device to VTP CLIENT mode.
Finance(config)#do sh vlan brief
VLAN      Name                          Status      Ports
----  -------------------------------  ---------  ----------------------------
-------
1         default                       active    Fa0/2, Fa0/3, Fa0/4, Fa0/5
                                                  Fa0/6, Fa0/7, Fa0/8, Fa0/9
                                                  Fa0/10, Fa0/11, Fa0/12, Fa0/13
                                                  Fa0/14, Fa0/15, Fa0/16, Fa0/17
                                                  Fa0/18, Fa0/19, Fa0/20, Fa0/21
                                                  Fa0/22, Fa0/23, Fa0/24, Gig0/1
                                                  Gig0/2
100       sales                         active
101       finance                       active
102       hr                            active
103       acct                          active
1002      fddi-default                  active
1003      token-ring-default active
1004      fddinet-default               active
1005      trnet-default                 active
Finance(config)#int range f0/2-10
Finance(config-if-range)#switchport mode access
Finance(config-if-range)#switchport access vlan 101
Finance(config-if-range)#exit
Finance(config)#exit
Finance#
%SYS-5-CONFIG_I: Configured from console by console
```

Now, let's verify that the VLANs were assigned to the desired ports:

```
Finance#sh vlan brief
VLAN      Name                          Status      Ports
----  -------------------------------  ---------  ----------------------------
----
1         default                       active    Fa0/11, Fa0/12, Fa0/13, Fa0/14
                                                  Fa0/15, Fa0/16, Fa0/17, Fa0/18
                                                  Fa0/19, Fa0/20, Fa0/21, Fa0/22
                                                  Fa0/23, Fa0/24, Gig0/1, Gig0/2
100       sales                         active
101       finance                       active    Fa0/2, Fa0/3, Fa0/4, Fa0/5
                                                  Fa0/6, Fa0/7, Fa0/8, Fa0/9
                                                  Fa0/10
```

```
102       hr                  active
103       acct                active
1002      fddi-default        active
1003      token-ring-defaultactive
1004      fddinet-default     active
1005      trnet-default       active
```

The HR switch configuration:

```
Switch(config)#hostname HR
HR (config)#vtp mode client
Setting device to VTP CLIENT mode.
HR (config)#do sh vlan brief
HR (config)#int range f0/2-10
HR (config-if-range)#switchport mode access
HR (config-if-range)#switchport access vlan 102
HR (config-if-range)#exit
HR (config)#exit
HR#
%SYS-5-CONFIG_I: Configured from console by console
HR #copy run start
Destination filename [startup-config]?
Building configuration...
[OK]
HR #sh vlan brief
```

```
VLAN    Name                      Status        Ports
----    -------------------------------- --------- --------------------------------
-----------
1       default                   active        Fa0/11, Fa0/12, Fa0/13, Fa0/14
                                                Fa0/15,Fa0/16, Fa0/17, Fa0/18
                                                Fa0/19, Fa0/20, Fa0/21, Fa0/22
                                                Fa0/23, Fa0/24, Gig0/1, Gig0/2

100     sales                     active
101     finance                   active
102     hr                        active        Fa0/2, Fa0/3, Fa0/4, Fa0/5
                                                Fa0/6, Fa0/7, Fa0/8, Fa0/9
                                                Fa0/10

103     acct                      active
1002    fddi-default              active
1003    token-ring-default        active
1004    fddinet-default           active
1005    trnet-default             active
```

The ACCT Switch configuration:

```
Switch(config)#hostname acct
acct(config)#vtp mode client
Setting device to VTP CLIENT mode.
acct(config)#do sh vlan brief
VLAN    Name                     Status     Ports
----  ------------------------------  ---------  --------------------------
----
1       default                  active     Fa0/2, Fa0/3, Fa0/4, Fa0/5
                                            Fa0/6, Fa0/7, Fa0/8, Fa0/9
                                            Fa0/10, Fa0/11, Fa0/12, Fa0/13
                                            Fa0/14, Fa0/15, Fa0/16, Fa0/17
                                            Fa0/18, Fa0/19, Fa0/20, Fa0/21
                                            Fa0/22, Fa0/23, Fa0/24, Gig0/1
                                            Gig0/2
100     sales                    active
101     finance                  active
102     hr                       active
103     acct                     active
1002    fddi-default             active
1003    token-ring-default  active
1004    fddinet-default     active
1005    trnet-default       active
acct(config)#
```

Now let's assign the VLANs to the desired ports:

```
acct(config)#int range f0/2-10
acct (config-if-range)#switchport mode access
acct (config-if-range)#switchport access vlan 103
acct (config-if-range)#exit
acct (config)#exit
acct #
%SYS-5-CONFIG_I: Configured from console by console
acct #copy run start
Destination filename [startup-config]?
Building configuration...
[OK]
acct #sh vlan brief
VLAN    Name                     Status       Ports
----  ------------------------------  ---------  --------------------------
--------
1       default                  active       Fa0/11, Fa0/12, Fa0/13, Fa0/14
                                              Fa0/15, Fa0/16, Fa0/17, Fa0/18
                                              Fa0/19, Fa0/20, Fa0/21, Fa0/22
                                              Fa0/23, Fa0/24, Gig0/1, Gig0/2
100     sales                    active
```

```
101           finance         active
102           hr              active
103           acct            active      Fa0/2, Fa0/3, Fa0/4, Fa0/5
                                          Fa0/6, Fa0/7, Fa0/8, Fa0/9
                                          Fa0/10
1002          fddi-default       active
1003          token-ring-default active
1004          fddinet-default    active
1005           trnet-default     active
HR#
```

Well, that was not so hard. We simply named the switch, turned the switch mode to `client`, and assigned the VLAN to the appropriate ports. As usual, you must verify everything you do, which is why you will always see me doing `show` commands to make sure that the commands I typed worked.

Believe me, I have been in 9,000 and 10,000 ASR routers and after doing my configuration, I try to save, and it errors out on me. To be honest, 80% was a typo, but the other 20% is just the IOS being wacky. So, always check and double-check your work. As far as your certification goes, please check your work and see whether what you configured gets the intended outcome before you hit next.

One thing I should also mention is to remember that we trunked the ports on the layer 3 switch, so does the Layer 2 switch need any trunking or is it done dynamically? Let's see:

```
acct#sh int trunk
Port       Mode         Encapsulation      Status       Native  vlan
Fa0/1      auto         n-802.1q           trunking               1
```

Remember, all ports by default are `Dynamic Auto` so it will mirror its neighbor port. That's why the lower ports are trunked `Dynamically`.

Before we move on to inter-VLAN routing, I want to define certain VLANs that we have seen but not mentioned. The following VLANs are reserved and you must be in transparent mode to use them:

VLAN	Name	Status	Ports
1002	fddi-default	active	
1003	token-ring-default	active	
1004	fddinet-default	active	
1005	trnet-default	active	

The preceding 1002-1005 VLAN range cannot be used, changed, renamed, or deleted. These VLANs are called extended VLANs and won't be saved in the database, unless your switch is set to `transparent mode` using the `vtp mode transparent` command. You should be familiar with this command, since we switched the Layer 2 switches to *client* mode.

If you try to create a VLAN within this range or higher, you will get an error and it will not allow you to create the VLAN. If you are using a simulator, you will get a bogus error:

```
HR(config)#vlan 4100
          ^
% Invalid input detected at '^' marker
```

In a real-world scenario using an actual IOS, you would get the following:

```
Core(config)#vlan 4100
Core(config-vlan)#^Z
% Failed to create VLANs 4100
Extended VLAN(s) not allowed in current VTP mode.
Failed to commit extended VLAN(s) changes
```

VLAN 1 also falls into this category; it cannot be created, changed, renamed, or deleted, by default that is the native VLAN. If you want to change the native VLAN, you must create another VLAN and make it the native VLAN using the following command:

```
Core(config-if)#switchport native vlan 600
```

Once you make VLAN 600 in this case, you must assign all ports to that VLAN, so no ports are left on VLAN 1.

Be careful when changing the native VLAN, it must be the same across the entire switched network, or you will have a `Native VLAN mismatch` error.

Now that we have configured all our VLANs, assigned them to their appropriate ports, and have trunked the ports that need to be trunked using the 802.1q protocol, we are ready for inter-VLAN connectivity. We will first do it using the router and then I will show you how to do it on the Layer 3 switch:

Configuring the core router for Inter-vlan communication

```
CORE(config)#INT F0/0
CORE(config-if)#NO SHUT
```
> On the physical interface all you need to do is turn it on.

```
CORE(config-if)#
%LINK-5-CHANGED: Interface FastEthernet0/0, changed state to up

%LINEPROTO-5-UPDOWN: Line protocol on Interface FastEthernet0/0, changed state to up

CORE(config-if)#INT F0/0.100
CORE(config-subif)#
```
> How you create a sub-interface the number SHOULD match the vlan id.

```
%LINK-5-CHANGED: Interface FastEthernet0/0.100, changed state to up

%LINEPROTO-5-UPDOWN: Line protocol on Interface FastEthernet0/0.100, changed state to up

CORE(config-subif)#ENCAP DOT1Q 100
```
> Encapsulation must match the 802.1q protocol and the number is required to match the vlan id.

```
CORE(config-subif)#IP ADDRESS 192.168.100.254 255.255.255.0
CORE(config-subif)#
CORE(config-subif)#INT F0/0.101
CORE(config-subif)#
```
> The IP address is the default gateway address for all devices on this network.

```
%LINK-5-CHANGED: Interface FastEthernet0/0.101, changed state to up

%LINEPROTO-5-UPDOWN: Line protocol on Interface FastEthernet0/0.101, changed state to up

CORE(config-subif)#ENCAP DOT1Q 101
CORE(config-subif)#IP ADDRESS 192.168.101.254 255.255.255.0
CORE(config-subif)#
CORE(config-subif)#INT F0/0.102
CORE(config-subif)#
%LINK-5-CHANGED: Interface FastEthernet0/0.102, changed state to up

%LINEPROTO-5-UPDOWN: Line protocol on Interface FastEthernet0/0.102, changed state to up

CORE(config-subif)#ENCAP DOT1Q 102
CORE(config-subif)#IP ADDRESS 192.168.102.254 255.255.255.0
CORE(config-subif)#
CORE(config-subif)#INT F0/0.103
CORE(config-subif)#
%LINK-5-CHANGED: Interface FastEthernet0/0.103, changed state to up

%LINEPROTO-5-UPDOWN: Line protocol on Interface FastEthernet0/0.103, changed state to up

CORE(config-subif)#ENCAP DOT1Q 103
CORE(config-subif)#IP ADDRESS 192.168.103.254 255.255.255.0
CORE(config-subif)#DO WR
Building configuration...
[OK]
CORE(config-subif)#
```

Now that we have created the sub interfaces for each VLAN, and the correct encapsulation type and VLAN ID, we have also assigned the correct IP address, which will act as the default gateway for all devices. Let's verify that everything is working properly.

You will be typing three different commands to verify your work:

```
Show ip interface brief
CORE#sh ip int brief
Interface                 IP-Address    OK?  Method Status      Protocol
FastEthernet0/0           unassigned    YES  unset  up          up
FastEthernet0/0.100 192.168.100.254     YES  manual up          up
FastEthernet0/0.101 192.168.101.254     YES  manual up          up
FastEthernet0/0.102 192.168.102.254     YES  manual up          up
FastEthernet0/0.103 192.168.103.254     YES  manual up          up
Show ip route
CORE#sh ip route
Codes: C - connected, S - static, I - IGRP, R - RIP, M - mobile, B - BGP
D - EIGRP, EX - EIGRP external, O - OSPF, IA - OSPF inter area
N1 - OSPF NSSA external type 1, N2 - OSPF NSSA external type 2
E1 - OSPF external type 1, E2 - OSPF external type 2, E - EGP
i - IS-IS, L1 - IS-IS level-1, L2 - IS-IS level-2, ia - IS-IS inter area
* - candidate default, U - per-user static route, o - ODR
P - periodic downloaded static route
Gateway of last resort is not set
C 192.168.100.0/24 is directly connected, FastEthernet0/0.100
C 192.168.101.0/24 is directly connected, FastEthernet0/0.101
C 192.168.102.0/24 is directly connected, FastEthernet0/0.102
C 192.168.103.0/24 is directly connected, FastEthernet0/0.103
Show Startup-config
CORE#sh start
*Some output omitted*
    interface FastEthernet0/0
    no ip address
    duplex auto
    speed auto
    !
    interface FastEthernet0/0.100
    encapsulation dot1Q 100
    ip address 192.168.100.254 255.255.255.0
    !
    interface FastEthernet0/0.101
    encapsulation dot1Q 101
    ip address 192.168.101.254 255.255.255.0
    !
    interface FastEthernet0/0.102
    encapsulation dot1Q 102
    ip address 192.168.102.254 255.255.255.0
    !
    interface FastEthernet0/0.103
    encapsulation dot1Q 103
    ip address 192.168.103.254 255.255.255.0
```

So, based on our configurations, we should be able to communicate with all the VLANs. Let's verify by pinging all the network's gateway addresses, so we will need to add a PC to one of the VLANs, or all of them if you prefer. I will only add one PC and ping all the gateway addresses.

We will use the Finance VLAN to perform our test:

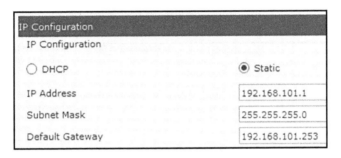

```
C:\>PING 192.168.100.254
Pinging 192.168.100.254 with 32 bytes of data:
Reply from 192.168.100.254: bytes=32 time=1ms TTL=255
Reply from 192.168.100.254: bytes=32 time<1ms TTL=255
Ping statistics for 192.168.100.254:
Packets: Sent = 2, Received = 2, Lost = 0 (0% loss),
Approximate round trip times in milli-seconds:
Minimum = 0ms, Maximum = 1ms, Average = 0ms
Control-C
^C
C:\>PING 192.168.101.254
Pinging 192.168.101.254 with 32 bytes of data:
Reply from 192.168.101.254: bytes=32 time=4ms TTL=255
Reply from 192.168.101.254: bytes=32 time<1ms TTL=255
Ping statistics for 192.168.101.254:
Packets: Sent = 2, Received = 2, Lost = 0 (0% loss),
Approximate round trip times in milli-seconds:
Minimum = 0ms, Maximum = 4ms, Average = 2ms
Control-C
^C
C:\>PING 192.168.102.254
Pinging 192.168.102.254 with 32 bytes of data:
Reply from 192.168.102.254: bytes=32 time<1ms TTL=255
Reply from 192.168.102.254: bytes=32 time<1ms TTL=255
Ping statistics for 192.168.102.254:
Packets: Sent = 4, Received = 4, Lost = 0 (0% loss),
Approximate round trip times in milli-seconds:
Minimum = 0ms, Maximum = 0ms, Average = 0ms
Control-C
```

```
^C
C:\>PING 192.168.103.254
Pinging 192.168.103.254 with 32 bytes of data:
Reply from 192.168.103.254: bytes=32 time<1ms TTL=255
Reply from 192.168.103.254: bytes=32 time<1ms TTL=255
Ping statistics for 192.168.103.254:
Packets: Sent = 4, Received = 4, Lost = 0 (0% loss),
Approximate round trip times in milli-seconds:
Minimum = 0ms, Maximum = 0ms, Average = 0ms
```

So, our configurations are on the money. We are able to ping all the end devices on every network.

That was easy to configure on the router, but if we want to use the Layer 3 switch, instead of the router, for inter-VLAN communications, we need to configure a couple more things on router all our switches.

The Layer 3 switch will be the main one we need to concentrate on since we are going to enable the routing feature on it. But we must also assign the switches an IP address and default gateway.

Let's get to work! The first thing we must do in the Layer 3 switch is assign all the VLANs an IP address:

```
interface Vlan100
mac-address 0060.5c66.3701
ip address 192.168.100.253 255.255.255.0
!
interface Vlan101
mac-address 0060.5c66.3702
ip address 192.168.101.253 255.255.255.0
!
interface Vlan102
mac-address 0060.5c66.3703
ip address 192.168.102.253 255.255.255.0
!
interface Vlan103
mac-address 0060.5c66.3704
ip address 192.168.103.253 255.255.255.0
```

```
!
interface Vlan600  ◄───────────────    New VLAN was added for the G0/2
mac-address 0060.5c66.3705             interface that goes to the router.
ip address 192.168.1.253 255.255.255.0   We must create a network there also
```

The command to do that is very simple:

```
Interface vlan 100
Ip address 192.168.100.253 255.255.255.0
No shut
```

You would do the same command to all the VLANs, so do not forget to turn on the VLAN interface. Well, really we should have turned on routing first, but we can do that now:

```
Core(config)#ip routing
```

Assign the default gateway to the outside world, which is the router:

```
Core(config)#IP DEFAULT-GATEWAY 192.168.1.254
```

We can then choose a routing protocol that we will configure on the Layer 3 switch and router:

```
router eigrp 100
network 192.168.1.0
network 192.168.100.0
network 192.168.101.0
network 192.168.102.0
network 192.168.103.0
no auto-summary
```

Now we test whether we have connectivity across the network:

ping 192.168.101.253   My gateway address

```
Pinging 192.168.101.253 with 32 bytes of data:
Reply from 192.168.101.253: bytes=32 time<1ms TTL=255
Reply from 192.168.101.253: bytes=32 time<1ms TTL=255
Ping statistics for 192.168.101.253:
Packets: Sent = 2, Received = 2, Lost = 0 (0% loss),
Approximate round trip times in milli-seconds:
Minimum = 0ms, Maximum = 0ms, Average = 0ms
Control-C
^C
```

C:\>ping 192.168.100.253   VLAN 100 address

```
Pinging 192.168.100.253 with 32 bytes of data:
Reply from 192.168.100.253: bytes=32 time=1ms TTL=255
Reply from 192.168.100.253: bytes=32 time<1ms TTL=255
Ping statistics for 192.168.100.253:
Packets: Sent = 2, Received = 2, Lost = 0 (0% loss),
Approximate round trip times in milli-seconds:
Minimum = 0ms, Maximum = 1ms, Average = 0ms
Control-C
^C
```

C:\>ping 192.168.102.253	VLAN 102 address

```
Pinging 192.168.102.253 with 32 bytes of data:
Reply from 192.168.102.253: bytes=32 time<1ms TTL=255
Reply from 192.168.102.253: bytes=32 time=2ms TTL=255
Ping statistics for 192.168.102.253:
Packets: Sent = 2, Received = 2, Lost = 0 (0% loss),
Approximate round trip times in milli-seconds:
Minimum = 0ms, Maximum = 2ms, Average = 1ms
Control-C
^C
```

C:\>ping 192.168.103.253	VLAN 103 address

```
Pinging 192.168.103.253 with 32 bytes of data:
Reply from 192.168.103.253: bytes=32 time<1ms TTL=255
Reply from 192.168.103.253: bytes=32 time=1ms TTL=255
Ping statistics for 192.168.103.253:
Packets: Sent = 2, Received = 2, Lost = 0 (0% loss),
Approximate round trip times in milli-seconds:
Minimum = 0ms, Maximum = 1ms, Average = 0ms
Control-C
^C
```

C:\>ping 192.168.1.254	Core Router address

```
Pinging 192.168.1.254 with 32 bytes of data:
Reply from 192.168.1.254: bytes=32 time=1ms TTL=254
Reply from 192.168.1.254: bytes=32 time<1ms TTL=254
Ping statistics for 192.168.1.254:
Packets: Sent = 2, Received = 2, Lost = 0 (0% loss),
Approximate round trip times in milli-seconds:
Minimum = 0ms, Maximum = 1ms, Average = 0ms
Control-C
^C
C:\>
```

So, we have connectivity across our network, but by no means is this the only way of checking the connectivity across the network. In the advanced switching chapter, I will show you how to do the same thing, but using a different method with the Layer 3 switch.

Summary

In this chapter, I showed you not only how to create a VLAN, but also how to name the VLAN and assign the VLAN to a port or range of ports. We also learned the importance of trunking a port, going between switches or from a switch to a router, so it can carry multiple VLANs across, using the 802.1q protocol, which is the one Cisco is now using. Then, we learned how to make separate VLANs talk to each other in two different ways: using a router and configuring subinterfaces, or using the Layer 3 switch and enabling routing on it.

If you remember anything from this chapter, let it be the importance of creating VLANs in your network. That way, your network can run more efficiently because you have reduced the amount of broadcast on your network.

Later in the book, we will continue talking about switching and we will learn other methods we can use to make layers more streamlined and secure.

14
Introduction to the EIGRP Routing Protocol

By now, you should have an idea of how routing works and whether we use static routes, default routes, or dynamic routing protocols. We have already configured EIGRP for IPv6, but we did not get into the details for this unique routing protocol.

One of the more confusing questions is: Are the EIGRP routing protocols still proprietary to Cisco? Not any more! For more information on open standard EIGRP used by multiple vendors, refer to the following link: `http://tools.ietf.org/html/draft-savage-eigrp-00`

It's not only a challenge for real-world networks and their devices, but what about the CCNA certification exam? How do we answer that question, if asked? As far as the CCNA 200-125 is concerned, EIGRP still remains proprietary to Cisco, and that is the way you must think and answer in the exam.

In the real world, that will be completely up to your company's SOP and what they are going to use across their WAN. In this chapter, our focus will be on how EIGRP works, its features, and configuring EIGRP for single autonomous systems and multiple autonomous systems.

We will cover the following topics in this chapter:

- EIGRP features and operations
- **Reliable Transport Protocol (RTP)**
- Diffusing the update algorithm, or DUAL
- Route discovery and maintenance

- Configuring EIGRP for IPv4
- VLSM support and summarization
- Controlling EIGRP traffic
- Split horizon
- Verifying and troubleshooting EIGRP

EIGRP features and operations

Before we begin discussing EIGRP, we need to understand where it came from. It originated from Interior Gateway Routing Protocol (**IGRP**). The problem with IGRP is that it had no support for **Variable Length Subnet Masking** (**VLSM**) and it was broadcast-based. With the Enhance Interior Gateway Routing Protocol, we now have support for VLSM and the updates are sent via a multicast using the following multicast address: 224.0.0.100 for IPv4.

EIGRP has a lot more to offer than its predecessor. Not only is it a classless routing protocol with VLSM capabilities, it has a maximum hop count of 255, but by default this is set to 100. It is also considered a hybrid or advanced distance-vector routing protocol. That means that it has the better of two worlds, with a links state and **distance vector** (**DV**). The DV features are just like RIPv2, where it has limited hop counts. It will send out the complete routing table to its neighboring routers the first time it tries to converge, and it will summarize the route. So, you would have to use the no auto-summary command so that it sends out the subnet mask along with the updates.

It has link state features, such as triggered updates, after it has fully converged, and the routing table is complete. EIGRP will maintain neighbor relationships or adjacencies, using *hello* messages and when a network is added or removed, it will only send that change.

EIGRP also has a very intelligent algorithm. The Dual algorithm will consider several attributes to make a more efficient or reliable decision as to which path it will send out the packet on to reach the destination faster. Also, EIGRP is based on autonomous systems, with a range from 1-65,535. You can only have one autonomous system, which means all the routers are sharing the same routing table, or you can have multiple autonomous systems, at that point you would have to redistribute the routes into the other AS, for the routers to communicate with each other.

So, EIGRP is a very powerful routing protocol and it has a lot of benefits to allow us to run our network more efficiently. So, let's create a list of the major features:

- Support for VLSM or CIDR
- Summarization and discontinuous networks
- Best path selection using the DUAL
- No broadcast; we use multicast now
- Supports IPv4 and IPv6
- Efficient neighbor discovery

Neighbor discovery

All routing protocols have a process that they use to create neighbor relationships with the router that they are directly connected to. EIGRP is no different; it has its own process or set of rules that it must follow to create that relationship. Essentially, it follows these three criteria:

- Hello or ACK received
- AS numbers must match
- Identical metrics (these are the *K* values *bandwidth, delay, reliability, load, and MTU*)

The following diagram will give you a visual of how exactly *neighbor discovery* works:

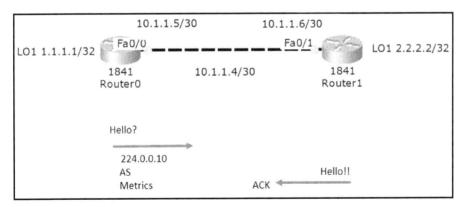

If you were to type the `show ip eigrp neighbors` command, this is what you would see:

```
R0#sh ip eigrp neighbors
IP-EIGRP neighbors for process 100
H   Address   Interface   Hold   Uptime    SRTT  RTO  Q  Seq
                          (sec)             (ms)  Cnt    Num
0  10.1.1.6    Fa0/0    11 00:12:01 40    1000  0      13
R1#sh ip eigrp neighbors
IP-EIGRP neighbors for process 100
H   Address   Interface   Hold  Uptime  SRTT RTO  Q  Seq
                          (sec)          (ms) Cnt Num
0  10.1.1.5    Fa0/1      12    00:17:22 40  1000 0  19
```

Another command that is very helpful is the `show ip protocols` command:

```
R0#sh ip protocols
Routing Protocol is "eigrp 100 "
Outgoing update filter list for all interfaces is not set
Incoming update filter list for all interfaces is not set
Default networks flagged in outgoing updates
Default networks accepted from incoming updates
EIGRP metric weight K1=1, K2=0, K3=1, K4=0, K5=0
EIGRP maximum hopcount 100
EIGRP maximum metric variance 1
Redistributing: eigrp 100
Automatic network summarization is not in effect
Maximum path: 4
Routing for Networks:
10.0.0.0
1.0.0.0
Routing Information Sources:
Gateway Distance Last Update
10.1.1.6 90 0
Distance: internal 90 external 170
R1#sh ip protocols
Routing Protocol is "eigrp 100 "
Outgoing update filter list for all interfaces is not set
Incoming update filter list for all interfaces is not set
Default networks flagged in outgoing updates
Default networks accepted from incoming updates
EIGRP metric weight K1=1, K2=0, K3=1, K4=0, K5=0
EIGRP maximum hopcount 100
EIGRP maximum metric variance 1
Redistributing: eigrp 100
Automatic network summarization is not in effect
Maximum path: 4
Routing for Networks:
```

```
10.0.0.0
2.0.0.0
Routing Information Sources:
Gateway Distance Last Update
10.1.1.5 90 0
Distance: internal 90 external 170
```

As you can see from the output of `sh ip eigrp neighbors` *and the* **sh ip protocols**, they are on the neighbor routers, share and are on the same subnet. They are using the same autonomous system and their metrics are the same.

The link state property of EIGRP sends Hellos to its neighboring router to maintain that adjacency, instead of sending the entire routing table periodically. If you were to do a `debug ip eigrp packets` command, you would see those *hello messages* being sent and received.

Look at the following screenshot to see an example of hello messages:

```
R0#debug eigrp packets
EIGRP Packets debugging is on
    (UPDATE, REQUEST, QUERY, REPLY, HELLO, ACK )
R0#
EIGRP: Sending HELLO on Loopback0
  AS 100, Flags 0x0, Seq 4/0 idbQ 0/0 iidbQ un/rely 0/0

EIGRP: Received HELLO on Loopback0 nbr 1.1.1.1
  AS 100, Flags 0x0, Seq 4/0 idbQ 0/0

EIGRP: Packet from ourselves ignored

EIGRP: Sending HELLO on FastEthernet0/0
  AS 100, Flags 0x0, Seq 4/0 idbQ 0/0 iidbQ un/rely 0/0
```

One of the best things about using `Hello` messages is that it reduces the amount of information that gets sent out on the network. If you are in a single autonomous system, Hello messages are automatically used, but if you are not in a single autonomous network, then you would need to do a redistribution and that would involve inputting the metrics, which need to be identical.

The advantage of the hello messages, even in a multiple AS network, is that hello messages would still be sent out to maintain the adjacency instead of the entire routing table. With EIGRP, that only happens when they first learn about each other's network; after that, it is simply maintaining the adjacency.

EIGRP timers

Just like all routing protocols, EIGRP has different timers, such as hold time interval, smooth round-trip-timer, and queue information. They are all kept in the **neighbor table** to include the IP address:

```
R1#sh ip eigrp neighbors
IP-EIGRP neighbors for process 100
H     Address    Interface Hold   Uptime    SRTT   RTO   Q    Seq
                           (sec)                    (ms)  Cnt  Num
0    10.1.1.5    Fa0/1     12     00:17:22  40     1000  0    19
```

Before we keep moving forward with EIGRP, there is some terminology you need to know. The following table will help you understand these terms:

Term	Definition
Reported Distance or Advertised Distance	The RD or AD is the metric of the remote network as your neighbor reports it, but also it is the routing table metric, and it's the second number in the parenthesis in your topology table

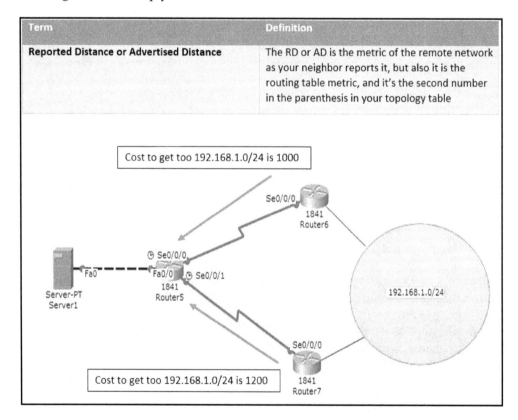

The preceding diagram is theoretical. It is showing you that your neighbor routers are giving you a *reported distance* or *advertised distance* to get to the remote network of 192.168.1.0, which is called a **cost**.

The R5 router must now decide, based on that cost, and place the faster or lower cost on the routing table and the higher cost or slower path in the topology table. This brings us to our next term, feasible distance or FD:

Term	Definition
Feasible Distance or FD	Bottom line the FD is the route with the lowest cost or fastest path that is on the routing table

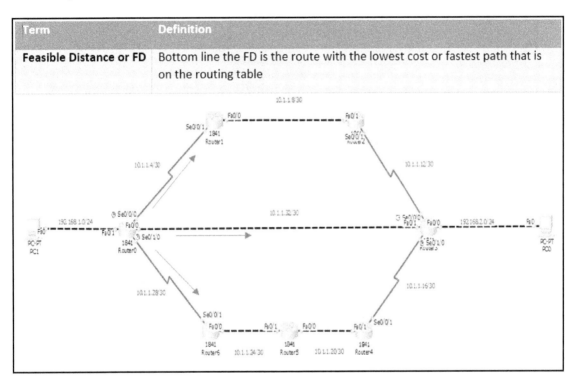

The preceding diagram shows three separate paths to get to the `192.168.2.0/24` network. So, how does EIGRP choose which path to take? Remember, it uses the FD from the neighbor routers, but it also takes into consideration the metrics or *K* values bandwidth, delay, reliability, load, and MTU.

Let's look at the routing table, since only the fastest and best routes end up on the routing table:

```
R0#sh ip route
The Gateway of last resort is not set.
10.0.0.0/8 is variably subnetted, with nine subnets and two masks.
D 10.0.0.0/8 is a summary; 00:02:34, Null0
C 10.1.1.4/30 is directly connected; Serial0/0/0
D 10.1.1.8/30 [90/540160] via 10.1.1.6, 00:02:29; Serial0/0/0
D 10.1.1.12/30 [90/2684416] via 10.1.1.6, 00:02:27, Serial0/0/0
D 10.1.1.16/30 [90/2686976] via 10.1.1.29, 00:02:24, Serial0/1/0
D 10.1.1.20/30 [90/2174976] via 10.1.1.29, 00:02:24, Serial0/1/0
D 10.1.1.24/30 [90/2172416] via 10.1.1.29, 00:02:24, Serial0/1/0
C 10.1.1.28/30 is directly connected, Serial0/1/0
C 10.1.1.32/30 is directly connected, FastEthernet0/0
C 192.168.1.0/24 is directly connected, FastEthernet0/1
D 192.168.2.0/24 [90/2686976] via 10.1.1.6, 00:02:27, Serial0/0/0
```

Pay close attention to the number highlighted.

Now, let's look at the topology table, but I will omit information not related to what we are looking for:

```
R0#sh ip eigrp topology
P 192.168.2.0/24, 1 successors, FD is 2686976
via 10.1.1.6 (2686976/2174976), Serial0/0/0
via 10.1.1.29 (2689536/2177536), Serial0/1/0
via 10.1.1.34 (40005120/28160), FastEthernet0/0
```

As you can plainly see, the three different routes are in the topology table, but the one with the lowest FD is the one that makes it to the routing table because it is the fastest path to the destination network based only on your neighbors' reported distance and your own calculation using the *K* values. Just so you know, out of the five *K* values, by default, only bandwidth and delay are the ones that are on.

If you go back to the diagram, you would think it would go across the FastEthernet link, since it's 100 Mps and serial links are usually smaller. That should make you think that someone must have changed the bandwidth on serial links.

Let's look at the bandwidth of the 10.1.1.6 interface, since that is the direction that our traffic is flowing:

```
R0#sh int s0/0/0
Serial0/0/0 is up, line protocol is up (connected)
Hardware is HD64570
Internet address is 10.1.1.5/30
MTU 1500 bytes, BW 10000000 Kbit, DLY 20000 usec,
reliability 255/255, txload 1/255, rxload 1/255
```

Bingo! That is not the default of a serial link. For a WIC2T card, it should be 1.544 Mbps. Now let's look at the FastEthernet link:

```
FastEthernet0/0 is up, line protocol is up (connected)
Hardware is Lance, address is 0006.2a77.0401 (bia 0006.2a77.0401)
Internet address is 10.1.1.33/30
MTU 1500 bytes, BW 64 Kbit, DLY 100 usec,
reliability 255/255, txload 1/255, rxload 1/255
```

64 Kbit on a Fast Ethernet link? I think not. That is why the traffic is flowing in the direction that it is flowing.

So, EIGRP uses a combination of different variables to find the best path to the destination network. But what still holds true, after the calculation is done, is that the lowest FD will be the best path to the destination network when multiple paths exist.

Let's look at some more terms, so we can move forward with EIGRP:

Term	Definition
Feasible successor or FS	The FS is the path that its AD is less than the FD of the current successor and it considered a backup route. In other words, the FS is the path that is slower, and it came in second place
Successor Route	The Successor is the route that will make it to the Routing table, it has the fastest route to the destination network.
Neighbor Table	Keeps the information about adjacent neighbors, if a new neighbor is found the information is kept in the Neighbor table
Topology Table	The topology table has all routes it has learned through the DUAL algorithm, so the Feasible Successor routes and Successor routes will be in the topology table. Since these routes are volatile, the topology table is kept in RAM. The routing table get its information from the topology table.
Reliable Transport Protocol or RTP	The RTP protocol was designed by Cisco, to ensure proper communication between routers configured with EIGRP. Its purpose is to use the multicast and unicast addresses to ensure updates are sent reliably. This process is often called the "Reliable Multicast."

One thing you need to keep in mind is that EIGRP is all about changes in the topology and any updates that may happen on the network. It synchronizes routing databases at startup, while at the same time maintaining the consistency of the existing databases over time.

The following are five different types of packets used in EIGRP:

- **Update**: Update packets contain routing information. When updates are sent, they use RTP. This also means that if only one router within the single AS needs an update, it will use a unicast address instead of multicast and only that router gets updated. Always remember that regardless of whether it's multicast or unicast, you will always need an ACK to create that reliable transport.
- **Query**: A query is used when a router loses a path to an existing destination. It will always be multicast in nature and will always use RTP. Keep in mind that the query is coming from the topology table.

- **Reply**: If you send a query, you want a reply in return and this is done via a unicast address. If a reply is being used normally, it is because a path was lost to a specific destination.
- **Hello**: Hello messages are used to discover and maintain neighbor relationships. They are sent via unreliable multicast, which means they do not require ACKs.
- **ACK**: An ACK is short for **acknowledgement**; it lets you know the packet got there and back.

Diffusing Update Algorithm or DUAL

This is the algorithm that allows EIGRP to have all the features it has and allows traffic to be so reliable. The following is a list of the essential tasks that it does:

- Finds a backup route if the topology permits
- Support for VLSM
- Dynamic route recovery
- Query its neighbor routers for other alternate routes

EIGRP routers maintain a copy of all their neighbors' routes, so they can calculate their own cost to each destination network. That way, if the successor route goes down, they can query the topology table for alternate or backup routes. This is what makes EIGRP so awesome, since it keeps all the routes from their neighbors and, if a route goes down, it can query the topology table for an alternate route.

But, what if the query to the topology table does not work? Well, EIGRP will then ask its neighbors for help to find an alternate path! The DUAL strategy, and the reliability and leveraging of other routers, makes it the quickest to converge on a network.

For the DUAL to work, it must meet the following three requirements:

- Neighbors are discovered or noted as dead within a distinct time
- Messages that transmitted should be received correctly
- Messages and changes received must be dealt with in the order they were received

The following command will show you those hello messages received, and more:

```
R1#sh ip eigrp traffic
IP-EIGRP Traffic Statistics for process 100
Hellos sent/received: 56845/37880
Updates sent/received: 9/14
Queries sent/received: 0/0
Replies sent/received: 0/0
Acks sent/received: 14/9
Input queue high water mark 1, 0 drops
SIA-Queries sent/received: 0/0
SIA-Replies sent/received: 0/0
```

If you wanted to change the default hello timer to something greater, the command would be the following:

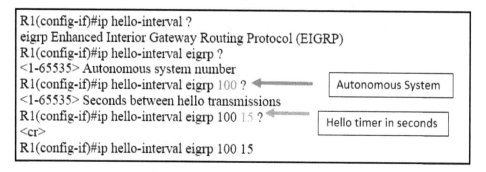

Remember that this command is typed under interface configuration mode.

Configuring EIGRP

Well, I think we have said enough about EIGRP; we now know that it is based on autonomous systems, being either single or multiple. It is an enhanced routing protocol, due to the fact that it has both distance-vector and link state features. The maximum number of routers a packet can travel is 255 routers, but, by default, this is set to 100.

It uses a very sophisticated algorithm called **diffused update algorithm**, or **DUAL**, which makes lots of decisions based on metrics, such as the five **K** values of *bandwidth, delay, load, reliability, and MTU*. It also gets AD, or advertised distance, from its neighbor routers to calculate the distance to remote networks.

EIGRP also works with tables. The routing table, topology table, and neighbor table, all work together to make sure if a path to a destination network fails then the routing protocol will always have an alternate path to that network.

The alternate path is chosen by the FD, or feasible distance. If you have the lowest FD, then you are the *successor route* and will be placed in the routing table. If you have a higher FD, you will remain in the topology table as a feasible successor.

So, EIGRP is a very reliable protocol. Let's configure it.

The following topology is going to be a full mesh, with LANs on each router. This will add to the complexity of the lab, so we can look at everything we have talked about. Before we begin configurations, we must know the IP addressing scheme of each device. The following table shows the addresses, gateways, and masks of each device:

IP Scheme for PC's

NODE	IP ADDRESS	SUBNET MASK	GATEWAY
PC0	192.168.1.1	255.255.255.0	192.168.1.254
PC1	192.168.1.2	255.255.255.0	192.168.1.254
PC2	192.168.2.1	255.255.255.0	192.168.2.254
PC3	192.168.2.2	255.255.255.0	192.168.2.254
PC4	192.168.3.1	255.255.255.0	192.168.3.254
PC5	192.168.3.2	255.255.255.0	192.168.3.254
PC6	192.168.4.1	255.255.255.0	192.168.4.254
PC7	192.168.4.2	255.255.255.0	192.168.4.254

IP Scheme for Routers

INTERFACE	R1	R2	R3	R4	CIDR
F0/0	192.168.1.254	192.168.2.254	192.168.3.254	192.168.4.254	/24
F0/1	10.1.1.21	10.1.1.25	10.1.1.22	10.1.1.26	/30
S0/0/0	10.1.1.5	10.1.1.10	10.1.1.18	10.1.1.14	/30
S0/0/1	10.1.1.9	10.1.1.17	10.1.1.13	10.1.1.6	/30

The routing protocol in use must learn to use our show commands:

```
R1#sh ip protocols
Routing Protocol is "eigrp 100 "
Outgoing update filter list for all interfaces is not set
Incoming update filter list for all interfaces is not set
Default networks flagged in outgoing updates
Default networks accepted from incoming updates
EIGRP metric weight K1=1, K2=0, K3=1, K4=0, K5=0
EIGRP maximum hopcount 100
EIGRP maximum metric variance 1
Redistributing: eigrp 100
Automatic network summarization is not in effect
Maximum path: 4
Routing for Networks:
192.168.1.0
10.0.0.0
Routing Information Sources:
Gateway Distance Last Update
10.1.1.10 90 1739292
10.1.1.22 90 1755881
10.1.1.6 90 1774985
Distance: internal 90 external 170
```

Okay, you have the topology, the IP scheme, and which routing protocol to use, and its autonomous system. As you can see, I already configured the lab, but now it's your turn.

You are going to have to configure it to follow along with the show command we are about to do.

Don't worry about including any administrative commands. That is not the purpose of this chapter. You should, by now, know your admin commands. The first thing you need to worry about is connectivity, so I will show you the output of the sh ip int brief command from each router:

```
R1
R1>EN
R1#SH IP INT BRIEF
Interface              IP-Address      OK? Method Status
Protocol
FastEthernet0/0        192.168.1.254   YES manual up                    up
FastEthernet0/1        10.1.1.21       YES manual up                    up
Serial0/0/0            10.1.1.5        YES manual up                    up
Serial0/0/1            10.1.1.9        YES manual up                    up

R2
R2#SH IP INT BRIEF
Interface              IP-Address      OK? Method Status
Protocol
FastEthernet0/0        192.168.2.254   YES manual up                    up
FastEthernet0/1        10.1.1.25       YES manual up                    up
Serial0/0/0            10.1.1.10       YES manual up                    up
Serial0/0/1            10.1.1.17       YES manual up                    up

R3
R3#SH IP INT BRIEF
Interface              IP-Address      OK? Method Status
Protocol
FastEthernet0/0        192.168.3.254   YES manual up                    up
FastEthernet0/1        10.1.1.22       YES manual up                    up
Serial0/0/0            10.1.1.18       YES manual up                    up
Serial0/0/1            10.1.1.13       YES manual up                    up

R4
R4#SH IP INT BRIEF
Interface              IP-Address      OK? Method Status
Protocol
FastEthernet0/0        192.168.4.254   YES manual up                    up
FastEthernet0/1        10.1.1.26       YES manual up                    up
Serial0/0/0            10.1.1.14       YES manual up                    up
Serial0/0/1            10.1.1.6        YES manual up                    up
```

As you can see, all my interfaces have the correct IPv4 addresses and they are all up up; your configuration should be the same. If you also want to see the subnet mask of the command you could have done, which is like `sh ip int brief`, it is `sh protocols`:

```
R4#sh protocols
Global values:
  Internet Protocol routing is enabled
FastEthernet0/0 is up, line protocol is up
  Internet address is 192.168.4.254/24 ←—
FastEthernet0/1 is up, line protocol is up
  Internet address is 10.1.1.26/30 ←—
Serial0/0/0 is up, line protocol is up
  Internet address is 10.1.1.14/30 ←—
Serial0/0/1 is up, line protocol is up
  Internet address is 10.1.1.6/30 ←—
```

It gives you the same information, but you can also see your mask as well.

After you have checked that all your interfaces are up and running, it is now time to configure the routing protocol. We will be doing a single autonomous system using the number 100 on all the routers, so they can share the same routing table. Through the uses of hello messages, they can discover their neighbors. The configuration of the EIGRP protocol should look like this per router:

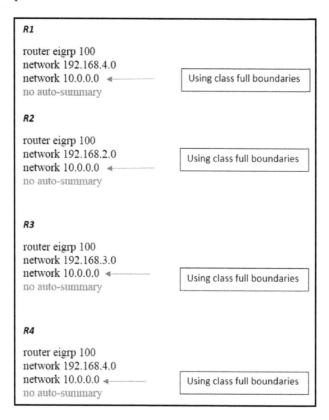

As you can see, we are using the 100 autonomous system number for all routers and when we advertise the networks, especially the 10.1.1.0 network, we use the classfull boundary, which is a Class A network. We must not forget the no auto-summary command or it will not send out the subnet mask on the updates.

Now, let's check out our routing tables to see if we have converged fully, meaning we have found all our networks:

```
R1
R1#sh ip route

Gateway of last resort is not set

      10.0.0.0/30 is subnetted, 6 subnets
C        10.1.1.4 is directly connected, Serial0/0/0
C        10.1.1.8 is directly connected, Serial0/0/1
D        10.1.1.12 [90/2172416] via 10.1.1.22, 00:25:02, FastEthernet0/1
D        10.1.1.16 [90/2172416] via 10.1.1.22, 00:25:10, FastEthernet0/1
C        10.1.1.20 is directly connected, FastEthernet0/1
D        10.1.1.24 [90/2172416] via 10.1.1.10, 00:25:02, Serial0/0/1
                   [90/2172416] via 10.1.1.6, 00:25:01, Serial0/0/0
C     192.168.1.0/24 is directly connected, FastEthernet0/0
D     192.168.2.0/24 [90/2172416] via 10.1.1.10, 00:25:02, Serial0/0/1
D     192.168.3.0/24 [90/30720] via 10.1.1.22, 00:25:10, FastEthernet0/1
D     192.168.4.0/24 [90/2172416] via 10.1.1.6, 00:25:01, Serial0/0/0
```

R2
```
R2#SH IP ROUTE
Gateway of last resort is not set
10.0.0.0/30 is subnetted, 6 subnets
D 10.1.1.4 [90/2172416] via 10.1.1.26, 02:27:38, FastEthernet0/1
C 10.1.1.8 is directly connected, Serial0/0/0
D 10.1.1.12 [90/2172416] via 10.1.1.26, 02:27:38, FastEthernet0/1
C 10.1.1.16 is directly connected, Serial0/0/1
D 10.1.1.20 [90/2172416] via 10.1.1.9, 02:27:39, Serial0/0/0
[90/2172416] via 10.1.1.18, 02:27:39, Serial0/0/1
C 10.1.1.24 is directly connected, FastEthernet0/1
D 192.168.1.0/24 [90/2172416] via 10.1.1.9, 02:27:39, Serial0/0/0
C 192.168.2.0/24 is directly connected, FastEthernet0/0
D 192.168.3.0/24 [90/2172416] via 10.1.1.18, 02:27:39, Serial0/0/1
D 192.168.4.0/24 [90/30720] via 10.1.1.26, 02:27:38, FastEthernet0/1
```
R3
```
R3Gateway of last resort is not set
10.0.0.0/30 is subnetted, 6 subnets
D 10.1.1.4 [90/2172416] via 10.1.1.21, 02:28:49, FastEthernet0/1
D 10.1.1.8 [90/2172416] via 10.1.1.21, 02:28:49, FastEthernet0/1
C 10.1.1.12 is directly connected, Serial0/0/1
C 10.1.1.16 is directly connected, Serial0/0/0
C 10.1.1.20 is directly connected, FastEthernet0/1
D 10.1.1.24 [90/2172416] via 10.1.1.17, 02:28:50, Serial0/0/0
[90/2172416] via 10.1.1.14, 02:28:50, Serial0/0/1
D 192.168.1.0/24 [90/30720] via 10.1.1.21, 02:28:49, FastEthernet0/1
D 192.168.2.0/24 [90/2172416] via 10.1.1.17, 02:28:50, Serial0/0/0
C 192.168.3.0/24 is directly connected, FastEthernet0/0
D 192.168.4.0/24 [90/2172416] via 10.1.1.14, 02:28:50, Serial0/0/1
```
R4
```
R4#SH IP ROUTE
Gateway of last resort is not set
10.0.0.0/30 is subnetted, 6 subnets
C 10.1.1.4 is directly connected, Serial0/0/1
```

```
D    10.1.1.8 [90/2172416] via 10.1.1.25, 02:29:51, FastEthernet0/1
C    10.1.1.12 is directly connected, Serial0/0/0
D    10.1.1.16 [90/2172416] via 10.1.1.25, 02:29:51, FastEthernet0/1
D    10.1.1.20 [90/2172416] via 10.1.1.5, 02:29:52, Serial0/0/1
     [90/2172416] via 10.1.1.13, 02:29:52, Serial0/0/0
C    10.1.1.24 is directly connected, FastEthernet0/1
D    192.168.1.0/24 [90/2172416] via 10.1.1.5, 02:29:52, Serial0/0/1
D    192.168.2.0/24 [90/30720] via 10.1.1.25, 02:29:51, FastEthernet0/1
D    192.168.3.0/24 [90/2172416] via 10.1.1.13, 02:29:52, Serial0/0/0
C    192.168.4.0/24 is directly connected, FastEthernet0/0
```

It seems that EIGRP has found all our different networks and has applied the best metric to each destination. If you look closely at the routing table, you will see that two networks have multiple paths to it: `10.1.1.20` and `10.1.1.24`. The path that it takes is determined by the router that is learning it.

So, what does that mean? EIGRP has two successor routes or two feasible distances that are equal, so they must go to the routing table. All other routes to include the successor routes will be in the topology table.

I have highlighted the networks that have the multiple paths, which means they can go in either direction, but EIGRP will load balance by default when it has multiple paths:

```
R4#sh ip protocols
Routing Protocol is "eigrp 100 "
Outgoing update filter list for all interfaces is not set
Incoming update filter list for all interfaces is not set
Default networks flagged in outgoing updates
Default networks accepted from incoming updates
EIGRP metric weight K1=1, K2=0, K3=1, K4=0, K5=0
EIGRP maximum hopcount 100
EIGRP maximum metric variance 1
Redistributing: eigrp 100
Automatic network summarization is not in effect
Maximum path: 4   <-----------
Routing for Networks:
192.168.4.0
10.0.0.0
Routing Information Sources:
Gateway Distance Last Update
10.1.1.5 90 117075464
10.1.1.25 90 117075471
10.1.1.13 90 117075493
Distance: internal 90 external 170
```

We need to see exactly which path it is taking to this network: `10.1.1.20`. This is from the R4 viewpoint. It could go via `10.1.1.5` or `10.1.1.13`, so let's use the tools we have at hand, such as `traceroute`:

```
R4#traceroute 10.1.1.20
Type escape sequence to abort.
Tracing the route to 10.1.1.20
1 10.1.1.5 7msec 1 msec 6 msec
```

So, even if they have the identical metric of `2172416`, it will choose the first path from top to bottom, to send the packet to the destination. If that path is shut down or is disconnected, it will still have an alternate route to get to the destination.

In your lab, if you followed the configuration exactly as I did it, you should get the same results. But, this is where your curiosity should come in. Shut down the `10.1.1.5` interface and see what happens. What will your routing table look like then? Will it have only one route to the destination or will it have more than one? Remember that when a successor route goes down, EIGRP will query the topology table to find an alternate route, but in this situation, will it do that, since an alternate route exists?

Let's take a look:

```
R1(config)#int s0/0/0
R1(config-if)#shut
```

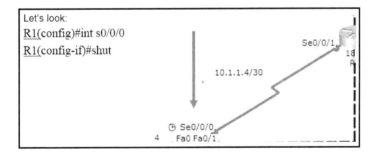

Now let's take a look at the routing table from the R4 perspective.

The first thing that happens is the following:

```
R4#
%LINK-5-CHANGED: Interface Serial0/0/1, changed state to down
%LINEPROTO-5-UPDOWN: Line protocol on Interface Serial0/0/1, changed state
to down
%DUAL-5-NBRCHANGE: IP-EIGRP 100: Neighbor 10.1.1.5 (Serial0/0/1) is down:
interface down
R4#sh ip route
Gateway of last resort is not set
10.0.0.0/30 is subnetted, 5 subnets
D    10.1.1.8 [90/2172416] via 10.1.1.25, 02:57:14, FastEthernet0/1
C    10.1.1.12 is directly connected, Serial0/0/0
D    10.1.1.16 [90/2172416] via 10.1.1.25, 02:57:14, FastEthernet0/1
D    10.1.1.20 [90/2172416] via 10.1.1.13, 02:57:15, Serial0/0/0
C    10.1.1.24 is directly connected, FastEthernet0/1
D    192.168.1.0/24 [90/2174976] via 10.1.1.13, 02:57:14, Serial0/0/0
D    192.168.2.0/24 [90/30720] via 10.1.1.25, 02:57:14, FastEthernet0/1
D    192.168.3.0/24 [90/2172416] via 10.1.1.13, 02:57:15, Serial0/0/0
C    192.168.4.0/24 is directly connected, FastEthernet0/0
```

Only one route exists, which is 10.1.1.13. It had the same metric as 10.1.1.5. So, in this situation, there was no need to query the topology table, since an existing alternate route already existed in the routing table. But, let's verify this with the traceroute command:

```
R4#traceroute 10.1.1.20
Type escape sequence to abort.
Tracing the route to 10.1.1.20
1 10.1.1.13 0 msec 5 msec 1 msec (alternate path)
1 10.1.1.5 7msec 1 msec 6 msec (original path)
```

Since it only had one path to get to the 10.1.1.20 network, it was quicker in getting there, but when it had multiple paths, it took longer. Now I know we are talking about milliseconds, but still, it is a delay, none the less.

So, what does this tell us? Redundancy is not always a good thing. This is a full-mesh topology, which is very costly and we are running into delays. So, be careful in your design of the network. There is such a thing as too much redundancy and you can easily create Layer 3 loops and delays.

We looked at the routing table, but not the topology table, so I am going to turn on the s0/0/0 interface again and look at the routing table once more to make sure all is as it was and then look at the topology table.

Almost immediately after turning on the s0/0/0 interface on R1, I receive the following message:

```
R4#
%LINK-5-CHANGED: Interface Serial0/0/1, changed state to up
%LINEPROTO-5-UPDOWN: Line protocol on Interface Serial0/0/1, changed state
to up
%DUAL-5-NBRCHANGE: IP-EIGRP 100: Neighbor 10.1.1.5 (Serial0/0/1) is up: new
adjacency
Let us peek at the routing table on R4:
R4#sh ip route
Gateway of last resort is not set
10.0.0.0/30 is subnetted, 6 subnets
C 10.1.1.4 is directly connected, Serial0/0/1
D 10.1.1.8 [90/2172416] via 10.1.1.25, 03:08:05, FastEthernet0/1
C 10.1.1.12 is directly connected, Serial0/0/0
D 10.1.1.16 [90/2172416] via 10.1.1.25, 03:08:05, FastEthernet0/1
D 10.1.1.20 [90/2172416] via 10.1.1.13, 03:08:05, Serial0/0/0
             [90/2172416] via 10.1.1.5, 00:01:45, Serial0/0/1
C 10.1.1.24 is directly connected, FastEthernet0/1
D 192.168.1.0/24 [90/2172416] via 10.1.1.5, 00:01:45, Serial0/0/1
D 192.168.2.0/24 [90/30720] via 10.1.1.25, 03:08:05, FastEthernet0/1
D 192.168.3.0/24 [90/2172416] via 10.1.1.13, 03:08:05, Serial0/0/0
C 192.168.4.0/24 is directly connected, FastEthernet0/0
```

Notice that the first path in the network is through 10.1.1.13 and not 10.1.1.5, as before.

Now let us look at the topology table:

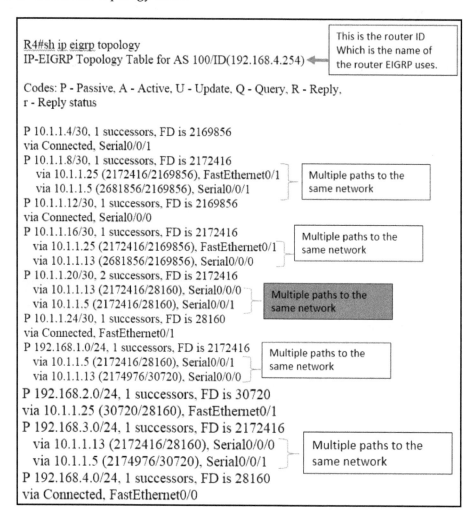

Keep in mind that the topology has all possible routes to all destination networks. Only the ones with the lowest FD make it to the routing table and earn the title of the successor route. If you notice the highlighted networks, they are the same as the ones on the routing table. They both have the exact same metric, so they would both earn the title of successor route.

But let's analyze another network. Let's choose that last one on the list, `192.168.3.0`. It has multiple routes, but the metrics are not the same. If you notice, the FD is `2172416`, so `10.1.1.13` would be the successor route, but `10.1.1.5` has a metric of `2174976`, which truly makes it a feasible successor and will remain in the topology table.

So, what does that mean to us? Well, if the successor route was to go down, then it would have to query the topology table in order to acquire an alternate path. What does the routing table show us about the `192.168.3.0` network, from the R3 perspective?

```
R4#sh ip route
D 192.168.3.0/24 [90/2172416] via 10.1.1.13, 03:28:10, Serial0/0/0
```

There is only one route, the one with the lowest FD, so it's true that, in this case, if this route goes down, a query to the topology table must take place.

So, you see it all depends on how you set up your network topology; you may have a feasible successor, or you may not. So, you must analyze the network you are working with to make it an effective network.

We have not even changed the bandwidth of any of the interfaces or used the variance command in order to include other routes in our load balancing.

EIGRP is a very complete protocol and it allows you to do a lot of tweaking, so you can get the most out of your network.

Bandwidth Control

We said that EIGRP uses metrics, such as bandwidth, delay, reliability, load, and MTU, so we can manipulate these **K** values or metrics to force packets to go in the direction we want them to go. Essentially, we would be manipulating the outcome of the routing table by changing just one of the **K** values. In the following example, I will be changing the bandwidth on R4 `s0/0/1` to 64 Kb and the `s0/0/0` to 10000000 and then see what the outcome will be.

Router 4 changing the bandwidth on serial interfaces:

```
R4(config)#int s0/0/1
R4(config-if)#bandwidth 64
R4(config-if)#
%DUAL-5-NBRCHANGE: IP-EIGRP 100: Neighbor 10.1.1.5 (Serial0/0/1) is down:
interface down
R4(config-if)#int s0/0/1
%DUAL-5-NBRCHANGE: IP-EIGRP 100: Neighbor 10.1.1.5 (Serial0/0/1) is up: new
adjacency
```

```
R4(config-if)#bandwidth 10000000
R4(config-if)#
%DUAL-5-NBRCHANGE: IP-EIGRP 100: Neighbor 10.1.1.5 (Serial0/0/1) is down:
interface down
[
R4(config-if)#
%DUAL-5-NBRCHANGE: IP-EIGRP 100: Neighbor 10.1.1.5 (Serial0/0/1) is up: new
adjacency
```

The second I change the bandwidth, the interface goes down and before I get to the next interface, it comes back up; that is how quickly EIGRP works. Now, let's see if that had an impact on our routing and topology table:

```
R4#sh ip route
Gateway of last resort is not set
10.0.0.0/30 is subnetted, 6 subnets
C 10.1.1.4 is directly connected, Serial0/0/1
D 10.1.1.8 [90/2172416] via 10.1.1.25, 07:31:57, FastEthernet0/1
C 10.1.1.12 is directly connected, Serial0/0/0
D 10.1.1.16 [90/2172416] via 10.1.1.25, 07:31:57, FastEthernet0/1
D 10.1.1.20 [90/540160] via 10.1.1.5, 00:03:32, Serial0/0/1
C 10.1.1.24 is directly connected, FastEthernet0/1
D 192.168.1.0/24 [90/540160] via 10.1.1.5, 00:03:32, Serial0/0/1
D 192.168.2.0/24 [90/30720] via 10.1.1.25, 07:31:57, FastEthernet0/1
D 192.168.3.0/24 [90/542720] via 10.1.1.5, 00:03:32, Serial0/0/1
C 192.168.4.0/24 is directly connected, FastEthernet0/0
```

It sure did. Before, on the routing table, the destination network had two paths it could choose, the 10.1.1.5 and 10.1.1.3 paths. That is not the case now. There is only one successor route with a metric of **540160**.

Let us see what the topology table looks like:

```
R4#sh ip eigrp topology
IP-EIGRP Topology Table for AS 100/ID(192.168.4.254)
Codes: P - Passive, A - Active, U - Update, Q - Query, R - Reply,
r - Reply status
P 10.1.1.4/30, 1 successors, FD is 512256
via Connected, Serial0/0/1
P 10.1.1.8/30, 1 successors, FD is 2172416
   via 10.1.1.25 (2172416/2169856), FastEthernet0/1
   via 10.1.1.5 (2681856/2169856), Serial0/0/1
P 10.1.1.12/30, 1 successors, FD is 2169856
via Connected, Serial0/0/0
P 10.1.1.16/30, 1 successors, FD is 2172416
   via 10.1.1.25 (2172416/2169856), FastEthernet0/1
   via 10.1.1.13 (2681856/2169856), Serial0/0/0
P 10.1.1.20/30, 1 successors, FD is 540160
```

```
   via 10.1.1.5 (540160/28160), Serial0/0/1
   via 10.1.1.13 (2172416/28160), Serial0/0/0
P 10.1.1.24/30, 1 successors, FD is 28160
via Connected, FastEthernet0/1
P 192.168.1.0/24, 1 successors, FD is 540160
   via 10.1.1.5 (540160/28160), Serial0/0/1
   via 10.1.1.13 (2174976/30720), Serial0/0/0
P 192.168.2.0/24, 1 successors, FD is 30720
via 10.1.1.25 (30720/28160), FastEthernet0/1
P 192.168.3.0/24, 1 successors, FD is 542720
   via 10.1.1.5 (542720/30720), Serial0/0/1
   via 10.1.1.13 (2172416/28160), Serial0/0/0
P 192.168.4.0/24, 1 successors, FD is 28160
via Connected, FastEthernet0/0
```

The topology table has multiple paths, but the difference you need to be aware of is the FD number, which is drastically lower than the one for the `10.1.1.13` path. So, what does this little experiment tell us? Simply by changing the bandwidth on the router interfaces, we manipulated the routing table and topology table. We now have a true feasible successor route and alternate path if the successor route fails.

To use that backup or alternate route, EIGRP must query the topology table to put that path in the routing table.

One thing I have failed to mention thus far is the letter *P* next to all these routes. What does that mean? That is a good thing. It means it is passive; it has found all the networks and EIGRP has fully converged. What you don't want to see is *A*, which means **Active**. It is actively looking for a destination network with no luck. In this case, when the topology table is getting an *A*, it is a bad thing.

So, let's sum up what we have done so far with EIGRP.

We have configured EIGRP in a single autonomous system environment, which means the same AS number for all the routers:

```
router eigrp 100
network 192.168.4.0
network 10.0.0.0
no auto-summary
```

This method of configuration is only one way, and this is the way you will configure it for the CCNA certification. There is another way of doing it and I will show you now, but:

Warning ! This is not the way of the certification, only a real-world application.

```
ROUTER EIGRP 100
NETWORK 192.168.4.0 0.0.0.255
NETWORK 10.1.1.4 0.0.0.3
NETWORK 10.1.1.12 0.0.0.3
NETWORK 10.1.1.24 0.0.0.3
NO AUTO-SUMMARY
```

EIGRP allows you to use a wildcard mask, so the protocol knows exactly what network is assigned to it. You will still want to put the `auto-summary` command, so it sends that mask out on the updates.

Warning ! This is not the way of the certification, only a real-world application.

Now that we have clarified that, we then checked our routing table to make sure we have converged with all the networks and we did. We verified it using the `traceroute` command. One interesting thing we found was that some networks had multiple paths to it, but they still showed up on the routing table, which means they are not real FS.

When we changed the metric of R4 on its serial interfaces, we saw that the routing table only had one route for the `10.1.1.20` network, but the topology table had multiple paths. The reason for this is that the FD was not the same. One had a lower FD, which will become the successor route and the larger FD will remain in the topology table as a backup route.

Finally, I explained the difference between the *P for passive*, and *A for active* outputs shown in the topology table. Just keep in mind *P* is good and *A* is bad, at least in this instance.

We are not done yet with tweaking our beloved EIGRP. If you remember back at the beginning of the chapter, I stated that EIGRP has a maximum hop count of 255, but, by default, it is set to `100`. We see this information here:

```
R4#sh ip protocols
Routing Protocol is "eigrp 100"
Outgoing update filter list for all interfaces is not set
Incoming update filter list for all interfaces is not set
```

```
Default networks flagged in outgoing updates
Default networks accepted from incoming updates
EIGRP metric weight K1=1, K2=0, K3=1, K4=0, K5=0
EIGRP maximum hopcount 100
EIGRP maximum metric variance 1
Redistributing: eigrp 100
Automatic network summarization is not in effect
Maximum path: 4
Routing for Networks:
192.168.4.0
10.0.0.0
Routing Information Sources:
Gateway Distance Last Update
10.1.1.25 90 117075471
10.1.1.13 90 117075493
10.1.1.5 90 143982070
Distance: internal 90 external 170
```

If our network is using more than 100 routers, we will run into an issue. Our packets will start dropping and we don't want that. So, how can we fix this problem? Let's see:

```
(config)#router eigrp 10
(config)#metric maximum-hops 255
```

Typing in that command will allow you to reach 255 routers in your network. EIGRP is very scalable.

We talk about small, medium, and enterprise networks, but where do draw the line? It is my personal belief that if you have anything over 25 routers and underneath those routers you have at least 10 subnets, you have a large network, which EIGRP is very capable of handling.

Never forget your OSI model. Layer 1 is extremely important. When you build a building, you do not start at the top floor; you begin with the foundations. The same goes for a network.

If you create a good infrastructure, especially in your cabling and network devices, and your topology has proper redundancy, everything else will fall into place.

One more command I would like to talk about (and in this mesh or mess network, it would come in very handy), is the `variance` command. This little command allows you to load balance across routes simply by using a number, which is a **multiplier**. Let's take a look at the power of this command.

This time, let's look at R1's routing table:

```
R1#sh ip route
Gateway of last resort is not set
10.0.0.0/30 is subnetted, 6 subnets
C  10.1.1.4 is directly connected, Serial0/0/0
C  10.1.1.8 is directly connected, Serial0/0/1
D  10.1.1.12 [90/2172416] via 10.1.1.22, 14:00:48, FastEthernet0/1
D  10.1.1.16 [90/2172416] via 10.1.1.22, 14:00:48, FastEthernet0/1
C  10.1.1.20 is directly connected, FastEthernet0/1
D  10.1.1.24 [90/2172416] via 10.1.1.10, 14:00:49, Serial0/0/1
               [90/2172416] via 10.1.1.6, 10:54:28, Serial0/0/0
C  192.168.1.0/24 is directly connected, FastEthernet0/0
D  192.168.2.0/24 [90/2172416] via 10.1.1.10, 14:00:49, Serial0/0/1
D  192.168.3.0/24 [90/30720] via 10.1.1.22, 14:00:48, FastEthernet0/1
D  192.168.4.0/24 [90/2172416] via 10.1.1.6, 10:54:28, Serial0/0/0
```

As we already know, this destination network has no feasible successor, so let's take a look at the topology table to see all the routes and make a better decision on how we are going to load balance the network:

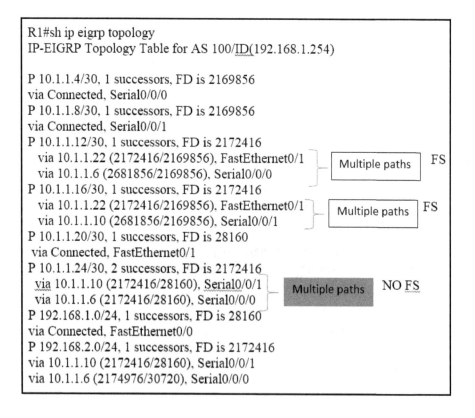

We are going to load balance for 10.1.1.16 and we are going to add another route to that network by using the variance command. We can do up to 32 equal-cost paths, but let's not get crazy. Let's first understand what this command can actually do:

```
R1(config)#router eigrp 100
R1(config-router)#variance ?
<1-128> Metric variance Multiplier
R1(config-router)#variance 2
```

So what happened to our routing table? Remember that this was the original entry on the routing table with a metric of 1:

```
D 10.1.1.16 [90/2172416] via 10.1.1.22, 14:00:48, FastEthernet0/1
```

Now it will look like the following:

```
D 10.1.1.16 [90/2172416] via 10.1.1.22, 00:00:08, FastEthernet0/1
  [90/2681856] via 10.1.1.10, 00:00:10, Serial0/0/1
```

Since we input the variance or multiplier of the FD, it included the FS as the successor route, so now it appears in the routing table. There's no more FS in the topology table for this network. Let's verify this:

```
P 10.1.1.16/30, 2 successors, FD is 2172416
via 10.1.1.22 (2172416/2169856), FastEthernet0/1
via 10.1.1.10 (2681856/2169856), Serial0/0/1
```

Even though they have different metrics, they both show up in the topology table, because when I used the variance of 2, it multiplied the lowest FD and that included the higher metric, making them both successor routes and no FS was required.

All that we have talked about is needed for certification purposes and real-world scenarios, but we have only talked about single autonomous systems. In a real-world network, a single autonomous system may work for small networks but not for large networks, meaning you have a branch office around your city or around the state or in different states or even globally. That is a game changer.

So, with that said, I am going to show how to configure multiple autonomous systems using EIGRP.

We are going to keep it simple, since this is not a requirement for the CCNA 200-125, but I would like you to at least have an understanding of how this would work, for when you get to the workforce, or simply to enhance your knowledge level.

The following is going to be the topology we are using. Like I said, it is very simple and straightforward:

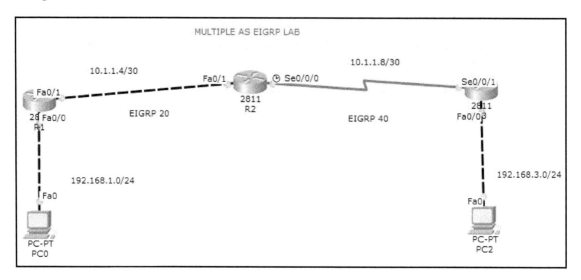

As you can see in the preceding diagram, we have AS 20 and AS 40. We are using three routers. What you need to understand here is that the interfaces that are touching or connecting to the AS. Notice that on R1, the interfaces F0/0 and F0/1 are in AS 20, but on R2, only F0/1 is part of AS 20.

On R2 the S0/0/0 is part of AS 40, on R3 the interfaces S0/0/1 and F0/0 will be participating on AS 40. So, R2 is the key router that will communicate back and forth from different autonomous systems.

One step at a time, first, let's configure connectivity. Just by looking at the routing tables, we know we have connectivity, but we should still ping. What will do is go to R2 and ping its neighbors:

```
R1

R1#sh ip int brief
Interface              IP-Address      OK? Method Status
Protocol
FastEthernet0/0        192.168.1.254   YES manual up                            up
FastEthernet0/1        10.1.1.5        YES manual up                            up

R2

R2#SH IP INT BRIEF
Interface              IP-Address      OK? Method Status
Protocol
FastEthernet0/0        unassigned      YES unset   administratively down
down
FastEthernet0/1        10.1.1.6        YES manual up                            up
Serial0/0/0            10.1.1.9        YES manual up                            up

R3

R3#SH IP INT BRIEF
Interface          IP-Address      OK? Method Status
Protocol
FastEthernet0/0    192.168.3.254   YES manual up                up
FastEthernet0/1    unassigned      YES unset   administratively down
down
Serial0/0/0        unassigned      YES unset   administratively down
down
Serial0/0/1        10.1.1.10       YES manual up                up

R2#ping 10.1.1.5

Type escape sequence to abort.
Sending 5, 100-byte ICMP Echos to 10.1.1.5, timeout is 2 seconds:
!!!!!
Success rate is 100 percent (5/5), round-trip min/avg/max = 0/0/0 ms

R2#ping 10.1.1.10

Type escape sequence to abort.
Sending 5, 100-byte ICMP Echos to 10.1.1.10, timeout is 2 seconds:
!!!!!
Success rate is 100 percent (5/5), round-trip min/avg/max = 1/4/13 ms
```

We are good to go. Now we can start configuring the EIGRP routing protocol for multiple ASes. What we will do is start from R2, since its interfaces will be on different AS numbers:

```
router eigrp 20
redistribute eigrp 40
network 10.1.1.4 0.0.0.3
auto-summary
!
router eigrp 40
redistribute eigrp 20
network 10.1.1.8 0.0.0.3
auto-summary
```

You may be asking yourself, how does EIGRP know which interface to use? Good question. All you need to do is look at the network that is being advertised for each AS; they are not the same. Remember, you assigned the IP addresses to the interfaces that belong to a network, and what you see here are those networks. Also, look at how I am configuring EIGRP. I am using a wildcard mask and using the `redistribute` command to allow AS 40 to talk to AS 20 and the reverse. All metrics are the same, so there is no need to change or add any of that information, which is something I said that YOU DO NOT DO for the CCNA. This configuration will not be on your CCNA. I am just giving you a peak into the future and helping you in your work environment.

Let us move now to the R1 configuration of EIGRP:

```
router eigrp 20
network 192.168.1.0
network 10.1.1.4 0.0.0.3
auto-summary
```

This should seem familiar and is straightforward.

Now we move to the last router, which is R3:

```
router eigrp 40
network 10.1.1.8 0.0.0.3
network 192.168.3.0
auto-summary
```

Once again, it's a very straightforward configuration.

In this simple topology, your biggest challenge is to remember which interface or network faces what AS number.

Now, for the moment of truth. Has EIGRP understood and discovered the neighbors?

```
R1#sh ip route
Gateway of last resort is not set
10.0.0.0/8 is variably subnetted, 3 subnets, 2 masks
D 10.0.0.0/8 is a summary, 00:29:40, Null0
C 10.1.1.4/30 is directly connected, FastEthernet0/1
D EX 10.1.1.8/30 [170/6780416] via 10.1.1.6, 00:29:39, FastEthernet0/1
C 192.168.1.0/24 is directly connected, FastEthernet0/0
D EX 192.168.3.0/24 [170/6806016] via 10.1.1.6, 00:29:31,
FastEthernet0/1
```

Notice that it is learning about AS 40 as an external route:

```
R3#sh ip route
Gateway of last resort is not set
10.0.0.0/8 is variably subnetted, 3 subnets, 2 masks
D    10.0.0.0/8 is a summary, 00:29:15, Null0
D EX 10.1.1.4/30 [170/2195456] via 10.1.1.9, 00:29:14, Serial0/0/1
C    10.1.1.8/30 is directly connected, Serial0/0/1
D EX 192.168.1.0/24 [170/2221056] via 10.1.1.9, 00:29:14, Serial0/0/1
C    192.168.3.0/24 is directly connected, FastEthernet0/0
```

R3 is learning about AS 20 as an external route, but what about R2? What would its routing table look like?

```
R2#sh ip route
Gateway of last resort is not set
10.0.0.0/30 is subnetted, 2 subnets
C    10.1.1.4 is directly connected, FastEthernet0/1
C    10.1.1.8 is directly connected, Serial0/0/0
D    192.168.1.0/24 [90/30720] via 10.1.1.5, 00:35:47, FastEthernet0/1
D    192.168.3.0/24 [90/2172416] via 10.1.1.10, 00:35:39, Serial0/0/0
```

Since R2 knows about both AS numbers, they would not be external to R2.

Summary

Well, we have talked and configured EIGRP extensively. You should have a pretty good foundation for the different types of configurations of EIGRP and dealing with its features, such as tweaking the bandwidth, which in turn will change the metrics, successor routes in the routing table, and feasible successors in the topology table. We have also learned about whether we have an FS or not based on the location.

We even did a simple multiple AS with EIGRP using the redistribution command, but just remember that this will not be in your certification. Please pay more attention and practice the single AS lab and be curious and change things, but only after you get it to work like mine.

15
The World of Open Shortest Path First (OSPF)

The OSPF interior routing protocol is a very popular protocol in enterprise networks. This chapter will present a brief history of OSPF and provide a comparison with the IS-IS routing protocol, since this is also a link state routing protocol.

We will be learning the basics of OSPF, its features and configuration, and much more. We will be creating multiple labs, since OSPF has different aspects that we need to learn for the certification and the real world. Not only will we be looking at single-area OSPF, but also multi-area OSPF.

The following topics will be covered in this chapter:

- History of OSPF
- SPF tree calculation
- OSPF metrics
- Configuring OSPF
- Wildcard calculations
- Configuring OSPF in our network
- OSPF DR and BDR
- Verifying OSPF
- OSPF scalability
- Categories of multi-area components

- OSPF router roles
- Types of LSAs
- OSPF Hello protocol
- Neighbor states
- Basic multi-area configuration

Brief history

The origins of OSPF date back to the late 1980s by the IETF. OSPFv1 was published in 1989 and OSPF was published in 1991. OSPFv3 for IPv6 was first published in 1997, and a later revision came out in 1999. For the RFC aficionados, RFC2740 was really the one that introduced OSPFv3 for IPv6 in 1999, but it was replaced by RFC5340 in 2008.

So, OSPF has been around for a long time and even the IPv6 version of it has been around for ten years, although we still have not fully embraced it.

There is another link state protocol that I will briefly touch upon, which is IS-IS. This protocol has be around since the late 1970s but not until 2008 was RFC5308 ready to go for IPv6. This is still a long time and very little has been spoken about it.

When you get to your CCNP or CCIE studies, you will get somewhat deeper into the protocol, but really it would take working for a company that uses IS-IS to get a real understanding about the protocol.

Both OSPF and IS-IS are IGP; they distribute routing information between neighbor routers belonging to a single AS.

They both support the following:

- CIDR
- VLSM
- Authentication
- Multi-pat
- IP unnumbered links

Their terminology differs somewhat, as shown in the following table:

OSPF	IS-IS
Host	End systems or ES
Router	Intermediate Systems (IS)
Link	Circuit
Packet	Protocol Data Unit (PDU)
Designated Router (DR)	Designated IS (DIS)
Backup DR (BDR)	N/A (no BDIS is used)
Link-State Advertisements (LSA)	Link-State PDU (LSP)
Hello Packet	IIH PDU
Database Description (DBD)	Complete Sequence number PDU(CSNP)
Area	Sub domain (area)
Non-Backbone area	Level-1 area
Backbone area	Level-2 Sub domain (backbone)
Area Border Router (ABR)	L1L2 Router
Autonomous System Boundary Router (ASBR)	Any IS

I like to compare apples to apples; that is why I choose to compare OSPF with IS-IS, as both are link state routing protocols. Even though they do not have the same terminology or configuration, the purpose is still the same. Within the comparisons of OSPF, it is normally compared to RIPv2, which doesn't make sense since these two protocols are completely different from each other; it's like comparing apples and oranges. One of them is a distance vector (RIP) and the other is a link state (OSPF). They work completely differently to each other. Just the fact of me stating to you that one is DV and the other is an LS should say it all.

I believe, the reason the literature compares these two protocols is due to the fact that, at the time, EIGRP was Cisco proprietary and could only be used with Cisco equipment, so you had no choice but to use RIP or OSPF, even though IS-IS has been around since the 1970s.

But that is no longer the case. Cisco opened its EIGRP routing protocol as an open standard for multi-vendor use. This was an update on the Cisco website on March 7, 2013 (Document ID: **1518931547541273**). It released a basic portion of the protocol to the IETF and is still a work in progress. Not everyone is willing to change to the open EIGRP protocol just yet.

So, because Cisco is making the EIGRP routing protocol available for all to use, I believe that we should compare LS with LS and DV with DV. That is not to mention the benefits or disadvantages of running a DV versus LS on a WAN. That would be a completely different story.

One of the advantages that OSPF has over RIPv2 is that it can subdivide the networks into smaller areas. It means that, in the OSPF world, you must have a backbone area that is the first area created, and then you can create all other areas, but they must all communicate back to area zero. The following diagram will show you the hierarchy that is possible with OSPF and not RIP:

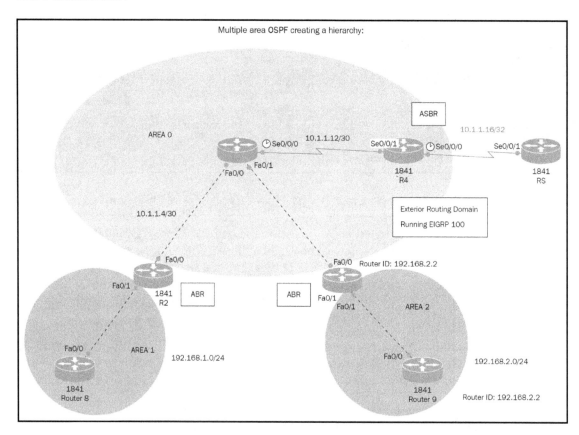

As you can see from the preceding topology, we are using both ABR and ASBR, we have our backbone **AREA 0** and we have **AREA 1** and **AREA 2**. Since **AREA 1** and **AREA 2** are connected to an ABR, which is connected directly to the backbone or **AREA 0**, we do not really need any special configuration and will learn the routes automatically.

You need to make sure that in the ABR routers, you assign the proper area to the correct network. This is how the **AREA 1** routers sees all the routes:

```
R8#sh ip route

Gateway of last resort is not set

      10.0.0.0/30 is subnetted, 4 subnets
O IA   10.1.1.4 [110/2] via 192.168.1.1, 02:20:28, FastEthernet0/0
O IA   10.1.1.8 [110/3] via 192.168.1.1, 02:20:28, FastEthernet0/0
O IA   10.1.1.12 [110/66] via 192.168.1.1, 02:20:28, FastEthernet0/0
O IA   10.1.1.16 [110/130] via 192.168.1.1, 00:29:08, FastEthernet0/0
C      192.168.1.0/24 is directly connected, FastEthernet0/0
O IA 192.168.2.0/24 [110/4] via 192.168.1.1, 02:19:51, FastEthernet0/0
```

The router sees all networks outside its own area as inter area routes, but the one we want to focus on is 10.1.1.16, because that network is running EIGRP, so we had to configure redistribution in R4. This is what it looks like:

```
router eigrp 100
redistribute ospf 1 metric 5000 10 255 255 65535 (Beyond the scope of the
CCNA)
network 10.0.0.0
no auto-summary
!
router ospf 1
log-adjacency-changes
redistribute eigrp 100 (Beyond the scope of the CCNA)
network 10.0.0.0
network 10.1.1.16 0.0.0.3 area 0
network 10.1.1.12 0.0.0.3 area 0
```

So, let us see how R5, the external routing domain, sees the other networks:

```
R5#sh ip route

      10.0.0.0/30 is subnetted, 2 subnets
D        10.1.1.12 [90/2681856] via 10.1.1.17, 00:35:50, Serial0/0/1
C        10.1.1.16 is directly connected, Serial0/0/1
D EX 192.168.1.0/24 [170/2172416] via 10.1.1.17, 00:25:40, Serial0/0/1
D EX 192.168.2.0/24 [170/2172416] via 10.1.1.17, 00:25:40, Serial0/0/1
```

It sees AREA 1 and AREA 2 as external routes. Notice the AD is 170.

This is simply to show you that you can configure a true hierarchy in OSPF and include multiple routing protocols. But there is more to that. Let's first get into some OSPF terminology:

Term	Definition
Link	This is the interface of the router.
Router ID	This is also called the RID. It is the highest physical IP address that identifies the router. Unless you configure a loopback address, then that logical address will become the RID or you can hardcode your own RID.
Neighbor	These are the interfaces on routers that share the same network. But to become a neighbor, you must meet the following criteria: area ID, stub area flag, authentication password (optional), Hello and Dead Timers.
Adjacency	This would be a relationship with two or more OSPF routers that allow routing table exchange. If you met all the criteria, it will only share information with neighbors that have established an adjacency. OSPF is nitpicky.
Designated router	A DR only exists in a broadcast or multi-access network. It follows an election process to pick the DR. OSPF will first look for the highest IP address on any physical interface. If you have a loopback interface, it will use the highest loopback. You could manipulate the election by putting a higher priority number on an interface, which will become the DR but if there is a match, RID would be the tie breaker.
Backup designator router	Just like the DR, the BDR would be the next highest and it will also publicize routing information. It is a hot standby in case the DR goes down, but it will not dispense any LSAs
Hello protocol	This provides dynamic neighbor discovery and maintains neighbor relationships. A combination of hellos and LSAs builds and maintains the topological database. The hello protocol uses the `224.0.0.5` multicast address.
Neighborship database	This is a list of all OSPF routers where hello packets have been seen. The RID and state are in the neighborship database.
Topological database	This contains information from all of the LSA packets that have been received for an area.
Link state advertisements	LSA packets will only be exchanged with routers that have build adjacencies with other OSPF routers. They contain link state and routing information about those neighbor routers.

OSPF areas	In OSPF, routers that belong to the same area ID will not only share that same area ID but will belong to the same topology table. So, in a multi-area ID configuration, each area would have their own topology table and it is a requirement that you must configure AREA 0 first, as this is the backbone area.
Broadcast or multi-access	This is simply a broadcast domain. Think of multiple OSPF routers connecting to the same broadcast domain; an example would be if they all connect to the same switch. When this happens, an election process happens to designate a DR and BDR and it will base its decision on the highest IP address on any physical interface. The highest loopback address is configured, the highest priority number, which is in the range of 0-255, and, lastly, you could put in your own RID manually. This election process only happens in Ethernet networks.
Non-broadcast multi-access	This type of access is usually found in frame relay or ATM networks and special OSPF configurations must be used so it can function properly.
Point-to-point	As the term states, these are two routers usually connected by a serial cable or circuit through frame relay, which will eliminate the DR and BDR election.
Point-to-multipoint	This type of topology or connection type is interesting, because all routers share a single point connection leading to multiple destination routers. It could be that they are all in the same area or not, or share the same network or not. This will definitely challenge the OSPF configuration you can deploy.

OSPF operation

Now that you have some foundation knowledge about OSPF, we need to understand in more detail about how exactly OSPF discovers, propagates, and finally chooses a route. OSPF does a very good job in calculating cost values to choose the Shortest Path First to its destinations.

Basically, OSPF operations can be separated into three categories:

- Neighbor and adjacency initialization
- LSA flooding
- SPF tree calculation

Neighbor and adjacency initialization

This is the very first part of OSPF operations. The router at this point will allocate memory for this function as well as for the maintenance of both the neighbor and topology tables. Once the router discovers which interfaces are configured with OSPF, it will begin sending hello packets throughout the interface in the hope of finding other routers using OSPF.

Let's look at a visual representation:

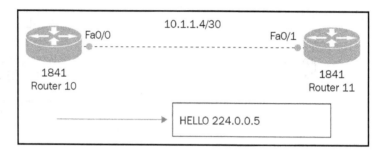

To be honest a lot more than that happens, especially since we are using Ethernet. Remember this would be considered a broadcast in between the routers so the election needs to run to choose DR and BDR, but you don't have to believe me, let me show you.

Before I configured these routers, I turned on `debug ip ospf adj`.

```
00:03:06: OSPF: DR/BDR election on FastEthernet0/0
00:03:06: OSPF: Elect BDR 10.1.1.5
00:03:06: OSPF: Elect DR 10.1.1.6
00:03:06: OSPF: Elect BDR 10.1.1.5
00:03:06: OSPF: Elect DR 10.1.1.6
00:03:06: DR: 10.1.1.6 (Id) BDR: 10.1.1.5 (Id)
```

One thing to keep in mind is that if you are using Ethernet, as we are, the hello packet timer is set to 10 seconds. If it is not an Ethernet connection, the hello packet timer will be set to 30 seconds. Why is this so important to know? Because the hello packet timer must be identical to its adjacent router or they will never become neighbors.

Link State Advertisements and Flooding

Before we begin to start talking about LSA flooding and how it uses LSUs to create the OSPF routing table, let's elaborate on this term.

There is not just one type of LSA either. Let's have a look at the following table:

Type	Name	Description
1	Router LSA	The routers publicize presence and lists the links to other routers on the same network.
2	Network LSA	The DR on a broadcast segment lists which routers are joined together by the segment.
3	Summary LSA	ABR takes information it has learned on one of its attached areas and summarizes it before sending it out on other areas.
4	ASBR-Summary LSA	ASBR is where the type 5 LSA originated and would give more detailed information.
5	External LSA	Contains important information about OSPF from other routing processes. They are flooded into all areas except NSSA

By no means are these the only LSAs that exist. There are 11 LSAs, but for the CCNA, you must know about the ones that I highlighted, do not dismiss the rest.

LSA updates are sent via multicast addresses. Depending on the type of network topology you have, that multicast address is used.

For the point-to-point networks, the multicast address is 224.0.0.5. In a broadcast environment, 224.0.0.6 is used. But as we get further into OSPF and start discussing DR/BDR routers in a broadcast environment, the DR uses 224.0.0.5 and the BDR uses 224.0.0.6. In any case, remember that these two multicast addresses are used within OSPF.

The network topology is created via LSAs updates, for which the information is acquired through LSUs or link state updates. So, OSPF routers, after they have converged, send hellos via LSAs. If any new change happens, it is the job of the LSU to update the LSA of the routers in order to keep routing tables current.

SPF Tree Calculation

Each area will calculate the best path of a destination network using the SPF algorithm and the topology database. It creates a tree, where the router is the center, or root, and all other networks are arranged as the branches and leaves of that tree. The SPF is used to insert the routing information into the routing table. It's good to know that if you have multiple areas, then you have multiple trees. OSPF then needs to calculate the best path to a different area or routing domain.

Also, OSPF uses cost as its metric, which the SPF will provide. The faster the link, the lower the cost, which would mean the slower, the link the higher the cost. But, you can always override the calculation by using the `ip ospf cost` command, which has a range of 1-65,535.

Configuring the basics of OSPF

You have already had a sneak peek into the configuration of OSPF, but let's take it back to the basics. The following diagram shows the topology:

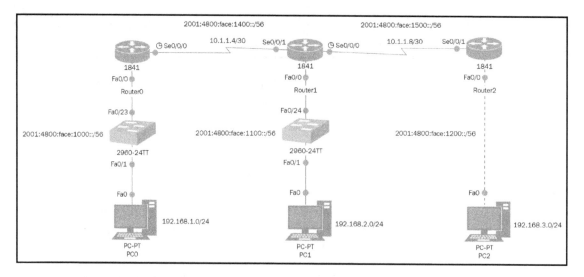

Yes, this is the basic topology, but we will do a dual stack, shown as follows:

Configuration of R1:

```
R1(CONFIG)#INT F0/0
R1(CONFIG-IF)#IP ADDRESS 192.168.1.254 255.255.255.0
R1(CONFIG-IF)#NO SHUT
R1(CONFIG-IF)#INT S0/0/0
R1(CONFIG-IF)#IP ADDRESS 10.1.1.5 255.255.255.252
R1(CONFIG-IF)#CLOCK RATE 4000000
R1(CONFIG-IF)#NO SHUT
R1(CONFIG-IF)#EXIT
R1(CONFIG)#ROUTER OSPF 1
R1(CONFIG-ROUTER)#NETWORK 10.1.1.4 0.0.0.3 AREA 0
R1(CONFIG-ROUTER)#NETWORK 192.168.1.0 0.0.0.255 AREA 0
R1(CONFIG-ROUTER)#EXIT
R1(CONFIG)#EXIT
R1#COPY RUN START
```

Configuration of R2:

```
R2(CONFIG)#INT F0/0
R2(CONFIG-IF)#IP ADDRESS 192.168.2.254 255.255.255.0
R2(CONFIG-IF)#NO SHUT
R2(CONFIG-IF)#INT S0/0/0
R2(CONFIG-IF)#IP ADDRESS 10.1.1.9 255.255.255.252
R2(CONFIG-IF)#CLOCK RATE 4000000
R2(CONFIG-IF)#NO SHUT
R2(CONFIG-IF)#INT S0/0/1
R2(CONFIG-IF)#IP ADDRESS 10.1.1.6 255.255.255.252
R2(CONFIG-IF)#EXIT
R2(CONFIG)#ROUTER OSPF 1
R2(CONFIG-ROUTER)#NETWORK 10.1.1.4 0.0.0.3 AREA 0
R2(CONFIG-ROUTER)#NETWORK 10.1.1.8 0.0.0.3 AREA 0
R2(CONFIG-ROUTER)#NETWORK 192.168.2.0 0.0.0.255 AREA 0
R2(CONFIG-ROUTER)#EXIT
R2(CONFIG)#EXIT
R1#COPY RUN START
```

Configuration of R3:

```
R3(CONFIG)#INT F0/0
R3(CONFIG-IF)#IP ADDRESS 192.168.3.254 255.255.255.0
R3(CONFIG-IF)#NO SHUT
R3(CONFIG-IF)#INT S0/0/1
R3(CONFIG-IF)#IP ADDRESS 10.1.1.10 255.255.255.252
R3(CONFIG-IF)#NO SHUT
R3(CONFIG-IF)#EXIT
R3(CONFIG)#ROUTER OSPF 1
R3(CONFIG-ROUTER)#NETWORK 10.1.1.8 0.0.0.3 AREA 0
R3(CONFIG-ROUTER)#NETWORK 192.168.3.0 0.0.0.255 AREA 0
R3(CONFIG-ROUTER)#EXIT
R3(CONFIG)#EXIT
R3#COPY RUN START
```

So, what did we do? We put the IP addresses on each interface and since we are using serial cables, on the DCE side of the cable, we must use the clock rate command and assign the clock rate for synchronization and encapsulation.

Then we configured OSPF with basic configuration, which means that all we did was advertise the networks we are attached to using the process ID number, which is local to the router. The complete network ID address we are partly using is a wildcard mask and since this is the first area, we must use area 0.

We can verify several ways to use the ping command. Use the sh ip protocols or sh ip route, but let's look at how this would look.

Verifying from R1, you will get the following:

```
R1#ping 192.168.3.1

Type escape sequence to abort.
Sending 5, 100-byte ICMP Echos to 192.168.3.1, timeout is 2 seconds:
!!!!!
Success rate is 100 percent (5/5), round-trip min/avg/max = 2/7/12 ms

R1#ping 192.168.2.1

Type escape sequence to abort.
Sending 5, 100-byte ICMP Echos to 192.168.2.1, timeout is 2 seconds:
!!!!!
Success rate is 100 percent (5/5), round-trip min/avg/max = 1/3/7 ms
```

R1#sh ip protocols

Routing Protocol is "ospf 1"
Outgoing update filter list for all interfaces is not set
Incoming update filter list for all interfaces is not set
Router ID 192.168.1.254
Number of areas in this router is 1. 1 normal 0 stub 0 nssa
Maximum path: 4
Routing for Networks:
192.168.1.0 0.0.0.255 area 0
10.1.1.4 0.0.0.3 area 0
Routing Information Sources:
Gateway Distance Last Update
192.168.1.254 110 00:03:20
192.168.2.254 110 00:03:18
192.168.3.254 110 00:03:20
Distance: (default is 110)

The highlight text are what you need to pay attention to. The Process ID number, the Router ID, the networks we are routing for and the default AD.

R1#sh ip route

Gateway of last resort is 0.0.0.0 to network 0.0.0.0

10.0.0.0/30 is subnetted, 2 subnets
C 10.1.1.4 is directly connected, Serial0/0/0
O 10.1.1.8 [110/128] via 10.1.1.6, 07:38:23, Serial0/0/0
C 192.168.1.0/24 is directly connected, FastEthernet0/0
O 192.168.2.0/24 [110/65] via 10.1.1.6, 07:38:23, Serial0/0/0
O 192.168.3.0/24 [110/129] via 10.1.1.6, 07:38:23, Serial0/0/0
S* 0.0.0.0/0 is directly connected, Serial0/0/0

The highlight text is what you need to pay attention to. We are using a default route and the "O", tell us we are learning OSPF routes.

There are three simple commands that we could use to verify that our configuration of OSPF is correct. One thing you need to know very well is wild card masking, so let me show you a couple of examples:

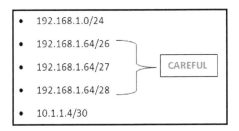

- 192.168.1.0/24
- 192.168.1.64/26 ⎤
- 192.168.1.64/27 ⎬— CAREFUL
- 192.168.1.64/28 ⎦
- 10.1.1.4/30

Before we begin, let me you present a very simple way of doing wildcard masking. All you must do is use the constant number 255.255.255.255 and subtract your subnet mask from it:

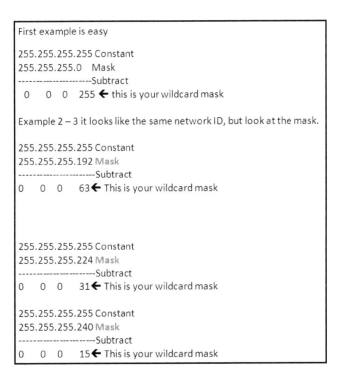

```
First example is easy

255.255.255.255 Constant
255.255.255.0   Mask
--------------------Subtract
  0    0   0   255 ← this is your wildcard mask

Example 2 – 3 it looks like the same network ID, but look at the mask.

255.255.255.255 Constant
255.255.255.192 Mask
--------------------Subtract
0    0   0     63← This is your wildcard mask



255.255.255.255 Constant
255.255.255.224 Mask
--------------------Subtract
0    0   0     31← This is your wildcard mask

255.255.255.255 Constant
255.255.255.240 Mask
--------------------Subtract
0    0   0     15← This is your wildcard mask
```

So, as you can plainly see, your mask will determine the wildcard mask. The network ID may look the same but you will have three different wildcard masks. That would be a lot of different hosts pointing to a specific interface.

Finally, let's look at another example, which is a subnetted Class A address:

```
255.255.255.255 Constant
255.255.255.252 Mask
-----------------------Subtract
0    0    0    3 ← this is your wildcard mask.
```

It's extremely simple, with no physics needed.

So, that was a basic configuration of OSPF, but you can configure OSPF in many ways. I just explained wildcard masking, but remember that zeros need to match exactly, so what can you tell me about the following configuration, using a different topology?

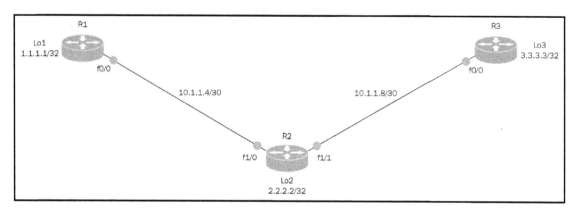

```
R1(config)#router ospf 1
R1(config-router)#net 0.0.0.0 0.0.0.0 area 0
R2(config)#router ospf 2
R2(config-router)#net 10.1.1.6 0.0.0.0 area 0
R2(config-router)#net 10.1.1.9 0.0.0.0 area 0
R2(config-router)#net 2.2.2.2 0.0.0.0 area 0
R3(config)#router ospf 3
R3(config-router)#net 10.1.1.0 0.0.0.255 area 0
R3(config-router)#net 3.3.3.0 0.0.0.255 area 0
```

We configured OSPF in three different ways, so let's explain each one.

In this new topology, we are playing around with the wildcard mask. You can see in the first configuration that when we create the network statement, we use all zeros, 0.0.0.0 0.0.0.0, and then we put in the area number.

Using all zeros means matching all interfaces, so any IP address that exists on the router will be matched by OSPF, placed in area 0, and advertised to the neighbor routers.

In the second example, when we create our network statement, we put the actual IP address of the interface and then use a wildcard mask of all zeros, `192.168.1.254 0.0.0.0`. In this case, OSPF will know exactly what interface is going to participate in the OSPF process, because we are matching exactly each octet.

In the last example, the network state created was using the network ID and then we only matched the first three octets and we used 255 on the last octet, which states *whatever number*.

So, OSPF has tremendous flexibility in its configurations, to meet your needs on the network. You just need to know what those needs are.

By the way, I hope you spotted that I used a different process ID number on each router. Keep in mind for the CCNA and even most "real-world" networks that the process ID number is only locally significant. The other routers do not care, so this number can be whatever you want it to be.

 THIS NEW TOPOLOGY WAS CREATED IN GNS3. IT WILL ONLY WORK IN GNS3, VIRL, OR LIVE EQUIPMENT. PACKET TRACER WILL ALLOW YOU TO ENTER THE COMMANDS, BUT THE ROUTING PROTOCOL WILL NOT CONVERGE.

To further prove that the three new ways of configuring OSPF work, here are the routers' output:

```
R1#sh ip route
Gateway of last resort is not set
      1.0.0.0/32 is subnetted, 1 subnets
C        1.1.1.1 is directly connected, Loopback1
      2.0.0.0/32 is subnetted, 1 subnets
O        2.2.2.2 [110/2] via 10.1.1.6, 18:41:09, FastEthernet0/0
      3.0.0.0/32 is subnetted, 1 subnets
O        3.3.3.3 [110/3] via 10.1.1.6, 18:41:09, FastEthernet0/0
      10.0.0.0/30 is subnetted, 2 subnets
O        10.1.1.8 [110/2] via 10.1.1.6, 18:41:09, FastEthernet0/0
C        10.1.1.4 is directly connected, FastEthernet0/0
R1#sh ip protocols
  Routing Protocol is "ospf 1"
    Outgoing update filter list for all interfaces is not set
    Incoming update filter list for all interfaces is not set
    Router ID 1.1.1.1
    Number of areas in this router is 1. 1 normal 0 stub 0 nssa
    Maximum path: 4
```

```
    Routing for Networks:
      0.0.0.0 255.255.255.255 area 0
    Reference bandwidth unit is 100 mbps
    Routing Information Sources:
      Gateway          Distance        Last Update
      3.3.3.3             110           18:41:42
      2.2.2.2             110           18:41:42
    Distance: (default is 110)
  R1#ping 2.2.2.2
Type escape sequence to abort.
  Sending 5, 100-byte ICMP Echos to 2.2.2.2, timeout is 2 seconds:
  !!!!!
  Success rate is 100 percent (5/5), round-trip min/avg/max = 16/20/24 ms
  R1#ping 3.3.3.3
  Type escape sequence to abort.
  Sending 5, 100-byte ICMP Echos to 3.3.3.3, timeout is 2 seconds:
  !!!!!
  Success rate is 100 percent (5/5), round-trip min/avg/max = 36/52/72 ms
```

As you can see, I have full connectivity and by looking at my routing table, I am learning about all the routes. But I want to show the differences in the configuration of the network statements for the three routers using the `sh ip protocols` command:

```
    R2#sh ip protocols
    Routing Protocol is "ospf 2"
      Outgoing update filter list for all interfaces is not set
      Incoming update filter list for all interfaces is not set
      Router ID 2.2.2.2
      Number of areas in this router is 1. 1 normal 0 stub 0 nssa
      Maximum path: 4
      Routing for Networks:
        2.2.2.2 0.0.0.0 area 0
        10.1.1.6 0.0.0.0 area 0
        10.1.1.9 0.0.0.0 area 0
      Reference bandwidth unit is 100 mbps
      Routing Information Sources:
        Gateway          Distance        Last Update
        3.3.3.3             110           18:31:18
        1.1.1.1             110           18:31:18
      Distance: (default is 110)
    R3#sh ip protocols
    Routing Protocol is "ospf 3"
      Outgoing update filter list for all interfaces is not set
      Incoming update filter list for all interfaces is not set
      Router ID 3.3.3.3
      Number of areas in this router is 1. 1 normal 0 stub 0 nssa
      Maximum path: 4
      Routing for Networks:
```

```
      3.3.3.0 0.0.0.255 area 0
      10.1.1.0 0.0.0.255 area 0
   Reference bandwidth unit is 100 mbps
    Routing Information Sources:
      Gateway          Distance      Last Update
      2.2.2.2               110      18:47:13
      1.1.1.1               110      18:47:13
    Distance: (default is 110)
```

To look at other features that OSPF uses, we are going to explore the `passive-interface` command. This is very useful in preventing updates being sent out. But be warned, this command works differently with other routing protocols. For example, if you were to configure it on EIGRP, it will not send or receive updates. In OSPF, it simply prevents updates from being sent out, but will receive updates for neighbor routers. It will not update its routing table, so essentially that interface is down.

Let's look from the perspective of R2:

```
R2(config-router)#passive-interface f1/0
*Oct  3 04:47:01.763: %OSPF-5-ADJCHG: Process 2, Nbr 1.1.1.1 on
FastEthernet1/0 from FULL to DOWN, Neighbor Down: Interface down or
detached
```

Almost immediately, it took the `F1/0` interface down. What's happening is that the router is not sending any hellos. Let's further investigate by using the `debug ip ospf hello` command:

```
R2#debug ip ospf hello
OSPF hello events debugging is on
R2#
*Oct  3 04:49:40.319: OSPF: Rcv hello from 3.3.3.3 area 0 from
FastEthernet1/1 10.1.1.10
*Oct  3 04:49:40.319: OSPF: End of hello processing
R2#
*Oct  3 04:49:43.723: OSPF: Send hello to 224.0.0.5 area 0 on
FastEthernet1/1 from 10.1.1.9
R2#
*Oct  3 04:49:50.319: OSPF: Rcv hello from 3.3.3.3 area 0 from
FastEthernet1/1 10.1.1.10
*Oct  3 04:49:50.323: OSPF: End of hello processing
R2#
*Oct  3 04:49:53.723: OSPF: Send hello to 224.0.0.5 area 0 on
FastEthernet1/1 from 10.1.1.9
R2#
*Oct  3 04:50:00.327: OSPF: Rcv hello from 3.3.3.3 area 0 from
FastEthernet1/1 10.1.1.10
*Oct  3 04:50:00.331: OSPF: End of hello processing
```

It is no longer sending updates out to the `F1/0` interface, so let's look at the routing table now and see what networks we know about:

```
R2#sh ip route
Gateway of last resort is not set
      2.0.0.0/32 is subnetted, 1 subnets
C        2.2.2.2 is directly connected, Loopback2
      3.0.0.0/32 is subnetted, 1 subnets
O        3.3.3.3 [110/2] via 10.1.1.10, 00:05:12, FastEthernet1/1
      10.0.0.0/30 is subnetted, 2 subnets
C        10.1.1.8 is directly connected, FastEthernet1/1
C        10.1.1.4 is directly connected, FastEthernet1/0
R2#ping 2.2.2.2
Type escape sequence to abort.
Sending 5, 100-byte ICMP Echos to 2.2.2.2, timeout is 2 seconds:
!!!!!
Success rate is 100 percent (5/5), round-trip min/avg/max = 1/1/4 ms
R2#ping 3.3.3.3
Type escape sequence to abort.
Sending 5, 100-byte ICMP Echos to 3.3.3.3, timeout is 2 seconds:
!!!!!
Success rate is 100 percent (5/5), round-trip min/avg/max = 20/24/40 ms
```

So, what are we looking at? We are only learning about the `3.3.3.3` network, which is the loopback address on R3. We have stopped learning about the `1.1.1.1` network, and we do not have connectivity to it. We can ping our own loopback, obviously, and we can ping the loopback on R3.

Okay, let's remove the `passive interface` command and compare the difference:

```
R2(config)#router ospf 2
R2(config-router)#no passive-interface f1/0
R2(config-router)#
*Oct  3 04:57:34.343: %OSPF-5-ADJCHG: Process 2, Nbr 1.1.1.1 on
FastEthernet1/0 from LOADING to FULL, Loading Done
```

We have now recreated our neighbor relationship with R1 once more. Let's debug again:

```
R2#debug ip ospf hello
OSPF hello events debugging is on
R2#
*Oct  3 05:03:48.527: OSPF: Send hello to 224.0.0.5 area 0 on
FastEthernet1/0 from 10.1.1.6
R2#
*Oct  3 05:03:50.303: OSPF: Rcv hello from 3.3.3.3 area 0 from
FastEthernet1/1 10.1.1.10
*Oct  3 05:03:50.303: OSPF: End of hello processing
```

```
R2#
*Oct  3 05:03:52.143: OSPF: Rcv hello from 1.1.1.1 area 0 from
FastEthernet1/0 10.1.1.5
*Oct  3 05:03:52.143: OSPF: End of hello processing
R2#
*Oct  3 05:03:53.723: OSPF: Send hello to 224.0.0.5 area 0 on
FastEthernet1/1 from 10.1.1.9
```

Once again, we are sending and receiving hellos from R1, so let's ping the loopback on R1, but also look at the routing table:

```
R2#sh ip route
Gateway of last resort is not set
      1.0.0.0/32 is subnetted, 1 subnets
O 1.1.1.1 [110/2] via 10.1.1.5, 00:06:50, FastEthernet1/0
      2.0.0.0/32 is subnetted, 1 subnets
C        2.2.2.2 is directly connected, Loopback2
      3.0.0.0/32 is subnetted, 1 subnets
O        3.3.3.3 [110/2] via 10.1.1.10, 00:06:50, FastEthernet1/1
      10.0.0.0/30 is subnetted, 2 subnets
C        10.1.1.8 is directly connected, FastEthernet1/1
C        10.1.1.4 is directly connected, FastEthernet1/0
R2#ping 1.1.1.1
Type escape sequence to abort.
Sending 5, 100-byte ICMP Echos to 1.1.1.1, timeout is 2 seconds:
!!!!!
```

Once more, we have connectivity, so with the `passive-interface` be very careful how you are going to use it and which protocol you are going to use it with.

Now let's explore another feature, which is the `default-information originate`. This is used in conjunction with a static-default route to create an OSPF default static route. It is like advertising a static default route. To let all the routers know if you want to get to a destination network, this is the way to go.

So, how would you configure something like that? Let's take a look.

Use the following topology:

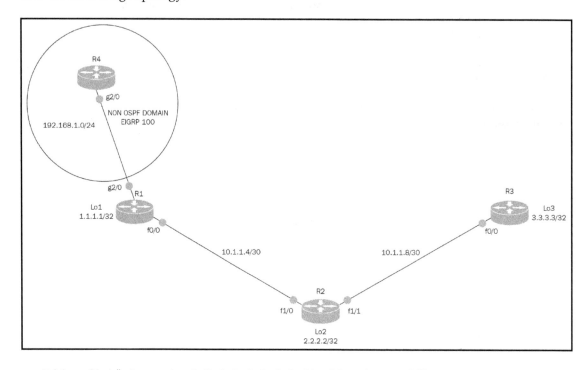

```
R1(config)# ip route 0.0.0.0 0.0.0.0 GigabitEthernet2/0
R1(config)#router ospf 1
R1(config-router)#default-information originate
```

Now that we have created a static route to an external network and we did the default-information originate command, what would the routing tables of the other routers look like?

```
R2#sh ip route
Codes: C - connected, S - static, R - RIP, M - mobile, B - BGP
       D - EIGRP, EX - EIGRP external, O - OSPF, IA - OSPF inter area
       N1 - OSPF NSSA external type 1, N2 - OSPF NSSA external type 2
       E1 - OSPF external type 1, E2 - OSPF external type 2
       i - IS-IS, su - IS-IS summary, L1 - IS-IS level-1, L2 - IS-IS
level-2
       ia - IS-IS inter area, * - candidate default, U - per-user static
route
       o - ODR, P - periodic downloaded static route
    Gateway of last resort is 10.1.1.5 to network 0.0.0.0
1.0.0.0/32 is subnetted, 1 subnets
O        1.1.1.1 [110/2] via 10.1.1.5, 00:16:35, FastEthernet1/0
```

```
          2.0.0.0/32 is subnetted, 1 subnets
C         2.2.2.2 is directly connected, Loopback2
          3.0.0.0/32 is subnetted, 1 subnets
O         3.3.3.3 [110/2] via 10.1.1.10, 00:16:35, FastEthernet1/1
          10.0.0.0/30 is subnetted, 2 subnets
C         10.1.1.8 is directly connected, FastEthernet1/1
C         10.1.1.4 is directly connected, FastEthernet1/0
O      192.168.1.0/24 [110/2] via 10.1.1.5, 00:16:35, FastEthernet1/0
O*E2 0.0.0.0/0 [110/1] via 10.1.1.5, 00:16:35, FastEthernet1/0
R3#sh ip route
Codes: C - connected, S - static, R - RIP, M - mobile, B - BGP
       D - EIGRP, EX - EIGRP external, O - OSPF, IA - OSPF inter area
       N1 - OSPF NSSA external type 1, N2 - OSPF NSSA external type 2
       E1 - OSPF external type 1, E2 - OSPF external type 2
       i - IS-IS, su - IS-IS summary, L1 - IS-IS level-1, L2 - IS-IS
level-2
       ia - IS-IS inter area, * - candidate default, U - per-user static
route
       o - ODR, P - periodic downloaded static route
Gateway of last resort is 10.1.1.9 to network 0.0.0.0
     1.0.0.0/32 is subnetted, 1 subnets
O        1.1.1.1 [110/3] via 10.1.1.9, 00:17:17, FastEthernet0/0
         2.0.0.0/32 is subnetted, 1 subnets
O        2.2.2.2 [110/2] via 10.1.1.9, 00:17:17, FastEthernet0/0
         3.0.0.0/32 is subnetted, 1 subnets
C        3.3.3.3 is directly connected, Loopback3
         10.0.0.0/30 is subnetted, 2 subnets
C        10.1.1.8 is directly connected, FastEthernet0/0
O        10.1.1.4 [110/2] via 10.1.1.9, 00:17:17, FastEthernet0/0
O      192.168.1.0/24 [110/3] via 10.1.1.9, 00:17:17, FastEthernet0/0
O*E2 0.0.0.0/0 [110/1] via 10.1.1.9, 00:17:17, FastEthernet0/0
R4#sh ip route
Codes: C - connected, S - static, R - RIP, M - mobile, B - BGP
       D - EIGRP, EX - EIGRP external, O - OSPF, IA - OSPF inter area
       N1 - OSPF NSSA external type 1, N2 - OSPF NSSA external type 2
       E1 - OSPF external type 1, E2 - OSPF external type 2
       i - IS-IS, su - IS-IS summary, L1 - IS-IS level-1, L2 - IS-IS
level-2
       ia - IS-IS inter area, * - candidate default, U - per-user static
route
       o - ODR, P - periodic downloaded static route
Gateway of last resort is 192.168.1.1 to network 0.0.0.0
     1.0.0.0/32 is subnetted, 1 subnets
D EX   1.1.1.1 [170/5376] via 192.168.1.1, 00:12:38, GigabitEthernet2/0
         2.0.0.0/32 is subnetted, 1 subnets
D EX   2.2.2.2 [170/5376] via 192.168.1.1, 00:12:38, GigabitEthernet2/0
         3.0.0.0/32 is subnetted, 1 subnets
```

```
D EX   3.3.3.3 [170/5376] via 192.168.1.1, 00:12:38, GigabitEthernet2/0
         10.0.0.0/30 is subnetted, 2 subnets
D EX   10.1.1.8 [170/5376] via 192.168.1.1, 00:12:38, GigabitEthernet2/0
D EX   10.1.1.4 [170/5376] via 192.168.1.1, 00:12:38, GigabitEthernet2/0
C      192.168.1.0/24 is directly connected, GigabitEthernet2/0
D*EX 0.0.0.0/0 [170/5376] via 192.168.1.1, 00:12:38, GigabitEthernet2/0
```

So, this is how you would advertise a default route to external route, using OSPF.

Obviously, you must configure EIGRP on R1 and R4 and do some redistribution. That is why all the routes are external, but you are advertising a way out using a static default route.

OSPF and loopback interfaces

You have seen that I have configured a loopback address in the previous lab, so let me explain to you why we really use them. We can use them for a variety of reasons. Laziness is one reason. I don't want to create a LAN, so I use loopback interfaces instead. They can be used for real purposes, such as diagnostics. You can always source a loopback address. Also, you would have an interface that never goes down, because it is virtual.

Most importantly, they are used in the election process of the designated router and back-up designated router, but we will get to that in a little bit. So, loopback interfaces can help us a lot and configuring them is very simple.

This is how you would configure a loopback address:

```
R4(config)#int Lo400
R4(config-if)#ip a
*Oct 4 04:01:51.272: %LINEPROTO-5-UPDOWN: Line protocol on Interface
Loopback400, changed state to up
R4(config-if)#ip address 4.4.4.4 255.255.255.255
```

It is a straightforward configuration. You use the Lo, which is short for loopback and a number. The range you have is 0-2147483647, so take your pick. There is no need to do a no shut command since it turns on all by itself.

I choose to use a host mask of all 255s, but you don't have to.

Loopback addresses are simply used for sourcing, diagnostics, OSPF elections, or creating a quick LAN for labs purposes. One thing to remember, just like any other interface, you need to advertise it on whatever routing protocol you are using.

The following are some show commands that you could use to troubleshoot OSPF:

```
R2#sh ip route
Gateway of last resort is 10.1.1.5 to network 0.0.0.0
     1.0.0.0/32 is subnetted, 1 subnets
O       1.1.1.1 [110/2] via 10.1.1.5, 15:49:15, FastEthernet1/0
     2.0.0.0/32 is subnetted, 1 subnets
C       2.2.2.2 is directly connected, Loopback2
     3.0.0.0/32 is subnetted, 1 subnets
O       3.3.3.3 [110/2] via 10.1.1.10, 15:49:15, FastEthernet1/1
     10.0.0.0/30 is subnetted, 2 subnets
C       10.1.1.8 is directly connected, FastEthernet1/1
C       10.1.1.4 is directly connected, FastEthernet1/0
O    192.168.1.0/24 [110/2] via 10.1.1.5, 15:49:15, FastEthernet1/0
O*E2 0.0.0.0/0 [110/1] via 10.1.1.5, 15:49:15, FastEthernet1/0
R2#sh ip ospf
 Routing Process "ospf 2" with ID 2.2.2.2
 Start time: 00:07:57.248, Time elapsed: 1d19h
 Supports only single TOS(TOS0) routes
 Supports opaque LSA
 Supports Link-local Signaling (LLS)
 Supports area transit capability
 Router is not originating router-LSAs with maximum metric
 Initial SPF schedule delay 5000 msecs
 Minimum hold time between two consecutive SPFs 10000 msecs
 Maximum wait time between two consecutive SPFs 10000 msecs
 Incremental-SPF disabled
 Minimum LSA interval 5 secs
 Minimum LSA arrival 1000 msecs
 LSA group pacing timer 240 secs
 Interface flood pacing timer 33 msecs
 Retransmission pacing timer 66 msecs
 Number of external LSA 1. Checksum Sum 0x00E4AD
 Number of opaque AS LSA 0. Checksum Sum 0x000000
 Number of DCbitless external and opaque AS LSA 0
 Number of DoNotAge external and opaque AS LSA 0
 Number of areas in this router is 1. 1 normal 0 stub 0 nssa
 Number of areas transit capable is 0
 External flood list length 0
    Area BACKBONE(0)
        Number of interfaces in this area is 3 (1 loopback)
        Area has no authentication
        SPF algorithm last executed 15:49:56.552 ago
        SPF algorithm executed 19 times
        Area ranges are
        Number of LSA 5. Checksum Sum 0x023969
        Number of opaque link LSA 0. Checksum Sum 0x000000
        Number of DCbitless LSA 0
```

```
                Number of indication LSA 0
                Number of DoNotAge LSA 0
                Flood list length 0
        R2#sh ip ospf database
                OSPF Router with ID (2.2.2.2) (Process ID 2)
                    Router Link States (Area 0)
    Link ID         ADV Router      Age       Seq#          Checksum Link count
    1.1.1.1          1.1.1.1        609       0x80000059 0x0051CB 3
    2.2.2.2          2.2.2.2        156       0x80000056 0x008CC9 3
    3.3.3.3          3.3.3.3         50       0x8000004F 0x001E66 2
                    Net Link States (Area 0)
    Link ID         ADV Router      Age         Seq#          Checksum
    10.1.1.6         2.2.2.2         156         0x8000002B 0x009D4F
    10.1.1.9         2.2.2.2         401         0x8000004E 0x009D21
                Type-5 AS External Link States
    Link ID         ADV Router      Age         Seq#          Checksum Tag
    0.0.0.0          1.1.1.1         609         0x8000001D 0x00E4AD 1
```

In the preceding show commands, pay attention to the highlighted portions; that is what you need to focus on.

Before I show you some more show commands, we first need to discuss designated routers and back-up designated routers.

OSPF runs an election to choose these routers, but only on an Ethernet network, multi-cast network, and broadcast network; whatever terminology you want to use. It will not do it on a serial connection.

The election follows a particular order. It first looks for the highest IP address on any physical interface of the router, unless you configured a loopback address, which at that point it will ignore the physical interfaces and choose the highest loopback address, but it does not stop there. If you want to have control over the election, you can set the priority on an interface to its highest value of 255. The range is 0-255; 0 means no elections and on all other numbers an election is run. The router will always be the DR; the second highest priority would be the BDR.

But why do we need DRs and BDRs in these multi-networks? The answer is control of data flow. Routers that are not DRs or BDRs are known as DROTHERS, which means designated others. They will send their updates to the DR via 224.0.0.5 and the DR will disseminate that information to all the DROTHERs via 224.0.0.6 to include the BDR.

We will look at a simple topology of two routers to prove the point of when an election takes place:

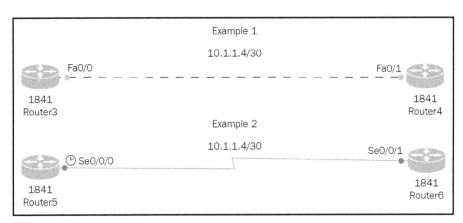

Let's analyze example 1, which is using a crossover cable to create an Ethernet network:

```
ERouter1#sh ip ospf int f0/0
FastEthernet0/0 is up, line protocol is up
Internet address is 10.1.1.5/30, Area 0
Process ID 1, Router ID 10.1.1.5, Network Type BROADCAST, Cost: 1
Transmit Delay is 1 sec, State BDR, Priority 1
Designated Router (ID) 10.1.1.6, Interface address 10.1.1.6
Backup Designated Router (ID) 10.1.1.5, Interface address 10.1.1.5
Timer intervals configured, Hello 10, Dead 40, Wait 40, Retransmit 5
Hello due in 00:00:02
Index 1/1, flood queue length 0
Next 0x0(0)/0x0(0)
Last flood scan length is 1, maximum is 1
Last flood scan time is 0 msec, maximum is 0 msec
Neighbor Count is 1, Adjacent neighbor count is 1
Adjacent with neighbor 10.1.1.6 (Designated Router)
Suppress hello for 0 neighbor(s)
```

In the preceding example, you need to memorize that show command. First of all, the router ID is the address of the router. It is the only address on that router, so there is no higher address to choose, and that address becomes the RID. Next, pay attention to the network type **broadcast**. Automatically, the priority number becomes a number one, forcing an election.

Finally, look at the DR and BDR. The DR is your neighbor router because its IP address is higher than yours.

So, for this example, OSPF is following the rules of the election process.

Let's now look at example 2:

```
SRouter1#sh ip ospf int s0/0/0
Serial0/0/0 is up, line protocol is up
Internet address is 10.1.1.5/30, Area 0
Process ID 1, Router ID 10.1.1.5, Network Type POINT-TO-POINT, Cost: 64
Transmit Delay is 1 sec, State POINT-TO-POINT, Priority 0
No designated router on this network
No backup designated router on this network
Timer intervals configured, Hello 10, Dead 40, Wait 40, Retransmit 5
Hello due in 00:00:09
Index 1/1, flood queue length 0
Next 0x0(0)/0x0(0)
Last flood scan length is 1, maximum is 1
Last flood scan time is 0 msec, maximum is 0 msec
Neighbor Count is 1 , Adjacent neighbor count is 1
Adjacent with neighbor 10.1.1.6
Suppress hello for 0 neighbor(s)
```

In example 2, it states that the network type is a point-to-point and any book for CCNA you read, except for this one, will tell you that OSPF elections will not happen on point-to-point and that is not true. The reason there is no election in this example is that the priority number is ZERO and allows OSPF not to run an election.

In the first example, it is a point-to-point, but the difference is the cabling. It sees it as an Ethernet network, so the priority number is 1 and the election is processed.

So, we have proven our point, when an OSPF election takes place.

Now I can show you one more command, since you now understand the concept of the OSPF DR/BDR election process:

```
R3#sh ip ospf neighbor
Neighbor  ID    Pri   State       Dead    Time Address      Interface
3.3.3.3    1     FULL/DROTHER  00:00:37   192.168.1.3   FastEthernet0/0
2.2.2.2    255   FULL/DR       00:00:37   192.168.1.2   FastEthernet0/0
4.4.4.4    1     FULL/DROTHER  00:00:37   192.168.1.4   FastEthernet0/0
R3#sh ip ospf int f0/0

FastEthernet0/0 is up, line protocol is up
Internet address is 192.168.1.1/24, Area 0
Process ID 1, Router ID 1.1.1.1, Network Type BROADCAST, Cost: 1
Transmit Delay is 1 sec, State BDR, Priority 254
Designated Router (ID) 2.2.2.2, Interface address 192.168.1.2
Backup Designated Router (ID) 1.1.1.1, Interface address 192.168.1.1
Timer intervals configured, Hello 10, Dead 40, Wait 40, Retransmit 5
Hello due in 00:00:02
```

```
Index 2/2, flood queue length 0
Next 0x0(0)/0x0(0)
Last flood scan length is 1, maximum is 1
Last flood scan time is 0 msec, maximum is 0 msec
Neighbor Count is 3, Adjacent neighbor count is 3
Adjacent with neighbor 3.3.3.3
Adjacent with neighbor 2.2.2.2 (Designated Router)
Adjacent with neighbor 4.4.4.4
Suppress hello for 0 neighbor(s)
```

The preceding `show` commands of `sh ip` neighbors. They are giving you the DR with the priority number that was used to make it the DR and the DROTHER numbers.

The `sh ip ospf int f0/0` command shows everything we have discussed previously and if you look at the DR and BDR, they are using loopback addresses.

So, when doing a lab like this, be curious and use not only IP addresses on the physical interface, but also configure loopbacks and priorities and look at the outcome. That is the only way you are going to fully understand this process.

For the preceding commands, I used a different topology, as shown in the following diagram:

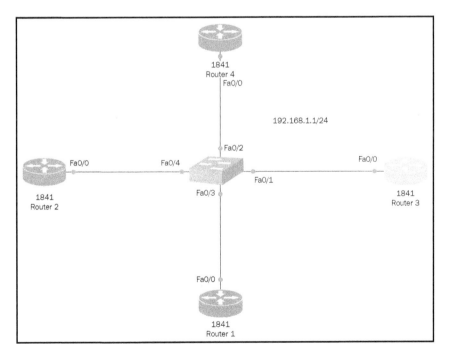

Multi-area OSPF configuration

In the beginning of the chapter, I showed you a sneak peek into the world of multi-area OSPF. It is time to get a little deeper into the configuration of multi-area OSPF and the advantages gained by doing this type of configuration.

Before you continue into this advanced configuration of OSPF, you must have a good understanding of single-area OSPF, the process that it takes to create neighbor relationships, topological databases, and the different ways you can configure OSPF.

Multi-area OSPF gives scalability in our network, and a better way to manage the WAN. You can separate areas by building, county, and state; it is completely up to you how you create your hierarchy.

Like I said before, too many routers in one area creates a big problem. If one link goes down, or if a subnet is added, some sort of change happens to the topology, and the entire area has to recalculate its topological database, which means recalculating the SPF tree and updating the routing table. That means LSAs type 1 flooding your links.

If you are in a single area or multi-area, do not let that area get too big simply because of the processing overhead you are going to put on your routers. So the advantage, if used correctly, is in creating multiple areas with less routers, which sounds similar to VLANs.

When there is an issue or an update in a specific area that is maintained in that area and will not interrupt any other area.

Multi-area terminology

- **Backbone area**: This is the center or backbone of the OSPF areas. All other areas must communicate to the backbone area. So, essentially, when creating this type of topology, it is like a hub and spoke and it eliminates redundant paths and counts to infinity.
- **ABR**: This is an area border router that connects directly to the backbone area and to another area. It is the go-between for AREA 1 and AREA 0. That way, everyone in Area 1 can communicate with Area 0. Both routers would be running OSPF.
- **ASBR**: This is an autonomous system router, which connects to an ABR and, through redistribution, it will bring external routes into the OSPF domain.

It is very important to understand LSAs also. Early on in the chapter, I included a table on LSAs, so I will include it here as well, since it plays an even more important role:

Type	Name	Description
1	Router LSA	The routers publicize presence and lists the links to other routers on the same network.
2	Network LSA	The DR on a broadcast segment lists which routers are joined together by the segment.
3	Summary LSA	ABR takes information it has learned on one of its attached areas and summarizes it before sending it out on other areas.
4	ASBR-Summary LSA	**ASBR is where the type 5 LSA originated and would give more detailed information.**
5	External LSA	**Contains important information about OSPF from other routing processes. They are flooded into all areas except NSSA**

In a multi-area OSPF, these LSAs are the ones to focus on and how to find them.

So, with that said, let's configure a multi-area OSPF, as shown in the following diagram:

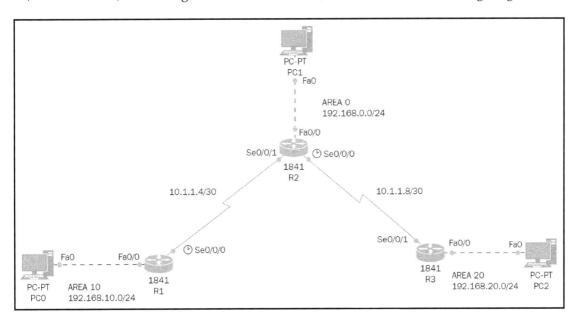

```
R2(config)#ROUTER OSPF 1
R2(config-router)#NET 192.168.0.0 0.0.0.255 AREA 0
R2(config-router)#NET 10.1.1.4 0.0.0.3 AREA 0
R2(config-router)#NET 10.1.1.8 0.0.0.3 AREA 0
R2(config-router)#DO WR
R1#CONFIG T
Enter configuration commands, one per line. End with CNTL/Z.
R1(config)#ROUTER OSPF 10
R1(config-router)#NET 192.168.10.0 0.0.0.255 AREA 10
R1(config-router)#NET 10.1.1.4 0.0.0.3 AREA 0
R1(config-router)#DO WR
00:24:07: %OSPF-5-ADJCHG: Process 10, Nbr 192.168.0.254 on Serial0/0/0
from LOADING to FULL, Loading Done
R3(config)#ROUTER OSPF 20
R3(config-router)#NET 192.168.20.0 0.0.0.255 AREA 20
R3(config-router)#NET 10.1.1.8 0.0.0.3 AREA 0
R3(config-router)#DO WR
Building configuration...
[OK]
R3(config-router)#
00:26:10: %OSPF-5-ADJCHG: Process 20, Nbr 192.168.0.254 on Serial0/0/1
from LOADING to FULL, Loading Done
```

As you can see, we have the message FULL, Loading Done; that is a good thing.

Let's look at the R1 and R3 routing tables, as follows:

```
R1#sh ip route
10.0.0.0/30 is subnetted, 2 subnets
C 10.1.1.4 is directly connected, Serial0/0/0
O 10.1.1.8 [110/128] via 10.1.1.6, 00:03:45, Serial0/0/0
O 192.168.0.0/24 [110/65] via 10.1.1.6, 00:03:45, Serial0/0/0
C 192.168.10.0/24 is directly connected, FastEthernet0/0
O IA 192.168.20.0/24 [110/129] via 10.1.1.6, 00:01:17, Serial0/0/0
R3#sh ip route
10.0.0.0/30 is subnetted, 2 subnets
O 10.1.1.4 [110/128] via 10.1.1.9, 00:02:05, Serial0/0/1
C 10.1.1.8 is directly connected, Serial0/0/1
O 192.168.0.0/24 [110/65] via 10.1.1.9, 00:02:05, Serial0/0/1
O IA 192.168.10.0/24 [110/129] via 10.1.1.9, 00:02:05, Serial0/0/1
C 192.168.20.0/24 is directly connected, FastEthernet0/0
```

We are getting inter-area routes, which is a good thing. Now we ping from host to host. We will be pinging from Area 10, shown as follows:

```
C:\>ping 192.168.0.1
Pinging 192.168.0.1 with 32 bytes of data:
Reply from 192.168.0.1: bytes=32 time=7ms TTL=126
Reply from 192.168.0.1: bytes=32 time=1ms TTL=126
Reply from 192.168.0.1: bytes=32 time=1ms TTL=126
Reply from 192.168.0.1: bytes=32 time=3ms TTL=126
C:\>ping 192.168.20.1
Pinging 192.168.20.1 with 32 bytes of data:
Reply from 192.168.20.1: bytes=32 time=2ms TTL=125
Reply from 192.168.20.1: bytes=32 time=2ms TTL=125
Reply from 192.168.20.1: bytes=32 time=8ms TTL=125
Reply from 192.168.20.1: bytes=32 time=6ms TTL=125
```

So, we have full connectivity across our network, and the hosts are on different areas. As far as the CCNA is concerned, this is as far as you need to go.

Redistribution and even virtual links are beyond the scope of the CCNA. You should know what they are, but you will not be configuring or looking at them.

Summary

This chapter covered a lot of OSPF configurations, from the basic single area to multi-area OSPF. We covered terminology, the features of OSPF, and different ways we can advertise the networks.

Make sure you know how to configure a single-area OSPF and how to find out if it's working using the show commands we used in the chapter. Don't forget about the election of DR and BDR. That only happens in Ethernet networks.

One last thing: memorize all the LSAs given in the table; you may come across them.

In our next chapter, we will learn about **Border Gateway Protocol (BGP)** eBGP.

16
Border Gateway Protocol

The **Border Gateway Protocol** (**BGP**) allows us to connect to systems around the globe. In this chapter, we will be looking at BGP, specifically the **External Border Gateway Protocol** (**eBGP**). To cover BGP in its entirety would take a book of its own. So, we will briefly cover BGP overall and then compare iBGP and eBGP to understand their differences. We will configure BGP, and by doing so, you will see how huge and powerful this protocol is.

Topics that will be covered in the chapter include the following:

- A brief history of BGP
- Comparing BGP to EGP and OSPF
- Configuring iBGP
- Configuring eBGP
- Verifying BGP

A brief history of BGP

BGP has been around since the early days of the internet, all the way back to the days of ARPANET.

BGP dates to 1969, where it sent a message through the internet and only a portion of the message was received, but it was considered a success.

In 1971, ARPANET implemented more internet protocols. These were early data packet switching-type protocols, which in turn provided us with the TCP/IP.

In 1982, an attempt was made to create an internet protocol and the GGP, or the Gateway-to-Gateway Protocol, came to be. Unfortunately, it did not scale well and suffered from excessive overhead in the managing of routing tables, and troubleshooting a non-centralized system proved to be extremely difficult.

To fix these deficiencies, the **Exterior Gateway Protocol (EGP)** was developed, which started the concept of autonomous systems. The purpose of this protocol was to ensure the flow of traffic over multiple AS by exchanging routing information.

The BGP protocol that we embrace today has its roots in EGP, but it builds upon it.

Good to know: BGPv4 was released in 1995 under RFC 1771. We still use it today.

BGP versus OSPF

The major differences between BGP and OSPF protocols are shown in the following table:

Characteristics	BGP	OSPF
Routing algorithm	Distance vector	Link state
Classless support	Yes	Yes
Summarization	Yes	Yes
VLSM	Yes	Yes
Metric	Various attributes	Bandwidth
Hierarchy	No	Yes
Building blocks	AS	Areas
Base protocol	TCP using port 179	IP protocol port 89
Traffic type	Unicast	Multicast
Neighbors	Manually assigned	Discovered
Route exchange	Only with neighbors	With adjacent neighbors
Initial update	Synchronized DB	Synchronized DB
Hello timers	60 seconds	10 - 30 seconds
Hold timers	180 seconds	40 - 120 seconds
Internal route exchange	iBGP session	LSA types 1 and 2
External route exchange	eBGP session	LSA types 3, 4, and 5
Routing updates	Attributes and AS path	Metric LSA 3 and 4
Network statements	Advertises network	Activates OSPF on interface
Unique features	Route reflectors	Stub, totally stubby, and NSSA area

So, now that we can see the differences between OSPF and BGP, as you should already know, BGP is the routing protocol of the internet and really can't be compared to any IGP, but some network administrators do use OSPF in their backbone wide area network, so I compared the differences between these two protocols.

Just so you understand, to run BGP, you must get permission from your ISP. Why? Because you will be sharing routing tables with them.

As far as the certification goes, you will only need to worry about eBGP, but I want to give you a wider view of the protocol. So, here we go.

Overview of BGP specification

BGP is a distance-vector routing protocol, which advertises its routing table periodically. These updates will include networks advertised, attributes used that influence the path of the packet, the next hop address that allows us to reach the destination network, and the AS through which the route update has passed.

BGP uses a list of AS to try to ensure a loop-free path by enforcing a rule that *no AS path may contain the same AS number twice*. The following characteristics of BGP will allow it to create summaries of networks to reduce the size of the routing tables:

- BGP uses lots of attributes to choose the best path to a destination network. If multiple AS numbers are used, BGP also takes this into consideration when choosing a path. When using multiple AS numbers, this is considered eBGP and the path distance would be longer compared to an iBGP, which uses a single AS number.
- BGP is a non-hierarchical networking structure, which means there is no backbone area. This is what makes BGP very scalable and complicated to configure. With BGP, you don't need a neighbor router to be physically connected to you. Neighbors could be routers that are not physically connected to you, simply by inputting the neighbor command, and if you wanted to bypass a router so it will not participate in your BGP networks, you can simply use the `route reflector` command. But that goes beyond the scope of the CCNA certification.
- As you are by now aware, BGP uses autonomous systems to create boundaries of networks but does not treat the communication completely differently depending on the AS they belong to.
- BGP use AS numbers to advertise routes and to learn about the reachability of routers by listening to advertisements from all AS numbers. You could create policies to advertise the routes you want and in which direction.

BGP is dependent on TCP for connection-oriented, acknowledged communication using port 179. When using BGP, you manually configure your neighbors. One advantage of BGP is that you could bypass a router between two router and make them neighbors.

BGP uses a variety of different stages when they first try to converge. Once the initial neighbor connection is established, BGP will simply send triggered updates via keepalives.

BGP is very interesting and the configurations you can create could turn into some monstrous complexities, but not for the CCNA. It will pose very simple questions, and it is highly doubtful you will even need to configure it. But, just so you know how BGP works, let's look at some interesting facts about iBGP and eBGP:

- **iBGP**: The routers must be configured as a neighbor to all other iBGP routers in the same area
- **eBGP**: It is not a requirement that every router be a neighbor to every other eBGP router

We still need to advertise our networks using the `Network` command, but there are synchronization rules that BGP uses to be able to interact with IGP routing protocols.

So, with all that said, we have just scratched the surface with BGP. But for CCNA, we only need to know the very basics of it and the best way to understand it is to do it.

So, let's configure BGP. We will first do the same AS, then we will do different AS, and compare the differences using our `show` commands.

The following is our topology:

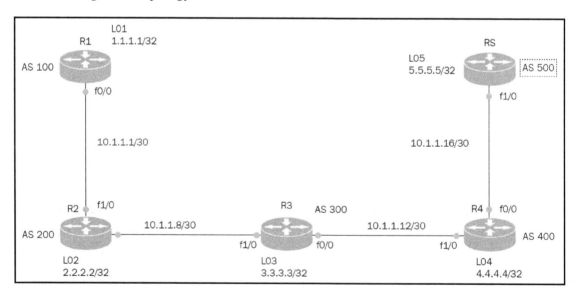

```
R1(config)#ROUTER BGP 100
R1(config-router)#NEIGHBOR 10.1.1.6 REMOTE-AS 100
R1(config-router)#NETWORK 10.1.1.4 MASK 255.255.255.252
R1(config-router)#NET WORK 1.1.1.1 MASK 255.255.255.255
R1(config-router)#DO WR
R2(config)#ROUTER BGP 100
R2(config-router)#NEIGHBOR 10.1.1.5 REMOTE-AS 100
R2(config-router)#NEIGHBOR 10.
*Oct  6 06:37:40.729: %BGP-5-ADJCHANGE: neighbor 10.1.1.5 Up
R2(config-router)#NEIGHBOR 10.1.1.10 REMOTE-AS 100
R2(config-router)#NETWORK 10.1.1.4 MASK 255.255.255.252
R2(config-router)#NETWORK 10.1.1.8 MASK 255.255.255.252
R2(config-router)#NETWORK 2.2.2.2 MASK 255.255.255.255
R2(config-router)#DO WR
R3# CONFIG T
Enter configuration commands, one per line.  End with CNTL/Z.
R3(config)#ROUTER BGP 100
R3(config-router)#NEIGHBOR 10.1.1.9 REMOTE-AS 100
R3(config-router)#NEIGHBOR 10.1.1.14 REMOTE-AS 100
R3(config-router)#
*Oct  6 06:39:23.509: %BGP-5-ADJCHANGE: neighbor 10.1.1.9 Up
R3(config-router)#NETWORK 10.1.1.8 MASK 255.255.255.252
R3(config-router)#NETWORK 10.1.1.12 MASK 255.255.255.252
R3(config-router)#NETWORK 3.3.3.3 MASK 255.255.255.255
R3(config-router)#DO WR
R4(config)#ROUTER BGP 100
R4(config-router)#NEIGHBOR 10.1.1.13 REMOTE-AS 100
R4(config-router)#NEIGHBOR 10.1.1.18 REMOTE-AS 100
*Oct  6 06:43:32.253: %BGP-5-ADJCHANGE: neighbor 10.1.1.13 Up
R4(config-router)#NETWORK 10.1.1.12 MASK 255.255.255.252
R4(config-router)#NETWORK 10.1.1.16 MASK 255.255.255.252
R4(config-router)#NETWORK 4.4.4.4 MASK 255.255.255.255
R4(config-router)#DO WR
R5#CONFIG T
Enter configuration commands, one per line.  End with CNTL/Z.
R5(config)#ROUTER BGP 100
R5(config-router)#NEIGHBOR 10.1.1.17 REMOTE-AS 100
R5(config-router)#NETWORK 10.1.1.16 MASK 2
*Oct  6 06:36:02.749: %BGP-5-ADJCHANGE: neighbor 10.1.1.17 Up
R5(config-router)#NETWORK 10.1.1.16 MASK 255.255.255.252
R5(config-router)#NETWORK 5.5.5.5 MASK 255.255.255.255
R5(config-router)#DO WR
```

What we just did was simple configuration of iBGP in AS 100. All we did was choose an autonomous system number, tell it who its neighbors are, and the neighbors' remote-as, which is the same. Then we simply advertise the networks to which we are connected, but it would be slightly different as we must use the MASK command to enter the mask.

Now, let's verify it is working using the following commands:

- show ip bgp summary
- show ip bgp
- show ip bgp neighbors

```
R1#sh ip bgp summary
BGP router identifier 1.1.1.1, local AS number 100
BGP table version is 3, main routing table version 3
2 network entries using 234 bytes of memory
3 path entries using 156 bytes of memory
3/2 BGP path/bestpath attribute entries using 372 bytes of memory
0 BGP route-map cache entries using 0 bytes of memory
0 BGP filter-list cache entries using 0 bytes of memory
BGP using 762 total bytes of memory
BGP activity 2/0 prefixes, 3/0 paths, scan interval 60 secs
Neighbor V  AS Msg Rcvd MsgSent TblVer InQ OutQ Up/Down State/PfxRcd
10.1.1.6 4 100 19  18    3      0    0 0:13:19                    2
```

This information is to verify that BGP sessions are up and working and to verify the IP address(es) and the AS of our neighbor(s):

```
R2#sh ip bgp summary
BGP router identifier 2.2.2.2, local AS number 100
BGP table version is 6, main routing table version 6
3 network entries using 351 bytes of memory
5 path entries using 260 bytes of memory
3/2 BGP path/bestpath attribute entries using 372 bytes of memory
0 BGP route-map cache entries using 0 bytes of memory
0 BGP filter-list cache entries using 0 bytes of memory
BGP using 983 total bytes of memory
BGP activity 3/0 prefixes, 5/0 paths, scan interval 60 secs
Neighbor  V AS MsgRcvd MsgSent TblVer InQ OutQ Up/Down State/PfxRcd
10.1.1.5  4 100 23      24      6   0   0    00:18:05     1
10.1.1.10 4 100 21      2       6   0   0    00:15:22     2

R3#sh ip bgp summary
BGP router identifier 3.3.3.3, local AS number 100
BGP table version is 5, main routing table version 5
4 network entries using 468 bytes of memory
6 path entries using 312 bytes of memory
3/2 BGP path/bestpath attribute entries using 372 bytes of memory
0 BGP route-map cache entries using 0 bytes of memory
0 BGP filter-list cache entries using 0 bytes of memory
BGP using 1152 total bytes of memory
BGP activity 4/0 prefixes, 6/0 paths, scan interval 60 secs
Neighbor  V AS MsgRcvd MsgSent TblVer InQ OutQ Up/Down State/PfxRcd
```

```
10.1.1.9  4 100 23      24 5    0        0 00:18:15            2
10.1.1.14 4 100 19      19 5    0        0 00:14:56            2

   R4#sh ip bgp summary
   BGP router identifier 4.4.4.4, local AS number 100
   BGP table version is 4, main routing table version 4
   3 network entries using 351 bytes of memory
   5 path entries using 260 bytes of memory
   3/2 BGP path/bestpath attribute entries using 372 bytes of memory
   0 BGP route-map cache entries using 0 bytes of memory
   0 BGP filter-list cache entries using 0 bytes of memory
   BGP using 983 total bytes of memory
   BGP activity 3/0 prefixes, 5/0 paths, scan interval 60 secs
Neighbor  V  AS MsgRcvd MsgSent TblVer InQ OutQ Up/Down State/PfxRcd
10.1.1.13 4  100 22      22      4      0   0   00:17:58    2
10.1.1.18 4  100 20      20      4      0   0   00:15:57    1

   R5#sh ip bgp summary
   BGP router identifier 5.5.5.5, local AS number 100
   BGP table version is 5, main routing table version 5
   2 network entries using 234 bytes of memory
   3 path entries using 156 bytes of memory
   3/2 BGP path/bestpath attribute entries using 372 bytes of memory
   0 BGP route-map cache entries using 0 bytes of memory
   0 BGP filter-list cache entries using 0 bytes of memory
   BGP using 762 total bytes of memory
   BGP activity 2/0 prefixes, 3/0 paths, scan interval 60 secs
Neighbor  V AS MsgRcvd MsgSent TblVer InQ OutQ Up/Down State/PfxRcd
10.1.1.17 4 100 23      23       5      0   0   00:18:28   2
```

OK, we see all our neighbors, we are using version 4 of BGP, and if `State/PfxRcd` is some number other than zero, that would be bad. All you need to do is to pay attention to the highlighted portion; when running the `show ip bgp summary` command that is what you are looking for, certification purposes.

Let's continue checking our iBGP configuration:

```
R1#show ip bgp
BGP table version is 3, local router ID is 1.1.1.1
Status codes: s suppressed, d damped, h history, * valid, > best, i -
internal,
r RIB-failure, S Stale
Origin codes: i - IGP, e - EGP, ? - incomplete
Network          Next Hop        Metric LocPrf  Weight Path
*  i10.1.1.4/30  10.1.1.6          0      100    0      i
*>               0.0.0.0           0             32768  i
*>i10.1.1.8/30   10.1.1.6                 100    0      i
```

The `show ip bgp` command is supposed to show us the entire BGP table. This should show us all the routes to all the networks. I only see two routes, so let's ping and see how far we can go:

```
R1#ping 10.1.1.6
Type escape sequence to abort.
Sending 5, 100-byte ICMP Echos to 10.1.1.6, timeout is 2 seconds:
!!!!!
Success rate is 100 percent (5/5), round-trip min/avg/max = 16/20/24 ms
R1#ping 10.1.1.9
Type escape sequence to abort.
Sending 5, 100-byte ICMP Echos to 10.1.1.9, timeout is 2 seconds:
!!!!!
Success rate is 100 percent (5/5), round-trip min/avg/max = 20/24/36 ms
R1#ping 10.1.1.10
Type escape sequence to abort.
Sending 5, 100-byte ICMP Echos to 10.1.1.10, timeout is 2 seconds:
!!!!!
Success rate is 100 percent (5/5), round-trip min/avg/max = 32/67/104 ms
R1#ping 10.1.1.12
Type escape sequence to abort.
Sending 5, 100-byte ICMP Echos to 10.1.1.12, timeout is 2 seconds:
.....
Success rate is 0 percent (0/5)
```

So, we can only ping about the neighbors that we are connected to, which is only R2.

Let's look at that last `show` command:

```
R1#sh ip bgp neighbors
BGP neighbor is 10.1.1.6,  remote AS 100, internal link
  BGP version 4, remote router ID 2.2.2.2
  BGP state = Established, up for 00:14:34
  Last read 00:00:34, last write 00:00:34, hold time is 180, keepalive
interval is 60 seconds
  Neighbor capabilities:
    Route refresh: advertised and received(old & new)
    Address family IPv4 Unicast: advertised and received
  Message statistics:
    InQ depth is 0
    OutQ depth is 0
                            Sent        Rcvd
    Opens:                  1           1
    Notifications:          0           0
    Updates:                1           1
    Keepalives:             16          16
    Route Refresh:          0           0
    Total:                  18          18
```

Default minimum time between advertisement runs is 0 seconds.
For address family: IPv4 Unicast
BGP table version 3, neighbor version 3/0
Output queue size : 0
Index 1, Offset 0, Mask 0x2
1 update-group member
Sent Rcvd
Prefix activity: ---- ----
Prefixes Current: 1 2 (Consumes 104 bytes)
Prefixes Total: 1 2
Implicit Withdraw: 0 0
Explicit Withdraw: 0 0
Used as bestpath: n/a 1
Used as multipath: n/a 0
Outbound Inbound
Local Policy Denied Prefixes: -------- -------
Bestpath from this peer: 1 n/a
Total: 1 0
Number of NLRIs in the update sent: max 1, min 1
Connections established 1; dropped 0
Last reset never
Connection state is ESTAB, I/O status: 1, unread input bytes: 0
Connection is ECN Disabled, Mininum incoming TTL 0, Outgoing TTL 255
Local host: 10.1.1.5, Local port: 34745
Foreign host: 10.1.1.6, **Foreign port: 179**
Enqueued packets for retransmit: 0, input: 0 mis-ordered: 0 (0 bytes)
Event Timers (current time is 0xA01F140):
Timer Starts Wakeups Next
Retrans 19 0 0x0
TimeWait 0 0 0x0
AckHold 18 1 0x0
SendWnd 0 0 0x0
KeepAlive 0 0 0x0
GiveUp 0 0 0x0
PmtuAger 0 0 0x0
DeadWait 0 0 0x0
    iss: 4047372662   snduna: 4047373087   sndnxt: 4047373087   sndwnd:
15960
    irs: 1675119061   rcvnxt: 1675119491   rcvwnd: 15955   delrcvwnd:
429
    SRTT: 276 ms, RTTO: 466 ms, RTV: 190 ms, KRTT: 0 ms
    minRTT: 16 ms, maxRTT: 300 ms, ACK hold: 200 ms
    Flags: active open, nagle
    IP Precedence value : 6
    Datagrams (max data segment is 1460 bytes):
    Rcvd: 36 (out of order: 0), with data: 18, total data bytes: 429
    Sent: 22 (retransmit: 0, fastretransmit: 0, partialack: 0, Second
Congestion: 0), with data: 19, total data bytes: 424

What this command shows us, in a nutshell, is that we can only get to our neighbors that we created in BGP. There is other highlighted information that you need to look at, but this command is only really for when you get to the real world; it's doubtful you will need it for the CCNA certification .

The iBGP was configured on purpose, to show you that the CCNA exam will not cover this portion of the protocol and will not go into any kind of depth. BGP is a huge routing protocol, which is used by your ISP and more likely than not, eBGP is what the ISP is using. This is what the CCNA certification will be on, and it will still be the basics of it.

If you configure iBGP, the rule states that you must have a full mesh, but I can show you how we can fix this situation. However, let's first look at the routing table, as it is so far:

```
R1#sh ip route
Gateway of last resort is not set
1.0.0.0/24 is subnetted, 1 subnets
C 1.1.1.0 is directly connected, Loopback1
10.0.0.0/30 is subnetted, 2 subnets
B 10.1.1.8 [200/0] via 10.1.1.6, 00:26:26
C 10.1.1.4 is directly connected, FastEthernet0/0
```

Learning only one BGP route, which is a configured neighbor, let's fix this situation. I configured the IGP routing protocol, RIPv2, on all the routers. Let's look at bgp summary:

```
R1#sh ip bgp summary
BGP router identifier 1.1.1.1, local AS number 100
BGP table version is 5, main routing table version 5
2 network entries using 234 bytes of memory
3 path entries using 156 bytes of memory
3/2 BGP path/bestpath attribute entries using 372 bytes of memory
0 BGP route-map cache entries using 0 bytes of memory
0 BGP filter-list cache entries using 0 bytes of memory
BGP using 762 total bytes of memory
BGP activity 2/0 prefixes, 3/0 paths, scan interval 60 secs
Neighbor V AS MsgRcvd MsgSent TblVer InQ OutQ Up/Down State/PfxRcd
10.1.1.6 4 100 35      35        5    0   0    00:31:25  2
```

Nothing changed. Why? As per the rules of iBGP, you must make a neighbor relationship with all routers running in the same AS, so you can then it would work properly, but that is not entirely true. Keep reading through, and you will see why. OK, here we go again:

```
R1#sh ip bgp summary
BGP router identifier 1.1.1.1, local AS number 100
BGP table version is 12, main routing table version 12
4 network entries using 468 bytes of memory
8 path entries using 416 bytes of memory
3/2 BGP path/bestpath attribute entries using 372 bytes of memory
```

```
0 BGP route-map cache entries using 0 bytes of memory
0 BGP filter-list cache entries using 0 bytes of memory
BGP using 1256 total bytes of memory
BGP activity 5/1 prefixes, 10/2 paths, scan interval 60 secs
Neighbor   V  AS MsgRcvd MsgSent TblVer InQ OutQ Up/Down State/PfxRcd
10.1.1.6   4  100 1462    1462    12     0    0   00:06:50 2
10.1.1.10  4  100 9       9       12     0    0   00:04:17 2
10.1.1.14  4  100 8       8       12     0    0   00:03:04 2
10.1.1.18  4  100 6       6       12     0    0   00:01:30 1
```

Now, I have all my neighbors, so what did I do to make this happen? I created neighbor statements to all the highlighted IP addresses. Even though they have no physical connection, it is the IGP RIPv2 that is making this possible by sending its updates out. Remember the rule of iBGP: it must be a full mesh, all iBGP routers must be connected to all other iBGP routers.

 iBGP will not be on the CCNA EXAM and it is not the only way to make this work.

If we look at the routing table, who is responsible for sending the routes across? Check out the following code:

```
R1#sh ip route
Gateway of last resort is not set
     1.0.0.0/24 is subnetted, 1 subnets
C       1.1.1.0 is directly connected, Loopback1
     2.0.0.0/24 is subnetted, 1 subnets
R       2.2.2.0 [120/1] via 10.1.1.6, 00:00:17, FastEthernet0/0
     3.0.0.0/24 is subnetted, 1 subnets
R       3.3.3.0 [120/2] via 10.1.1.6, 00:00:17, FastEthernet0/0
     4.0.0.0/24 is subnetted, 1 subnets
R       4.4.4.0 [120/3] via 10.1.1.6, 00:00:17, FastEthernet0/0
R    5.0.0.0/8 [120/4] via 10.1.1.6, 00:00:17, FastEthernet0/0
     10.0.0.0/30 is subnetted, 4 subnets
R       10.1.1.8 [120/1] via 10.1.1.6, 00:00:17, FastEthernet0/0
R       10.1.1.12 [120/2] via 10.1.1.6, 00:00:17, FastEthernet0/0
C       10.1.1.4 is directly connected, FastEthernet0/0
R       10.1.1.16 [120/3] via 10.1.1.6, 00:00:18, FastEthernet0/0
```

So, enough about iBGP. Let's get rid of BGP and RIP and configure eBGP from scratch, with different autonomous systems and see how that works. But to make sure we do not mess up, here is the same topology with the AS numbers:

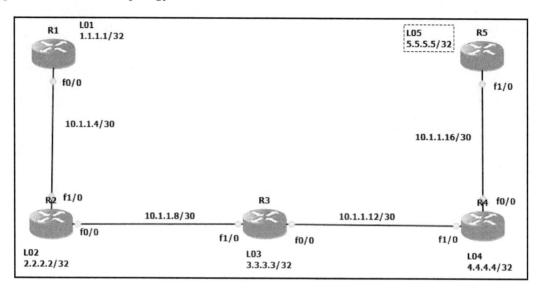

```
R1#config t
Enter configuration commands, one per line.  End with CNTL/Z.
R1(config)#router bgp 100 //Local AS
R1(config-router)#neighbor 10.1.1.5 remote-as 200   //Remote AS
% Cannot configure the local system as neighbor
R1(config-router)#neighbor 10.1.1.6 remote-as 200       //Remote AS
R1(config-router)#net 10.1.1.4 mask 255.255.255.252
R1(config-router)#net 1.1.1.1 mask 255.255.255.255

R2(config)#router bgp 200   //Local AS
R2(config-router)#neighbor 10.1.1.5 remote-as 100       //Remote AS
*Oct 8 08:19:01.777: %BGP-5-ADJCHANGE: neighbor 10.1.1.5 Up
R2(config-router)#neighbor 10.1.1.10 remote-as 300   //Remote AS
R2(config-router)#net 10.1.1.4 mask 255.255.255.252
R2(config-router)#net 10.1.1.8 mask 255.255.255.252
 R2(config-router)#net 2.2.2.2 mask 255.255.255.255
R2(config-router)#do wr

R3(config)#router bgp 300 //Local AS
R3(config-router)#neighbor 10.1.1.9 remote-as 200    //Remote AS
*Oct 8 08:19:54.957: %BGP-5-ADJCHANGE: neighbor 10.1.1.9 Up
R3(config-router)#neighbor 10.1.1.14 remote-as 400 //Remote AS
R3(config-router)#net 10.1.1.8 mask 255.255.255.252
R3(config-router)#net 10.1.1.12 mask 255.255.255.252
```

```
R3(config-router)#net 4.4.4.4 mask 255.255.255.255
R3(config-router)#do wr

R4(config)#router bgp 400  //Local AS
R4(config-router)#neighbor 10.1.1.13 remote-as 300   //Remote AS
R4(config-router)#neighbor 10.1.1.18 remote-as 500   //Remote AS
*Oct 8 08:22:56.069: %BGP-5-ADJCHANGE: neighbor 10.1.1.13 Up
R4(config-router)#net 10.1.1.12 mask 255.255.255.252
R4(config-router)#net 10.1.1.16 mask 255.255.255.252
R4(config-router)#net 4.4.4.4 mask 255.255.255.255

R5(config)#router bgp 500 //Local AS
R5(config-router)#neighbor 10.1.1.17 remote-as 400 //Remote AS
R5(config-router)#net 10.1.1.16 mask 255.255.255.2 //Remote AS
*Oct 8 08:14:08.221: %BGP-5-ADJCHANGE: neighbor 10.1.1.17 Up
R5(config-router)#net 10.1.1.16 mask 255.255.255.252
R5(config-router)#net 5.5.5.5 mask 255.255.255.255
R5(config-router)#do wr
```

OK, we have configured all the routers with their local AS and their neighbor's AS. We have configured eBGP, now let's verify whether it is working:

```
R1#sh ip bgp summary
BGP router identifier 1.1.1.1, local AS number 100
BGP table version is 5, main routing table version 5
4 network entries using 468 bytes of memory
5 path entries using 260 bytes of memory
5/4 BGP path/bestpath attribute entries using 620 bytes of memory
3 BGP AS-PATH entries using 72 bytes of memory
0 BGP route-map cache entries using 0 bytes of memory
0 BGP filter-list cache entries using 0 bytes of memory
BGP using 1420 total bytes of memory
BGP activity 4/0 prefixes, 5/0 paths, scan interval 60 secs
Neighbor V AS MsgRcvd MsgSent TblVer InQ OutQ Up/Down State/PfxRcd
10.1.1.6 4 200 32      30     5      0    0   00:26:27    4
```

We have our neighbor and we have `State/PfxRcd`.

Check this out, though:

```
R1#sh ip bgp
BGP table version is 5, local router ID is 1.1.1.1
Network          NextHop    Metric LocPrf Weight Path
*   10.1.1.4/30  10.1.1.6      0            0   200  i
*>               0.0.0.0                    0 32768  i
*> 10.1.1.8/30   10.1.1.6      0            0   200  i
*> 10.1.1.12/30  10.1.1.6      0          200   300  i
*> 10.1.1.16/30  10.1.1.6      0      200 300   400  i
```

That did not happen with iBGP, so does that mean we can ping? Look at the following code:

```
R1#ping 10.1.1.17
Type escape sequence to abort.
Sending 5, 100-byte ICMP Echos to 10.1.1.17, timeout is 2 seconds:
!!!!!
Success rate is 100 percent (5/5), round-trip min/avg/max = 36/81/128 ms
R1#ping 10.1.1.18
Type escape sequence to abort.
Sending 5, 100-byte ICMP Echos to 10.1.1.18, timeout is 2 seconds:
!!!!!
Success rate is 100 percent (5/5), round-trip min/avg/max = 80/87/96 ms
R1#ping 10.1.1.13
Type escape sequence to abort.
Sending 5, 100-byte ICMP Echos to 10.1.1.13, timeout is 2 seconds:
!!!!!
Success rate is 100 percent (5/5), round-trip min/avg/max = 48/55/64 ms
```

We can ping. How was it possible? Because the external AS is part of the path to get to the destination networks. That is what you need to remember for the CCNA certification. So, let's have a look at the routing table:

```
R1#sh ip routeGateway of last resort is not set
     1.0.0.0/24 is subnetted, 1 subnets
C       1.1.1.0 is directly connected, Loopback1
     10.0.0.0/30 is subnetted, 4 subnets
B       10.1.1.8 [20/0] via 10.1.1.6, 00:38:08
B       10.1.1.12 [20/0] via 10.1.1.6, 00:35:45
C       10.1.1.4 is directly connected, FastEthernet0/0
B       10.1.1.16 [20/0] via 10.1.1.6, 00:34:04
```

It's simple. No IGP is needed. BGP is the routing protocol that is being used.

Summary

In this chapter, you learned about the differences between iBGP and eBGP, mainly that an iBGP network would need to have a full mesh or create neighbor relationships with all the other iBGP routers because they are all in the same AS.

If we use eBGP, the AS is a part of the path, so there is no need to configure an IGP, such as RIP, to create the routing table. BGP is the routing protocol of choice to get to remote networks.

Now that we have discussed BGP and configured it, it is time to create an access list to secure our network. In the next chapter, we will be discussing the rules and how to create ACLs.

17
Access-Control List

Security is the most vital part of any network. We must make sure that our information is secure from the outside as well as from the inside. Not only do we have to worry about unauthorized personnel coming in through our WAN connections, we also must be concerned about the employees who are already present inside our network. There could be a potential threat to the company inside as well.

In this chapter, we will cover how to create an Access-Control List that will mitigate threats externally and internally. We will cover standard ACLs, Extended ACLs, Named ACLs, and Remarks. We will briefly cover some aspects of firewalls and their policies.

While going through this chapter, keep in mind that security is done in layers. You need to ask yourself, *How vital is the information I am trying to secure*, and, *How determinedly are people trying to get in?*

The following topics will be covered in this chapter:

- Concepts of security
    - Confidentiality
    - Integrity
    - Availability
- Risk Assessments
- Rules of ACLs
- Standard ACLs
- Extended ACLs
- Named ACLs
- Remarks

Concepts of security

As I said at the beginning of this chapter, securing your network should be one of your main concerns as an IT professional. But security is done for steps—you must secure the data of whatever company you work in—as it is their most valuable asset.

The concept here is called **CIA**, which stands for **Confidentiality**, **Integrity**, and **Availability**. We must keep the data within the confines of the company or devices they reside in. It must remain confidential, it should be treated as **Top Secret**. Imagine you work for a company that invents a product for cars that never breaks, or gets worn down, it would never have to be replaced. Well, the information would make that company millions if not billions of dollars. Not only would industrial spies want it, even internal employees would love to get their hands on it and sell it to the highest bidder. So you must protect it, not only with firewalls, policies, or ACLs, but with a physical limitation of who can access the information; those individuals would be vetted, and sign so many contracts to keep them from ever thinking of doing the wrong thing.

When it comes to integrity, this means we need to ensure that the formula for what was invented does not get altered in any way, shape, or form. We must protect the integrity of the original document as it was created, so that the company can thrive from its invention and you don't lose your job. But this also means keeping the data that we send across a WAN intact, so that no malevolent individual acquires our data as it passes through our WAN and changes the original message.

Lastly, availability means who has access to this **top secret** information. Securing our network is not just about creating policies on a Firewall or an Active Directory server but physical security. Don't leave important documents just laying around, don't leave your workstation open so anyone can gain access to your files. Everyone plays an important role when we speak of security.

An ACL is simply one of the layers of security we can implement in our network to permit or deny access to certain locations and how they can access information.

Risk management

We have many tools and protocols at our disposal to understand the risk a company takes when they create a network. If you are ever called in to asses the risk factor of a company, meaning how vulnerable we are to an attack, or our information being stolen, there is no simple answer to this question.

You must perform a risk assessment. When performing this task, you must not only look at the infrastructure of the company and the software policies involved, you must also interview all department heads and employees that may have access to the network and can inadvertently retrieve your *top secret* information for their own benefit.

The company must also accept the fact that there is some risk and you must make them understand that. As a security professional, all we can do is mitigate the threat and lessen the vulnerabilities that users, hackers, and spies can exploit.

Keep in mind that companies can not only lose money, which is something tangible, they could also lose time, which is intangible, but can cost money if you have to perform disaster-recovery.

With all that said, let's look at what ACLs can do for us.

Rules of Access Control Lists

Before we get into the rules that govern ACLs, we need to understand what an ACL is, the different types of ACLs, and how they work. An ACL is nothing more than an IF and Then statement; IF this happens Then take this action. But the type of ACL in use would allow you to this in many different fashions. There are two types of ACLs: Standard and Extended. A third extension or mutation is a named ACL, and we will be covering all three. Let's break them down using a table so we can clearly see the differences between them:

Type of ACL	Range	Description
Standard	1 – 99	With this type of ACL, we can only use source addresses. That means if we wanted to deny a source address or network to a destination, we would need to create and apply the ACL at the destination.
Extended	100 – 199	This type of ACL is more flexible than a standard ACL, because it can use a protocol, source address, destination address, and port number. You can be very specific about what type of traffic you want to permit or all and you can place it nearest the source address. Pay attention to the topology you are in before applying the ACL.

Named (mutated standard/extended)	Word/number	This type of ACL is the most common in the real world, because it is easier to understand its purpose—humans understand names better than numbers. But the funny thing about it when creating it you can use a word or a number to make it standard or extended.
Remarks	N/A	This you can use with any of the ACLs, it is a more descriptive of what the ACL is used for. That is the purpose for a remark, but for whatever reason the powers that be want you to know this crucial bit of information.

OK, now that we know about the different types of ACLs, we can get to rules, or, how exactly an ACL would work once configured.

First, I need to tell you that you can create hundreds of thousands of ACLs, but until you assign an ACL to an interface or a Line, it will not take effect, however it will take up space in your router. ACLs, if applied to an interface, you can only apply one ACL per interface, per protocol, per direction, which simply stated you can only apply one ACL going IN to router or OUT of the router. The good new is that an ACL can multiply lines long and they are read line by line in a top-to-bottom approach until a match is made.

You may ask, *"Laz, how many lines can you have on an ACL?"* Well, there is no literature that states a limitation exist, but there is literature that states that the more lines you have, the more of an impact it will have on your routers processing the ACL. But for this to happen, you would need thousands of lines.

The recommendation is that it is better to have 2 separate ACLs with 1,000 entries than 1 ACL with 2,000 entries, that way the processor would be able to better handle the data.

Also, one very important thing to note is that at the end of every ACL, there is an implicit deny, or as I like to call it, an Invisible deny. So what? Well, if your ACL starts with a deny, you must end your ACLs with a permit statement; otherwise, all information will be denied, essentially making that port useless.

OK, standard numbered ACLs are rarely used, but for certification purposes, you will need to know how to create one and probably troubleshoot it. Here is what the syntax looks like:

```
R1(config)#access-list 1 deny host 192.168.1.0
R1(config)#access-list 1 permit any
R1(config)#exit
R1#copy run start
```

Let's break down the syntax:

Command	Number of ACLs	Action	Source
Access-list	1	Deny	Host `192.168.1.0`
Access-list	1	Permit	Any

What this standard ACL is doing is denying 3 host `192168.1.0`, from doing what? Therefore, it must be created and placed at the destination. But let's see an example of this in our topology.

Now we can ping from R3 to R1 `10.1.1.5` IP address:

```
R3#ping 10.1.1.5
Type escape sequence to abort.
Sending 5, 100-byte ICMP Echos to 10.1.1.5, timeout is 2 seconds:
!!!!!
Success rate is 100 percent (5/5), round-trip min/avg/max = 8/43/72 ms
```

So, let's create a standard ACL that would not allow R3 to that.

We would need to go to R1 and create and apply the ACL on that router:

```
R1(config)#access-list 1 deny host 10.1.10
R1(config)#access-list 1 permit any
R1(config)#Int f0/0
R1(config-if)#ip access-group 1 in
R3#ping 10.1.1.5
Type escape sequence to abort.
Sending 5, 100-byte ICMP Echos to 10.1.1.5, timeout is 2 seconds:
UUUUU
Success rate is 0 percent (0/5)
```

So, our ACL is working thus far, let's try pinging from R5 and see what we get:

```
R5#ping 10.1.1.5
Type escape sequence to abort.
Sending 5, 100-byte ICMP Echos to 10.1.1.5, timeout is 2 seconds:
!!!!!
Success rate is 100 percent (5/5), round-trip min/avg/max = 84/96/120 ms
```

Since the ACL is only blocking that one host, and everything else is permitted, that is why we can ping. Remember the ACL is read from top to bottom until it makes a match.

Just so you know, we could have also written the same ACL, to get the same results using the following:

```
R1(config)#access-list 1 deny 10.1.1.10 0.0.0.0 ç This also means host
R1(config)#access-list 1 permit any
R1(config)#Int f0/0
R1(config-if)#ip access-group 1 in
```

If you want to block the entire 10.1.1.8 network, try the following:

```
R1(config)#access-list 2 deny  10.1.1.8 0.0.0.3
R1(config)#access-list 2 permit any
R1(config)#Int f0/0
R1(config-if)#ip access-group 2 in
```

Let's test our hypothesis:

1. Get rid of the first ACL that is assigned to the f0/0 interface:

```
R1(config)#int f0/0
R1(config-if)#no ip access
R1(config-if)#no ip access-group 1 in
```

2. Create the ACL the we create above to block the entire 10.1.1.8 network:

```
R1#config t
Enter configuration commands, one per line.  End with CNTL/Z.
R1(config)#acc
R1(config)#access-list 2 deny 10.1.1.8 0.0.0.3
R1(config)#access-list 2 permit any
R1(config)#int f0/0
R1(config-if)#ip access-group 2 in
R1(config-if)#
R3#ping 10.1.1.5
Type escape sequence to abort.
Sending 5, 100-byte ICMP Echos to 10.1.1.5, timeout is 2 seconds:
UUUUU
Success rate is 0 percent (0/5)
R3#ping
Protocol [ip]:
Target IP address: 10.1.1.5
Repeat count [5]:
Datagram size [100]:
Timeout in seconds [2]:
Extended commands [n]: y
Source address or interface: 10.1.1.9
Type of service [0]:
Set DF bit in IP header? [no]:
```

```
Validate reply data? [no]:
Data pattern [0xABCD]:
Loose, Strict, Record, Timestamp, Verbose[none]:
Sweep range of sizes [n]:
Type escape sequence to abort.
Sending 5, 100-byte ICMP Echos to 10.1.1.5, timeout is 2 seconds:
UUUUU
```

In this example, we must use an extended ping, so we source the IP address within the range of the network we are blocking.

The point we are trying to make here is that we could play all day with the wildcard mask and block the entire 10.0.0.0 network, or simply deny any and no traffic will go to R1. You can see that standard ACLs are limited because not only can they not ping, they can't access R1 through any port.

You could use a standard ACL to block telnet, but I just said you are limited to source addresses, so let me show you how that is done.

First, let's configure R4 so we can telnet into the router:

```
R4#config t
Enter configuration commands, one per line.  End with
CNTL/Z.(config)#enable password cisco
R4(config)#line vty 0 15
R4(config-line)#password cisco
R4(config-line)#login
R4(config-line)#do wr
```

This configuration will allow us to fully log in to the router and access the privilege mode prompt:

```
R5#telnet 10.1.1.17
Trying 10.1.1.17 ... Open
User Access Verification
Password:
R4>enable
Password:
R4#I am in the router
```

Now we will configure a standard ACL to allow on one host to telnet all others would be blocked from telnetting to R4:

```
R1#telnet 10.1.1.13
Trying 10.1.1.13 ... Open
[Connection to 10.1.1.13 closed by foreign host]
R1#telnet 10.1.1.9
Trying 10.1.1.9 ...
R3#telnet 10.1.1.13
Trying 10.1.1.13 ... Open
[Connection to 10.1.1.13 closed by foreign host]
```

So, you can use a standard ACL to permit or deny telnet traffic by simply applying to the line instead of the interface.

Now let's get into extended ACLs. We will use a different topology for this example:

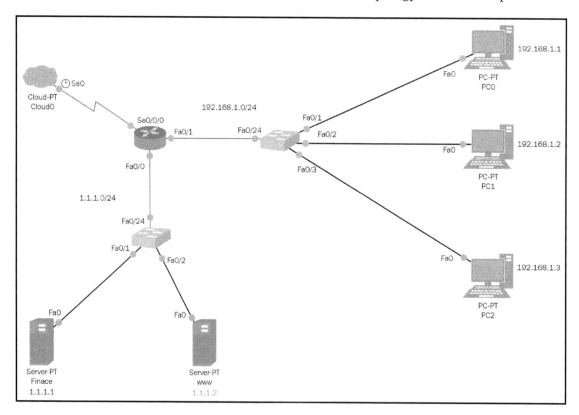

In the preceding topology, we will create an extended ACL that will do the following:

- Allow only PC0 web access to the WWW server
- Deny all other nodes from accessing the WWW using web access
- Permit all other types of we will use a different topology for this `example.traffic` from anyone

```
RX(config)#access-list 100 permit tcp host 192.168.1.1 host 1.1.1.2 eq 80
RX(config)#access-list 100 deny tcp any host 1.1.1.2 eq 80
RX(config)#access-list 100 permit ip any any
RX(config)#int f0/0
RX(config-if)#ip access-group 100 out
```

Let's check to see whether this ACL will work. Everyone should be able to have connectivity to the WWW server, but only PC0 should have web access to PC0; all others would be denied:

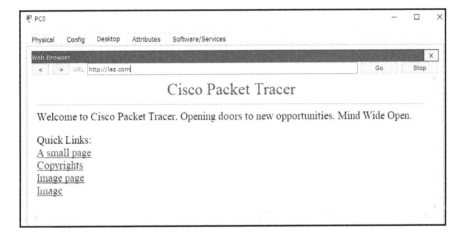

So far, we can use port `80` from PC0 as planned:

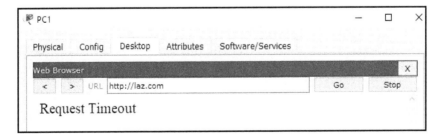

As per the ACL, we cannot reach the WWW server through port 80, but can we ping the server? Let's check:

```
Packet Tracer PC Command Line 1.0
C:\>ping 1.1.1.2

Pinging 1.1.1.2 with 32 bytes of data:

Reply from 1.1.1.2: bytes=32 time=1ms TTL=127
Reply from 1.1.1.2: bytes=32 time<1ms TTL=127
Reply from 1.1.1.2: bytes=32 time<1ms TTL=127
Reply from 1.1.1.2: bytes=32 time<1ms TTL=127
```

We certainly can ping the server, which means the ACL is doing what it is supposed to do, block port 80 from all other nodes, but allow all other types of connectivity. We can check this in our router, by using `show` commands:

```
RX#sh access-lists 100
Extended IP access list 100
permit tcp host 192.168.1.1 host 1.1.1.2 eq www (5 match(es))
deny tcp any host 1.1.1.2 eq www (35 match(es))
permit ip any any (7 match(es))
```

Look at the highlighted portions, which is the key point regarding how ACLs work: they read line by line until a match is made. The first time we tried to get to the WWW server, the first line of the ACL looked at the first line and made a match, it said, *You are 192.168.1.1 so you are permitted.*

The second time, we tried to get to the WWW server through port 80, it did not make a match on the first line, but it made a match on the second line stating, *You are not 192.168.1.1, so I will deny access since we are using port 80.*

Finally, the last verification of this ACL is to see whether we have connectivity by using the `ping` command, so it did not make a match on the first line, it did not make a match on the second line, but the last line allows all other types of traffic to anyone through all other ports and that is where it made a match and we were able to ping the WWW server.

One thing you should be asking yourself is, why did I apply the ACL nearest the destination, when the rule states that extended ACLs since they are so specific, you need to apply them nearest the source.

Well, Cisco is test your deductive reasoning. You must look at the topology and understand that the router is connected to links. For all who come to this router seeking access to the WWW through port 80, they need to be confronted with the ACL and must go through port F0/0.

Let's look at a visual:

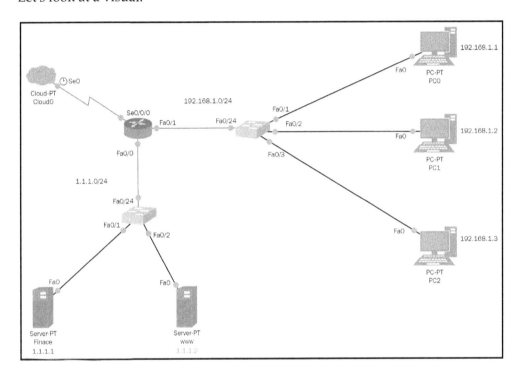

The main reason in this example, we have some remote network attached to our S0/0/0, if we do not apply the ACL at the F0/0 and instead apply it a the F0/1, which is what the book states we should do if it's a extended ACL, then any traffic coming from the remote network, will never be filtered by the ACL, so that is why we must apply it at the funnel or the F0/0.

So, when you are taking you certification or dealing with real-world situations, use your logic before creating and applying an ACL, so you can get the intended results.

Named ACLs

A named ACL is not different than a numbered ACL, except that instead of giving the ACL a number, you give it a name, so humans can understand what that ACL's purpose is. Of course, the syntax will begin differently, so let's create the same ACL, but this time we will give it a name.

Let's see the step-by-step breakdown:

```
RX(config)#IP Access-list ?
extended   Extended Access List
standard   Standard Access List
RX(config)#IP Access-list
RX(config)#IP Access-list extended ?
<100-199> Extended IP access-list number
WORD       name
RX(config)#IP Access-list extended Block_Port80
RX(config-ext-nacl)# ?
<1-2147483647>      Sequence Number
default                     Set a command to its defaults
deny                        Specify packets to reject
exit                         Exit from access-list configuration mode
no                          Negate a command or set its defaults
permit                   Specify packets to forward
remark                  Access list entry comment
RX(config-ext-nacl)#permit ?
ahp            Authentication Header Protocol
eigrp          Cisco's EIGRP routing protocol
esp            En capsulation Security Payload
gre            Cisco's GRE tunneling
icmp          Internet Control Message Protocol
ip             Any Internet Protocol
ospf          OSPF routing protocol
tcp            Transmission Control Protocol
udp           User Datagram Protocol
RX(config-ext-nacl)#permit tcp ?
A.B.C.D Source address
any Any source host
host A single source host
RX(config-ext-nacl)#permit tcp host 192.168.1.1 ?
A.B.C.D         Destination address
any              Any destination host
eq               Match only packets on a given port number
gt               Match only packets with a greater port number
host             A single destination host
lt               Match only packets with a lower port number
neq             Match only packets not on a given port number
```

```
range              Match only packets in the range of port numbers
RX(config-ext-nacl)#permit tcp host 192.168.1.1 host 1.1.1.2 ?
eq                 Match only packets on a given port number
established  established
gt                 Match only packets with a greater port number
lt                 Match only packets with a lower port number
neq               Match only packets not on a given port number
range             Match only packets in the range of port numbers
<cr>
RX(config-ext-nacl)#permit tcp host 192.168.1.1 host 1.1.1.2 eq 80
RX(config-ext-nacl)#?
<1-2147483647>    Sequence Number
default                Set a command to its defaults
deny                   Specify packets to reject
exit                    Exit from access-list configuration mode
no                     Negate a command or set its defaults
permit              Specify packets to forward
remark              Access list entry comment
RX(config-ext-nacl)#deny tcp host any host 1.1.1.2 eq 80
RX(config-ext-nacl)#permit ip any any
RX(config-ext-nacl)#exit
RX(config)#int f0/0
RX(config-if)#ip access-group Block_Port80 out
Extended IP access list Block_Port80
10 permit tcp host 192.68.1.1 host 1.1.1.2 eq www
20 deny tcp any host 1.1.1.2 eq www
30 permit ip any any
```

As you can see from the highlighted portion of code, this extended ACL has a name not a number, but the outcome would be the same as the numbered ACL. Cisco does not stop there; now it wants you to give a more detailed description of the intended purpose of the access list, whether it be a numbered or a named ACL.

Remarks

This is very straightforward and simple: when creating an ACL, you will come to a point where you can put in a remark and describe what the ACL is meant to be used for. Let's use the named access list as an example:

```
RX(config)#ip access-list extended Block_Port80
RX(config-ext-nacl)#?
<1-2147483647>    Sequence Number
default                Set a command to its defaults
deny                   Specify packets to reject
exit                    Exit from access-list configuration mode
no                     Negate a command or set its defaults
```

```
permit                          Specify packets to forward
remark                          Access list entry comment
RX(config-ext-nacl)# remark This is access-list is to block the boss from
accessing the www server from using port 80
RX#sh start
(Certain output was omitted)
deny tcp any host 1.1.1.2 eq www
permit ip any any
```

remark: This access list is to block the boss from accessing the WWW server from using port 80.

Summary

There you have it! We looked at standard, extended, and named ACLs, as well as remarks, so you can better describe the what the ACL is really doing. We also discussed security concepts. One thing that you need to keep in mind for the certification or the real world is that totally secure networks *do not exist*; it comes down to how determined an individual is to hack your network. Security is based on layers of different types of obstacles, such as ACLs, firewall policies, AD policies, intrusion-detection systems, and network intrusion-prevention systems. For the certification, if you know your ACLs, you'll be fine, but for the real world, be prepared to learn a whole lot more.

See you in the next chapter.

18
Network Address Translation

What is NAT and why do we use it? In this chapter, we will be discussing the **Network Address Translation (NAT)** protocol and its configuration. We will also look at the pitfalls that we must be aware of while configuring NAT so that we know how to troubleshoot problems if should they arise.

The following are the topics that this chapter will cover:

- A brief history of NAT
- The types of NAT we use:
  - Static
  - Dynamic
  - NAT overload or PAT
- How NAT works
- Configuring NAT
- Troubleshooting NAT

A brief history of NAT

NAT was set up simply to slow down the depletion of public IPv4 addresses. When the commercialization of the internet started, we found ourselves running out of public assigned IP addresses. No one could have imagined that 4.2 billion addresses were going to fall short of the mark.

So, the concept of NAT was introduced, with its purpose of taking a private IPv4 address and translating it into a public IPv4 address, so that it could go onto the internet and allow users to do whatever they need to do.

If you want to get specific as to what NAT can help us do, besides go play online video games, here are some points that you should keep in mind:

- NAT enables you to connect to the internet and your end devices have only private IP addresses
- When you change to a new ISP, you do not need to change your internal addressing
- NAT helps if you are bringing networks together that have the same addressing scheme

These three points say it all but let's get a visualization of NAT with the following diagram:

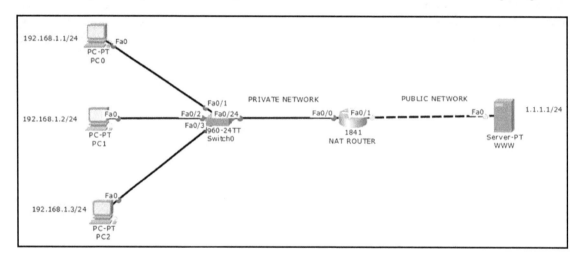

Types of NAT and its configuration

As you can see from the preceding diagram, we have a private network using the private IP address 192.168.1.0/24 and public network using the public IP address 1.1.1.0/24 network. The public network is using a web server that I configured with DNS, so we can see different ports when NAT translates the private address to public.

We can configure using three different methods, so I will explain the three different types and compare them. The first one I am going to break down is **static NAT**, which is neither very feasible nor efficient. While configuring static NAT, you must manually pair up each private address with a public address.

If you have 1,000 nodes that need internet access, you will have to purchase 1,000 public IPs and in today's technological era, it will run into thousands of dollars. This is how you would configure static NAT if you have deep pockets and nothing else to do but type:

```
NAT_ROUTER(config)#ip nat inside source static 192.168.1.1 1.1.1.254
```

Now, just imagine typing that 999 times with a different private address and public address!

You still need to tell the router which interface is `ip nat inside` and `ip nat outside`.

Static is not the way you would want to go, so the next type of NAT is slightly better.

With dynamic NAT, you can create an actual pool of addresses, so no typing of thousands or even hundreds of addresses. Awesome! Hold on though, no reason for celebration yet; you still need to purchase those 1,000 IPs so it is still going to burn a hole in your pocket.

This what dynamic NAT would look like. This time I will include the interfaces:

```
NAT_ROUTER(config)#int f0/0
NAT_ROUTER(config-if)#ip nat inside
NAT_ROUTER(config-if)#int f0/1
NAT_ROUTER(config-if)#ip nat outside

NAT_ROUTER(config)#ip nat pool DYNAMIC 1.1.2.1 1.1.3.254 Netmask 255.255.254.0
NAT_ROUTER(config)#access-list 10 permit 1.1.2.0 0.0.3.255
NAT_ROUTER(config)#ip nat inside source list 10 pool DYNAMIC
```

The interfaces must be configured so that the router knows what the private address is and what the public address is, with any type of NAT, so the preceding configurations would be the same. You must tell the router which interface is facing your inside or outside interface for NAT to work properly.

When using dynamic NAT, you create a pool of as many IP addresses as you need. In the preceding example, you have 1,022 addresses available, and you would also pay a pretty penny for that too.

The standard access list is permitting those 1,022 addresses with the wildcard mask configured.

Even though this is more effective, it's still not feasible. The next form of NAT is the most used in any company, as it is feasible and effective.

NAT overload or PAT uses a pool just like dynamic NAT, but it is a pool of one address, so it's cheaper and effective. Let's see how that configuration would be done:

```
NAT_ROUTER(config)#int f0/0
NAT_ROUTER(config-if)#ip nat inside
NAT_ROUTER(config-if)#int f0/1
NAT_ROUTER(config-if)#ip nat outside

NAT_ROUTER(config)#ip nat pool LAZ 1.1.1.254 1.1.1.254 Netmask 255.255.255.0
NAT_ROUTER(config)#access-list 10 permit 192.168.1.0 0.0.0.255
NAT_ROUTER(config)#ip nat inside source list 10 pool LAZ overload
```

Okay, you have seen the three different configurations, but before we get into the router, let's look at the advantages and disadvantages of using NAT:

Advantages	Disadvantages
Conserves legally registered addresses	Translation results in switching path delays
Increases flexibility when connecting to the internet	Causes loss of end -to-end IP traceability
Eliminates address renumbering as a network evolves	Creating tunnels using protocols, such as IPsec, adds complexity due to modification to the headers

How NAT works

There's still some information I need you to know before we start configuring the routers. The following is just some basic terminology, but it is important for the certification:

Term	Definition
Inside local	Your PC in the private network before translation
Outside local	Destination PC as it appears to your internal network
Inside global	Your PC translated by the NAT router with a public school
Outside global	Destination PC with the actual internet address

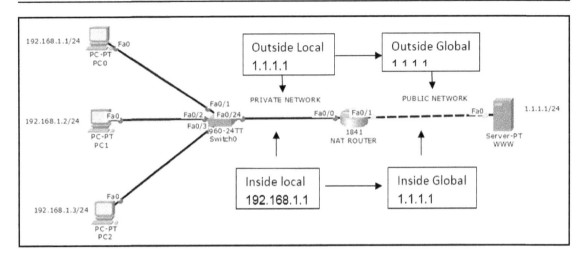

The labels in the preceding diagram depict the process of NAT. It takes your *inside local* private address and translates it to the *inside global* public address. The destination address which is the web server will always be the same; what does change is the source port, which is randomly chosen above a number of 1024, but the destination port will be the same, because we are all going to the same web page through port 80.

Configuring NAT inside the router

Using the same topology we have been looking at, we are now going to go inside the router and configure NAT overload:

```
NAT_ROUTER(config)#int f0/0
NAT_ROUTER(config-if)#ip nat inside
NAT_ROUTER(config-if)#int f0/1
NAT_ROUTER(config-if)#exit
NAT_ROUTER(config)#ip nat pool laz 1.1.1.254 1.1.1.254 netmask 255.255.255.0
NAT_ROUTER(config)#access-list 30 permit 192.168.1.0 0.0.0.255
NAT_ROUTER(config)#ip nat inside source list 30 pool laz overload
NAT_ROUTER(config)#do wr
```

When configuring NAT overload, make sure you use the word overload at the end of the third line. You also need to be careful when typing in the pool name, as it's case sensitive, and make sure you point to the correct ACL. You must be aware of all these pitfalls when you configure PAT. Now we need to test and verify that NAT is translating. We will access the web server through the browser on all three PC's.

PC0:

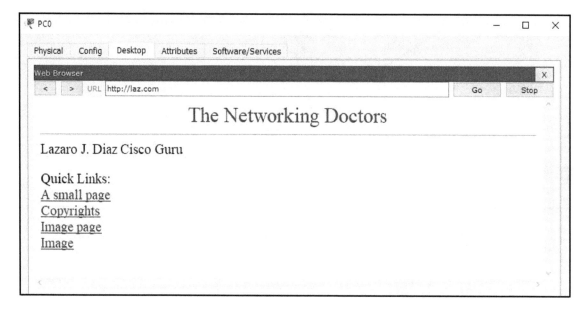

PC1:

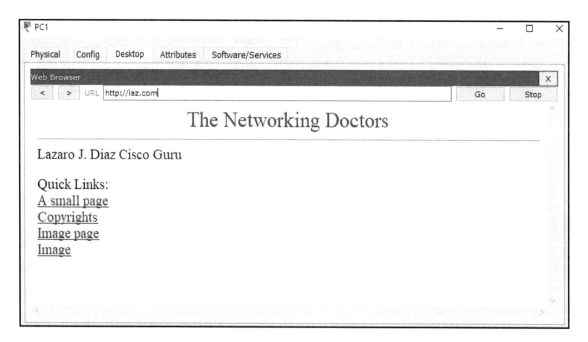

PC2:

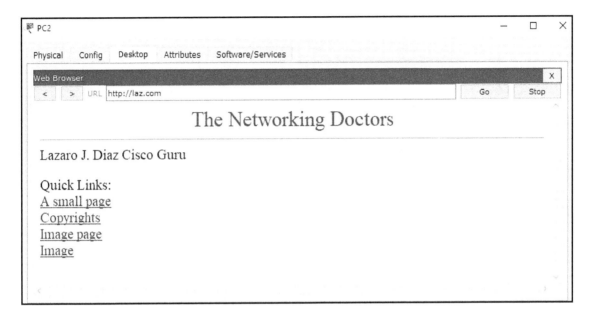

Okay, all computers were able to reach the website using the DNS domain name.

Troubleshooting NAT

To check or troubleshoot NAT, you must send data through the router so NAT can translate the addressees, we hope. Now let's check that NAT overload or PAT has translated the addresses from private to public.

Our NAT configuration is working and, as you can see from following screenshot, so it's a success and the router is translating our inside local address to the inside global address using different port numbers. The destination address remains the same, but look at the protocol column. It is using both UDP and TCP. The reason for that is DNS uses both of these protocols:

```
NAT_ROUTER#sh ip nat translation
```

Pro	Inside global	Inside local	Outside local	Outside global
udp	1.1.1.254:1026	192.168.1.2:1026	1.1.1.1:53	1.1.1.1:53
udp	1.1.1.254:1027	192.168.1.1:1027	1.1.1.1:53	1.1.1.1:53
udp	1.1.1.254:1028	192.168.1.3:1028	1.1.1.1:53	1.1.1.1:53
tcp	1.1.1.254:1026	192.168.1.2:1026	1.1.1.1:80	1.1.1.1:80
tcp	1.1.1.254:1027	192.168.1.1:1027	1.1.1.1:80	1.1.1.1:80
tcp	1.1.1.254:1028	192.168.1.3:1028	1.1.1.1:80	1.1.1.1:80

You could also do a debug command to check if NAT is translating. But, for certification purposes, that would be a waste of time that you don't have. But here is the command and its output, anyway:

```
NAT_ROUTER#debug ip nat
NAT_ROUTER#NAT: s=192.168.1.3->1.1.1.254, d=1.1.1.1 [98]
NAT_ROUTER#NAT*: s=1.1.1.1, d=1.1.1.254->192.168.1.3 [96]
NAT_ROUTER#NAT: s=192.168.1.3->1.1.1.254, d=1.1.1.1 [99]
NAT_ROUTER#NAT*: s=1.1.1.1, d=1.1.1.254->192.168.1.3 [97]
NAT_ROUTER#NAT: s=192.168.1.3->1.1.1.254, d=1.1.1.1 [100]
NAT_ROUTER#NAT: s=192.168.1.3->1.1.1.254, d=1.1.1.1 [98]
NAT_ROUTER#NAT*: s=1.1.1.1, d=1.1.1.254->192.168.1.3 [96]
```

Here the s is the source address the -> is translated to, and the d is the destination address.

Summary

This chapter was short and easy. We saw how NAT works, and how to configure static NAT, dynamic NAT, and NAT overload, or PAT. We also learned some terminology, so if someone asked, you would know what the inside local address and the inside global addresses are. We also verified that NAT was working using the show ip nat translation command or debug ip nat.

You now can configure NAT and troubleshoot without an issue. Time to move to Chapter 19, *Wide Area Networks*, looking at WAN and all its wonders.

19
Wide Area Networks

I hope you are ready for the magnitude of the amount of information that WANs are made up of. Cisco supports numerous types of WAN designs, which means the hardware, protocols and topologies that can get created, would fill up a whole library.

We are going to focus on some of the basics of WAN technologies and protocols that you will encounter in the CCNA certification but also in real-world scenarios. We will discuss the different types of connection options that a WAN can create. In LAN, you were pretty much in control and if you needed to add other links to connect to new offices, it was as easy as running wire through your infrastructure and making sure the cables were properly created and terminated. Connectivity would not be an issue and you would simply create the IP scheme. Wide Area Networks are not so simple. If you are a company that has branch offices, you must be able to connect to those offices on a daily basis.

When we talk about speed, our internal network may be running at gigabit speed, but what if your internet connection has running speeds such as 56 Kbps, 512 Kbps, 1.544 Mbps, or even 100 Mbps? Is that upload or download speed? Is it dedicated or shared and can you guarantee me that speed all the time.

What about redundancy? We spoke of switching loops because we have redundancy in our LAN switches, but what about redundancy in WAN? Do you need redundancy? So, these and many more questions are going to be addressed in this chapter.

The following topics will be covered in the chapter:

- Understanding WANs
- Need for WANs
- Topologies that make up a WAN
- WAN terminology
- Bandwidth connections used in a WAN
- Types of connection used in a WAN

- WAN protocols:
    - HDLC
    - PPP
    - Frame-Relay
    - MPLS
    - VPN
    - GRE tunnels
    - DMVPN
- Redundancy protocols:
    - HSRP
    - VRRP
    - GLBP

Understanding WAN

We must first understand the differences between a LAN and a WAN. In a LAN, we own our infrastructure, and we have full control of every aspect of it. In a WAN, we must lease the infrastructure from a provider and have little to no control of what happens to our packets as they go through the provider's networks.

Although, in today's modern era of networking, where everything is moving to the cloud and we have services such as PaaS, IaaS, and SaaS, which vary in the amount of control we can have on the software and even the hardware, we still are paying for the services for a provider to take us across to our branch networks or use their software or hardware. One of the issues we face is bandwidth. Luckily for us, our technology has grown to the point where bandwidth is not an issue, if you have the money. Therefore, you really need to understand the needs of the company when you are choosing a provider connectivity for your branch offices located at remote locations.

I will give a simple example. When you move into a home and you want internet access, so you can send email, connect to social media, or simply browse the internet for information, you must find a provider to do that. Just because the devices in your home are wireless and they connect to your wireless access point/router does not mean you can get online. It is your provider's modem/router that allows you to surf the web. The question is how much are you willing to pay for that?

There are various companies that provide this service and they break it down by download speed and upload speed. The download will generally be faster than the upload; speeds vary for download from 1.544 Mbps to 1 Gbps and prices can vary just as greatly, from $10 a month to $300 a month. Keep in mind that this is for home use. Now imagine that you run a business, where you depend on internet connectivity and you need the fastest upload and not only download.

Your company is holding webinars, you have storage online, and you must be able to upload large files quickly from one geographical location to another quickly. So, a WAN in a business is extremely important. We need to consider what our needs as a company are before we start choosing a provider.

A provider we contract would help us with connectivity to our remote networks, can have storage space for us, can handle our infrastructure to free us from having networking equipment in our offices, as simply as using Microsoft Office online. Again, they are in control, so know what you're signing and remember if something goes wrong, you must contact them and open a trouble ticket and see how quickly they resolve the issue.

After reading so far, you might be thinking, is a WAN really needed? Well keep on reading; the next topic will answer that question for you.

Need of WAN

To be direct and give you a straightforward answer, yes. WANs are a crucial part of today's business. If you own a business, no matter what it is, you will at least have a web page or some sort of social media to advertise yourself. The days of using the newspaper really does not work anymore. TV and radio are good options, but those also exist online.

So, even the smallest of businesses must have something online, to advertise themselves so their business can grow; that is the ultimate reason we get into a business. If you want to stay current and competitive in today's business world, you must have a presence online and if you have multiple locations for your business and they are located in different locations, you need to have access to those branches through the internet to see what is going on.

With the growth of the internet and the fact that we can access all our personal and business information online, security is a huge concern. Well your provider can also give you that service, for a price of course, but you can't really put a price on your personal or business information; you need to have it secure.

To sum up all this, we need WANs, we have no choice, unless you are going to purchase your own equipment, take out the proper licensing required to be able to run cabling from one location to another, or if you are doing Wide Area Wireless Networking, you must stay within the FCC regulations.

If you are in the business of education, architecture, baking cupcakes, or whatever, you don't have the time or the money to create your extremely large local area network. It is just not feasible. So yes, WANs are here to stay and this chapter will focus on the main topics you need to be aware of to make proper decisions and to pass your certification.

Topologies that make up a WAN

In general, we have two types of topologies: the *physical topology*, which is the actual layout of your network, and the *logical topology*, which describes how your traffic is going to flow, and which direction your traffic is going to take to reach its intended destination. In a Wide Area Network, we have several topologies we can create, based on the business needs, but here we will discuss three basic WAN topology designs:

Hub and spoke

This design is based on a centralized router (hub), and several branch or remote routers (spokes) that communicate with the hub and all other routers through the hub:

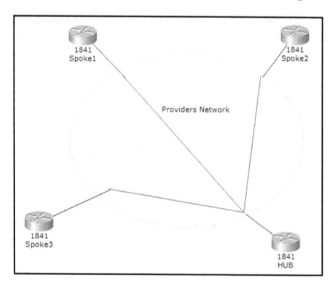

An advantage to creating this type of topology is that it makes it easier to administer and keep the costs down, but the disadvantages can outweigh the advantages:

- If the hub routers go down, the spokes have no way to communicate. There is a single point of failure.
- The hub limits overall performance to the shared resources on it.
- A single connection to the hub router for all remote networks consumes bandwidth.

Fully meshed topology

This type of topology would be the utopia of networking. You would have every customer edge router directly connected to every other customer edge router. The following diagram shows what this would like:

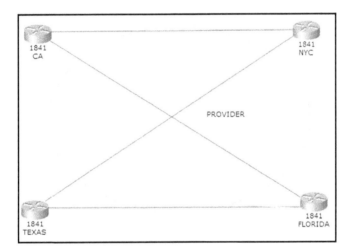

Like I said previously, this would be awesome, but this will never be reality, because of the cost factor. In my experience, it seems that companies would rather spend their money on sandalwood or African blackwood for their offices than purchase STP cabling for the lab or a decent internet connection to carry their data across the world. I have even seen companies go from IP phones back to analog, because it was a better service.

Anyway, this would be great because you would have complete redundancy. The configuration maybe more complex but it would be worth it. But we, as IT professionals, must learn to *adapt and overcome* to what is given to us to work with.

There is one more topology we could use, which is a partial mesh and that means taking out one link from the preceding diagram, and there you go, you have a partial mesh. The general consensus is that the partial mesh has the best of both worlds, since you have redundancy and it is not as expensive as a full mesh.

WAN terminology

Before we start defining each term, let's look at a visual of what a WAN connection would look like from the company to the provider. You need to understand this before you decide to order you're WAN, because it is contract that you will be signing, and they will not explain all the details.

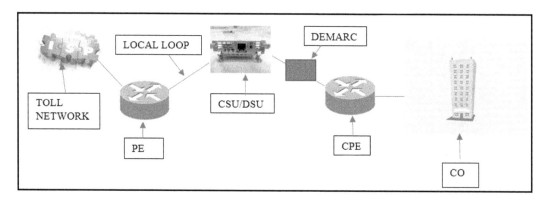

Let's define the terms you must know for your certification, and also for real-world, so they don't fool you:

Term	Definition
CPE or Customer Premises Equipment	This is your router, the equipment in your company.
CSU/DSU Channel Service Unit/Data Service Unit	This provides the clocking of the line to the router. This connects to the serial of your router, there are several types of CSU/DSU you can use, but in todays network, we use Ethernet, and this has become obsolete. Keep in mind that for the CCNA certification is still in used, all you need to know if you don't have a clock rate on the DCE portion of your cable, you will not connect to your neighbor router. You will be getting Layer 2 errors such as, line is up down, encapsulation errors, synchronization errors also. Certification only. All routers are DTE
DCE	Data Communication interface on the router, where you would put the clock rate on, if using crossover serial cable.
DTE	Data Terminal Equipment interface on the router, no clocking needed. All devices are DTE, that is why clocking was needed to either an internal or external CSU/DSU was needed. That is not the case now.
Demarcation Point	This is where the provider connects to and there responsibility ends and yours begins.
Local Loop	This connects the closest switching office, which is your provider.
Toll Network	This is a trunk line inside the WAN providers network. Anytime you see a cloud image that is the WAN providers network, which is a collection of routers, switches and other networking equipment. All of this is owned by the ISP.
Optical Fiber Converters	This connects to the demarcation point, which will convert optical signals to electrical signals. But again, today we have the capability of running Fiber straight into your home. Routers/Modems have the technology to the conversion of those signals.

Bandwidth connections used in a WAN

In a WAN, you also must know the bandwidth terminology used. You should be able to recognize the bandwidth you are getting by the lines you are given. The following table will give you the more common lines in use.

Line	Bandwidth
DS0 Digital Signal 0	64Kbps
T1 or DS1	24 DS0 gives you 1.544Mbps
E1 same as T1 but in Europe	30 DS0 gives you 2.048Mbps
T3 or DS3	28 DS1 or 672 DS0 44.736Mbps
OC-3 Optical Carrier	3 DS3 or 2,016 DS0 155.52Mbps
OC-12	4 OC3 8,064 DS0 622.08Mbps
OC-48	4 OC12 32,256 DS0 2488.32Mbps
OC-192	4 OC48 129,024 DS0 9,953.28Mbps
Metro Ethernet (Todays technology)	10Gbits, 40Gbits, 100Gbits, 400Gbits or 400Gbps

The preceding table pay more attention to the highlighted portion, since these are the most commonly used.

Types of connection used in a WAN

So, now that you have an idea of how WAN data gets from one side to the other and the speed available, you now need to understand the types of connections they use. We basically have three types of connection, as shown in the following diagram, and then we will break down each one:

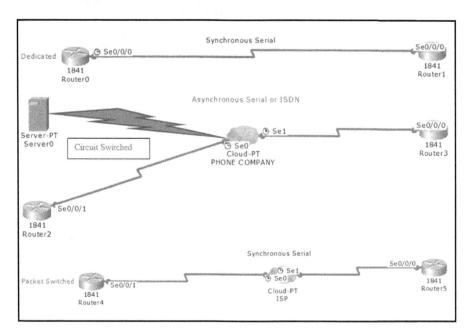

So, let's break down these types of connections, starting with the following:

- **Dedicated or leased lines**: This type of connection is what we would call a point-to-point connection and it is a dedicated connection. It is simple connection going from one CPE through the DCE to another CPE, and you would have bandwidth up to 45 Mbps. But this type of connection is very expensive, as you always have a dedicated line just for you; therefore, you need to know your network. In this type of connection, you would use either the HDLC or PPP encapsulation types. I will discuss these two protocols later in the chapter.

- **Circuit switched:** With this type of connection, think of dial-up and modems. This type of technology is not in use, but you will see it in your certification, and you just may find this type of connection as a backup in some networks in the form of an ISDN, which is used for low bandwidth data transfer. The bandwidth on ISDN differs if you have a BRI interface, which is 128 kbits, or you could have 144 kbits if you have two bearer channels running at 64 kbits and a signaling channel at 16 kbits. The advantage is that it is low cost.

- **Packet switched:** This type of connection is a hybrid of both a dedicated and circuit switch connection types. Basically, you pay for what you use; the lines in the company are sharing the bandwidth of the line. You could theoretically have the bandwidth of a T3 or 56K. Since you are sharing the medium, if no one is on the WAN then you have full reign but when people start getting online, then you start to slow down.

WAN protocols

I am going to show you next, what type of encapsulation routers have on their serial link, by default, and then I will break down the differences between HDLC and PPP:

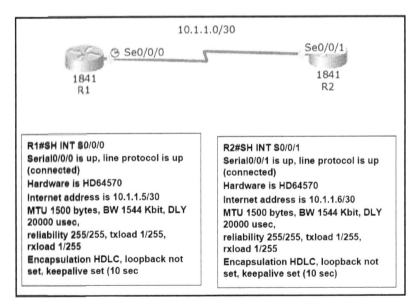

HDLC and PPP

So, let's talk about HDLC encapsulation. It is proprietary to each vendor; it was not intended to encapsulate different network layer protocols, so each individual vendor had to put in the header of HDLC their own specific way to identify the network layer protocols.

What does this mean? If you are going to use HDLC, you must have the same vendor on both sides.

So, how do we circumvent this issue, so that we can use whatever vendor we want? Well we use the point-to-point, or PPP, encapsulation open standard protocol. It uses a network control protocol field in layer 2 of the OSI model, to identify the network layer protocol. It also allows for authentication and multilink connections over asynchronous links.

Let's look at PPP in action:

If properly configured, this is what you should see. If you do not see Link Control Open, or LCP open, or a different encapsulation, you will not be able to communicate. Pay attention to these screenshots. But, anyway, let me show you how I configured PPP to work on both routers.

PPP has many different features. One of them is authentication, which you will need to know about if a connection is not happening. So, enough talk, let's proceed:

```
R1(config)#int s0/0/0
R1(config-if)#encap ppp
R1(config-if)#
%LINEPROTO-5-UPDOWN: Line
protocol on Interface Serial0/0/0,
changed state to down
R1(config-if)#ppp authentication chap
pap
```

```
R2(config)#int s0/0/1
R2(config-if)#encap ppp
R2(config-if)#ppp authentication
chap pap
R2(config-if)#username R1
password cisco
%LINEPROTO-5-UPDOWN: Line
protocol on Interface Serial0/0/1,
```

Notice that when we change the encapsulation type on R1, the link immediately changes to down. Then we added `ppp authentication chap pap`. We use chap as our first choice of authentication because it is encrypted. pap is just the backup in case chap fails. We also create a username and password. The username will be the hostname of your neighbor router and then you can make up any password, but just note that it is case sensitive.

In R2 we have a little different outcome. The line is already down, and it does not come up until we complete the configuration, by putting in the username and password. What this should tell you is that even if you are using PPP on both routers and you decide to use authentication, it must be the same on your directly connected routers.

OK, let's look at a popular method used and maybe still in use today, which is the connection type, packet switching. What happen here is that you share your bandwidth with everyone in the building, but you are guaranteed what is in your contract.

Yes, you must create a contract and after you have analyzed your network, you came up with the conclusion that you must have 512 kbps at minimum. This speed must be guaranteed and it will be your *CIR* committed information rate. But, if possible, you would like a *burst rate* of a T1. What does that mean, if possible? Well, if no one in the building is using the line and the bandwidth is available, it allows you to burst to the maximum.

If you are doing a frame-relay network, then you will be using a PVC, or permanent virtual circuit, which is really a point-to-point sub-interface, and a DLCI number, which is assigned by your provider. This stands for Data Link Connection Identifier. This is the preferred method of configuring frame-relay.

So, let's look at the frame-relay topology and configuration:

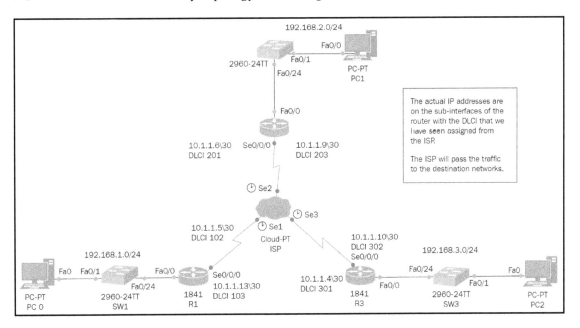

Let's look at the serial configuration, router by router, and then we will configure the ISP. This is a lab, after all.

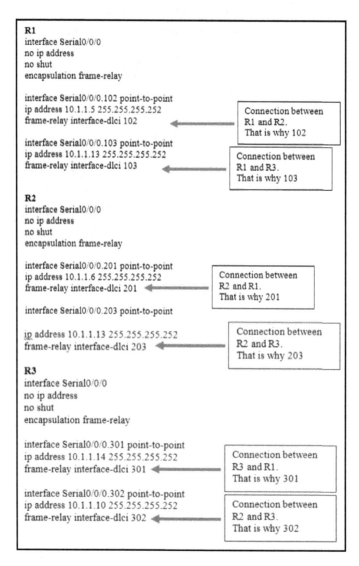

```
R1
interface Serial0/0/0
no ip address
no shut
encapsulation frame-relay

interface Serial0/0/0.102 point-to-point
ip address 10.1.1.5 255.255.255.252
frame-relay interface-dlci 102
```
Connection between R1 and R2. That is why 102

```
interface Serial0/0/0.103 point-to-point
ip address 10.1.1.13 255.255.255.252
frame-relay interface-dlci 103
```
Connection between R1 and R3. That is why 103

```
R2
interface Serial0/0/0
no ip address
no shut
encapsulation frame-relay

interface Serial0/0/0.201 point-to-point
ip address 10.1.1.6 255.255.255.252
frame-relay interface-dlci 201
```
Connection between R2 and R1. That is why 201

```
interface Serial0/0/0.203 point-to-point

ip address 10.1.1.13 255.255.255.252
frame-relay interface-dlci 203
```
Connection between R2 and R3. That is why 203

```
R3
interface Serial0/0/0
no ip address
no shut
encapsulation frame-relay

interface Serial0/0/0.301 point-to-point
ip address 10.1.1.14 255.255.255.252
frame-relay interface-dlci 301
```
Connection between R3 and R1. That is why 301

```
interface Serial0/0/0.302 point-to-point
ip address 10.1.1.10 255.255.255.252
frame-relay interface-dlci 302
```
Connection between R2 and R3. That is why 302

At this point, your job would be complete, and your ISP would have to do the rest of the work on their side to connect the dots, but since this is a lab, you would need to go inside the cloud and create the DLCI's per serial interface and under frame-relay create the actual connections, as shown in the following screenshots:

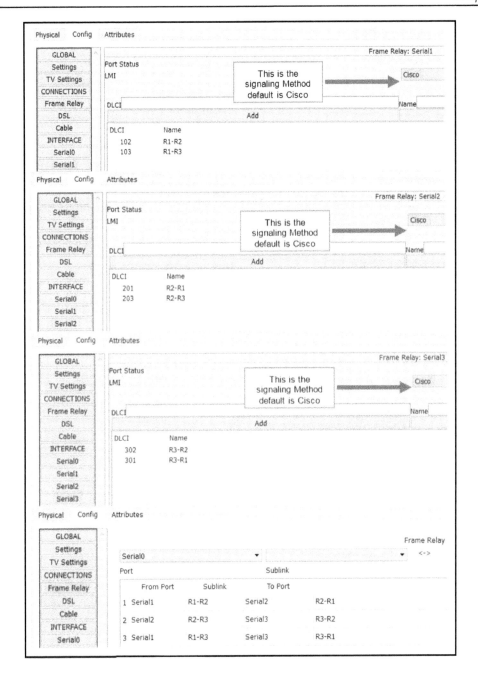

This last screenshot is the actual frame-relay connections to the different DLCIs.

But still, to get connectivity across, you would need an IGP. You can use RIP, EIGRP, or OSPF.

But now you need to check if frame-relay is working, and you would do so using the following commands:

```
R1#sh frame-relay lmi
LMI Statistics for interface Serial0/0/0 (Frame Relay DTE) LMI TYPE = CISCO
Invalid Unnumbered info 0          Invalid Prot Disc 0
Invalid dummy Call Ref  0          Invalid Msg Type 0
Invalid Status Message 0            Invalid Lock Shift 0
Invalid Information ID 0             Invalid Report IE Len 0
Invalid Report Request 0            Invalid Keep IE Len 0
Num Status Enq. Sent 729           Num Status msgs Rcvd 728
Num Update Status Rcvd 0           Num Status Timeouts 16
LMI Statistics for interface Serial0/0/0.102 (Frame Relay DTE) LMI TYPE =
CISCO
LMI Statistics for interface Serial0/0/0.103 (Frame Relay DTE) LMI TYPE =
CISCO

R1#sh frame-relay pvc
PVC Statistics for interface Serial0/0/0 (Frame Relay DTE)
DLCI = 102, DLCI USAGE = LOCAL, PVC STATUS = ACTIVE, INTERFACE =
Serial0/0/0.102
input pkts 14055 output pkts 32795 in bytes 1096228
out bytes 6216155 dropped pkts 0 in FECN pkts 0
in BECN pkts 0 out FECN pkts 0 out BECN pkts 0
in DE pkts 0 out DE pkts 0
out bcast pkts 32795 out bcast bytes 6216155
DLCI = 103, DLCI USAGE = LOCAL, PVC STATUS = ACTIVE, INTERFACE =
Serial0/0/0.103
input pkts 14055 output pkts 32795 in bytes 1096228
out bytes 6216155 dropped pkts 0 in FECN pkts 0
in BECN pkts 0 out FECN pkts 0 out BECN pkts 0
in DE pkts 0 out DE pkts 0
out bcast pkts 32795 out bcast bytes 6216155
```

- **FECN**: Forward Explicit Congestion Notification. This is the source requesting that the destination slows down its request for data.
- **BECN**: Backward Explicit Congestion Notification. This is the destination requesting that the source sends data more slowly.
- **DE bits**: These are the bits that went off the CIR , and congestion could be happening. If you see a lot of DE bits, packets are being dropped.

MPLS

This is the next packet switched WAN protocol. People are moving from frame-relay and going to multiple protocol label switching, or MPLS. The reason for this is the need for speed. In this type of communication, only the edge routers are the ones that do routing lookup of all other routers. The core routers do label switching with a mechanism called POP HOP and SWAP. Routers will have their own local label and forward a new label to their neighbor router, which in turn will swap for their own label until it reaches the customer edge router and then it POPs the label and just does a naked IP. The labels carry all the layer 3 destination addresses.

MPLS works in combination with CEF, Cisco Express Forwarding, which will make looking for routes much faster. There is no need for serial connections anymore because MPLS supports Ethernet technology.

Virtual Private Networks

In a nutshell, VPNs are a way for remote users to connect to the company's network in a secure fashion. A tunnel would be created encapsulating the data using some sort of security protocols. The packets should not be sniffed out.

This technology has really picked up, since lots of people are working from home and you can connect to the company's resources as if you were right at your desk.

Companies can use VPNs internally, but that is not what they are made for. They are for WANs. When you must traverse the dangerous waters of the internet, you should create VLANs. That way, we can pass information securely, to a certain degree.

There are three different types of VPN categories:

- **Remote-access**: This allows remote users to securely access the company's network and use its resources, always having to authenticate with a username and password.
- **Site-to-site VPN**: This type of VPN is also called an intranet VPN. It allows a company to connect its remote sites to the corporate backbone. I can tell you that in telecommunications, site-to-site VPNs are used on frequent basis, connecting to remote sites from the actual main switch plant.
- **Extranet VPN**: This allows an organization's client, business partners, and suppliers to be connected to the corporation, but in a very limited way. This is also called a B2B.

We also have layer 2 VPNs that use the MPLS labels to transport data, as well as layer 3 VPNs that you use the IP layer, so it takes advantage of the routing protocols in use.

When securing VPNs, you would use IPSec or security protocols, such as AH or ESP, along with encryption, such as symmetric encryption and asymmetric encryption. But this is more a topic for the CCNA security or Security+ certifications. Here, just understand what a VPN is and its benefits. Simply stated, it can securely take your data across the public internet safely.

GRE Tunnels

Generic Encapsulation Tunnels is a tunneling protocol that has the capabilities of encapsulating many network layer routing protocols, such as, RIP, EIGRP, or OSPF.

A GRE tunnel interface can support a header for passenger protocols for the following:

- IPv4 or IPv6
- GRE itself
- The transport delivery protocol is usually IP

GRE tunnels do have their own unique characteristics:

- GRE provides no security
- GRE has no support for IP multicast or IP broadcast

So, using GRE tunnels, together with IPSec, allows you to run routing protocols, IP multicast, as well as multiprotocol traffic across your network.

Configuring GRE Tunnel

Now let us see how to configure the GRE protocol:

```
R1(config)#int tunnel 0
R1(config-if)#
*Oct 24 04:25:41.799: %LINEPROTO-5-UPDOWN: Line protocol on Interface
Tunnel0, changed state to down
R1(config-if)#tunnel mode gre ip
R1(config-if)#ip address 172.16.1.1 255.255.255.0          Tunnel IP
R1(config-if)#tunnel source 10.1.1.1
R1(config-if)#tunnel destination 10.1.1.2       Actual IP address on Physical interface
R1(config-if)#

*Oct 24 04:28:18.827: %LINEPROTO-5-UPDOWN: Line protocol on Interface
Tunnel0, changed state to up

R2(config)#int tunnel 0
R2(config-if)#ip address
*Oct 24 04:29:55.431: %LINEPROTO-5-UPDOWN: Line protocol on Interface
Tunnel0, changed state to down
R2(config-if)#ip address 172.16.1.2 255.255.255.0
R2(config-if)#tunnel mode gre ip
R2(config-if)#tunnel source 10.1.1.2
R2(config-if)#tunnel destination 10.1.1.1
R2(config-if)#
*Oct 24 04:31:14.759: %LINEPROTO-5-UPDOWN: Line protocol on Interface
Tunnel0, changed state to up
```

How to verify if the GRE Tunnel is Operational

Now that we have configured GRE Tunnel, let us see how to check whether it is operational or not.

```
R1#sh ip int brief
Interface     IP-Address     OK? Method Status      Protocol
Tunnel0        172.16.1.1    YES manual up          up

R2#sh ip int brief
Interface     IP-Address     OK? Method Status      Protocol
Tunnel0        172.16.1.2    YES manual up          up

R1#sh int tun 0
Tunnel0 is up, line protocol is up
   Hardware is Tunnel
   Internet address is 172.16.1.1/24
   MTU 1514 bytes, BW 9 Kbit, DLY 500000 usec,
```

```
        reliability 255/255, txload 1/255, rxload 1/255
    Encapsulation TUNNEL, loopback not set
    Keepalive not set
    Tunnel source 10.1.1.1, destination 10.1.1.2
    Tunnel protocol/transport GRE/IP
      Key disabled, sequencing disabled
      Checksumming of packets disabled
    Tunnel TTL 255
    Fast tunneling enabled
    Tunnel transmit bandwidth 8000 (kbps)
    Tunnel receive bandwidth 8000 (kbps)
    R1#sh ip route
Gateway of last resort is not set
      172.16.0.0/24 is subnetted, 1 subnets
C        172.16.1.0 is directly connected, Tunnel0
      10.0.0.0/30 is subnetted, 1 subnets
C        10.1.1.0 is directly connected, Serial3/0

R1#ping 172.16.1.2
Type escape sequence to abort.
Sending 5, 100-byte ICMP Echos to 172.16.1.2, timeout is 2 seconds:
!!!!!
Success rate is 100 percent (5/5), round-trip min/avg/max = 60/61/64 ms
```

DMVPN

This is a Cisco proprietary protocol. The Dynamic Multipoint Virtual Point Network feature allows you to easily scale your enterprise network. Even small companies use DMVPN with IPSec.

DMVPN allows you to configure a single GRE tunnel interface and one IPSec profile on the hub router that would manage all other routers. This feature will automatically create the tunnels for you from hub to spoke or spoke to spoke, making your life a lot easier. It does so with the help of the following protocols:

- NHRP
- Multipoint GRE

DMVPN comes in three phases. I will show a Phase 1 configuration, which is not on the test at all:

```
hub:
int tunnel0
ip address 10.1.0.5 255.255.255.0
ip nhrp authentication hush
```

```
ip nhrp map multicast dynamic
ip nhrp network-id 99
tunnel source gig1.100
tunnel mode gre multipoint
tunnel key 100000
spoke:
interface tunnel0
ip address 10.1.0.1 255.255.255.0
ip nhrp authentication hush
ip nhrp network-id 99
ip nhrp map 10.1.0.5 169.254.100.5
nhrp map multicast 169.254.100.5
ip nhrp nhs 10.1.0.5
tunnel source gig1.100
tunnel destination 169.254.100.5    (tunnel mode gre multipoint)**
tunnel key 100000
```

So, we are creating a GRE tunnel with security on it and the best part about that, is that it is secured.

Redundancy Protocol

We all know that having redundancy in our network is crucial. If one interface goes down, we should have another path of getting to the destination network, unknowingly to the customer. Your clients, customers, or users should not be aware of what is going on behind the scene; they may experience a hiccup, but that is all.

In networking, we could use three redundancy protocols that work on your routers or layer 3 switches, so if one of the links goes down, they would automatically switch over to the next layer 3 device and continue to transmit data.

I have outlined the protocol here, along with some questions that you need to ask yourself:

How fast can the fail over happen?

- How is the client aware to switch?
- What if a WAN link fails?

HSRP:

- Cisco only created 1994
- Uses, by default, hello timers of 3 seconds and a hold timer 10

VRRP (industry standard):

- IETF in 1999
- Multiple vendor,
- Faster timers (hello, 1 second, hold 3 seconds

GLBP:

- Cisco only, created 2005
- Just like HSRP, allows active to active connections, which adds load balance

Let's break this down even further. We will look at HSRP, which is the Cisco preferred protocol, and most likely be on your exam.

HSRP:

- Gateways organized into standby groups
- One active, one standby
- Virtual router ID and MAC address generated
- Hello messages sent once every 3 seconds,4

```
Dead after 10 seconds
VIP IP: 10.1.1.1
VIP MAC:0000.0c07.ac01
Format of MAC:
0000.0c = cisco vendor ID
07.AC = HSRP ID
X.X = STANDBY GROUP#
```

Clients that have the above VIPs, will change routers when AR does not respond.

Now that you are familiar with HSRP, how would you configure it on your network?

HSRP initial config:

- Create standby group
- Clients have normal default-gateways
    - Primary
    - Secondary
- Create a priority number, default 100
- Re-assign IP addresses on clients
- Verify
- Tweeking
- Clients have normal default-gateways:

```
Active
standby 1 ip 10.1.1.1
standby 1 priority 120 (default 100) 0-255
interface FastEthernet0/0
ip address 192.168.100.254 255.255.255.0
duplex auto
speed auto
standby version 2
standby 1 ip 192.168.100.100
standby 1 priority 200
standby 1 preempt
standby 1 track FastEthernet0/1
preempt: bring back the original active router
        - standby 1 preempt
tracking: tracks an interface if it goes down
          subtract a predetermined number from
        the priority
        - standby 1 track f0/1
```

As you can see there is no HSRP command. Everything is done under the interface and to start the configuration, you must use the `standby` command. To verify that HSRP is working, you could use the following two commands:

```
R0#sh standby f0/0
FastEthernet0/0 - Group 1 (version 2)
State is Active
4 state changes, last state change 00:00:17
Virtual IP address is 192.168.100.100
Active virtual MAC address is 0000.0C9F.F001
Local virtual MAC address is 0000.0C9F.F001 (v2 default)
Hello time 3 sec, hold time 10 sec
Next hello sent in 0.925 secs
Preemption enabled
```

```
Active router is local
Standby router is 192.168.100.253
Priority 180 (configured 190)
Track interface FastEthernet0/1 state Down decrement 10
Group name is hsrp-Fa0/0-1 (default)
R0#sh standby briefP
indicates configured to preempt.
Interface Grp  Pri P  State  Active   Standby     Virtual IP
Fa0/0     1    180  P   Active   local   192.168.100.253
192.168.100.100
```

By no means is this the only redundancy protocol. I briefly mentioned VRRP and GLBP, but these are really not mentioned in any detail in the exam, but for your own personal knowledge I will give you a sneak peek.

VRRP

The following are the characteristics of VRRP:

- Active/standby now master/backup
- Standby group is a vrrp group
- Master router can share virtual IP
- 1 sec hello, 3 sec down time (no config)
- Advertise/learn master only
- Config vrrp group
- Optimize settings
- Verify

```
int f0/0
vrrp 20 ip 172.31.6.80
vrrp 20 preempt
vrrp 20 timers adverties msec 100
```

GLBP

The following are the characteristics of GLBP:

- Single VIP with multiple MACS
- Active virtual gateway
- Manages virtual gateway

- Other routers act as active. Really are active virtual forwarders
- More than one router can be active
- Single VIP
- Multiple virtual MAC

```
INT F0/0
GLBP 1 IP 172.31.6.90
GLBP 1 PRIORITY 150 (AVG)
GLBP 1 LOAD-BALANCING
      HOST-DEPENDENT*** (based on host mac)
      ROUND-ROBIN**
   WEIGHTED (choose a portion assigned macs)
```

So, these are your redundancy protocols that are used on very large to small medium networks. Using these protocols, you should have very little loss of connectivity to your clients. Just so you can have a visual of what the topology may look like, here is an example of the concept:

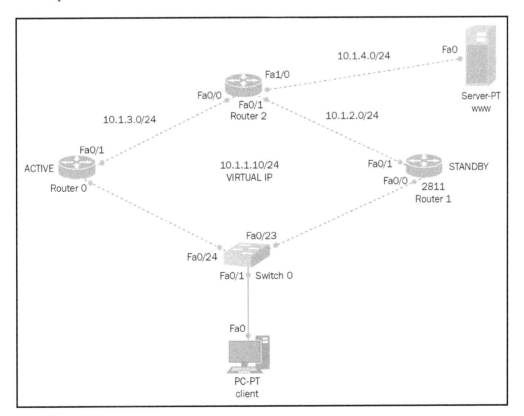

Summary

We have covered a lot of information in this chapter and you have learned that WANs are extremely important. We need to choose the right type of connection, security, protocols, and, most importantly, our provider. In the next chapter, we will go into some advanced topics of the overall technologies we have already discussed.

We have learnt about the HDLC protocol and its drawbacks when compared to PPP, which you will be configuring and learning the process and the components that make up PPP. We have also briefly touch upon VPN's and their importance when using remote users. We have also discussed GRE tunnels, and gain the understanding of their use and how to configure GRE on our network.

Advanced Networking Topics 20

Yes!! You made it to the last chapter. Here, we will be covering several topics throughout the book that are more advanced. You will be creating a topology that will have everything you will need, to pass your certification and hit the ground running in the work force. We will create a large topology to include what you would need in your LAN and WAN.

This chapter will cover the following topics:

- Layer 2 configurations
    - Spanning-Tree
    - VTP
    - Changing Native VLAN
- Layer 3 configurations
    - MPLS configuration
    - Wireless

We will be configuring everything we learned in this book, along with the topics covered in this chapter.

Layer 2 configurations

Let's analyze the topology. First thing notice the hardware we have layer 2 and a router which will be doing the routing, obviously. Second thing, it is not the typical **Laz network**. You now have the networks, which are subnetted, but I did not put the NetID toward the root switch. We will have to consider that. Also, it states that all native VLANs will be in 100, so we need to make those changes and then we need to worry about the routing between all these networks and secure them. Let's look at the following diagram:

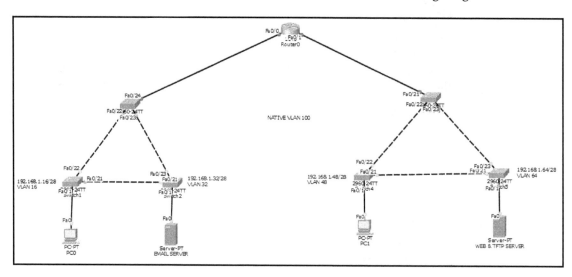

I already put the IP addresses on the PCs, but remember that all networks are subnetted, so be careful when assigning the addresses; we also have email servers, and a web and TFTP server, so you need to configure those as well.

Let's proceed step by step. Let's look at the PCs and IP configurations:

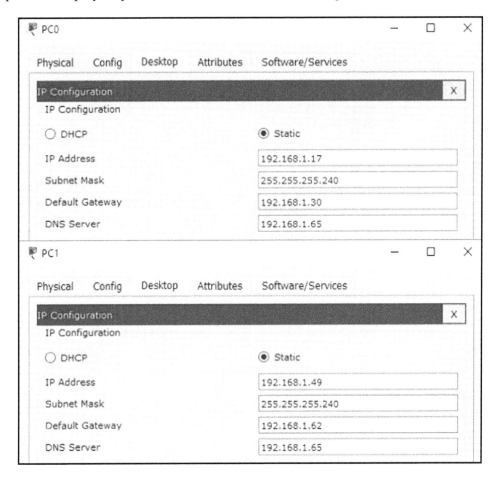

We have the correct IPs on the PCs. Let's do the same for the servers, and we need to configure the servers for the type of job they are going to do.

We will start with the email server:

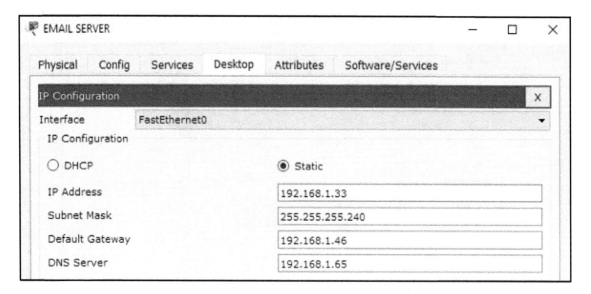

Now let's configure the email:

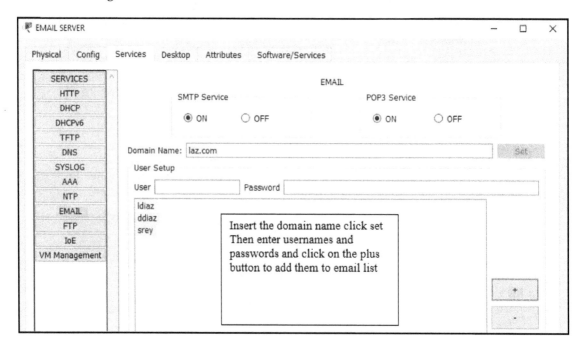

Here's how to configure your PC to be able to send an email. You need to fill in the text-box for your name, email address, IP addresses for the incoming and outgoing mail, and at the bottom you must put a username and password. Once this is complete, you should see a window like the following:

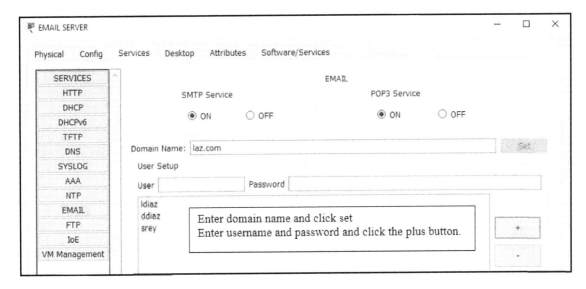

So, are you ready to send emails?

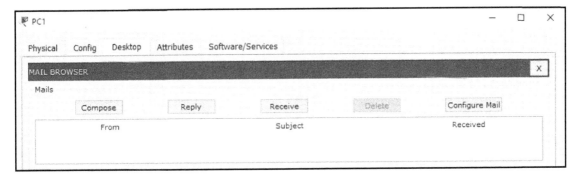

All right, let's round this off configuring the WEB/DNS/TFTP server. The following screenshot shows IP configuration:

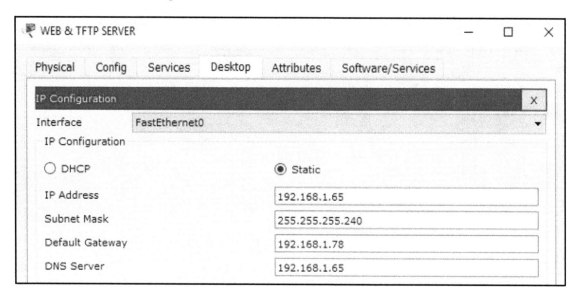

In web server configuration, all you really need to do is set up the DNS, but I made some changes in the HTTP category on the HTML (you don't have to do this):

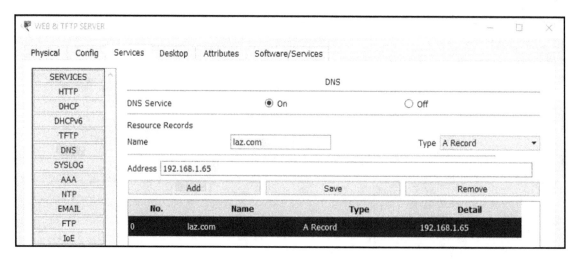

This is nowhere near a real DNS server, but understand the concept. Now we have all the end devices set up, it's time to start the Layer-2 switches.

Layer 2 switch

We are going to start configuring the LAN on the left. We will configure some of the basic administrative commands that have an instance of STP for all VLANs. Our root bridge will always be the core switch. We will tweak the VTP protocols, trunk ports, and create the VLANs on the core switch, but we will not assign them. Let's get started.

Here is the code for the core L2 switch:

```
CORE(config)#hostname CORE1
CORE1(config)#ENABLE PASSWORD CISCO
CORE1(config)#IP DOMAIN-NAME CISCO.COM
CORE1(config)#USERNAME LDIAZ PRIVilege 15 PASSword 0 CISCO
CORE1(config)#IP SSH Authentication-retries 3
CORE1(config)#IP SSH TIme-out 120
CORE1(config)#CRYPTO KEY GENERATE RSA
The name for the keys will be: CORE1.CISCO.COM
Choose the size of the key modulus in the range of 360 to 2048 for your
general purpose keys. Choosing a key modulus greater than 512. This may
take a few minutes.
How many bits in the modulus [512]:
% Generating 512 bit RSA keys, keys will be non-exportable...[OK]
CORE1(config)#LINE CON 0
*Mar 2 17:35:41.679: RSA key size needs to be at least 768 bits for ssh
version 2
*Mar 2 17:35:41.679: %SSH-5-ENABLED: SSH 1.5 has been enabled
CORE1(config-line)#LOGIN LOCAL
CORE1(config-line)#PASSWORD CISCO
CORE1(config-line)#LINE VTY 0 15
CORE1(config-line)#LOGIN LOCAL
CORE1(config-line)#PASSWORD CISCO
CORE1(config-line)#TRAnsport Input ALL
CORE1(config)#SPAnning-tree MODE Rapid-pvst
CORE1(config)#SPANning-tree VLAN 16,32,100 PRIority 0
CORE1(config)#VTP DOMAIN CISCO
Changing VTP domain name from NULL to CISCO
CORE1(config)#VLAN 16
CORE1(config-vlan)#NAME STUDENTS
CORE1(config-vlan)#VLAN 32
CORE1(config-vlan)#NAME SCHOOL
CORE1(config-vlan)#VLAN 100
```

```
CORE1(config-vlan)#NAME MANAGEMENT
CORE1(config-vlan)#DO WR
Building configuration...
[OK]
CORE1(config-vlan)#EXIT
CORE1(config)#INT RANGE F0/22-24
CORE1(config-if-range)#SWITCHPORT MODE TRUNK
```

Spanning Tree Protocol

Spanning Tree Protocol (STP) is a protocol that stops switching loops at layer 2 of the OSI; it comes alive when it realizes that there are redundant links on the network.

An STP run goes through an election process; based on the lowest bridge priority number, that switch will become the root bridge, and all information will be sent to the root bridge and then sent back out. But what is the criteria used to select the root bridge, and if you are not the root bridge, what are you designated as and your ports on the switches also have to in a certain mode/status.

By default, STP is on and it is watching all the ports; that is why when you connect something to a port, it first goes amber and then it turns green, because the STP is looking at the port. The election process is only complete when you have redundant links connected to each of the switches. The STP looks at the priority number first, which by default is 32769 on all Cisco Catalyst switches, so it cannot decide based on that number, so it looks for the switch with the lowest MAC address, and makes that switch the root bridge. On the root bridge, all ports are Designate Forwarding ports. So now it needs to find a switch to block ports on, the switch with the highest MAC address, will be chosen and it will pick the port with highest MAC address or the slowest bandwidth. Something to be aware of when STP is doing its election and you have more than two switches is that all ports that face the root bridge must be the root port for all other ports that can be ALT BLK or Designated Forwarding ports so, in making its election decisions it takes that into account as well.

In our network, I chose the switch called Core1 to always be the root bridge, and I want only one instance of the STP for all the VLANs that will exists. Type the following command so no matter what the Core1 switch will always be the root bridge:

```
CORE1(config)#SPANning-tree VLAN 16,32,100 PRIority 0
```

Let's look at a visual of what I am actually talking about. To look at the STP information, you must type the show spanning-tree command.

As you can see, the VLAN0001 is not part of the STP election, since it does not say *this is the root bridge.* The reason is when I chose the VLANs that are going to take part in this STP instance, VLAN 1 was not included. Remember that I am going to change the native VLAN to 100, which will be the management VLAN.

I want you to pay close attention to the highlighted portions. Notice that the spanning-tree was changed from PVST to RPVST. All switches must be changed to the newer STP mode or you will run into compatibility issues. The following table include the different types of STP; memorize them for the test and when you are hired, change the STP to the most current one if that will make the network more efficient. Remember the old adage, *If it ain't broke, don't fix it.*

Spanning-Tree Protocol Types		
Protocol	Standard body	Number of Instances
STP/CST (Common STP)	802.1D	1
PVST+	Cisco	One for every VLAN
RSTP	802.1W	1
Rapid PVST+	Cisco	One for every VLAN

What would be the deciding factor for you to decide which STP to run? Well, if you run one instance of STP for all VLANs, your thousands of VLANs could create a problem. Rapid PVST+ is the ultimate; it has a faster convergence and allows you to have a root bridge per VLAN. The CCNA 200-125, wants you to know that there are different STP types and how to do a basic configuration as we did previously.

VTP

We also created a VTP domain called CISCO, but do not think of this as a domain name, as this is simply a name, a neighborhood all the switches can participate in, but to really have it secure, you must also use the VTP PASSWORD LAZ. The domain name due to the trunk ports will travel down to all switches, but the password must be manually configured.

Let's look at the VTP output and highlight the important points you need to focus on:

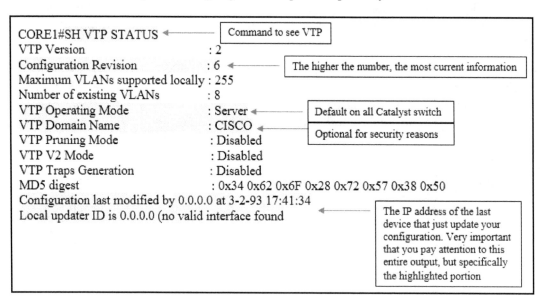

OK, we do the same to all the switches, and we will change the default VLAN for the last one:

```
Switch(config)#VTP MODE CLIENT
Setting device to VTP CLIENT mode.
Switch(config)#DO SH VLAN BRIEF
VLAN Name Status Ports
---- -------------------------------- --------- ----------------------------
---
1 default active Fa0/1, Fa0/2, Fa0/3, Fa0/4
Fa0/5, Fa0/6, Fa0/7, Fa0/8
Fa0/9, Fa0/10, Fa0/11, Fa0/12
Fa0/13, Fa0/14, Fa0/15, Fa0/16
Fa0/17, Fa0/18, Fa0/19, Fa0/20
Fa0/21, Fa0/23, Fa0/24, Gig0/1
Gig0/2
16 STUDENTS                 active
32 SCHOOL                   active
100 MANAGEMENT              active
1002 fddi-default           active
1003 token-ring-default     active
1004 fddinet-default        active
1005 trnet-default          active
Switch(config)#HOSTNAME STUDENTS
STUDENTS(config)#INT RANGE F0/1-15
```

```
STUDENTS(config-if-range)#SWITCHPORT MODE ACCESS
STUDENTS(config-if-range)#SWITCHPORT ACCESS VLAN 16
STUDENTS(config-if-range)#SWITCHPORT PORT-SECURITY
STUDENTS(config-if-range)#SWITCHPORT PORT-SECURITY MAC STICKY
STUDENTS(config-if-range)#SWITCHPORT PORT-SECURITY MAX 1
STUDENTS(config-if-range)#SWITCHPORT PORT-SECURITY VIOLATION SHUT
STUDENTS(config-if-range)#SPANNING-TREE PORT FAST
                                        ^
% Invalid input detected at '^' marker.
STUDENTS(config-if-range)#SPANNING-TREE PORTFAST
%Warning: portfast should only be enabled on ports connected to a single
host. Connecting hubs, concentrators, switches, bridges, etc... to this
interface when portfast is enabled, can cause temporary bridging loops.
Use with CAUTION
%Portfast will be configured in 15 interfaces due to the range command
but will only have effect when the interfaces are in a non-trunking mode.
STUDENTS(config-if-range)#SPANNING-TREE BPDUGUARD ENABLE
STUDENTS(config-if-range)#DO WR
```

The bottom switches will have VTP MODE CLIENT, which means no one can change, delete, or access the VLAN database. But it will send and receive updates; this is why the revision number is so important, as you could be a client or a server, and if your revision is higher, you will update all other switches and overwrite their configuration. If they are in transparent mode, then it won't accept or send updates. OK, this was the STUDENT switch. Now for the SCHOOL switch:

```
Switch(config)#VTP MODE CLIENT
Setting device to VTP CLIENT mode.
Switch(config)#DO SH VLAN BRIEF
VLAN Name Status Ports
---- ------------------------- --------- ----------------------------
----
1 default active Fa0/1, Fa0/2, Fa0/3, Fa0/4
Fa0/5, Fa0/6, Fa0/7, Fa0/8
Fa0/9, Fa0/10, Fa0/11, Fa0/12
Fa0/13, Fa0/14, Fa0/15, Fa0/16
Fa0/17, Fa0/18, Fa0/19, Fa0/20
Fa0/21, Fa0/22, Fa0/24, Gig0/1
Gig0/2
16 STUDENTS              active
32 SCHOOL                active
100 MANAGEMENT           active
1002 fddi-default         active
1003 token-ring-default active
1004 fddinet-default     active
1005 trnet-default       active
Switch(config)#HOSTNAME SCHOOL
```

```
SCHOOL(config)#INT RANGE F0/1-15
SCHOOL(config-if-range)#SWITCHPORT MODE ACCESS
SCHOOL(config-if-range)#SWITCHPORT ACCESS VLAN 32
SCHOOL(config-if-range)#SWITCHPORT PORT-SECURITY
SCHOOL(config-if-range)#SWITCHPORT PORT-SECURITY MAC STICKY
SCHOOL(config-if-range)#SWITCHPORT PORT-SECURITY MAX 1
SCHOOL(config-if-range)#SWITCHPORT PORT-SECURITY VIOLATION SHUT
SCHOOL(config-if-range)#SPANNING-TREE PORTFAST
%Warning: portfast should only be enabled on ports connected to a single
host. Connecting hubs, concentrators, switches, bridges, etc... to this
interface when portfast is enabled, can cause temporary bridging loops.
Use with CAUTION
%Portfast will be configured in 15 interfaces due to the range command
but will only have effect when the interfaces are in a non-trunking mode.
SCHOOL (config-if-range)#SPANNING-TREE BPDUGUARD ENABLE
SCHOOL (config-if-range)#EXIT
SCHOOL(config)#DO WR
```

Remember, we need to change the STP mode from PVST to RAPID-PVST using the
following command:

```
STUDENTS(config)#SPANNING-TREE MODE RAPID-PVST
SCHOOL(config)#SPANNING-TREE MODE RAPID-PVST
```

Changing native VLAN

OK, one more thing we need to do is to change the Native VLAN to 100, which means we
need to turn VLAN 100 to the native VLAN and then assign all the ports on VLAN 1 on
VLAN 100. As we do this, we may see errors such as *mismatch native vlan*. Don't worry, once
we have finished, that will go away. This is the error you will get when you start changing
the native VLAN:

```
CORE1(config-if-range)#
%CDP-4-NATIVE_VLAN_MISMATCH: Native VLAN mismatch discovered on
FastEthernet0/23 (100), with SCHOOL FastEthernet0/23 (1).
%CDP-4-NATIVE_VLAN_MISMATCH: Native VLAN mismatch discovered on
FastEthernet0/24 (100), with Switch FastEthernet0/1 (1).
```

When you change the native VLAN, you need to go into the ports and make them part of
VLAN 100 and then run the following command:

```
CORE1(config-if-range)#SWITCHPORT TRUNK NATIVE VLAN 100
```

We assigned ports f0/16 20 to the new native VLAN 100; now, based on what you have read, you would need to do the InterVLAN and the other, triangle following the same commands.

Remember, the IP addresses are assigned on the end devices, so it is now up to you based on what you have learned to do InterVLAN connectivity.

For the following lab I will be using GN3. Packet tracer will not work.

Layer-3 configurations

The following topology is what we will be using for MPLS. It is a very simple lab; the point of the lab is for you to become more familiar with MPLS configurations and some of its components:

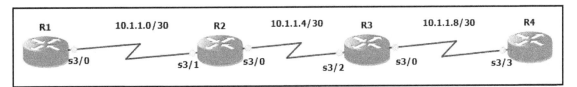

MPLS

Before we begin the configuration, the following table will show the terminology used with MPLS. Don't freak out, this will not be on your CCNA, but at least you have a heads-up on everything else. I highlighted the most common ones that you may run into:

Name	Description
MPLS	Multiple Protocol Label Switching WAN Technology.
FEC	Forward Equivalency Class.
CEF	Cisco Express Forwarding.
RIB	Routing Information Base.
FIB	Forwarding Information Base.

LFIB	Label Forwarding Information Base.
LDP	Label Distribution Protocol.
LSR	Label Switching Router.
LSP	Label Switched Path.
Labels	Corresponds to a single route and is locally significant to the router. Start at 16 and 1-15 are reserved.
Implicit NULL	Reserved for label 3.
PUSH	Deals with the Penultimate Hop Pop Process; where we *impose/push* the label learned to the downstream LDP neighbor.
SWAP	Deals with the Penultimate Hop Pop Process; where it will *swap* the label learned for a locally significant label.
POP	Deals with the Penultimate Hop Pop Process, if you are the PE router, you will *pop* or remove the label and send it downstream as an IP Packet.
P - Router	Provider router within the cloud.
PE - Router	Provider Edge Router; this router will be facing the customers.
CE = Router	Customer Edge Router; this router will be facing the PE routers.
Up Stream	Begins at the network that is being advertised; this is the CONTROL PLANE for LDP.
Down Stream	Transit Path is downstream toward the network the packets are trying to reach. (DATAPLANE).
Control Plane	SEE UP STREAM.
Data Plane	SEE DOWN STREAM.
VRF	Virtual routing and forwarding instance.
RD	Route Distinguishers.
RT	Route Targets allow for the more complex sharing of routes.
RR	A network-routing component that offers an alternative to the logical full-mesh requirement of **Internal Border Gateway Protocol (IBGP)**. An RR acts as a local point for IBGP sessions. The purpose of the RR is concentration.

Once again, the commands that I am going to show you here are the most basic commands, just to get MPLS up and running and so you can see the actual labels. Before you can start configuring MPLS, you must have connectivity in your network, so you can do static routing or dynamic routing, and it really does not matter which routing protocol you are using.

For this lab, I am using RIPv2, because it is just very easy to do. Here is a command of R4:

```
R4#sh ip route
Gateway of last resort is not set
     10.0.0.0/30 is subnetted, 3 subnets
C       10.1.1.8 is directly connected, Serial3/3
R       10.1.1.0 [120/2] via 10.1.1.9, 00:00:16, Serial3/3
R       10.1.1.4 [120/1] via 10.1.1.9, 00:00:16, Serial3/3
R4#ping 10.1.1.1
Type escape sequence to abort.
Sending 5, 100-byte ICMP Echos to 10.1.1.1, timeout is 2 seconds:
!!!!!
Success rate is 100 percent (5/5), round-trip min/avg/max = 88/90/96 ms
R4#
```

We have connectivity across the network, so let's configure MPLS:

```
R1(config)#MPLS IP
R1(config)#IP CEF
R1(config)#INT S3/0
R1(config-if)#MPLS IP
R1(config-if)#MPLS LABEL PROTOCOL LDP
R2(config)#MPLS IP
R2(config)#IP CEF
R2(config)#INT S3/1
R2(config-if)#MPLS IP
*Oct 25 09:22:59.028: %LDP-5-NBRCHG: LDP Neighbor 172.16.1.1:0 (1) is
UP
R2(config-if)#MPLS LABEL PROTOCOL LDP
R2(config)#INT S3/0
R2(config-if)#MPLS IP
R2(config-if)#MPLS LABEL PROTOCOL LDP
R3(config)#MPLS IP
R3(config)#IP CEF
R3(config)#INT S3/2
R3(config-if)#MPLS IP
R3(config-if)#MPLS LABEL PROTOCOL LDP
R3(config-if)#INT S3/0
R3(config-if)#MPLS IP
R3(config-if)#MPLS LABEL PROTOCOL LDP
R4(config)#MPLS IP
R4(config)#IP CEF
R4(config)#INT S3/3
R4(config-if)#MPLS IP
*Oct 25 10:33:29.103: %LDP-5-NBRCHG: LDP Neighbor 10.1.1.9:0 (1) is UP
R4(config-if)#MPLS LABEL PROTOCOL LDP
```

One interesting thing is that only the routers at the end get the notice of the LDP neighbor is up, so let's check to see whether MPLS is working, as we are actually switching labels:

```
R1#sh mpls forwarding-table
Local       Outgoing     Prefix      Bytes  tag      Outgoing      Next Hop
tag         tag or VC    or Tunnel   Id switched interface
16          16           10.1.1.8/30 0               Se3/0         point2point
17          Pop tag 10.1.1.4/30     0               Se3/0         point2point

R2#sh mpls forwarding-table
Local       Outgoing     Prefix      Bytes  tag      Outgoing      Next Hop
tag         tag or VC or Tunnel      Id     switched interface
16          Untagged 10.1.1.8/30     0      Se3/0              point2point

R3#sh mpls forwarding-table

Local  Outgoing     Prefix      Bytes    tag      Outgoing      Nex Hop
tag      tag or VC or Tunnel     Id   switched interface
16       Untagged    10.1.1.0/30           0       Se3/2         point2point

R4#sh mpls forwarding-table
Local    Outgoing     Prefix      Bytes  tag  Outgoing      Next Hop
tag         tag or VC or Tunnel Id  switched interface
16          16           10.1.1.0/30 0     Se3/3         point2point
17          Pop tag      10.1.1.4/30 0     Se3/3         point2point

R4#sh mpls ldp bindings
tib entry: 10.1.1.0/30, rev 4
    local binding: tag: 16
    remote binding: tsr: 10.1.1.9:0, tag: 16
tib entry: 10.1.1.4/30, rev 6
    local binding: tag: 17
    remote binding: tsr: 10.1.1.9:0, tag: imp-null
tib entry: 10.1.1.8/30, rev 2
    local binding: tag: imp-null
    remote binding: tsr: 10.1.1.9:0, tag: imp-null
```

This topology is very simple; you see, we only have labels 16 and 17, and the `imp-null` which is number 3 in the terminology table. Once MPLS sees you are a stub router, it will POP off the label and just send IP information.

But once again this information really goes beyond the scope of the CCNA 200-125 for now.

From here on, I will use packet tracer again.

Wireless

All right, one last topic and you're done. Even though I can almost guarantee you that you will not get asked anything about wireless, I have had students that have told me they have been asked, so I am going to create a simple wireless network for you and hit the main topics:

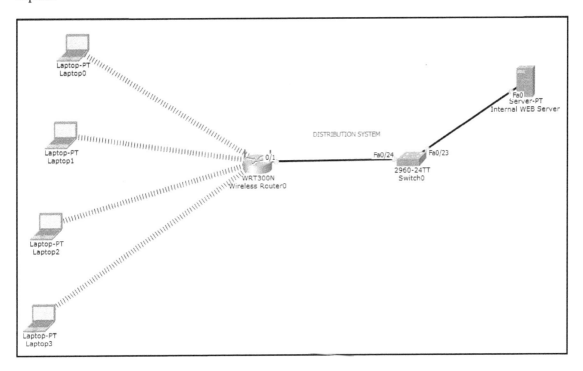

Before we get into the specifics of a wireless network, ask yourself why you would want or need a wireless network?

It is easy to set up, gain access to a physical network where I can't run wires, so I can do my work in bed. Wireless technology is great; just think of the phones we have today; we can do anything from anywhere if we have signal, and this is where IT comes in.

With wireless, we have options, so the first thing let's talk about is the standards we use today:

- 802.11g: Its 2.4 GHz band and uses **Orthogonal Frequency Division Multiplexing (OFDM)** based transmission, 54 Mbps, three non-overlapping channels: 1,3, and 11
- 802.11n: Its 2.4 and 5 GHz band uses MIMO, 54 Mbps to 600 Mbps

- `802.11ac`: Its 5 GHz band uses QAM, 54 Mbps up to 1 Gbps
- Soon to come will be `802.11ax`, which theoretically uses up to 2 Gbps

If you are implementing wireless, one thing you need to do is a physical site survey and a radio site survey. Doing this survey, it will allow you to know where you can physically put your APs and whether there are any other devices that would interfere with your wireless:

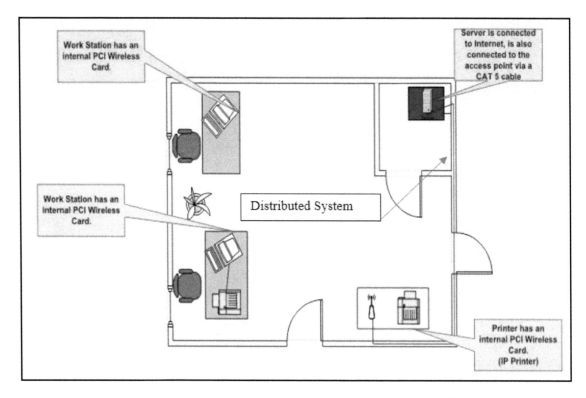

Since we have all these standards, the main thing is the wireless wave; the bigger the wave, the further it can travel, but less data can go on it, because it is not frequent. If the wave is smaller, but more frequent which means, more data can go on it.

This is called **Amplitude** modulation and **Frequency** modulation; the word modulation itself means putting data, information, or intelligence on a carrier wave, and a wave consists of a cycle, technically one cycle per second. Let's get a visual:

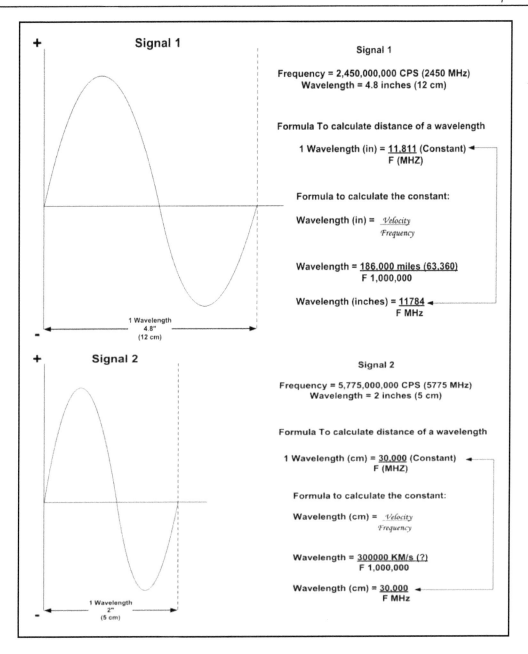

For all you physics freaks out there and for the rest of us, let's configure the wireless topology as shown in the following screenshot:

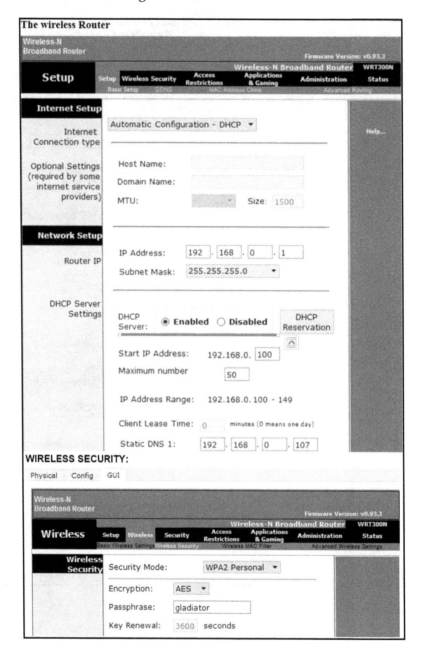

To join this wireless network, you must know the *Passphrase* gladiator.

You could secure it further by adding MAC filters, creating policies, disabling DHCP, and not broadcasting your SSID, which is your Security Set Identifier or the name you click on to join.

But that just creates more work for you; let me show you what I mean:

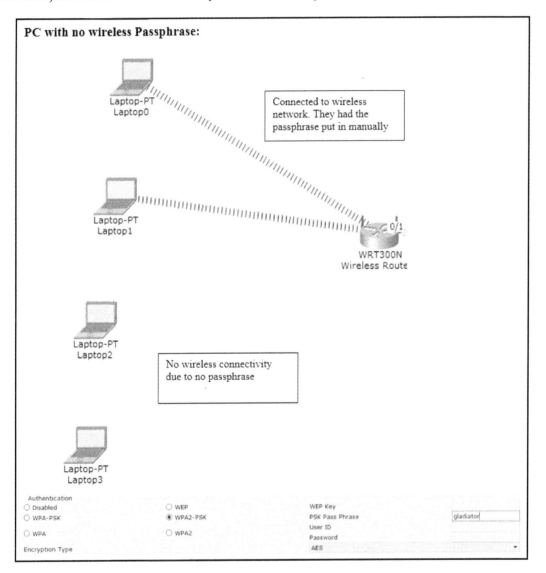

But this is just scratching the surface of wireless; there are endless ways to secure a network, but again this is not the CCNA Wireless Certification. So, there you have it; we have finished!!

Summary

First, congratulations on reading every chapter, doing every lab, and practicing everything that was required of you to obtain your CCNA 200-125 certification. The dedication and fortitude that you have shown will bear the fruits of your labor. In this book, we covered everything you need to know to pass your certification.

I have covered certain topics that you will not see, but I let you know ahead of time. We have covered logical models, IP addressing, switching, routing, security, NAT, and many sub-topics within those I mentioned.

If you did all the work and did research as you were reading, you will have no issues passing your certification , whether you take it in two parts or just one.

Always keep this in mind: no matter what certification you are taking, there is just no way you can know every possible scenario you may run into. You must understand the concepts of what I am teaching you, then you can apply a working and more logical theory to troubleshoot the problem.

To fix an issue within seconds, minutes, or even a couple of hours, you need to have prior knowledge of that issue. I have witnessed this myself, with experienced engineers that have decades of experience. So, go over the chapters repeatedly, practice the labs until it becomes second nature, create your own labs, and be curious to see what happens, as is best to make mistakes now than in the field.

I would like to thank you for choosing this book to prepare you for your exam, and my desire is to see all of you become successful as a network engineer.

Laz

21
Mock Test Questions

1. Which device runs at the network layer of the OSI model?

    A. Hub
    B. Repeater
    C. Router
    D. Switch

2. When data flows down the OSI model, what is the process called?

    A. Flowing down
    B. De-encapsulation
    C. Encapsulation
    D. Top down approach

3. Bus topologies are what we use in today's networks.

    A. True
    B. False

4. What does it mean when you are running at full duplex

    A. You can send and receive at the same time
    B. You can send and then receive
    C. You must wait a period to send or receive data
    D. The network is congested

5. What type of cable is used to connect two switches together?

    A. Straight through
    B. Rolled
    C. Console
    D. Cross over

6. If you were running a cable from building to building and its greater than 500ft, and do not want anything to interfere with it what type of cable would you use?

   A. Fiber Optic
   B. UTP
   C. STP
   D. Coax

7. In the Cisco Three Layer model, the core layer mains responsibility is what?

   A. Inter-vlan routing
   B. Routing Policies
   C. Passing information quickly
   D. Handling Thousands of routes

8. What layer of the OSI model maps over the host-to-host of the TCP/IP model?

   A. Network
   B. Data Link
   C. Transport
   D. Presentation

9. You need to create a network with 400 host, what CIDR would you use?

   A. /24
   B. /23
   C. /22
   B. /21

10. What is the broadcast address of the following host address `172.16.130.52` `255.255.240.0`?

   A. `172.16.130.255`
   B. `172.16.131.255`
   C. `172.16.144.255`
   D. `172.16.146.255`

11. When using a point to point connection what mask would you use and not waste IP address?

    A. /32
    B. /31
    C. /30
    D. None of the above

12. Which of the following prompts refers to user mode?

    A. #
    B. <
    C. >
    D. (config)#

13. Which of the following prompts will allow you to put an IP address in the interface?

    A. (config)#
    B. (config-router)#
    C. #
    D. (config-if)#

14. Which of the following Register values is the default setting?

    A. 0x2100
    B. 0x2142
    C. 0x2102
    D. 0x2101
    E. 0x2401

15. Static Default Routes can only be used on which routers?

    A. Any router on your network
    B. Default routes can only be used on switches
    C. You cannot use Default static routes, it must be through a routing protocol
    D. Stub routers only

16. What type of Routing protocol is RIPv2?

    A. Link State routing protocol
    B. Distance vector routing protocol
    C. Path vector routing protocol
    D. Static vector routing protocol

17. The EIGRP Routing protocol is based on Areas?

    A. True
    B. False

18. What is the range of the process ID number using OSPF?

    A. 4.2 billion
    B. 0 – 65,536
    C. 1 – 65,535
    D. 255

19. In a WAN you could use HDLC protocol when using Serial interfaces between any vendor?

    A. True
    B. False

20. What type of Access-list is needed if you are blocking port 443?

    A. Standard
    B. Extended
    C. Named
    D. You would need to create a policy on the firewall, an ACL can't be used

Assessments

1. Answer is C - Router
2. Answer is C - Encapsulation
3. Answer is B - False
4. Answer is A - You can send and receive at the same time
5. Answer is D - Cross over
6. Answer is A - Fiber Optic
7. Answer is C - Passing information quickly
8. Answer is C - Transport
9. Answer is B - `/23`
10. Answer is C - `172.16.144.255`
11. Answer is C- `/30`
12. Answer is C - `>`
13. Answer is D - `(config-if)#`
14. Answer is C - `0x2102`
15. Answer is D - Stub routers only
16. Answer is B - Distance vector routing protocol
17. Answer is B - False
18. Answer is C 1 – 65,535
19. Answer is B - False
20. Answer is B - Extended

For more questions and answers, please refer to `https://github.com/PacktPublishing/CCNA-Routing-and-Switching-200-125-Certification-Guide`.

Other Books You May Enjoy

If you enjoyed this book, you may be interested in these other books by Packt:

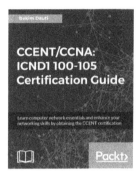

CCENT/CCNA: ICND1 100-105 Certification Guide
Bekim Dauti

ISBN: 978-1-78862-143-4

- Get to grips with the computer network concepts
- Understand computer network components and learn to create a computer network
- Understand switching and learn how to configure a switch
- Understand routing and learn how to configure a router
- Understand network services and the maintenance process
- Learn how to troubleshoot networking issues
- Become familiar with, and learn how to prepare for, the ICND1 100-105 exam

CCNA Security 210-260 Certification Guide
Glen D. Singh, Michael Vinod, Vijay Anandh

ISBN: 978-1-78712-887-3

- Grasp the fundamentals of network security
- Configure routing protocols to secure network devices
- Mitigate different styles of security attacks using Cisco devices
- Explore the different types of firewall technologies
- Discover the Cisco ASA functionality and gain insights into some advanced ASA configurations
- Implement IPS on a Cisco device and understand the concept of endpoint security

Leave a review - let other readers know what you think

Please share your thoughts on this book with others by leaving a review on the site that you bought it from. If you purchased the book from Amazon, please leave us an honest review on this book's Amazon page. This is vital so that other potential readers can see and use your unbiased opinion to make purchasing decisions, we can understand what our customers think about our products, and our authors can see your feedback on the title that they have worked with Packt to create. It will only take a few minutes of your time, but is valuable to other potential customers, our authors, and Packt. Thank you!

Index

Printed in the USA
CPSIA information can be obtained
at www.ICGtesting.com
JSHW052024270723
45527JS00001B/11